THE FULLNESS OF TIME IN A FLAT WORD

THEOPOLITICAL VISIONS

SERIES EDITORS:

Thomas Heilke
D. Stephen Long
and C. C. Pecknold

Theopolitical Visions seeks to open up new vistas on public life, hosting fresh conversations between theology and political theory. This series assembles writers who wish to revive theopolitical imagination for the sake of our common good.

Theopolitical Visions hopes to re-source modern imaginations with those ancient traditions in which political theorists were often also theologians. Whether it was Jeremiah's prophetic vision of exiles "seeking the peace of the city," Plato's illuminations on piety and the civic virtues in the Republic, St. Paul's call to "a common life worthy of the Gospel," St. Augustine's beatific vision of the City of God, or the gothic heights of medieval political theology, much of Western thought has found it necessary to think theologically about politics, and to think politically about theology. This series is founded in the hope that the renewal of such mutual illumination might make a genuine contribution to the peace of our cities.

OTHER VOLUMES IN THE SERIES:

Stanley Hauerwas and Romand Coles
Christianity, Democracy, and the Radical Ordinary: Conversations between a Radical Democrat and a Christian

Gabriel A. Santos
Redeeming the Broken Body: Church and State after Disasters

Bryan C. Hollon
Everything Is Sacred: Spiritual Exegesis in the Political Theology of Henri de Lubac

Nathan R. Kerr
Christ, History and Apocalyptic: The Politics of Christian Mission

Richard Bourne
Seek the Peace of the City: Christian Political Criticism as Public, Realist, and Transformative

The Fullness of Time in a
FLAT WORLD

Globalization

and the

Liturgical Year

SCOTT WAALKES

CASCADE *Books* • Eugene, Oregon

THE FULLNESS OF TIME IN A FLAT WORLD
Globalization and the Liturgical Year

Thepolitical Visions 6

Cascade Books
An Imprint of Wipf and Stock Publishers
199 W. 8th Ave., Suite 3
Eugene, OR 97401

www.wipfandstock.com

ISBN 13: 978-1-55635-863-0

Cataloguing-in-Publication data:

Waalkes, Scott.

The fullness of time in a flat world : globalization and the liturgical year / Scott Waalkes.

xxii + 362 p. ; 23 cm. Includes bibliographical references and index.

Thepolitical Visions 6

ISBN 13: 978-1-55635-863-0

1. Globalization—Religious aspects—Christianity. 2. Church year. 3. Economics—Religious aspects—Christianity. I. Title. II. Series.

BR115 .E3 W15 2010

Manufactured in the U.S.A.

To Michele, who encouraged me to
"obey the work."

Contents

Preface

The argument of this book is that the best way for Christians to respond to the ethical challenges of globalization is to observe the traditional church calendar. If that sounds strange to you, don't worry: I get that reaction all the time. But I ask the reader to wait and see if this idea makes more sense by the end of this preface and the next chapter.

It often helps to hear the story behind a book. The problem that motivated me to write *The Fullness of Time in a Flat World* began when I started teaching at a small Christian college in Northeast Ohio in 1998. I had recently finished a PhD in political science, I subscribed to the *Economist* magazine, I regularly read the work of *New York Times* columnist Thomas Friedman, and I assumed from my training and reading that globalization was an economic-political reality to which we all had to adapt. However, my students challenged me to rethink my acceptance of globalization's inevitability. When I presented globalization to them as a kind of irresistible natural force, they pressed me. They were skeptical, partly because many of their families' lives had been disrupted by choices that their bosses made to embrace globalization. Many students' parents worked as steelworkers, but foreign competition and technological change had decimated the steel industry and threatened their livelihoods. Local industries were facing stiff global competition, and international trade and outsourcing were easy targets, so my blithe assertions about globalization as an inevitable force—a force only in need of proper direction to make it benign—were met with some indignation in our corner of Ohio. Troubled students often asked point-blank whether I thought it was right that manufacturing jobs were moving overseas to areas with low wages. Was there anything we could do about the trend? Responding as a social scientist, I rehashed the classic arguments for free trade and free capital mobility from the discipline of economics: there are no alternatives in a globalizing world, and these processes shift resources from less-efficient to more-efficient uses. The government could compensate the "displaced workers" and we could all still be materially better off. Whether or not we liked it, I said, we had to adapt to this new economic reality. We had no other option.

But this answer hardly satisfied my students. They were not convinced by my responses to their serious moral questions, so they helped persuade me to write this book as a belated reply. However, students' positive experiences with globalization also persuaded me to write this book. Many of them had traveled across the world on short-term or long-term service-learning trips that made them more aware of their callings to love God and their neighbor. They were experiencing globalization personally and positively so much that many of them hoped to minister to people far from Ohio. Similarly, I spent a Fulbright year overseas with my wife and three children, an experience that affirmed healthy ways of connecting with others across the globe. People like us needed theological and ethical guidance to figure out how to live faithfully both with and against globalization.

So how does the Christian year help Christians respond ethically to globalization? How might it challenge us both to live differently and to affirm the positive aspects of globalization? I argue that it can initiate us into the alternative story of the gospels and thus form us in a story that strongly contrasts with the dominant narrative explaining economics, politics, ecology, and culture today. That dominant narrative is the story of increasing globalization and the story of a flat world, a story that captures the imagination of many of us who are enamored with fast-paced technological change and innovative business practices. In contrast to this flat-world narrative, the Christian year re-enacts the gospel narrative of the coming of God's peaceable Kingdom in the Fullness of Time in the person of Jesus Christ. It is this distinctly Christ-centered story that provides the standard for Christians to assess globalization and all other ethical issues. Rather than treating globalization as the reality to which the Christian must conform, the Christian story becomes the reality to which globalization must conform. While chapter 1 will offer further support for this argument, the rest of this preface clarifies the meaning of the key terms in this book's title as a way of clarifying what is to come.

Fullness refers both to a human experience of fulfillment and to the fullness of God's glory revealed in time through Jesus Christ. The human experience of fullness has been nicely described by the Catholic philosopher Charles Taylor in his most recent book: "Somewhere, in some activity, or condition, lies a fullness, a richness; that is, in that place (activity or condition), life is fuller, richer, deeper, more worth while, more admirable, more what it should be."[1] Related to such human experience, Christians claim that Jesus Christ is the fullness of God in human flesh. As an eminent Catholic theologian describes it, "Each moment of his life is more than itself; it is the presence of all things fulfilled: the 'fullness of time' in a qualitative sense, of time exalted to the plane of eternity."[2] Christians also claim that any human can experience some of the fullness that Taylor describes by worshipping God in orthodoxy (right belief) and orthopraxy (right practice). As an expression of both belief and practice, the seasons of the Christian year can connect worshippers to the fullness of Christ.

Time is a problematic word for busy contemporary people who all too rarely experience fullness in their hectic days. Unlike us, the ancient Greeks understood time in two different dimensions and used two different words for it: *chronos* and *kairos*. This book is about the ways in which the full *kairos* of Christ enters our *chronos* days. "*Chronos*," writes Jerry Sittser, "has to do with clocks, calendars, schedules, agendas, and pressure. . . . It demands efficiency, productivity, and punctuality. *Kairos*, by contrast, . . . is transcendent reality invading earthly reality, eternity revealing itself in time, the extraordinary manifesting itself in the ordinary. . . . We perform in *chronos*, but we truly live in *kairos*."[3] *Kairos*, then, is a synonym for the fullness of God in time, which brings us to the central question of this book: Can we experience the fullness of God in time within a world where practices of *chronos* time are spreading globally and threatening to dominate our daily lives? Can we begin to experience time as *kairos* and a gift from God?[4] The chapters of this book show how the liturgical year helps us reframe time so that we can re-imagine the flattening forces of our age and improvise alternatives that flow out of the fullness that we find in encountering Christ in time.

1. Taylor, *Secular Age*, 5.
2. Von Balthasar, *Theology of History*, 91–92.
3. Sittser, *Will of God as a Way of Life*, 191.
4. Bass, *Receiving the Day*, 1–14.

The flat world is best-selling author Thomas Friedman's term for the world transformed by global technological changes in which, he argues, "more people can plug, play, compete, connect, and collaborate with more equal power than ever before."[5] We will have occasion to hear from this prominent columnist and author throughout this book, since he is the leading interpreter of globalization for the wider public today, describing globalization in catchy terms that clearly outline the ethical problems we will address. Since Friedman openly admits some of the drawbacks of globalization, even as he proclaims it as the unavoidable reality to which all of us must adapt, he invites a dialogue that will run throughout this book. For now, it is sufficient to note that the problems of the flat world, which runs on *chronos* time, are symbolized by variations on the metaphor of flatness: the shrinking of history to "development" or a process to escape (covered in chapter 2), the reduction of value to monetary value (covered in chapter 3), the eclipse of a sense of the sacredness of Creation (covered in chapter 4), the diminution of work to wages (chapter 5), the distortion of our relationship with material objects in consumerism (chapter 6), the trampling upon other states by the hegemonic United States (chapter 7), the simplifying of the Good News to the preaching of free trade on a "level playing field" (chapter 8), the shrinking of the political authority of the church (chapter 9), and the homogenizing of culture through global media (chapter 10). Going beyond critique, however, each chapter responds to these problems of the flat world by sketching hope-filled, alternative practices that illustrate how the church can improvise practices of globalization by living out of the gospel story enacted each year in the church calendar.

Globalization is more than a buzzword, although it seems to be one of those malleable terms that can mean different things to different people.[6] Despite its ambiguity, the term itself helps us understand novel human experiences in the current day. To make this clear, we need to delve into some academic jargon that clarifies how the word "globalization" captures the experiences of everyday life. Globalization is in fact the best term to describe the multiplicity of interlinked processes that result in *increased economic, ecological, political, and cultural contacts between*

---

5. Friedman, *World is Flat*, x.

6. For a review of the history of the term's usage in English, see Chanda, *Bound Together*, 245–69.

peoples on the planet.[7] While such "transplanetary" contacts between peoples in different world regions are nothing new—humans have been migrating, trading, and conquering across the world since the dawn of recorded history—the *density, speed,* and *numbers* of relationships between regions of the globe are increasing in unprecedented ways.[8] Technology has helped compress space and time in ways that Europeans and North Americans recognize in their daily lives. We call our computer tech support line and end up talking with a person in India. We log into our accounts and shift money in seconds. We download African music in minutes, and we can fly to Africa in hours. Mexican food, sushi, and Thai food are readily available in most U. S. cities. We watch political revolutions unfold live on satellite television. We network with friends across the globe through the Internet. To put this more precisely, globalization increases our experiences of "supraterritorial" contacts, which are "social connections that substantially transcend territorial geography" and create situations of "*transworld simultaneity* (that is, they extend anywhere across the planet at the same time) and *transworld instantaneity* (that is, they move anywhere on the planet in no time)."[9] These admittedly heavy terms say more precisely that the world is speeding up and increasing the amount of contact between peoples across the globe, a trend reflected in the common description of trans-Atlantic travel to England as "crossing the pond." When you consider your everyday life, you might see the point: you can see how your life is affected by the flattening forces of globalization. You, like me, might even feel schooled more in the rhythms of the simultaneous and the instantaneous than in the rhythms of *kairos* time.

---

7. Held et al., *Global Transformations*, 14–21. The Globalization Index published by *Foreign Policy* magazine and A. T. Kearney Company captures *economics* (measuring per capita levels of foreign investment and foreign trade) and *politics* (counting memberships in international organizations, personnel and financial contributions to U.N. peacekeeping missions, international treaties ratified, and foreign aid transfers). Technology is included in per capita numbers of Internet users, Internet hosts, and secure servers, but as the next paragraph suggests, these are causes of globalization rather than manifestations of it. Notably absent from this list are measures of global *ecological* involvement and of *cultural* connections. See Kudrle, "Globalization by the Numbers," and Kluver and Fu, "Cultural Globalization Index."

8. Keohane and Nye, "Globalization"; Harvey, *Condition of Postmodernity*; Scholte, *Globalization*, 60–62. Scholte offers a comprehensive summary of rival definitions of globalization as well as a comprehensive description of "manifestations of globality" (67–75). His chapter on defining globalization is a seminal contribution in the literature.

9. Scholte, *Globalization*, 61. Emphasis in original.

The liturgical year refers to the Christian calendar of seasons that was largely in place for both Eastern and Western churches no later than the fourth century after Christ—a calendar that continues to be observed in Catholic, Lutheran, Anglican, and Orthodox traditions, and a calendar that operates on the practices of *kairos* time. The *Catechism of the Catholic Church* says that in the course of a liturgical year the church "unfolds the whole mystery of Christ."[10] Each episode in the life of Christ "is capable of supporting a lifetime of reflection," but the year does not merely promote reflection on the story of those episodes together.[11] It actually *re-enacts* the major chapters of the gospel narratives through a whole "carousel of sayings and stories, songs and prayers, processions and silences, images and visions, symbols and rituals, feasts and fasts in which the mysterious ways of God are not merely presented but experienced, not merely perused but lived through."[12] These re-enactments of the story help form Christians to re-imagine the world from within the story of Christ so that they can act according to that story. For Protestant readers unfamiliar with the experience of moving from Advent to Christmas, from Epiphany to Lent, and from Easter to Pentecost, this rhythm of the seasons moves from preparation for the Incarnation and birth of Jesus (the four Sundays of Advent) to the celebratory feast of that birth (the twelve days of Christmas). The next movement celebrates the appearance of Jesus to the Gentiles in person to the wise men (at Epiphany) and the revelation of God's glory through the ministry of Jesus (the Sundays after Epiphany). The calendar then moves to the central mystery of the Christian faith, the mystery of Jesus' suffering, passion, death, and resurrection. Lent is the season of preparation for Passion Week or Holy Week, followed by the triumphant feast day of Easter, followed forty days later by the Feast of the Ascension, which marks Jesus' disappearance into heaven. Around ten days later, the feast of Pentecost re-enacts the story of the descent of the promised Holy Spirit, followed by the Sundays of Ordinary Time, which account for almost half of the calendar year. Readers unfamiliar with the liturgical year are invited to turn to the Appendix at the end of the book for an overview of how the seasons fit into the conventional Western calendar. Moving through these liturgical seasons is an experience that only translates so

10. Catholic Church, *Catechism of the Catholic Church*, section 1163, p. 329. Also see Second Vatican Council, "Constitution on the Sacred Liturgy," section 102.

11. Farrow, *Ascension and Ecclesia*, x; also see von Balthasar, *Theology of History*, 72.

12. Searle, "Sunday," 59.

well onto the printed page, since much of the learning that occurs in the Christian year is tacit and embodied. To make this learning process more explicit, I focus on the gospel stories assigned for liturgical churches to read during each season, showing how the seasons re-enact the major chapters of the gospel story. Low-church readers who are unfamiliar with the seasons but familiar with Matthew, Mark, Luke, and John will find the seasons quite intelligible.

High-church readers familiar with the liturgical year might find the image of the Christian calendar as a "forward moving or ascending spiral" helpful.[13] This spiral image embodies both *chronos* and *kairos* time. The circular and cyclical element of the calendar comes from its repetition year after year—chronological recurrence. But there is also a sense of movement toward a destination, something of a linear element, as the church moves toward the Second Advent of Christ at the end of time— toward kairotic fullness. As a convert to the liturgical year who has lived through several cycles of the year now, I draw tacitly on my own experiences of how I grew in my understanding of the gospel narratives through the experience of repeatedly *re-enacting* them year after year, each time a little differently. Whereas globalization seeks to flatten the world into a homogeneous space of the global market, the Christian year embodies both homogeneous repetition and unique variety in each un-repeatable moment. From personal experience, we know that Christmas 1993 was different than Christmas 2007, but both were repetitions of Christmas activities such as singing carols, opening gifts, or eating festive meals. Christmas thus helps us find *kairos* right in the midst of *chronos*, and the same is true of the other seasons. Unlike Bill Murray's character in the film *Groundhog Day*, Christians do not experience time as a repetitive circle. But like his character, some Christians find subtle alterations in each repetition of the season, and like him they can learn to love better with each repetition.

Some evangelical readers might bring the same objections that evangelical scholar Robert Webber encountered in his own book on the spirituality of the church year. This was Webber's response to those readers:

> At this point you may be saying, "You're attaching too much significance to the Christian year. It is impossible for the discipline of the Christian year to accomplish so much for my spirituality." This objection has validity if the Christian year is seen as an end

13. Whalen, *Seasons and Fasts*, 8. Thanks also to Harry Winters for clarifying this point.

in itself. However, if we see the Christian year as an instrument through which we may be shaped by God's saving events in Christ, then it is not the Christian year that accomplishes our spiritual pilgrimage but Christ himself who is the very content and meaning of the Christian year.[14]

It is Christ, the fullness of God, who works through the year, and such practices of the church are, in Sam Wells' words, a Spirit-filled "pattern of making . . . dependence [on God] regular and faithful over time."[15] Both repetition and meaning, both *chronos* and *kairos*, inform Christian worship.

Although many theologians have focused on how the pattern of a Christian worship service informs Christian ethics and politics, this book reframes that weekly Sunday worship, including regular practices of preaching, baptism, and the Lord's Supper, through a vision of seasons of better and worse, joy and pain, noisy and quiet, fun and slogging, feasting and fasting.[16] "For everything there is a season," says the book of Ecclesiastes, "and a time for every matter under heaven: a time to be born, and a time to die" (Eccl 3:1–2a). In this sense, all humans experience seasons in life. As Joyce Zimmerman puts it, "the Liturgical Year clearly parallels our experience of life as a cadence of festivity (high points) and ordinariness (ebb points)."[17] The Christian calendar thus re-frames our weekly worship through the year and through both the ups and downs in life—knitting together our highs and lows that parallel the heights and depths of the journey of Jesus from birth to death, from resurrection to ascension, and from the Spirit's descent until the Second Advent. Throughout this journey of highs and lows, Christians believe that they can participate in the life of Christ—the fullness of God in human form—and his Kingdom at any moment. Or perhaps a better way of saying this is that the fullness of God abides with us, among us, and in the midst of our daily lives as individuals and communities of the church, whether things are going well or poorly. God's story of redemption is the story into which our lives are being conformed. In fact, Christians believe God's participation in their lives occurs through such simple

14. Webber, *Ancient-Future Time*, 24.

15. Wells, *God's Companions*, 50.

16. See the essays in Van Dyk, *More Profound Alleluia*; and Hauerwas and Wells, *Blackwell Companion*. Also, see Fodor and Hauerwas, "Performing Faith."

17. Zimmerman, *Liturgy as Living Faith*, 114.

activities as gathering, confessing sin, baptizing new members, preaching and listening to the Word, reciting confessions, passing the peace, sharing a meal, or going forth into the world.[18] These weekly activities occur within a larger pattern of yearly activity that gives narrative shape to our lives, helps us experience fullness, and gives us political direction. To find such direction, this book takes a journey through the calendar in order to show how re-enacting this alternative narrative helps the church improvise ethical responses to globalization.

Before continuing, I want to clarify two issues with my sources for reconstructing the church year. First, all biblical quotations are from the New Revised Standard Version of the Bible unless marked otherwise (e.g., KJV for the King James Version). Second, the "lectionary" is a cycle of scheduled readings for liturgical churches over a three-year rotation of Year A, Year B, and Year C. Year A draws most of its gospel lessons from Matthew, Year B draws most of its gospel lessons from Mark, and Year C draws most of its gospel lessons from Luke. Each Sunday not only has an assigned Gospel reading, but also an Old Testament text, a Psalm, and a New Testament epistle. I draw extensively on these readings in explaining each season. "*The* lectionary" to which I refer throughout the text is the Revised Common Lectionary (RCL), the revised version of an effort by mainline and Episcopal churches to align with the post-Vatican II schedule of assigned Scripture texts for each Sunday—an effort begun by an ecumenical committee in the 1970s.[19] In a few places where the Catholic and Protestant lectionaries differ, I typically follow the RCL schedule. Readers interested in finding out more about the liturgical year can find quick and easy access to the both RCL and the Catholic lectionaries at the *The Text This Week* Website (http://www.textweek.com), an excellent site that I came to depend upon while writing this book. Its creator, Jenee Woodard, deserves special praise and thanks. By making the lectionary so easily accessible in an interactive format, she has not only helped spread knowledge about the liturgical year to Protestants like me, but she has also performed a great service for the church.

18. For this movement within a single worship service, see Wells, *God's Companions*; and Hauerwas and Wells, *Blackwell Companion*.

19. Catholic Church, *Lectionary for Mass*; Allen, *On Common Ground*.

Acknowledgments

Appropriately enough, this book reflects a decade-long journey of living through the liturgical seasons in Christian communities. Chief among those communities, the people of the Akron Christian Reformed Church taught me by example how formation in the liturgical year breeds a certain way of being in the world. Harry Winters has done more than anyone else to help clarify this through his careful attention to the liturgy and the voice of God in it; he will recognize his imprint all over the pages that follow. The adult education class at ACRC in the Fall of 2006 forced me to clarify the ideas of each chapter and provided great questions and comments. Marcia Everett, Ginny Jensen, and Pamm Ohlinger picked up the ball when it was time to discuss communal action, getting our small group to join Mud Run CSA farm and buy local meats in 2007. Readers who think that this book idealizes what the church can do should join us to get a glimpse of how the church sometimes gets a few things right in living out of the Christian story. Nor do I believe that our church is alone. The adult education classes at First Mennonite Church of Canton and the First Sundays group from St Mark's Episcopal and Grace Lutheran of Wadsworth were helpful in allowing me to think out loud about the liturgical seasons and practical improvisations that the church could model. Thanks to all the generous church folk who discussed these ideas with interest.

Generous administrative support came from Malone University, which granted me a sabbatical in 2004–2005 and a Summer Research Grant in 2008 that aided in the completion of the manuscript. The drafting of the work began in earnest while on a Fulbright grant in Bahrain, for which I thank the Center for the International Exchange of Scholars. I also thank my colleagues for the year in the Department of Economics and Finance at the University of Bahrain for graciously including me and discussing globalization, even as we were practicing it. I need to thank the lively students who took International Economics with me in Bahrain, since they helped me think through a number of issues in a new context. Back at Malone, Becky Albertson has been a tireless administrative assistant who graciously put up with my absences over the summer and took time to proofread drafts of this project. The faculty development committee at Malone, chaired by Brock Reiman, arranged a helpful sabbatical presentation in the Spring 2008 semester.

I have been blessed with many supportive friends, colleagues, and students who helped this project along. Even if they are not named here, I hope they know how much I appreciate them. Of course, they should not be held responsible for the shortcomings that remain in this work, which are mine alone. Among the colleagues to name here, though, I must single out Jane Hoyt-Oliver, who team-taught three seminars on globalization and encouraged this work. Bill Cavanaugh's summer 2006 seminar on "Liturgy and Politics: Is the Church a *Polis*?" at the Calvin College Seminars in Christian Scholarship helped shore up my understanding of theology and pushed me to clarify the relationship between liturgy and life, church and world. In 2007, Steve Long and Mike Budde were delightful hosts for the Calvin Summer Seminar on "Liturgical Identities: Global, National, and Ecclesial," deepening my understanding of theology. Participation in that seminar also brought me into contact with Chad Pecknold, who recruited this book for the Theopolitical Visions series and supported its inclusion, along with Steve Long and Thomas Heilke. Chad, Steve, and Tom graciously offered detailed suggestions that greatly improved the final version. The other participants in that seminar were also tremendously helpful: Liza Anderson, Billy Daniels, Creston Davis, Mike Gulker, Peter Heltzel, Geoff Holsclaw, Steve Martin, Kent McDougal, Branson Parler, John Roth, Allyne Smith, and Keith Starkenburg. A hearty thanks to Jamie Smith and Joel Carpenter at the Calvin College Seminars in Christian Scholarship, as well as John Witvliet of the Calvin College Institute of Chrstian Worship, for funding both seminars.

Early drafts of this work appeared in a few places where I received helpful comments. Among them were two academic presentations: the *Secularity and Globalization: What Comes After Modernity?* conference at Calvin College in 2005 and the *World and Christian Imagination* conference at Baylor University in 2006. Some portions of the current manuscript first appeared in a chapter of the book *After Modernity? Secularity, Globalization, and the Re-Enchantment of the World* edited by James K. A. Smith and published by Baylor University Press in 2008. Baylor has granted permission to reproduce passages from that chapter which I gratefully acknowledge. Portions of Chapter 3 and chapter 5 also appeared in an article published in the Fall 2008 issue of *Christian Scholar's Review* entitled "Money or Business? A Case Study of Christian Virtue Ethics in Corporate Work." My thanks to CSR editor Don King for the copyright permission to reproduce passages from that work, and to Kenman Wong and an anonymous reviewer for helpful feedback. A number of people read earlier drafts of parts of the manuscript, among them the members of the Malone Writers Group—notably Jim Brownlee, Jay Case, David Dixon, Georgia Eshelman, Steve Jensen, Maria Lam, Matt Phelps, Fred Thomas, and Jacci Welling. Special thanks to Amy Milnes for reading a major chunk of the manuscript and offering comments. In the final stages of preparing the manuscript, Luke Thompson read an entire draft, provided crucial research assistance, created the bibliography, formatted the footnotes, and offered extremely helpful comments in response to chapter drafts.

And I must thank my family. They taught me more about living faithfully than anyone else. My parents, Tom and Joyce Waalkes, raised me in communities that formed me to understand that Christian theology and worship were to inform my whole life. I hope they and my siblings will better understand how my ranting at family gatherings about economics and politics flows from that training in the Christian life. My children—Michael, Bekah, and Kara—were patient with me as I took time away at the computer. Most importantly, my wife Michele encouraged me, in Madeleine L'Engle's words, to "obey the work," so this work is dedicated back to her.

CHAPTER 1

From Flatness to the Fullness of Time

The earth is the Lord's, and the fullness thereof;
the world, and they that dwell therein.

Psalm 24:1 (KJV)

In 1876, a Canadian engineer named Sir Sandford Fleming missed an
Irish train, and soon after the world ended up with standard time. Fleming
missed his train because of a mix-up in the timetables: he thought the
train departed at 5:35 PM, but it turned out to have departed at 5:35 AM.[1]
Most people would stay the night, live with the mistake, and move on.
But Fleming, being a good engineer, joined a growing campaign to stan-
dardize time itself. This campaign eventually succeeded when the United
States and European countries agreed in the Prime Meridian Conference
of 1884 to a system of twenty-four time zones, centered upon Greenwich,
England—the same system that still governs worldwide time today.
Representatives of these countries, like Fleming, found it necessary to pin
down the reckoning of time into longitudinal zones in order to coordinate
schedules for railroads, telegraphs, and steamships. Until time was fixed
this way, each locale reckoned time on its own and defined noon as the
time when the sun reached its highest point in that area. But this created
problems, since high noon occurred a minute later in locations twelve

1. Blaise, *Time Lord*, 75–76.

1

miles to the west. This was not a problem when people traveled slowly by foot or by horse, but it became a problem when railroads sped up travel: "Twelve noon on the schedule of the New York Central took place a little earlier than noon on the one of the Philadelphia Railroad, and both were still different from the local noon in the station in Pittsburgh. . . . High noon in Boston was twelve minutes earlier than high noon in New York City."[2] Needless to say, railroad travelers between these cities were often confused. Travelers arriving in Pittsburgh would find six different clocks set to different times.[3] They might arrive on Philadelphia time but need to transfer to a train running on Chicago time—and both times were different than the actual Pittsburgh time.[4]

With the help of Sir Sandford Fleming and much negotiation, the world's engineers and political leaders helped eliminate this confusion by standardizing time.[5] Even if the sun was not at its highest point where you lived, it was now noon when the standardized clocks said it was. Likewise, the sun now set at a later time on the western edge of a time zone than on the eastern edge: in mid-summer, people in Western Michigan now watched the sun set over Lake Michigan after 9:30 PM, while people in eastern Maine at the same latitude on the same day watched it set before 8:30 PM. Abstract standardized time began to rule—not one's intuitive feelings about when noon or sunset should fall in light of local realities. This standardized global time not only solved problems for travelers, but also facilitated further globalization. Once in place, it made possible higher-speed airplane travel, digital time-keeping, live satellite broadcasts, and global internet communication. However, it also eliminated human connections to the rhythms of the day and the seasons. It cut off time from its earthly roots and made it into an abstract, standardized measure. Instead of reckoning time locally with variety, people began to reckon time globally and according to a standardized grid. However, the results were good for business: "Displaying gratitude for the gods' gift of time became less important than showing up punctually for a day's work and collecting a guaranteed wage at the end of the week."[6] A work-

2. Yergin and Stanislaw, *Commanding Heights*, 400. Also see Blaise, *Time Lord*; and Bartky, *One Time*.

3. Pomeranz and Topik, *World that Trade Created*, 193.

4. Blaise, *Time Lord*, 70–71.

5. For details, see Bartky, *One Time*, 35–157.

6. Blaise, *Time Lord*, 5.

oriented, productivity-driven way of reckoning time was now the global standard. Travel was eased even as time was homogenized. But in this global system *chronos* time threatened to displace *kairos* time. The world became flatter, and the flattening process continues in earnest today.

Best-selling author Thomas Friedman writes, "The world is being flattened. I didn't start it and you can't stop it."[7] Friedman's metaphor of a "flat world" depicts globalization as a relentless, mechanical force sweeping across the globe that changes how we think, invest, eat, work, vote, and seek entertainment, among other things. At one level he provides a helpful description of how container ships, satellites, jet aircraft, the Internet, cell phones, electronic trading, and other technologies have knitted the globe together to make it smaller, faster, and flatter. Yet Friedman's description leads to a dead-end when he argues that opposing globalization is a bit like opposing the rising of the sun: "Even if I didn't much care for the dawn there isn't much I could do about it. I didn't start globalization, I can't stop it . . . and I'm not going to waste time trying."[8] Furthermore, he writes, "If you want to resist these changes, that is your business. . . . But if you think that you can resist these changes without paying an increasingly steep price . . . then you are deluding yourself."[9] So how, then, do Christians respond to globalization if it is such a powerful, unstoppable natural force? If Friedman is right, then it may be as difficult to address its moral shortcomings as it is to move back in time. It seems impossible to question the system of globalization. However, this book argues that the fullness of time in Christ, through the liturgical calendar, offers an escape from the flat world's dead end. As I noted in the preface, the liturgical year is itself neither a straight line nor a circle but a *spiral* that allows us to move forward while also moving through a cycle that repeats itself year after year. This cycle helps us re-imagine globalization so that we can improvise ethical responses out of the story embodied in the seasons.[10]

7. Friedman, *World is Flat*, 469.

8. Friedman, *Lexus and the Olive Tree*, xxii.

9. Ibid., 109.

10. Whalen, *Seasons and Fasts*, 8. Bass, *Receiving the Day*, 81, 111, notes that the repetitive cycle of the year is "round." Wolin, *Politics and Vision*, 112, notes that St. Augustine broke with the pagan understanding of time, adding a directional conception of history. Thanks to C. C. Pecknold for drawing my attention to Wolin.

The spiral of the liturgical year, which repeats itself each year but always uniquely, contrasts sharply with Friedman's image of a relentlessly flat world—an image that has a hold on many North American imaginations, especially in evangelicalism and in business and educational circles. For instance, *Harper's Magazine* reported in 2005 that Friedman's book *The Lexus and the Olive Tree* was one of the favorites of Pastor Ted Haggard, the former head of the National Association of Evangelicals.[11] Not unlike Friedman, the evangelical author Tom Sine depicts globalization as "an unprecedented tsunami racing toward us" that will "swamp all our boats if we don't make an effort to take the future seriously."[12] The image of an inevitable flat world is common outside the church, too. As my local paper reported, the chairman of the board of a prominent corporation headquartered in our city even preached the realities of a flat world to the leaders of our local city public schools. Taking his text from Friedman, this executive urged the educators "to impress upon students the importance of strong math and science skills, creativity and innovative thinking, teamwork, global awareness, flexibility and mobility." He elaborated on this last point, adding that students in India were "willing to move anywhere because 'they understand exactly how flat the world has become.'"[13] As the chairman of a corporation that operates in twenty-six countries, he hoped that tech-savvy local students would go wherever the jobs were. But there are problems in this discourse: in it, among other things, the earth becomes a flat space, a "level playing field" of buying and selling; people become commodities; God's Creation becomes natural resources; mobility breaks down political communities; and global electronic media increasingly shape culture. But is this the only story of our world? Christians believe that the "earth is the Lord's, and everything in it" (Ps 24:1). And where is God in relation to these processes of global integration? How does the story of God's redemption of all things in the fullness of time—the story re-enacted in the liturgical year—help us think and live out a Christian approach to globalization? This latter question drives this entire book. But first we must reflect on the meaning of "globalization."

---

11. Sharlet, "Soldiers of Christ I"; Stafford, "Evangelicals! Meet Ted Haggard."

12. Sine, *Mustard Seed versus McWorld*, 35.

13. Seeton, "Students." Emphasis added.

How the Term "Globalization" Helpfully Describes the World

When Friedman says that the world is flat, he is thinking of unstoppable technological forces that integrate the world; but his account takes God out of the story. Before we get to the problems, however, I want to acknowledge that there is a helpful truth in the use of the term *globalization*, as geographer David Harvey points out. He notes that the modern period has been the story of an ever-shrinking world, of "time-space compression." For example, from the year 1500 to the year 1840, the average speed of the main transportation means (horse-powered coaches or wind-powered ships) was ten miles per hour. By 1850, the average speed for steam locomotives was sixty-five miles per hour, and for steamships it was thirty-six miles per hour. And by the 1960s the world had jet aircraft that averaged over 500 miles per hour.[14] These technological changes, he argues, are closely linked to the "monetization" of time and the mapping of the earth from above in the modern period. Harvey argues that those with capital are interested in overcoming "spatial barriers" in order to maximize their returns, a process that has accelerated since the 1970s.[15] Simply put, if time is money, then those who desire more money have all the more reason to invest, produce, and sell more rapidly.

Although Friedman overstates the case when he writes that we cannot stop globalization, he correctly points out that patterns of globalization are already shaping the way we live, perhaps even our very experiences of space and time. The North American church has not avoided these trends. Globalization is, to some extent, inescapable—part of the system of global capitalism that delivers North Americans their daily food, clothing, and retirement savings (among other things). Our choices occur within daily lives that are regularly connected to global economic, ecological, political, and cultural patterns. Our groceries, our shoes, our cars, our computers, increasingly come from a web of overseas suppliers. We cannot escape the busy, globalized social world in which we live, and we already participate in globalization in our daily lives, even if we are doing nothing consciously. Merely depositing our paycheck in the bank makes us part of global finance. Merely shopping at a superstore and buying a t-shirt made in China connects us to the globalization of

14. Harvey, *Condition of Postmodernity*, 241.

15. Ibid., 228–31. For corroboration, see Glyn, *Capitalism Unleashed*.

work, consumption, and free trade. Merely buying our food from the local grocery store connects us to a global food supply chain. Merely fueling up our cars ties us to global oil markets and global politics. Merely voting or joining a non-governmental organization links us to global political communities. Merely viewing a Hollywood or a Bollywood film links us to products marketed across the globe. We cannot escape shaping, or being shaped by, practices of globalization. Whether or not we choose to do anything consciously, we are part of economic, ecological, political, and cultural systems with global connections. Our participation in this system creates both exciting possibilities and ethical challenges that this book will frame from within the liturgical year.

Ethical challenges have emerged as timesaving technology has made global capital movement and global production easier. Thus, globalization has pressed against ecological constraints. It has not only increased the pace of work and increased worker insecurity, but also forced producers to find new ways to sell, to get people to consume; producers now can produce more than people need. This pressure has led to increasing levels of marketing and advertising, to sell all the new goods and services.[16] The increasing flexibility or outsourcing of work and the ever-greater pressure to consume are thus two sides of the same problem of greater capital mobility, which speeds up time by valuing time in terms of money. As a result, while modern, affluent people often experience time as devoid of sacred meaning, they also experience increasing demands to work and to consume, which speed up time and reduces the search for meaning in public life to the shopping malls, websites, or churches that cater to "spiritual" consumers. At the same time, the world-as-space becomes flat when work can be outsourced across the globe. Workers suddenly feel that they are in a hurry and are competing with workers in China or India. And, well, often they are. One friend of mine left a post at the corporate office of a major U.S. retailer because an increasing amount of his time was spent supervising workers in India who did work he had previously done in the U.S., while he was constantly under pressure to outsource more work to them. I suspect this story would sound all too familiar to many North American workers. Their world *is* flat. We will return to this problem in a moment.

But first I want to sketch a brief overview of globalization, the process of integration between parts of the globe. Globalization clearly

16. Ibid., 284–86. Also see Budde, *The (Magic) Kingdom of God*, 16–52.

describes the shrinking of earthly space (through air travel, container ships, fiber optic cables, or the Internet) and the speeding up of time (measured in homogenous units). Both shrinking and speeding up the world, globalization flattens out the quirkiness and unpredictability and local cultures of the "old" round world.[17] But we need to distinguish four different types of global integration that have emerged over the last several hundred years. Each of these types can be expressed in terms of observable categories, each of which involves everyday activities directly or indirectly. [18] It is important to be specific and concrete about the type of globalization under discussion, as will be evident in the chapters to come. It is also important to understand how we experience these four types of globalization in everyday life and how constraining our imaginations to them can foreclose alternatives.

The first type of globalization is *economic*, and its subtypes are the globalizations of finance, labor, consumption, and trade. Economic globalization can be detected in levels of foreign investment, outsourcing, consumer purchases of foreign goods, and international trade levels. When we talk about global markets are we talking about money, work, consumption, or exchange across borders? Each of these intermeshes with our daily lives. We deposit money in financial institutions without thinking about where it goes. We buy food from all over the world without thinking about our connection to the land. We "consume" goods produced by outsourced subcontractors to retail chains, with workers laboring in conditions unknown. We purchase foreign-grown coffee without thinking of how the push for free trade affects the small farmers who grow the coffee. (Chapters 3–6 and chapter 8 will address these aspects of economic globalization.)

We participate in economic globalization in ways like these: "Your well-paying computer job has been outsourced to India; you are unable to pay your health insurance premiums; you discover that 80 percent of the food you eat is genetically modified, that all of your elected politicians are millionaires, and that corporate advertising is inundating your kids'

17. See Giddens, *Runaway World*.

18 For slightly different attempts to do just this, see "Measuring Globalization," 52; and the review of the *Foreign Policy* index by Kudrle, "Globalization by the Numbers." See also Alex Dreher's weighted index of economic, social, and political globalizations put out by the Swiss Federal Institute of Technology in Zurich on their website at http://www .globalization.kof.ch/.

schools."[19] Economic globalization connects all of these quite common situations, forming us, and yet it is difficult to identify the source of our troubles. Can we imagine creative ways of responding and practicing economic life that bring us closer to the fullness of Christ's time and space?

The second type of globalization is *ecological*. This moves us close to the realm of the earth sciences, notably the science of climate change, but measures of ozone depletion and global climate change also implicate the social sciences, illustrating the global consequences of social actions.[20] When pollution from China shows up in the atmosphere above North America, we are measuring an ecological pattern of globalization.[21] The globe's ecology connects the people who share this planet, yet our daily behavior often neglects such connections. We drive our cars without facing the potential costs of our personal contribution to greenhouse gas emissions, or we buy food grown overseas without considering the impact on fuel consumption, soil erosion, the effects on the climate, or the hunger of others. While consciousness of global ecological connections is closer to the Christian vision of Creation, our actions are framed in flat-world contexts that disconnect us from the consequences of our actions and discourage collective action to resolve planetary-scale problems. (Chapters 4 and 9 address ecological issues.)

We participate in global ecology when we buy produce at our local grocery store. Yet it is difficult, if not impossible, to discover the conditions under which this produce was grown. We have no face-to-face connections, no community, and no reference point to offer critique or point out alternatives. Can we imagine other ways of grocery shopping and eating that bring us closer to the fullness of Christ's time and space?

The third type of globalization is *political*, tied directly to the nation-state as a global institution that helps to frame our response to global problems such as climate change. The scope of political globalization is captured by numbers of sovereign states, abandoned currencies, nongovernmental organizations, or military bases overseas—as well as membership in international organizations, personnel and financial contributions to UN peacekeeping missions, international treaties ratified, and foreign aid transfers.[22] Political globalization is the increase in

19. Brubaker et al., "Introduction," in *Justice in a Global Economy*, 1.

20. Jackson, *Earth Remains Forever*, 69 and following.

21. Chea, "China's Air Pollution."

22 These latter four are part of the Foreign Policy index in "Measuring Globalization."

interactions *above, between,* or *below* state structures across the globe. Interaction that occurs above states implies truly supranational forms of authority; interaction at the level of states implies cooperation between states to carry out global actions; and interaction of peoples below and outside state structures implies cooperation between nongovernmental organizations in different countries or the migration of peoples from one state to another. At the supranational level there are few signs that state authority is being challenged. At the *inter-state* level, the United States currently plays a dominant role in the global politics and economics of the early twenty-first century, and we will see how this role is intricately tied to the *political-military globalization* (including colonialism) that occurred in the early modern period through the Cold War period.[23] After the Cold War, when the United States became the world's single military superpower and invaded Iraq, American citizens confronted more directly the question of whether the United States is a global empire. By contrast, when North Americans join global nongovernmental organizations or take mission trips overseas, they join movements that may be encouraging new forms of political solidarity *below* the state. But where does the church fit into these three levels of political globalization and how does it relate to the reconfiguration of global politics?

We participate in the globalization of politics when we see U.S. soldiers travel back from Iraq to our towns, both dead and alive. Yet Americans still put gasoline in their fuel tanks, even though they suspect there is a connection between the national appetite for petroleum, their government's quest for security in the Middle East, and issues of global climate change. Can we imagine other ways of seeing connections and acting politically that bring us closer to the fullness of Christ's time and space?

The final type of globalization is *cultural.* Cultural globalization shows up in exports and imports of books, periodicals, newspapers, films, and television news or entertainment programs.[24] The explosion of information and media technology allows people to view television

23. Abernethy, *Dynamics of Global Dominance,* 385, writes: "Much is made today of globalization as if it were a recent phenomenon. To say this is to ignore the history of most of the world. For most ex-colonial countries a high degree of openness and vulnerability to economic trends elsewhere—including flows of capital and advanced technology—has been a reality for centuries."

24. Kluver and Fu, "Cultural Globalization Index." They cite a UNESCO study estimating that exports of Hollywood films take around 85% of the global market. See UNESCO, *Survey on National Cinematography: Summary.*

programs and films, or read news reports produced around the world. A small indicator of the complexity of cultural globalization is the fact that one can now view the Arabic network al-Jazeera's news programs in English in the United States. Increasing numbers of cultural contacts across the globe raise the question of whether the world is facing U.S. cultural imperialism, the global homogenization of cultures, a violent backlash against such imperialism, or some kind of increased common identity and shared cultural understanding.

We participate in the globalization of culture when we purchase goods or services from any of the large multinational media firms that market "culture" around the world. Yet we can hardly imagine a world without Harry Potter books, Hollywood films, satellite television news, YouTube, or McDonalds. Can we imagine other forms of public culture? Can we imagine other ways of participating in global culture that bring us closer to the fullness of Christ's time and space?

At times the practices of globalization may be healthy for us and even orient us in the right direction, toward loving God and our neighbors. At other times, perhaps more often, they may be unhealthy for us. Either way, though, the object of Christian faith should form us more than anything else. Thus, as Jamie Smith puts it: "[O]ur worship and discipleship should be directed toward forming and directing [our] desire to find its *telos* [destiny] in God, countering the malformations of desire effected by the state and the market."[25] But how do ordinary North American Christians counter such malformations and orient their desires toward God? How do we engage (or disengage from) cultural, political, ecological, and economic globalizations so that our imaginations are formed in healthy ways that bring us into the fullness of God? The practice of the Christian year is one powerful way in which this forming can take place. By schooling us in the Christian story, the Christian year orients us to live in Christ's kingdom here and now, a kingdom that frames how we understand the flat world.

How Practicing the Liturgical Year Responds to the Flat World

What does it mean to say that the world is flat? I think it means four things for people: 1) a sense of powerlessness that comes from being

25. Smith, *Introducing Radical Orthodoxy*, 261.

disconnected from stories and communities that nourish an ethical imagination, 2) a sense of disenchantment, or the experience of life as bleak and soulless, with a decrease in sacred or transcendent meanings, 3) a sense of time scarcity, experienced in the increased pace of technological change, and 4) a sense of lost moral identity corresponding with a sense that life is experienced mostly individually rather than in a moral community. These are the deepest problems that come when we accept globalization as the master story governing our lives. Each of these problems pops up in Friedman's writings, and each can be addressed by the practice of the liturgical year, which helps us rethink these problems and begin to improvise alternative practices.

First, Friedman readily concedes that the forces of rootless globalization must be balanced by local "olive tree" cultures that root humans in local places. He is concerned that people will feel rootless and powerless to address the global systems affecting them. Yet the olive tree culture that he celebrates in his writings is an American one. He writes, "A healthy global society is one that can balance the Lexus and the olive tree all the time, and there is no better model for this on earth today than America. . . . [and America] not only can be, it must be, a beacon for the whole world."[26] By contrast, the liturgical year ushers us into a story that transcends the story of the United States and connects us to an alternative story—an alternative drama that helps empower ethical creativity. John Howard Yoder explains how this creativity, a gift of the Spirit, schools the church in "genuine innovation, surprise and paradox in the ways one learns to see reality, as over against the monolinear 'realism' of the established power system."[27] Such an alternative narrative helps Christians to read history differently, from the perspective of the losers rather than the winners.[28] Instead of reading history through the American story, which proclaims America to be a beacon, one reads history from the story of Christ and the church—a story that empowers creative ethical moves and proclaims the coming of the fullness of the Kingdom in Jesus as the beacon. Alasdair MacIntyre writes, "I can only answer the question 'What am I to do?' if I can answer the prior question 'Of what story or stories do I find myself a part?'"[29] The liturgical year, which offers the saving

26. Friedman, *Lexus*, 475.

27. Yoder, *Priestly Kingdom*, 94.

28. Ibid., 95.

29. Ibid., 216.

acts of Christ as a rich source for ethical re-imagination, helps us to find ourselves in the chapters of the gospel story (not the American story) and then answer the question of what we are to do about globalization.

To be more specific, the Christian year helps us to find ourselves in a *drama* that the church has re-enacted in *non-identical repetitions* for nearly 2,000 years.[30] That drama is the church re-enacting the gospel narratives, re-inhabiting them, making them present in the church's worship in such a way that they challenge individuals and the community to discern how to act in the future. The great Swiss theologian Hans Urs von Balthasar characterizes the participant's experience of Christian drama this way: "To these two experiences, that is, 'it is really true', and 'I am there', the theatrical element adds a further, perhaps more hidden aspect: the thought that here something is being acted out for me awakens the deeper realization that everything that has taken place is 'for me'; it happened on my account and so ultimately has a claim on me."[31] We realize that the drama of Jesus is present and has a personal claim on us, so we are challenged to live in fidelity to this claim. In each season, the church finds a different chapter of Jesus' life presented as a story into which the hearer must enter. The seasons return again and again to these stories, repeating them over and over, but not in vain. Von Balthasar notes the contrast between Jewish-Christian time and the pagan Gentiles' experience of time, in which they live "'having no hope and without God in the world' (Eph 2:12)—time as the eternal recurrence of the same thing being the same thing, the cumulative expression of meaningless existence."[32] Instead of vain repetition of the same thing over and over, the Christian year returns to the gospel stories, but each time in a different context. Lent in 1677 is different than Lent in 2007; Advent in 2028 will be different than Advent was in 1968. The stories encountered in worship will speak to churches differently. But each time it is Lent and each time it is Advent: repetition and regularity channel the novelty and uniqueness. Thus the church is always learning in each unique repetition of chapters of the yearly drama.

---

30. Wells, *Improvisation*; Vanhoozer, *Drama of Doctrine*, 16–19. Thanks to Creston Davis for pointing out the importance of the concept of non-identical repetition from Kierkegaard, *Repetition: An Essay in Experimental Psychology*, 52–56, 75–76. Also see Milbank, "Can a Gift Be Given?" 125, 150.

31. Von Balthasar, *Theo-Drama, Vol. 1*, 113.

32. Von Balthasar, *Theology of History*, 41.

Even those churches that do not follow the liturgical year can resonate with the idea that they are to live out of fidelity to the dramatic lessons found in the gospel narratives. With them, I do not want to romantically idealize the church's liturgical observance as a simple solution to globalization or any other political issue.[33] My argument is emphatically *not* that the practice of the liturgical year is sufficient to give us an ethic of globalization or that the liturgical churches have got it all right. Rather, the liturgical year regularly helps the church re-enter the gospel narratives as dramatic moments for ethical reflection. Liturgical and non-liturgical churches agree that *God is the author of the drama* of the gospel story, and the Christian church *responds* to the promptings of the Holy Spirit in its practices, which may sometimes need God's correction. Our feasts and fasts of the liturgical year could become as hollow as the New Moon festivals, liturgical feasts, and Sabbaths of Israel (Isa 1:13–14; Amos 5:21), so we must not make them into a means to achieve what only God can do through grace. However, repetition is not always a bad thing; it "provides vantage points from which to see beyond the present year," writes Dorothy Bass, "affording the specific footholds in time from which we look back and peer forward. Recurring dates are like pencil marks on the woodwork that record how much a child has grown from one birthday to the next."[34] The year helps us mark progress and failure. It guarantees neither. Indeed, Lent and Holy Week teach us that death and defeat might advance the story. Liturgical and non-liturgical Christians can also agree "that Christian existence is never stable or resolvable . . . but is ever-moving, always struggling along within the theodrama."[35] The church's struggle with globalization or other ethical issues is rightly an open-ended one until the end of time, when God shall end the struggle. But the repetitive cycle of the liturgical year—returning to Advent and Lent every year, for instance—helps reinforce this sense of continual struggle in an unfinished drama, toward a future not yet secured. We are still in the midst of the drama, the curtain has yet to drop, so we must act.

Second, Friedman fails to overcome the problem of disenchantment, the experience of a daily "practical atheism" that seems so common

33. This is an important critique leveled against Hauerwas by Nicholas M. Healy, "Practices and the New Ecclesiology," 287–308.

34. Bass, *Receiving the Day*, 111.

35. Healy, *Church, World and the Christian Life*, 185.

in modern life.[36] Put another way, this is the problem of secularization, the evacuation of God's activity from human life. Indeed, Friedman advocates a Jewish, ethical understanding of a "postbiblical view of God," which holds that "we make God present by our own choices and our own decisions."[37] Friedman says, "God celebrates a universe of such human freedom, because He knows that the only way He is truly manifest in the world is not if He intervenes, but if we all choose sanctity and morality in an environment in which we are free to choose anything."[38] So, in this view, we are truly on our own. But Christian theology and the practice of the liturgical year remind us that we are not on our own and that God does manifest himself by intervening. The Holy Spirit has come at Pentecost and will remain with us until the end. The world is not evolving in a secular process; it is somehow connected to God's plans to bring in his Kingdom with the help of the church.

The problem of secularization is a deep and nettlesome one that plagues the mainstream view of globalization (Friedman's view), because it treats the process of global integration as an autonomous natural, "secular" process that organizes social life, including the very time and space in which we live and work and worship. Simply put, it leaves out God.

How the world itself became secular, conceiving of itself without God, is a long and complicated story that will involve a brief review of the work of the philosopher Charles Taylor. How did the daily experience of work life and social life for ordinary people lose its fullness and become an experience of a bleak absence of God in daily activity? Taylor has spent several years trying to answer this question, and he recently expanded upon his answers in an 800-page book that throughout contrasts fullness with the secular flatness of modern life.[39] As part of his answer, Taylor points out that modern politics are shaped by secular "social imaginaries" that replaced the liturgical and theological notions of time that had dominated Western self-understandings through the medieval period, in which the world remained "enchanted." In contrast to an enchanted sense of time or liturgical time—time defined by its connection to the time of the gods—Taylor draws on Walter Benjamin's image of modern time as "homogeneous, empty time" in explaining how the world became

---

36. Gay, *Way of the (Modern) World*, 1–3.

37. Friedman, *Lexus and the Olive Tree*, 469.

38. Ibid., 469–70.

39. Taylor, *Secular Age*, 5, where he describes "fullness."

a secular political space.[40] The secular notion of time as simultaneous occurrences began to encompass "the way we live and order our lives,"[41] and it largely eclipsed earlier notions of higher time or liturgical time that people presumed as the basis for social life in the pre-modern era. In this earlier era, it was assumed that institutions existed "almost necessarily in more than one time-dimension, as though it were inconceivable that they have their being purely in the profane or ordinary time."[42] By contrast, a secular understanding of time exists in only one dimension—it flattens out time. It empties the public realm of God's potentially unpredictable agency and relegates that agency to the purely private, individual, and spiritual realm. Where does divine activity have a place in secular time? "It remained, if at all," Taylor writes, "only in an eschatological perspective" outside of time.[43] "Higher time," as Taylor puts it, no longer grounds public social space, and so the imagination of divine activity no longer shapes how people imagine and live in public space.[44] Thus, in the modern world, "all [public] social action takes place in profane time."[45] Humans forge political, cultural, and economic systems in time, and God has nothing to do with it. So the rise of a secular world is closely tied to globalization, which proclaims itself as an autonomous *system* to organize the world.

We now live in a "global market," as so many commentators suggest, and this image of an "impersonal order" becomes a crucial part of the way we imagine and act in the world, one of our most important social imaginaries.[46] As Taylor argues, it is not just an intellectual construct but a product of historical change (and here is where Taylor differs from theologian John Milbank who stresses intellectual change).[47] After all, self-made "sovereign" European states imposed such notions of secular space and secular time when they expanded their domains to include earth's entire surface in the nineteenth century (with the exceptions of

40. Ibid., 58–9, 124–25, 129; Taylor, *Modern Social Imaginaries*, 97–99. Also see Bader-Saye, "Figuring Time," 91–111; and Wells, *Transforming Fate into Destiny*, 141–50.

41. Taylor, *Secular Age*, 59.

42. Ibid., 195.

43. Taylor, *Modern Social Imaginaries*, 106.

44. Ibid., 155, 163.

45. Ibid., 194.

46. Taylor, *Secular Age*, 171–73, 294–95, 774–76.

47. Ibid., 294–95, 774–76. Milbank, *Theology and Social Theory*.

China, Iran, Japan, Korea, Thailand, and Ethiopia)—practices now link-ing the globe.[48] Indeed, the very concept of a unified global market is a notion of a public secular space. Contemporary North Americans, es-pecially those who read authors like Friedman, thus tend to think of the modern global system as flattened time and empty space: non-liturgical time with no public space for the actions of a trinitarian God whose fullness encompasses the earth and invites us into participation.

Whereas Christians had once lived and worked and worshiped in liturgical times and spaces that invited them regularly into participation in God's fullness, the practices of globalization in the modern world had truly flattened the world by marginalizing liturgical time and knitting our globe into an economic, ecological, political, and cultural unit that seemingly operated without God's activity. Thus globalization promises an integration that rivals the true integration that will occur at the end of time, when all the saints will be united in the worship of God. Prince Albert, the husband of Queen Victoria, said already in 1851 that "Nobody who has paid any attention to the peculiar features of the present era will doubt for a moment that we are living at a period of most wonderful transition which tends rapidly to accomplish that great end, to which indeed, all history points—the realization of the unity of mankind.... So man is approaching a more complete fulfillment of that great and sacred mission he has to perform in this world."[49] Prince Albert saw economic, political, and cultural globalization accomplishing God's purposes. But we should not assume too easily that God is always in globalization. If we do, we will be unable to discern its moral problems and we will be in danger of making the story of globalization a rival to the true story re-enacted in the Christian liturgical year—a story that is repeated each year but always differently in its own rhythms of grace. As we will see in the next chapter, Advent opens a space to begin to encounter the true story of integration.

Because the breakdown of communities living in liturgical time is closely associated with the rise of a globalizing, flat world, any hopeful Christian response to the flat world would seem to require a recovery of communal living in liturgical time, in *kairos* time.[50] To move from flatness

<hr />

48. Opello Jr. and Rosow, *Nation-State and Global Order*, 167–68.

49. Quoted in Dreher, *Crunchy Cons*, 105–6.

50. Pickstock, "Liturgy, Art and Politics," 164, writes: "traditional communities gov-erned by liturgical patterns of some sort are likely to be the only sources of resistance to

to the fullness of Christ requires that the church recover the practice of a liturgical time in which it participates in Christ's redemption in time—in the past, in our own time, and in the future. By participating in the liturgical year, Christians do just this and thereby combat the impression that God has evacuated a place in history, leaving history to powerful corporations and governments and not to the church.

A third dimension of flatness is found in Friedman's understanding of time. He states repeatedly and enthusiastically that globalization is increasing the speed of change: "This flattening process is happening at warp speed and directly or indirectly touching a lot more people on the planet at once."[51] But he says that there is little we can do about the process itself, which is "why the great challenge of globalization for our time will be to absorb these changes in ways that do not overwhelm people or leave them behind. None of this will be easy. But this is our task. It is inevitable and unavoidable."[52] So there is no hope, apart from absorbing the inevitable forces of change and adjusting to "reality." But is globalization the only reality that governs our time? Re-enacting the drama of the Christian year regularly, from Advent to Pentecost, helps us view the reality of the world from within the Christian story. It helps us to recover the *kairos* time of God's fullness dwelling in human history, in each season of the gospel narrative. Instead of rushing through time, the Christian year helps us to experience time as God's gift and to find our place in time as a place of fullness.

When God is detached from time, globalization becomes an unstoppable tsunami of fast-paced technological change, and it becomes the only reality. But this fast-paced tsunami makes time our enemy, something we fight to escape in a world of time scarcity. By contrast, the theologian von Balthasar makes the provocative point that "God intended man to have all good, but in his, God's time; and therefore all disobedience, all sin, consists essentially in breaking of time."[53] Instantaneous, quick changes are a hallmark of contemporary globalization, the introduction of technologies that promise to help us escape the limits of time and space. Unfortunately, the church has accommodated this modern

---

capitalist and bureaucratic norms." Thanks go to Mark Charlton for bringing my attention to this piece.

51. Friedman, *World Is Flat*, 49.

52. Ibid., 50.

53. Von Balthasar, *Theology of History*, 36–37.

way of being in time. A concern for the church's accommodation to modern rhythms is Alexander Schmemann's point: "We must understand . . . that the intensive, almost pathological preoccupation of our modern world with time and its 'problem' is . . . because of us, Christians. . . ." He contends that Christians allowed their faith to be "spiritualized" and made into "religion," and they thereby left behind the notion that Christ "redeemed—that is, made meaningful—time itself."[54] The church allowed time itself to be secularized, to lose its sacred connection to God. We view our days as empty of God's presence.

But liturgical time is a way of living in the fullness of time, embracing its limits, just as Jesus—the fullness of God—accepted limits by entering human time.[55] Theologian Catherine Pickstock evokes how the overtaking of liturgical time by modern commerce destroys a sense of rhythm and fullness and meaning. She writes, "American cities, for example, with few exceptions, are not focused around cathedrals (and so in a sense are not cities at all). People tend to eat at any time; shops are open all night long; and every week is a week without Sunday. To be non-liturgical means to have got rid of the differentiations of time and space, and to live in a perpetual virtual space of identical repetition."[56] Such a city fits well in a global capitalist system, but we can see the bleakness of such an empty world—a city without beauty, without truth, without Sabbath, without reminders of God's presence; a city of identical repetition, of homogeneity, of flat time. Time in the modern world becomes (in Thomas Merton's words) "no longer even a seasonal cycle. It's a linear flight into nothingness, a flight from reality and from God, without purpose and without objective, except to keep moving, to keep from having to face reality." Merton continues, "To live in Christ we must first break away from this linear flight into nothingness and recover the rhythm and order of man's real nature. . . . For man in Christ, the cycle of the seasons is something entirely new. It has become a *cycle of salvation*. The year is not just another year, it is the *year of the Lord*. . . ."[57]

In contrast to secular notions of constant, always-busy 24/7/365 time, the liturgical year, says Merton, "respects the flow of time and of

54. Schmemann, *For the Life of the World*, 49.

55. This is the central theme of von Balthasar, *Theology of History*.

56. Pickstock, "Liturgy, Art and Politics," 167. Thanks to Peter Heltzel, who reminded me of this passage.

57. Thomas Merton, *Seasons of Celebration*, 51. Emphasis in original.

history and yet, because it is in the 'fulness of time,' it anticipates the final accomplishment of all that time means to the Church."[58] Because Christ's saving actions enter time and history, they give shape to our own history as Christians. This does not mean simply that we date our years Anno Domini for the year of the Lord; it means that the church continually participates in Christ now. The best way to describe this mystery is to say that the church participates in the fullness of time in its worship, bringing worshippers into the Fullness of God and the Fullness of Time. Taylor says that the Christian liturgical year embodies a kind of higher time that "frequently could be ritually approached and its force partly reappropriated at certain privileged moments."[59] Such moments could include a baptism, a hymn, a reading, a sermon, a footwashing, or the Eucharist: these are moments in which past, present, and future meld together. Each liturgical moment, writes Michael Whalen, is "neither an exclusively past nor future event. It is an event which, though rooted in the past, is experienced in the present in such a way that the future is summoned."[60] Instead of a busy time-consciousness that excludes God, Christian worship brings us into contact with an abundance of time where we are brought into contact with the One who was the fullness of God in time.[61] We receive this abundance through a generous receptivity to time that was modeled by both Mary and Jesus. Instead of trying to control time, we receive it gratefully as a gift and hence "the abandonment of every sort of calculation is an essential feature of the 'fullness of time.'"[62] By giving up control of time, the church receives back the fullness of time from God.

The world has been flattened in a fourth way, in its loss of communities that foster moral life. Friedman describes globalization as empowering individuals but threatening to break down communities.[63] He admits concern about the effects this might have on morality. Thus he worries that "cyberspace" threatens to unify the world "without any value system, without any filters, without any alternative conception of meaning other than business and without any alternative view of human

58. Ibid., 57.

59. Taylor, *Secular Age,* 195; Taylor, *Modern Social Imaginaries,* 97–98.

60. Whalen, *Seasons and Fasts of the Church Year: An Introduction,* 8.

61. Webber, *Ancient-Future Time,* 179–81; von Balthasar, *Theology,* 26–27, 43.

62. Von Balthasar, *Theology,* 121.

63. Friedman, *Lexus and the Olive Tree,* 277–305, 348–64; *World is Flat,* 489–514.

beings other than as consumers looking for the lowest price."[64] But his solution is for people to learn "these much-needed values . . . off-line . . . in the olive groves of their parents' home or their community, church, synagogue, temple or mosque."[65] While the appeal to moral communities is admirable, it limits the role of religion to the sphere of "values" and personal behavior. A Christian understanding of moral community understands that the church must exist to help sustain the teaching of habits and practices that form members into disciples of Christ. In the Christian liturgical year the church teaches the story of the fullness of God's Kingdom coming in the person of Jesus of Nazareth—a story reinforced year after year that schools participants to live in the reality of that dawning kingdom. Simply put, the church year can teach Christians how to be better subjects of their king. This is a much clearer picture of morality tied to the purposes of real community, not a vague call for ethical "values." Living for the Kingdom is more distinctive and empowering than merely teaching values to ameliorate social problems, and the Christian year provides a clearer reason why Christians ought to live morally: It is part of their calling to join the community of disciples who follow their king. This community is not merely a shelter that instructs the young, but it is the primary identity for all ages, a kingdom that claims the loyalty of its disciples' entire lives. It connects entire church communities to the destiny of human history. We join the story of the disciples found in the gospels.

The liturgical year helps overcome the problem of individualism by fostering a moral community that seeks to live for the Kingdom and embody moral alternatives. The life of the Catholic convert and Cistercian monk Thomas Merton illustrates how his journey into the mystery of the liturgical calendar and into monastic community life coincided with his journey toward social reflection and social action that culminated in his opposition to the Vietnam War. We, like Merton, can be nurtured by the observation of the seasons in community, which can form individuals into becoming members of the body, can school them in the alternative story of redemption, can challenge conventional framings of political reality, and can orient members to live for Christ's kingdom. As Merton put it, "The liturgical year . . . is the great school of Christian living and the transforming force which reshapes our souls and our characters in

64. Friedman, *Lexus and the Olive Tree*, 470.

65. Ibid.

the likeness of Christ."[66] Re-enacting the church year is therefore not merely teaching or illustrating lessons about Christ; rather, it invites participation in fasting, feasting, and living in a community that forms us morally.[67] If the liturgical year were only a teaching tool, however, then churches could duplicate the calendar as a curriculum and skip the long, slow work of living and worshipping together. But it is necessary to undertake a long, slow work in community: the only way we can be formed into lasting habits and practices. Thankfully, this long slow work is inspired by our participation in the gospel story. Simon Chan points out how in the liturgical year we participate together in Christ: "we died and are buried with Christ; we are raised to life with him; we are filled with his Spirit; we advance the mission of God by the power of the Spirit; and we await Christ's return."[68] These are not merely themes to be imparted but are participatory truths re-enacted through immersion in the performance of the texts of the liturgy through gathering, entering, reading, listening, singing, praying, eating, and being sent forth each week. Participating in the Christian liturgy through the year is a whole way of life that connects individual spiritual formation to communal formation and the Spirit's leading; it is a shared journey toward the common purpose of becoming united with Christ. The seasons are not celebrations of abstract propositions about God; they actually help the church to *participate* in God's goodness.

By participating in God's goodness, the church learns to embody moral alternatives that are part of the journey toward becoming disciples of the king. Hendrik Berkhof captures the joyful spirit of embodying alternatives in his short book on the "powers and principalities" described by Paul. Berkhof says, "All resistance and every attack against the gods of this age will be unfruitful, unless the church . . . demonstrates in her life and fellowship how men can live freed from the Powers. We can only preach the manifold wisdom of God to Mammon if our life displays that we are joyfully freed from his clutches."[69] The liturgical year can help the church to live out such joyful alternatives year after year. Thus, we might say that the Christian calendar schools the community of disciples in a

---

66. Ibid., 53.

67. Schmemann, *For the Life of the World*, 52–53; Pieper, *In Tune With the World*, 18–19; also see Pieper, *Leisure, The Basis of Culture*, 53–54.

68. Chan, *Liturgical Theology*, 164–65. Also see Webber, *Ancient-Future Time*, 24.

69. Berkhof, *Christ and the Powers*, 51.

liturgical theology that grounds the political theology of a church community that participates in the Kingdom.[70] The church is not just a group of individuals who follow Jesus, but a group in communion with him. And this communal body together shows the world what it is like to live joyfully without being subservient to the Powers of the age, because this community of disciples is following a different master, the one we find in the seasons of the year. As Stanley Hauerwas puts it, "only by continually practicing, rehearsing, performing the faith will Christians have any chance of learning what it means to keep God's time."[71] We practice, rehearse, and perform the faith in the worshipping community.

So the liturgical year is an antidote to the problems of the lost narrative, of the loss of God in public life, the loss of liturgical time, and the loss of moral community. It also helps the church to re-imagine itself in time and to improvise ethical responses to challenges such as globalization.

RE-IMAGINATION AND IMPROVISATION

A few years ago, the theme for my college's freshmen orientation program was "Imagine the Kingdom." In order to live in a church community that participates in the Kingdom, one must imagine what that really means. Friedman writes, "You can flourish in this flat world, but it does take the right imagination and the right motivation."[72] Here I agree. However, he has in mind our ability to imagine ways of adapting to the alleged reality of the flat world. But the flat world offers the wrong imagination and motivation for the church, since it starts with the reality of the world around us rather than the reality of the Kingdom and the reality of its liturgical time: the time of the past that is always becoming present in non-identical repetition, thereby opening up a dramatic future that gives the church an abundance of time in which to discern its moral options as a political community.

Unlike the characters in Albert Camus' novel *The Plague*, we will need to recover a narrative imagination, which the liturgical year can help us do. Toward the end of the novel, Camus writes that the survivors

---

70. Kavanugh, "On Liturgical Theology," 95. For a similar argument about liturgy as theology in Chile after 1973, see Cavanaugh, *Torture and Eucharist*. On political theology, see O'Donovan, *Desire of the Nations*.

71. Fodor and Hauerwas, "Performing Faith," 98.

72. Friedman, *World Is Flat*, 469.

of the plague began to forget the loved ones they had lost in the plague: "In short, . . . their imagination had failed them. . . . Without memories, without hope, they lived for the moment only."[73] They sound a lot like many modern people: people who live without connection to the past or the future, without an imaginative connection to a story larger than themselves, people who live only for today.[74] Their world, like ours, is flat, in the sense that they can imagine no alternatives. They have no way to respond to encroaching plagues or to find fullness in their daily lives. To recover the story and ignite our imaginations of the Kingdom, to imagine empowering and joyful alternatives, we will need to find ourselves in the larger story, so that we do not live for the moment only. The Christian calendar helps to feed the Christian imagination by helping us find ourselves in the largest story of all: the divine action to redeem humanity and all of creation (with human participation in that action) until the final act.

In this encounter with an unknown future, the job of the church is to *improvise* in the drama of time between Christ's ascension and the end of time. As Samuel Wells puts it, the church must learn not to make the mistake of thinking that it is "in a one-act play rather than a five-act play."[75] An urgency to figure out easy answers to globalization in a hurry would reflect the idea that "everything must be squeezed into the unforgiving span of a single life"[76] Likewise, the church must place itself in the correct act. We live after the time of Jesus, who takes the leading role in redeeming. "The most important things have already happened. The Messiah has come, has been put to death, has been raised; and the Spirit has come. This is a great liberation for the church. It leaves Christians free, in faith, to make mistakes."[77] We are liberated to do our best in the knowledge that the world's redemption is not up to us. Liturgically, then, we learn to wait in Advent or Lent or after Pentecost, seeing the time of

---

73. Camus, *Plague*, 180, 182.

74. This loss of narrative imagination is a key theme of Alasdair MacIntyre, *After Virtue: A Study in Moral Theory*, 204–25.

75. Drawing on N. T. Wright, Wells argues that Act 1 of the world's drama was Creation, Act 2 was Israel, Act 3 was Jesus, Act 4 is the Church, and Act 5 will be the Eschaton. Wells, *Improvisation*, 55.

76. Ibid.

77. Ibid., 57

patient waiting as full of possibilities rather than empty.[78] Time becomes "not an enemy to be vanquished but . . . a friend to be embraced."[79] We can live peacefully and patiently in time, responding to globalization as best we know how, without worrying that we must get it exactly right.

The Christian calendar is an ongoing drama, a challenge to secularism, an experience of time abundance, and a community-forming narrative that calls for active participation on the part of the church community, who can respond to the ethical challenges of globalization primarily by worshipping God through time. Answers to globalization's problems will require the church to act creatively after reframing globalization in light of the larger story of redemption. This requires discernment so that we can discover lessons that flow from the liturgical year; we must let the lessons of the seasons guide us. While books like these can help nudge the conversation about globalization along, church communities will need to flesh out a multitude of ways in which to act faithfully in the drama of time. In each chapter, I will sketch out a few thoughts on what improvisation might look like, but these are not blueprints, only suggestions for how churches might live out responses to globalization that flow from observance of the Christian year.

What might improvisational discernment look like for a church facing globalization? To borrow from Wells, the church seems to be in a position similar to a person who has received a gift they do not like. That person can reject the gift, and the church can say no to globalization, but this threatens "to deny the goodness of God's creation and to declare war on society." That person can accept the gift and ask what the gift is *for* and what one is "*supposed* to do with it." But this puts the church in the position of treating globalization as part of a natural order, which assumes that "when [globalization] is employed about its correct purpose all is well." Such an argument (or natural law approach) urges us to direct the given reality of globalization to its proper ends, to find God in the midst of it, to make it good. By contrast, Wells argues for a third option:

> It is not a question of what the gift is *supposed* to be: it is a question of what the gift *can* be. One does not say, "What is this gift *for*?" —and even less, "Is this a good gift?"; one says, "How can this

---

78. Hauerwas and Coles, *Christianity, Democracy*, 343. For striking comments on how music can help us learn to "live peaceably with time," see Begbie, *Theology, Music and Time*, 144–54.

79. Fodor and Hauerwas, "Performing Faith," 105.

gift be understood or used in a faithful way? What does the way
we accept this gift say about the kind of people we are and want to
be? What can (or has) this gift become in the Kingdom of God?"
The ethical issues are less about the gift itself than about where
it is perceived to fit into the story of the way God deals with his
people and how that fitting-in takes place.[80]

In other words, to use Wells' term, the church can "overaccept" gifts such
as globalization by viewing them from within the church's place in the
Christian year and then improvising ethical practices once we have found
our place. To paraphrase MacIntyre's earlier statement, because the liturgical year helps us in the church to find ourselves in the drama, it allows
us to figure out what to do about globalization. It actively incorporates us
into the gospel narratives, making us participants in them, which helps
us to re-imagine globalization so that we can creatively improvise ethical
practices that help advance the drama. Thus, the following chapters seek
to demonstrate that Christians can improvise ethical responses when
they allow the liturgical year to reframe specific ethical problems with
globalization from within the church's seasons. But, as Romand Coles reminds us in his dialogue with Stanley Hauerwas, the church will need to
practice radical patience when the lessons from the story are not always
clear, even as the church re-enacts that story in each season; we may need
to wait and scale down our expectations of bold action.[81] Even within the
context of the church year, improvisation is no fast-acting panacea.

But if we let each season reframe our understanding of globalization,
we will be able to re-imagine it and start embodying joyful alternative
practices. Instead of thinking that there is no alternative to globalization
as it is currently practiced, we will find the space to live differently in line
with the story of the coming Kingdom.

80. Wells, *Improvisation*, 130. Emphases in original.

81. Hauerwas and Coles, *Christianity, Democracy*, 40–44, 178, 342–43.

CHAPTER 2

Advent and the End of History

Globalization isn't a choice. It's a reality.
—Thomas Friedman[1]

Restore us, O God; let your face shine, that we may be saved.
O Lord God of hosts, how long will you be angry with your people's
prayers?
Psalm 80:3–4

Cartoons can sometimes be prophetic. Take, for example, Bill Watterson's November 13, 1989, *Calvin and Hobbes* comic strip. It shows the young boy, Calvin, saying that he believes that "History is a force. Its unalterable tide sweeps all people and institutions along its unrelenting path. Everything and everyone serves history's single purpose."

"What is that purpose?" asks Hobbes, Calvin's pet tiger and sidekick.

"Why, to produce *me*, of course! I'm the end result of history," says Calvin. ". . . Now I'm here and history is vindicated."

"So now that history's brought you, what are you going to do?" asks Hobbes.

1. Friedman, *Lexus and the Olive Tree*, 112.

The answer is in the final panel of the strip: Calvin is watching Looney Tunes on television with Hobbes.[2] According to this cartoon, history culminates in us—and in us being entertained.

Publishing this strip just four days after the fall of the Berlin Wall, and at the very time that "the end of history" was being widely discussed, Watterson spotted complacency in the post-Cold War mood and discourse.[3] Twenty years later, we can see his profound, satirical points: Had history (or at least the Cold War struggle) ended so that people could be entertained in luxury? Was the world made safe for us to satisfy our material wants at leisure through entertainment technologies? Was consumer satisfaction the goal of history? The massive expansion of consumer spending in the 1990s, the abundance of goods and services available, the expansion of economic activities, the dizzying array of media choices, all suggested that the death of communism and ideological history in 1989 made it safe for affluent Americans to enjoy life, to enjoy material prosperity, to go shopping. Looking back now, Watterson does sound prophetic.

And despite the terrorist attacks of September 11, 2001, it is not clear that the complacency and narcissism Watterson spotted has abated. After those attacks, President George W. Bush asked Americans for their "continued participation and confidence in the American economy."[4] It seemed that Americans' patriotic duty was to go shopping and to be entertained. Thus Bush urged Americans to "Get down to Disney World in Florida. Take your families and enjoy life, the way we want it to be enjoyed."[5] On November 8, 2001, he said, "People are going about their daily lives, working and shopping and playing, worshiping at churches and synagogues and mosques, going to movies and to baseball games. Life in America is going forward—and . . . that is the ultimate repudiation of terrorism."[6] Even in the post 9/11 world, we see complacency, passivity, self-absorption, compulsive shopping, and a desire for entertainment— all packaged in the context of a growing economy and growing freedom,

2. Thanks to my colleague Jay Case for leaving this strip on his office door for years, until I finally noticed it.

3. A Lexis–Nexis search on "Fukuyama" and "end of history" reveals an avalanche of newspaper and magazine articles nationwide in the fall of 1989, following George Will's column "History's Last Word" in *Newsweek* on August 14, 1989.

4. "Address to a Joint Session," Line 153.

5. "At O'Hare," Lines 98–99.

6. "President Discusses War," Lines 107–10. Skocpol, "9/11 and the War on Terror," 538.

moving ever-forward. Our leaders believe that there is no alternative to our current system and that terrorism is simply hatred of that system or resentment of it. In fact, Friedman claims that Americans are plugged into globalization but the frustrated terrorists are not; the latter reside in the "unflat world."[7] They are resentful anti-globalizers, left behind by history, left outside the "upward and forward movement of history [that] is the unspoken premise of modern thought."[8]

For a long time, I had trouble figuring out how I could respond to globalization, since I shared the belief that it was an inevitable fate of history. I shared in the complacency that Watterson critiques. I was comfortable with the consumer abundance that the system brought me. Only when I began to appreciate how Advent breaks into our history was I able to overcome my complacency and begin to imagine alternatives. The problem of the globalization discourse is that it proclaims itself as the only alternative in history, which leaves us with two options: to accept it as part of an evolutionary process or try to escape from it by withdrawing from the world or attacking it.[9] But neither of these options does justice to the texts of Advent, which celebrate the coming of Jesus into time. His entrances into history (into first-century Palestine, into our lives, and at the end of time) are neither a logical development of evolution nor an escape from history. They are just the opposite: surprising breaks *into* history that liberate us to hope that the Kingdom is here. Observance of this season always prepares the church for this sharp jolt that celebrates how the fullness of God has entered, enters, and will enter history. This season of preparation can thus help the church find alternatives to globalization, because it lives out of the hope of the resurrection of the dead at Christ's return rather than out of an ideology of progress. By letting Christ's time break into our lives, we learn a proper relationship to time, which frees us to begin improvising ethically. While globalization is often proclaimed as an end-times kingdom that cannot be opposed, Christians who re-enact the true story of Advent wait and prepare for the beginning of God's rule. Advent prepares us for Christmas and the divine break into time that starts the spiral of redemption. It liberates the church's imagination so that it can see history's true point, re-imagine globalization, and envision new possibilities. Advent thus gives hope to those of us who

7. Friedman, *World is Flat*, 3rd ed., 555–70.

8. Conyers, *Eclipse of Heaven*, 174.

9. Wright, *Surprised by Hope*, 79–91.

feel powerless at times to respond to globalization constructively, creating a space for hopeful practices. Christ's Advent is the reality to which globalization conforms.

THE FLATNESS OF POST-COLD WAR TIME: THE TRIUMPH OF OPTIMISM OVER HOPE

Having risen to prominence after the Cold War, the globalization discourse proclaimed no alterative. But this proclamation flattens our relationship to time and reinforces our complacency and self-centeredness. It proclaims optimism while depriving the church of hope. By framing globalization as a process of evolution, it frames any opposition to globalization as opposing progress. Meanwhile, this view says, we can enjoy the fruits of progress since there is no alternative to the way we live in a globalized world. This discourse flattens out time's meaning and deadens the imagination by foreclosing any other framing of history's meaning and by avoiding any alternatives to the triumph of free-market globalization. Shane Claiborne and Chris Haw call this "the greatest sin of political imagination: thinking that there is no other way except the filthy rotten system we have today." [10]

Friedman writes, "People can talk about alternatives to the free-market and global integration, they can demand alternatives, they can insist on a 'third way,' but for now none is apparent." [11] If Friedman is right, then we are stuck with the flat world of globalization. Yet he is not alone here. When Margaret Thatcher was prime minister of the United Kingdom, she was fond of saying that "there is no alternative" to the economic reforms she instituted. [12] Both Friedman and Thatcher remind one of Francis Fukuyama's announcements in 1989 that history had ended, that we might be seeing "the end point of mankind's ideological evolution and the universalization of Western liberal democracy as the final form of human government." [13] Later, Fukuyama said of history that we would look back and "be forced to agree that there had only been one journey and one destination." [14] That destination was the ideological triumph of

10. Claiborne and Haw, *Jesus for President*, 153.

11. Friedman, *Lexus and the Olive Tree*, 103–4.

12. Bateman, "There are Many Alternatives," 307–11; Goudzwaard, *Globalization*, 35.

13. Fukuyama, "End of History," 4.

14. Fukuyama, *End of History*, 339.

the "universal homogenous state." He summarized this term memorably, and quaintly, as "liberal democracy in the political sphere combined with easy access to VCRs and stereos in the economic."[15] "The victory of the VCR" was a global market based on "the adoption of the principles of economic liberalism."[16] With communism gone in Russia and China on the road to capitalism, there it was. No serious ideological competitors were on the horizon. History had ended with the triumph of the ideology of a free global market. Globalization, capitalism, and democracy were the only reality; they were the goal of history. It is no surprise that Friedman calls Fukuyama's book "pathbreaking" and says that it most accurately described the novelty of globalization: it was "the triumph of liberalism and free-market capitalism."[17]

To be sure, Fukuyama lamented that history, defined as ideological struggle, had arrived at its end point. For him this triumph was tinged with sadness: "The struggle for recognition, the willingness to risk one's life for a purely abstract goal, the worldwide ideological struggle that called forth daring, courage, imagination, and idealism, will be replaced by economic calculation, the endless solving of technical problems, environmental concerns, and the satisfaction of sophisticated consumer demands."[18] As a result, the young Washington policy planner envisioned in 1989 the "prospect of centuries of boredom."[19] Later, he worried that the people of Romania and China, who had desired and struggled for recognition, "will all have dishwashers and VCRs and private automobiles. But would they also be *satisfied* with themselves?"[20] Both Fukuyama and Friedman reflected a common theme in political commentary at the end of the Cold War. Since they saw the end of the Cold War as a triumph of capitalism, they merely took the idea to its logical conclusion. With the main debate up to that point being framed as capitalism vs. socialism, there *was* no alternative that they could easily imagine. Hence Friedman proposed that the globalization system had replaced the old "Cold War

---

15. Fukuyama, "End of History," 8.

16. Fukuyama, *End of History*, 108. Thanks to Creston Davis for drawing this quote to my attention.

17. Friedman, *Lexus and the Olive Tree*, xxi.

18. Fukuyama, "End of History," 18.

19. Ibid.

20. Fukuyama, *End of History*, 312.

system" as "the defining international system."[21] And Fukuyama said, "We are at a unique juncture in history when, most people would admit . . . [t]here is only 'one language,' that of liberal democracy."[22] Even Marxists had to admit that there was no standpoint from which to criticize the newly emergent system of global capitalism: "Even Gorbachev agreed" that there was no alternative.[23] At one level, no one could understand what might come next. Without socialist or communist countries presenting live options, it seemed impossible to imagine serious rivals to global capitalist regimes in organizing social life. "[L]iberal democracy and free markets constitute the best regime," wrote Fukuyama, "or more precisely the best of the available alternative ways of organizing human societies (or again, if one prefers Churchill's formulation, the least bad way of doing so)."[24] Thus commentators might even concede the evils of global capitalism and democracy, and they might agree that it was necessary to tame globalization, to reform it, or to make it good; but they could not imagine a better alternative. Those who proclaimed globalization as the only reality merely failed to imagine alternatives. Instead, they proclaimed that globalization was the end of history, the culmination of all that had come before, the triumph of progress, the arrival of the end of times (the eschaton).

However, leaving aside theological problems for a moment, there is a political problem in this move: it reduces the hope for change by constraining us to imagine only the present systems or their future evolution. When Fukuyama, Friedman, and Thatcher posed no viable alternatives to free-market global capitalism, they sought to overcome any resistance with a variation on the argument from nature, the idea that all this is just the way the world is, and there is nothing we can do about it, because globalization was part of a natural process of evolutionary development. By proclaiming an inexorable trend toward globalization and integration, they ideologically justify the current power structure, which is convenient for those, such as Washington policy intellectuals, British prime ministers, or *New York Times* columnists, who rest at the top of that power structure, but less convenient for those at the bottom of the power structure who often suffer wrenching change that is supposedly

21. Friedman, *Lexus and the Olive Tree*, 7.
22. Fukuyama, "Reflections," 257.
23. Harvey, *Spaces of Hope*, 154.
24. Ibid.

inevitable. Friedman writes that we cannot stop globalization "except at a huge cost to human development."[25] This appears to be a bedrock principle for him. To resist the inevitable trend of globalization is to oppose higher living standards for humanity. We can only tame, re-direct, and reform this mighty force of change. Even if it harms the poor, unleashes violence, or harms the environment, it is the least bad alternative. It is all we have to work with, our starting point for the hope of change. Free-market globalization is our only hope.

Such a notion of open-ended development flattens history by reducing it to evolutionary progress and eliminating any transcendent hope. Viewing human history as either a linear or dialectical process of development reflects an Enlightenment teleology of history that explicitly sought to displace God as the providential agent of history. Karl Löwith aptly summarizes how thinkers like Voltaire, Kant, or Hegel secularized "the Christian hope of salvation into an indefinite hope of improvement and faith in God's providence into the belief in man's capacity to provide for his own earthly happiness."[26] Fukuyama's Hegelian approach explicitly reflects Kant's idea of "universal history," which Kant described as "a steadily advancing but slow development of man's original capacities."[27] When this conception of history took over, it became the "idolisation of historical evolution."[28] The motto for this view is that "progress is inevitable and there is no alternative."[29]

This secularization of providence—or, more accurately, this turning of transcendent divine providence into immanent human progress—is not merely confined to philosophers, but it has actually governed United

25. Friedman, *Lexus and the Olive Tree*, xxii, 112. And he repeats this same sentiment in his later book: "The world is being flattened. I didn't start it and you can't stop it, except at a great cost to human development and your own future." Friedman, *World is Flat*, 3rd ed., 635.

26. Löwith, *Meaning in History*, 111.

27. Kant, "Idea for a Universal History," 41. See Fukuyama, *End of History*, 126: "Modern natural science has provided us with a Mechanism whose progressive unfolding gives both a directionality and a coherence to human history over the past several centuries. In an age when we can no longer identify the experiences of Europe and North America with those of humanity as a whole, the Mechanism is truly universal."

28. O'Donovan, *Desire of the Nations*, 252. Also see 246. The equation of globalization and development is nicely deconstructed in Goudzwaard et al., *Hope in Troubled Times*, 143–46.

29. Harvey, *Spaces of Hope*, 176–77, comments on Thatcher's view as "nothing other than Smithian utopianism of process attached to a very Hegelian kind of teleology. . . ."

States foreign policy through the three most common and influential models for post-Cold War foreign policy—all of which ascended after the Cold War paradigm collapsed as an organizing framework.[30] In each case, we see progressivist themes underlying foreign policy discourse. First, the notion of the democratic peace, taken from Kant, suggested that no two countries that were both democracies had ever gone to war against each other, and hence the United States would advance world peace by promoting democratic forms of government.[31] As more countries became democratic, peace would advance—a central theme in President Bush's statements on the Iraq war. Second is the theme of economic development, which quickly replaced containing communism as a major goal of U.S. foreign policy. In fact, Fukuyama explicitly describes "economic modernization" based on the open-ended development of natural science as a universal goal of history.[32] Operating within these terms, post-Cold War leaders became heavily invested in bringing such "modernization," usually on favorable terms to U.S. economic interests, to the "developing world." As economies were developed with assistance from the economic scientists at the International Monetary Fund or World Bank, progress would result. A third emerged when Friedman and others revived John Stuart Mill's global economic peace argument, arguing that countries that traded with each other would not go to war against each other. As Mill put it in 1848, "the great extent and rapid increase of international trade, in being the principal guarantee of the peace of the world, is the great permanent security for the uninterrupted progress of the ideas, the institutions, and the character of the human race."[33] In typical catchy fashion, Friedman simplified the argument with his so-called Golden Arches theory of conflict prevention: "No two countries that both had McDonalds had fought a war against each other since each got its McDonald's."[34] For a time, like many in American political science, I was impressed by these broad generalizations about economic development, the democratic peace, and the liberal economic peace.[35] Each of them provided powerful

30. For an insightful overview of this transition, see Haley, *Strategies of Dominance*.

31. This began with Doyle, "Kant," 205–35, and 323–53. He sought to revive Kant, "Perpetual Peace," in *Kant's Political Writings*.

32. Fukuyama, "Reflections," 244–46.

33. Mill, *Principles of Political Economy*, 582.

34. Friedman, *Lexus and the Olive Tree*, 248.

35. See Waalkes, "Prescience and Paradigms," which argues that the liberal economic peace provided evidence against Samuel Huntington's "clash of civilizations" thesis.

simplifications that governed many research agendas in political science and many policy-planning discussions in Washington.

However, these models simplify and distort human history. As Fukuyama predicted, they suggest there may be some technical, bureaucratic problems to solve, but there is no longer a transcendent point to the story of history—apart from material life improving. They find the hope for peace more in a process of evolutionary change than in receiving gifts from God. Thus, they tempt us to live in a flat world that denies both God's transcendence and God's presence in history. They tempt us to deny that time and history could be punctuated by interruptions from God, by the presence of his fullness at the center of history, or by the indwelling of the Spirit in the church. Indeed, the church's only role appears to be adapting to the reality of globalization and providing moral instruction to those immersed in it. The real action in this view comes from the secular forces of armies, stock markets, corporations, and media outlets—not the church. God's agency and the church's agency are thus lost here. We have no hope, apart from the promise that things will get better through a process of development. Instead of holding the key to history, Advent, Christmas, Lent, Easter, and Pentecost have no bearing on how the world's story is told. Instead, "evolutionary optimism" assures us that steady progress is the story of the world.[36]

But theologian Oliver O'Donovan, among many others, points out that the myth of progress is theologically problematic. In his book *The Desire of the Nations,* O'Donovan even claims that modern, liberal societies risk becoming totalitarian antichrists when they proclaim themselves to be the only reality. As he puts it, "When believers find themselves confronted with an order that, implicitly or explicitly, offers itself as the sufficient and necessary condition of human welfare, they will recognize the beast."[37] With O'Donovan's help, then, I have come to see the dangerous complacency in a world in which free trade, economic development, and democracy become metaphors for—or the real instruments of—world peace, since their advocates claim that they are fundamental conditions for improving human welfare (rather than the rule of God). Although I will stop short of claiming that Thatcher, Friedman, or Fukuyama bear the mark of the beast, it is important to see how their progress myths obscure the crucial difference between optimism and hope. "Optimism,"

---

36. Wright, *Surprised by Hope,* 81–87.
37. O'Donovan, *Desire of the Nations,* 274.

writes A. J. Conyers, "anticipates the best possible outcome upon present conditions and circumstances. It stands upon the strength of the present and predicts a progressively better future. . . . Hope, however, is not produced by confidence; it produces confidence. It anticipates triumph in the future because it anticipates help, or grace."[38] As Conyers says, the good news of Christian faith offered "something different from optimism: it offered hope—the resurrection of the dead."[39] This hope for the return of Jesus and the resurrection of our bodies is the core of the Christian gospel, the reason for engaging the world now. Our hope attracts those who lose faith in progress and are left adrift. After all, not everyone today believes in progress: the wars and holocausts of the twentieth century helped destroy this myth, contributing to a loss of confidence that animates the postmodern mood, which Scott Bader-Saye describes as a loss of optimism: "The homogenous, empty time ushered in by the modern era continues to reign supreme, but now without the optimistic assumption that human beings could imprint order on its pristine sands."[40] Without evolutionary optimism, many have no hope for the future.

German theologian Johan-Baptist Metz argues that modern notions of evolutionary time and history form a "bourgeois eschatology" that assumes the present is a time of innocence. Such a view assumes that "everything will be all right in the end anyway, and all differences reconciled."[41] Indeed, Metz thus argues that a modern understanding of time as evolution leads to the kind of pessimism that Fukuyama exhibits when he discusses the boredom of the end of history.[42] In Metz's view, therefore, it is not surprising that modern people do not think about the end of time: "Taking everything into consideration, is it possible to look forward to the end of time? Or has the expectation of an end of time become no more than the expression of a mythical eschatology, because time itself has become a homogenous continuum that is without surprises, a bad infinity in which anything can happen?"[43] Understanding time as evolution paralyzes us because we cannot really imagine Christ's

---

38. Conyers, *Eclipse of Heaven*, 172.

39. Ibid.

40. Bader-Saye, "Figuring Time," 93.

41. Metz, "Messianic or 'Bourgeois Religion?'" 19. Miller, *Consuming Religion*, 131.

42. Metz, *Faith in History and Society*, 170.

43. Ibid., 174–75.

messianic breaking into our benign history of development. The modern understanding of time has made us complacent and self-centered.

So how might we recover an understanding of genuine hope for the world? For Metz, the hope of liberation comes in finding "the future in the memory of suffering," specifically through remembering the suffering, passion, death, and resurrection of Christ—all of which define our past, present, and future.[44] By recovering this alternative understanding of time's meaning, it is possible to recover an *imminent expectation* of Christ's presence in our lives. As he puts it, "It is not possible to imitate Jesus radically, that is, at the level of the roots of life, if 'the time is not shortened'. Jesus' call: 'Follow me!' and the call of Christians: 'Come, Lord Jesus!' are inseparable."[45] "Imminent expectation," writes Metz, "provides hope, which has been pacified and led astray by the evolutionary idea, with perspectives of time and expectation. It introduces the pressure of time and activity into Christian life. It does not deprive responsibility of its power, but rather provides it with motivation."[46] The central question is, "How much time do we (still) have?"[47]

This turn toward eschatology (the theology of time's end) might suggest to some that the church needs to escape from the prison of material history and hunker down until Jesus returns to bring Christians to heaven. Christians who talk about eschatology often present "Left Behind" scenarios in which "the present world is doomed to destruction while the chosen few are snatched up to heaven."[48] In light of such talk, it might sound as if attention to the future is there to help us escape from the present. We might concur with the student of mine who wrote about global climate change that

> I am not going to sit here and argue for or against global warming. If global warming is true and the world is going to end, then I am not going to lose sleep either because I know that the world is going to end. I know I am going to die. I also know God is in control and He sees the past, present, and future and if global warming was not in His plan then it would not happen. I believe

44. Metz, *Faith in History and Society*, 109–15.

45. Ibid., 176; also see McClendon, *Doctrine*, 90–92, on the foreshortening and compression of time, so that the future is closer.

46. Ibid., 176–77.

47. Ibid., 177.

48. Wright, *Surprised by Hope*, 120.

> it is a waste of my time and energy to worry. I would rather spend
> my time becoming the best person I can be in God's eyes.

This student has fallen into a common Gnostic trap for American evangelicalism, reducing Jesus' concern to the plight of one's individual soul
while shunning any concern for the external world. For this student, the
end of time is a certainty that has no bearing upon action the present, apart
from care of the soul. But a truly biblical eschatology involves discerning
(in John Howard Yoder's words) "the meaning which the future has for
the *present*."[49] And, as N. T. Wright argues, New Testament eschatology
reinforces the church's concern with activity in life here and now; Jesus
brings the future redemption back into our present.[50] Precisely because
the church believes that the resurrected and ascended Jesus will return
to judge the living and the dead, it is galvanized into action. Precisely because it believes that the resurrected and ascended Jesus is the first born
of the new creation, it can bear witness to the redemption of all things.
Precisely because it believes that a new Kingdom has already dawned
in Jesus, it tries to make disciples who live for that Kingdom in a peaceable community of social justice that bears witness to God's Kingdom
now. Because disciples know the end of the story, they know how to act
in the story. As Samuel Wells argues, eschatology should strongly shape
Christian theology and ethical imagination: "By providing an end to the
story it shows that the Christian narrative *is* indeed a story, not an endless sequence of events. Since the end is provided from outside, it is not
humanity's task to bring this end about." Christians are not called to bring
about a "desirable end" but are called to act in line with the already given
end.[51] That already given end is the coming of the Kingdom in Jesus, the
fulfillment of history and the beginning of redemption. Because God has
already redeemed all things in love through Christ, the church is free
to participate in witnessing to that redemption. The good news is about
redemption, which "is not simply making creation a bit better, as the
optimistic evolutionist would try to suggest. Nor is it rescuing spirits
and souls from an evil material world, as the Gnostic would want to say.
It is the remaking of creation, having dealt with the evil that is defac-
ing and distorting it."[52] As Wright says, "What creation needs is neither

---

49. Yoder, *Original Revolution*, 57; also see McClendon, *Doctrine*, 92.

50. Wright, *Surprised By Hope*, 26, 79–91, 117–45.

51. Wells, *Transforming Fate into Destiny*, 178.

52. Wright, *Surprised by Hope*, 97.

abandonment nor evolution but rather redemption and renewal."[53] The good news is that the redeeming and renewing has already begun; God's loving, harmonious reign is already in place, and the church participates in that reign through grace.

RE-ENACTING ADVENT: REMEMBERING OUR FUTURE

But how does the church begin to live into this reality of the dawning Kingdom that redeems and renews, that ushers in a new heaven and a new earth? Scott Bader-Saye commends the

> kind of active waiting and preparing [that] is practiced through-out the liturgical season of Advent. As we remember Christ's coming, we prepare for his return and situate ourselves in that time between the times, when the reign of God has begun in our midst but has not been consummated in the world. So we learn the hard lessons that yearn toward the future, and through the simple (but hard) practice of singing Advent hymns while the world (that is, the shopping mall) bombards us with Christmas carols.[54]

Advent turns our attention to the end of time and thus liberates us to re-imagine God acting in time, ushering in a Kingdom. So the season can help us re-imagine time and globalization in ways that will help us resist the false endings to history proclaimed by Friedman, Thatcher, and Fukuyama.

Episcopal priest Fleming Rutledge said in an Advent sermon that "in a very deep sense the entire Christian life in this world is lived in Advent, between the first and second comings of the Lord, in the midst of the tension between things the way they are and things they way they ought to be."[55] Because we understand the meaning of present history existing between Christ's first Advent and his final Advent at the end of time, we are liberated to view globalization as a far less important reality at work in time. We are liberated because we see where we stand in history. Thus, we discover the current age "as a period of the overlapping of two aeons . . . one points backwards to human history outside of (before) Christ; the other points forward to the fullness of the Kingdom of God,

---

53. Ibid., 107.

54. Bader-Saye, "Figuring Time," 110.

55. Rutledge, *Bible and the New York Times*, 29.

of which it is a foretaste."[56] Advent helps point us forward, provoking us to begin living in the fullness of Jesus' rule in the present by starting with the end of the story.

By the late seventh century Advent observance had taken root in the Western church year in the form we know now.[57] Oddly, both the daily office readings and the lectionary readings for the first days of Advent highlight the end times. But this makes sense as we enter the spiral of the year: we look ahead to where the story will end, and then we begin anew. So the new church year begins by proclaiming Christ's dramatic return to the earth to judge the living and the dead, making Advent not merely a season of preparation for Christmas (the first Advent), but a season of preparation for the final Advent of Christ. Embedded in this practice of the Christian year is the truth that we go forward by going backward, that we find our end at the beginning and our beginning at the end (to paraphrase T. S. Eliot's poem "East Coker"). Advent helps us to "remember the future" and situates us again in a proper relationship to time. Jesus already told his disciples what would happen, so all we must do is remember what he has already said.

When the church says "Come, Lord Jesus" in worship during Advent, it actually refers to *three* Advents, as St. Bernard of Clairvaux once described them: "In the first He came in the flesh and in weakness, in the second He comes in spirit and in virtue, and in the third He shall come in glory and majesty."[58] The first (fleshly) Advent was Jesus' coming at Christmas, a past event that also becomes a present and future event in the worship of the church. For instance, Christians look forward every year to re-enacting Christmas pageants that invite us into participation in this coming. Advent obviously prepares the church to commemorate Jesus' birth, his historical first coming, by inviting worshippers to participate in the story as if it were in the present. But the second, saving Advent is the coming of the redeeming Jesus into our individual and communal lives through the Spirit—a past, present, and future event. As with the first Advent, Christians must also prepare themselves to receive this coming of Christ through the Spirit into their bodies, hearts, minds, spirits, and actions. (Evangelicals are especially apt to focus on this need to have Christ personally present in one's individual heart, but we must

56. Yoder, *Original Revolution*, 58.

57. Cobb, "History," 468.

58. Bernard of Clairvaux, *St. Bernard's Sermons*, 40; also 22–31.

not lose sight of communities receiving and everyone embodying his grace in actions.) The model here is Mary, to whom Advent pays tribute near its end. The third, eschatological Advent is the coming of Christ at the end of time to judge the living and the dead, and it too requires that we prepare so that we may rightly receive it as a gift. As Samuel Wells notes, such an end is terrifying for those who live in the flat world of linear, evolutionary time. If time is a commodity that they control, they are about to lose it. But for Christians, it really is good news to know that God is in charge of history.[59] However, it requires traveling through Advent in order to prepare, to learn to wait, and to learn patience and vigilance in light of Christ's imminent third Advent. Christ's ancient-present-future coming infuses us with the sense of "imminent expectation" that Metz says introduces "the pressure of time and activity" into our lives.[60] Yet the repetition of Advent year after year also schools us in patience. By the time we sing "O Come, O Come Emmanuel" for the fiftieth year in a row, it may well have a less revolutionary, more plaintive meaning. We learn through the spiral of repetition that Jesus will come again in the fullness of his good time, not on our timetables, cultivating patience in the church. Interestingly, the current observance of a four-week Advent celebrates Bernard's Advents in reverse order, starting with the future advent, moving to the present advent, and concluding with the historical advent.

The Future Advent in Glory and Majesty: Energizing the Work of Healing and Justice

We follow the lectionary here, which begins with what we might call Apocalypse Sunday. It seems like a strange way to start the church year and start preparing for the coming of the baby Jesus, but it is appropriate because it jars us out of our complacency with the present age and prepares us to be renewed in grace. The *Book of Common Prayer* makes this link explicit in the prayer for the first Sunday of the season: "Almighty God, give us grace to cast away the works of darkness, and put on the armor of light . . . that in the last day, when he shall come again in his glorious majesty to judge both the living and the dead, we may rise to

---

59. Wells, *Transforming Fate into Destiny*, 148.

60. Metz, *Faith in History and Society*, 176.

the life immortal."[61] The future advent prepares us for a present advent of Christ.

It also jolts us out of complacency. As we have just seen, there is no shortage of commentators proclaiming that our present age is the best of all possible worlds and that peace will be upon us if we only embrace the present power structure. Such arguments are nothing new and were surely part of Roman discourse in the first century—the time of Jesus, John the Baptist, and Mary, the main actors in the Advent gospel drama.[62] If we enter that drama as complacent participants, it is important for us to let Jesus startle us into imminent expectation of his final coming as King.

And the Jesus we hear from at the beginning of Advent does give us a shock. All of the lectionary gospel selections allow us to hear Jesus in apocalyptic mode: "But about that day and hour no one knows, neither the angels of heaven, nor the Son, but only the Father" (Matt 24:36; Mark 13:32). In Luke, Jesus draws his disciples' attention to the parable of the fig tree sprouting leaves in the spring, which reminds us "that the kingdom of God is near" (Luke 21:31; also see Mark 13:28–31). If we listen carefully in worship, we should be puzzled or put on edge; in our present age of evolutionary time, this pronouncement sounds odd and out of place. What does it mean for us to watch the times in a way analogous to the way we would watch and wait for a tree to sprout leaves? Similarly, Jesus' imperatives in all three gospel accounts put the Advent listener on notice: "keep awake" (Matt 24:42; Mark 13:37); "be ready, for the Son of Man is coming at an unexpected hour" (Matt 24:44); "beware" (Mark 13:33); "keep alert" (Mark 13:33); "stand up and raise your heads, because your redemption is drawing near" (Luke 21:28); "be on guard" (Luke 21:34); "be alert at all times, praying that you may have the strength to escape all these things that will take place, and to stand before the Son of Man" (Luke 21:36). Jesus shocks the present-day listener into paying attention, increasing vigilance, watching for the signs of the times. We need the eschatological jolt that comes at the beginning of Advent.[63] We need to wake up. We need to have our imaginations liberated. Jesus puts us on notice that we need to connect his future Advent to our lives here and

61. Episcopal Church, *Book of Common Prayer*, 211.

62. On Roman imperial context, see Walsh and Keesmaat, *Colossians Remixed*; and Horsley, *Jesus and Empire*.

63. Webber, *Ancient-Future Time*, 37–53.

now. Put another way, the point is to find ourselves right in the *middle* of the Christian drama, taking our cues and improvising appropriately. Advent helps us by pointing us to the imminent end, which reminds us to live in light of the reality of what is still to come.

The practice of Advent thereby forms Christians to see the world anew and live for its royal redemption. As theologian James McClendon argued, the pictures of the end of time given in Scripture can give the Christian hope and patient endurance, as well as a heightened sense of the need to embody grace and peace here and now.[64] A prophetic imagination jolts us into action, leading people such as Gandhi or Martin Luther King Jr. to demonstrate "that suffering for a righteous cause can overturn principalities and powers."[65] Precisely because we follow a royal lamb who already rules, says McClendon, we can participate in this kingdom: "the sacrificial work of the earthly Jesus has already formed this 'royal' people; we exist; the new politics has begun."[66] One clear implication of the future Advent of Christ is that the church is to practice a politics of social justice and harmony within the church that witnesses to others.

This is no mere theory if we listen to the epistle readings in the lectionary for the Advent season. The sustaining of a peaceable community in light of Christ's coming is a key theme of the readings, suggesting that Christ's return was firmly yoked to right action in the early church. Paul reminds the Roman church, "Love does no wrong to a neighbor; therefore, love is the fulfilling of the law. . . . For salvation is nearer to us now than when we became believers; the night is far gone, the day is near" (Rom 13:10–11). James, too, links the coming of the Lord with unity in the church: "Strengthen your hearts, for the coming of the Lord is near. Beloved, do not grumble against one another, so that you may not be judged" (Jas 5:8b–9). And Peter likewise connects prophetic waiting to a peaceful, harmonious, right-living community: "Therefore, beloved, while you are waiting for these things, strive to be found by him at peace, without spot or blemish" (2 Pet 3:14). As the church listens to these and other texts in worship, it forges the link between a prophetic vision of the imminent return of Christ and the reasons for embodying a just and

---

64. A contextual reading of Revelation suggests that this is the main point of the unveiling (apocalypse): to give hope to the seven churches of Asia Minor.

65. McClendon, *Doctrine*, 98.

66. Ibid., 99.

peaceful community life. We need to embody peace as the day of Christ's fullness approaches, because our peace is a sign of the Kingdom's reality.

But we are always reminded that it is God who brings about the results. It is not up to the church alone, because the Spirit is there to sustain the peace of the church. Isaiah reminds us that true peace will not come from economic development, the increase in the number of democracies, or the global expansion of free trade. Rather, Isaiah says, God "shall judge between the nations, and shall arbitrate for many peoples; they shall beat their swords into plowshares, and their spears into pruning hooks; nation shall not lift up sword against nation, neither shall they learn war any more" (Isa 2:4). It is God who will judge with justice (Isa 11:4), "For as the earth brings forth its shoots, and as a garden causes what is sown in it to spring up, so the Lord God will cause righteousness and praise to spring up before all the nations" (Isa 61:11). Thus, any mechanism that seeks to replace God as an instrument of peace is potentially idolatrous. Democracy and economic development do not beat the swords into plowshares.[67] They may provide for an absence of conflict for a time, but this is not the same as resting in true peace and justice oriented toward the praise and worship of God. Rather, we learn from Jesus that he is the promised one who brings shalom, or wholeness, peace, healing, and redemption: "Go and tell John what you hear and see: the blind receive their sight, the lame walk, the lepers are cleansed, the deaf hear, the dead are raised, and the poor have good news brought to them. And blessed is anyone who takes no offense at me" (Matt 11:2–6).[68] It is Jesus who is the fullness of messianic time, both in the future and back then. His return to complete his reign on earth is the true end of history, and the church's job is to witness to this reign of healing. This understanding challenges the claims of those who believe in free-market globalization as the only reality in history.

The Present, Saving Advent in Spirit and Virtue: Preparing for Surprises

John the Baptist takes a central role in the gospel readings for the second and third Sundays of Advent, making clear how the church reads the

---

67. O'Donovan, *Desire of the Nations*, 252–71, opens the possibility that liberal societies may echo the "liberating summons" (253) of the gospel.

68. Jesus' words evoke Isaiah 35:5–6: "Then the eyes of the blind shall be opened, and the ears of the deaf unstopped; then the lame shall leap like a deer, and the tongue of the speechless sing for joy."

birth of Jesus as a fulfillment of Israel's hopes for redemption. John picks up the story where the book of Malachi left it: with a messenger to "prepare the way" (Mal 3:1).[69] John's message puts him squarely in line with the history of redemption: "He brings the people back to the wilderness again and immerses everyone who is ready to convert in the water of the Jordan at the very place where Israel stood before, under Joshua's leadership, it crossed over into the Land."[70] John must come to prepare the way for the one who is to come after him, the fullness of Israel's deliverance. So John appears to us in the wilderness of our lives and preaches again to us, "Repent, for the kingdom of heaven has come near" (Matt 3:2). The reality is that we must repent if we are to enter into the land of this kingdom of peace that is so near, because we are not ready to receive it and thus to share it. Advent is partly a school for re-conversion, repentance, and a return to divine hope.

The baptism of repentance that John preaches is preparation for what will come with the Kingdom: "Prepare the way of the Lord, make his paths straight. Every valley shall be filled, and every mountain and hill shall be made low, and the crooked shall be made straight, and the rough ways made smooth; and all flesh shall see the salvation of God" (Luke 3:4–6; Isa 40:3–5). This Kingdom is breaking in dramatically to our own world, so we had better repent and be ready—or so goes John's message. John even seems to imagine that the redemption of Israel was to be violent: "Even now the ax is lying at the root of the trees; every tree therefore that does not bear good fruit is cut down and thrown into the fire" (Matt 3:10).[71] He's partly right—after all, Herod and the Roman authorities violently opposed the coming of his Kingdom—but he also misses the humble, peaceful nature of Christ's coming as a newborn infant. This Jesus was a *surprising* redeemer for Israel. Hence, in Advent the church often reads Matthew 11 where John's disciples ask Jesus if he really is the Messiah. They are genuinely puzzled about how this Messiah is proceeding. We must be ready to admit that God's present and final breaking-in on globalization might look different than we expect. We must be prepared for surprises in the redemptive coming of the Kingdom on earth. At this point in Advent we are reminded that in our preparation

69. Lohfink, *Does God Need the Church?* 121–39.

70. Ibid., 126.

71. Thanks to Harry Winters for making this point clear.

we must look beyond to the one who is greater than the messenger.[72] We must repent in order to receive this coming of Christ through the Spirit, this redemption. As the church sometimes reads in Advent, "From his fullness we have all received grace upon grace. The law indeed was given through Moses; grace and truth came through Jesus Christ" (John 1:16–17). But this Jesus was a surprising Messiah.

As Robert Webber says, Advent is a time for the church to receive this message of the fullness of God's gracious redemption, to let "God break in on us in a fresh way."[73] Another Advent reading reminds us "that the one who began a good work among you will bring it to completion by the day of Jesus Christ" (Phil 1:6). The church is the beginning of this work, but its work is not yet done. We wait with John the Baptizer for the one who is to come. The church is now in John's position, heralding the coming of one who is much greater than the messenger, calling the world to repentance in advance of an imminent Kingdom. Advent observance prepares us to receive this surprising redemption into our own personal and communal lives in the present. It breaks us open to receive miraculous divine intervention, to receive the sharp break with history that Jesus' coming represents. But that requires the church to repent and be re-baptized with the Spirit.

The Historical, Fleshly Advent in the Holy Family

Yet this does not exhaust the full meaning of Advent for globalization. We have yet to touch upon for the commemoration of the incarnate Messiah's entry into time. As John the Baptist already signals to us, Jesus in the flesh is the embodiment of the hopes of Israel coming to life. His fullness is partly a fulfillment of past hopes. But this cosmic fulfillment takes a surprising turn. Not only does he enter into Israel's history, but he enters into a Jewish family from Galilee (the boondocks of Palestine in that day) and is born to young Mary, an unwed mother. Here is where the church can learn to abide with the poor and exiled, when it journeys into the final Sunday of Advent, the Sunday where attention is directed to the holy family's role in preparation for the first coming of Christ. If we want to know how to learn patience and trust amidst the darkness, if we want

---

72. In all four of the gospel accounts, John points beyond himself to Jesus (Matt 3:11; Mark 1:7; Luke. 3:16; John 1:27).

73. Webber, *Ancient-Future Time*, 39.

to prepare for Christ's coming, if we want to return from exile, if we want to gain hope in facing globalization, if we want to join the poor, then we must listen with Joseph and Mary. We must *wait* with them. We must receive Christ with them, in the realm of the personal (which, feminists remind us, is always political).

Matthew's account focuses on the disgrace that Joseph faced in being engaged to a woman who was pregnant with someone else's child. An angel appears in a dream to tell him, "The child conceived in her is from the Holy Spirit. She will bear a son, and you are to name him Jesus, for he will save his people from their sins" (Matt 1:20–21). Joseph, of course, listens to the angel, as he does when the angel warns him to flee to Egypt and later to return to Israel (Matt 2:13–23). Joseph's willingness to listen to the angels—his faith, trust, and obedience—make the nativity possible. Likewise, we must listen for God's words or visions and act on faith in responding to globalization. Similarly, Luke's lengthy account of the preparations for the nativity (split up and read on the fourth Sunday of Advent) focuses on Mary's faith, trust, and obedience. What does it mean for us to prepare for Christ's coming in the way that Mary did? And what would this mean for us in relation to globalization? Mary's affirmation of the divine plan in the Annunciation story provides a simple and powerful example. Despite her fear and confusion over the announcement from the Angel Gabriel, she says, "here am I, the servant of the Lord; let it be with me according to your word" (Luke 1:38).

Re-Imagining Globalization through Mary's Eyes

The dialogue in Luke raises four questions for those of us contemplating how to re-imagine globalization, by helping us attend closely to the dialogue between Mary and the angel Gabriel. First, God favors Mary (Luke 1:28) and is with her. Likewise, he favors us and is with us. This is grace, the undeserved favor with which God looks upon us. Are we able to accept that God's grace can break into our lives? Can we *receive* God's love and favor? This seems essential to our recovering the ability to face globalization constructively and creatively. We need to overcome the sense of powerlessness that often comes when we think of globalization as an irresistible reality. God's grace is the gift that frees us to respond, knowing that we are powerless on our own but that God can do amazing things through powerless, marginal people like us and Mary. Just as Mary and Joseph were receptive to the angel's startling messages, the church must learn to receive startling grace from God in order to figure out the situation the church is in, knowing that it is not all up to us to figure these things out, trusting in the hope that God will redeem his people in the fullness of time. Mary and Joseph allowed God to break into their present in a fresh and unexpected way. Likewise, the church must be open to receiving God's fullness through the Spirit so that it can live in accord with the end of the story it has already been given.[74] Instead of living in paralyzing worry, the church is liberated when it waits in prayerful attention. Such a practiced receptivity to grace is an essential part of Advent spiritual discipline. It makes us ready to receive surprises.

Second, can we receive God's gift of the Son through the Holy Spirit? What will it mean for us to allow the Spirit to come upon us and "overshadow" us as it did Mary (Luke 1:35) as we prepare for the arrival of the Son? What does it mean for us to allow the Holy Child to take root within us through the Spirit? In Luke's story, as in many icons of the Annunciation, there is a closeness and nearness of the Spirit—a hovering presence—that empowers us to break out of our pre-Advent complacency and to see our present as the time of the Lord. We need this gentle Spirit to help us overcome our hopelessness and listlessness. We need the Spirit to come near to help us respond in faith, trust, and action. As expectant or adoptive parents can attest, the imminent arrival of a child transforms the time, prompting the parents to purchase cribs, paint bedrooms, and pick out names. The parents trust that this good work, this growing presence inside the expectant mother, will be brought to completion. We must trust that Christ will live in us and give birth to good works in the body of the church through the Spirit. Just as Mary was receptive to the Spirit's overshadowing, the church must receive the Spirit in order to receive grace in the present. With the Spirit's help, the church can be more open to the fullness of God's life becoming present in time, just as the fullness of God became present in the womb of Mary. Then the church can see how the life of God is alive in the body of human time, how the Kingdom is coming into gestation and straining to be born (Rom 8:19–23)—right in the midst of our current day.[75] We can learn to see time as vibrantly alive and full of wonder and tension, with God's new creation bursting forth within the time of the present, rather than seeing

74. Wells, *Transforming Fate into Destiny*, 179.
75. Wright, *Surprised by Hope*, 103–4.

time as the flat stage for a process of evolutionary development—or as a place to be evacuated while we wait for the end. But this will require that the church do better than the congregation in the synagogue at Nazareth when it heard Jesus proclaim that Isaiah's healing promises were fulfilled in their midst, on that day. Gerhard Lohfink puts us in the complacent congregation at Nazareth:

> Apparently it makes people uncomfortable to have God appear concretely in their lives. It puts all their desires and favorite ideas in danger, and their ideas about time as well. It cannot be today, because in that case we would have to change our lives *today*. So we prefer to delay God's salvation to some future time. There it can rest, securely packaged, hygienic, and harmless.[76]

Unlike most everyone else in Nazareth, Mary believed that the fullness of time was present with her, and this receptivity to the Spirit liberated her, just as it can liberate the church. To emulate Mary, however, we in the church must be willing to change right now.

Third, however, to bring the work of the Spirit to completion requires our cooperation. Mary said yes to the angel's word, because she was a servant of the Lord. If we prepare ourselves to react to God as Mary did, then we will be prepared to say yes when our time comes for taking part in the coming of the fullness of time, the reign of Jesus the King. What will it mean for us to respond to globalization as humble servants of God, as people who wait and respond with Mary? How can we say yes to God? Just as Mary said yes, a liberated church must cooperate with God. It must say yes to the Spirit's leadings if there is to be a rebirth of hope in facing globalization. As the *Book of Common Prayer* puts it, we pray that "your Son Jesus Christ, at his coming, may find in us a mansion prepared for himself."[77] While divine initiative starts things off, there must be a human response that makes space for the fullness of God to take root in time. One of the most striking signs of a liberated church is its willingness to live differently in time than the conflict-ridden world, to live in harmony and justice with itself and with its neighbors. Embodying social justice is therefore a response to the question of what the church must do before the end; it is part of witnessing to the good news and making disciples until the end of the age. The imminence of the end of the age picks up on eschatological themes from the end of the year, Ascension and Pentecost.

76. Lohfink, *Does God Need the Church*, 136.

77. Episcopal Church, *Book of Common Prayer*, 212.

Because the church has the imminent expectation of Jesus' return it is always saying "both 'Have mercy on us—give us more time,' and 'Come Lord Jesus—give no more time to the oppressors.'"[78] What unites these contrasting attitudes toward the present is a desire to see God's will be done on earth, just as it is done in heaven. The first request—give us more time—reminds us that the church needs time to make disciples of all nations (Matt 28:19). The second request—bring justice to the oppressors—reminds us of Mary's song. As Mary did, the church hungers and thirsts for justice—for the people of God to be restored, for the poor to be lifted up, and for the haughty to be brought low—as it cooperates with God in the birth of redemption and recreation in a world so often enslaved by decay or lost hope.

Fourth, then, the church can learn to hunger for the justice of the kingdom as Mary did. We discover that she was anxious to take part in God's plans for the redemption of all things (not just souls), as we discover in Luke's account of her song (the Magnificat), which includes these strikingly political lines:

> He has shown strength with his arm; he has scattered the proud in the thoughts of their hearts. He has brought down the powerful from their thrones, and lifted up the lowly; he has filled the hungry with good things, and sent the rich away empty. He has helped his servant Israel, in remembrance of his mercy, according to the promise he made to our ancestors, to Abraham and to his descendants forever. (Luke 1:51–55)

This coming redemption of Jesus is both intensely personal and intensely political. On one side, Mary is a humble servant who has a deeply personal relationship with her God through the overshadowing Spirit, but on the other side she is also deeply committed to the historic understanding of God's redemption as more than just salvation from sins but as liberation of his covenant people from oppression. To Mary, the coming salvation is going to redeem the world in just the ways that Isaiah prophesied. God will lift up the humble and cut down the haughty; he will feed the hungry and give the rich nothing to eat. This salvation is going to be the re-creation of Israel, the fulfillment of the covenant promises to Abraham, Isaac, and Jacob. It will be the re-constitution of a true community of God's people. And this Jesus will be the one who will completely redeem his people from their troubles. He will rescue us from our

---

78. Knight, *Eschatological Economy*, 245.

exile and restore us to the land (to use Israel's biblical metaphor). He will be our only King. Just as Mary gave her primary allegiance to God, so the church must serve Jesus as its only king, must live in the Kingdom drama as its primary story of identity, and must begin practicing the politics of the Kingdom in the present. Oliver O'Donovan argues that Advent prepares us for a challenge to all other authorities.[79] It helps us to break free from those authorities in order to submit as servants, like Mary, to divine authority. But this submission does not occur in a vacuum or require us to take action under our own power. While Mary had only the history of Israel to draw on, the church can draw on the historical, fleshly Advent of Christ as a precedent and as a source of power. O'Donovan writes, "Christ the awaited King has come; he has assumed every structure of law and authority under his own command. He *has come*, we say. The predominant tense in Advent is past-perfect, not future. . . . God has done something which makes it impossible for us any more to treat the authority of human society as final and opaque."[80] Instead of accepting the reality of free-market globalization as the final authority, we can find ourselves in the new Kingdom of love that will have the final word. But we are thankful to discover that it is not up to us to bring about this Kingdom; rather, we receive it as the fruits of the redemption already brought by Christ's first Advent on earth. While Mary saw Jesus as the fulfillment of the hopes of Israel, the church understands Jesus also as the fulfillment of the world's hope for a liberating King. As the group of disciples constituted to serve that liberating the King, the church begins practicing the politics of the Kingdom now.

Mary's example illustrates how Advent helps us to re-imagine globalization's place in history, its supposed inevitability, and the supposed lack of alternatives to it. She had cultivated enough of an eschatological imagination to appreciate what she was hearing when she was told that she would bear one who would "save his people from their sins" (Matt 1:21). Thankfully, the practice of Advent can help the church to cultivate its eschatological imagination so that the church can be liberated to see that the alternative to the end of history is the coming of the Kingdom, God's loving reign breaking in to history, the restoration of Israel, the new creation, in which justice and peace reign. The eschatological jolts that come at the beginning of Advent wake up the church to see time

79. O'Donovan, *Desire of the Nations*, 253.
80. Ibid.

as alive with God's possibilities for renewal and redemption. Instead of accepting with equanimity the proclamation that resistance to globalization is futile, because globalization is the only evolutionary reality, the church is liberated to imagine that the Kingdom of God is the reality toward which history points, the culmination of history. And instead of trying to escape this supposedly unavoidable reality, the church is liberated to realize that God is at work reclaiming his rule over the world. Just as Mary did not see the Roman Empire, Herod, the Jewish leadership, or even her family as the final authorities, so also the church should not accept Thatcher, Fukuyama, or Friedman as the final authorities. Indeed, the church can see that anyone who proclaims history to be closed is proclaiming a rival kingdom to the true kingdom. Neither Caesar nor the VCR gets the final word. The final word belongs to the Word made flesh that dwelt among us in order to inaugurate a Kingdom community (John 1:14). The eschatological jolts at the beginning of Advent help prepare us to allow that Word to "find in us a mansion prepared for himself."

Here we see the deep continuity between all three Advents, the past arrival of the Son meeting the present coming of redemption turning us to the future coming, because we see that our salvation is not yet complete. Like Mary, the church on earth today is not yet united with its Father in heaven. Like Mary, we live under political authorities other than Jesus. Like Mary, we are waiting for redemption, waiting to be returned from exile. Like Mary, we might be as poor as or feel as helpless as an unwed mother. Unlike Mary, however, we do not always dwell in harmony with the Spirit. So we need to learn to wait with Mary, to abide with God in patience, to cooperate with the Creator in allowing the fullness of time to arrive and be borne out in our lives. By doing so, the church begins again to show the world its true King and its ultimate destiny.

Improvising Practices

But what will it mean to reframe globalization by living out of the dramas of Mary, Joseph, John the Baptist? I want to offer concrete practices that flow out of each season's worship in the hope that readers will brainstorm practices in their own church settings and improvise ethical responses to globalization's moral challenges. Two practices commend themselves in light of this chapter's analysis.

First, merely recovering practices of Advent can help churches respond to the monolithic claims for globalization as some kind of natural, evolutionary reality. Many Protestant churches have discovered the tradition of the Advent wreath, lighting a new candle on each of the four Sundays of the season. A tangible sign of anticipation, the candles remind us that we are waiting for the coming of Christmas Day, the beginning of twelve days of feasting to celebrate the incarnation of Christ. Our family has gotten into the habit of trying to light the candles of the Advent wreath most nights during the weeks before Christmas. We turn out all the lights in the house, we read an assigned Scripture passage (usually a prophetic passage), and then we sing Advent and Christmas songs. "O Come, O Come Emmanuel" is a personal favorite, since it captures the mood of Advent, the tone of expectant waiting for redemption. Although we permit ourselves to sing Christmas carols, the quiet songs in minor keys often fit the mood of hushed darkness and glowing candlelight. In the midst of the busy-ness of the secular Christmas shopping season, we try to make space for quiet anticipation. Like the people of Israel, we often long for the long-expected deliverer to break into time and establish his rule. This longing reminds us of our only true hope.

Advent songs and stories remind the church that its hope is rooted in the story of Christ's Kingdom, rather than in optimistic stories of the spread of markets, democracies, or economic development. As the church awaits its King's return, it can start to see globalization as something other than a natural order of the universe so that it can start to allow Christ's presence to inform its actions. The church can learn to embody justice now as a sign that points the way to the rule of God. Crafting creative ways of loving its neighbors, the church can demonstrate how the reign of God has begun. Advent practice therefore cultivates an eschatological imagination that liberates us to challenge the discourse of evolutionary development. If we prepare to receive this Kingdom yet again, we begin to realize that there *are* alternatives and that to challenge practices of globalization is not necessarily to challenge "human development." In fact, it might be necessary to challenge some of those practices in order to help people find the true end of history: the triumph of the Messianic Kingdom. Advent prepares us to receive this triumph as a surprising gift rather than a rude shock. Advent reminds the church that the future is not just a story of upward progress. Rather, it is the story of how Christ will come again. Yet in the early Advent gospel passages Christ tells us that he will come in surprising ways, teaching the church that there is a mysterious quality to the end of time, jolting us out of complacency, and cultivating postures of vigilance, expectancy, and patience. We learn that our King will come again from the transcendent realm to judge us, and so we want to be ready.

If we walk prayerfully through the season with Mary, then we will be closer to the humble who will be lifted up than the rich ones who will be turned away hungry. Advent stories remind us that God works more through young peasant girls in Palestine (when they allow him) than through Roman governors (despite their intentions). As we prepare to turn to the Christmas drama, we can take heart from the fact that God makes Mary a central player in accomplishing his purposes, while Quirinius (the governor of Syria who called a census) and Herod play only small roles in accomplishing his purposes. There was a crucial difference between Mary and those who participated in the Roman imperial power structure. Mary was able to understand what was happening because she was ready, whereas the imperial power structure of the day took no notice of the drama of redemption happening in one little corner of the empire. While the leaders of empire believed they were flattening the world and making perpetual peace possible, while they appeared to be fostering the conditions for stable evolutionary development, there was a Kingdom springing up inside it that would begin lifting the humble and bringing down the proud. But only those who practice prayerful attention will be able to see and receive this Kingdom. The true end of history will come when the rich and the poor are on the same level in the feast of the Lamb, when the King returns.

A second set of practices, then, will be to embody hopeful works of social justice while "building for the kingdom," to use N. T. Wright's formulation.[81] This will help us transcend the dualism with which we began this chapter and which often divides the church. The social gospel side of the church often hopes to build social justice through incremental, evolutionary change. They argue that it is up to the church to build the Kingdom through intervention in the forces of history as we see them. But this approach un-creatively accepts the terms that make globalization inevitable. The church is only left to re-direct or reform something that it must accept as given. "At the other end of the scale there are those who declare that nothing can be done until the Lord returns and everything

---

81. Wright, *Surprised by Hope*, 213–22.

is put to rights. The forces of evil are too entrenched, and nothing save a great apocalyptic moment of divine power can address them or change the deep structures of the way things are."[82] But this approach to social justice "banishes the continuing healing activity" of the Triune God in the world.[83] It evacuates Christian concern for the world to the realm of the hereafter. Instead of hungering and thirsting for the fulfillment of justice in time, as Mary did, the church allows complacency to take over. It is all too easy to abandon concern for the world while we cultivate our "personal relationships with Jesus." This is not biblical Christianity, which finds great comfort and energy to do the work of justice in eschatology: those who trust "in God making a whole new world in which everything will be set right at least, are unstoppably motivated to work for that new world in the present."[84] Like Mary, we must hope for this and be ready to cooperate in receiving it.

How could God challenge the dominant power structure of globalization through humble servants? How could he bring his liberating summons to the world through the church, which appears marginal to the sweep of global history? In the fleshly Advent he did it through Mary, in a surprising way that even John the Baptist did not expect. Through small actions of social justice, the world might begin to see the unexpected, micro-politics of the Kingdom in our local churches—a politics that works through marginalized people to give genuine hope to the downtrodden. But this will require a present Advent of Christ, a rebirth of him in our lives. This readiness to receive Christ into our midst again thus opens us to the future Advent of power and glory.

Can the world see hints of the justice to come, hints of what God's reign looks like, when it looks at our local churches? Will we be ready to receive God's reign when it comes? It is the point of Advent to reflect upon questions like these and to prepare the body of the church to make space for God's gifts of redemption before the fullness of God arrives again in the fullness of time.

---

82. Ibid., 215.

83. Ibid., 216.

84. Ibid., 214.

CHAPTER 3

Christmas and the Globalization of Finance

Neither a borrower nor a lender be: For loan oft loses both itself and friend,
And borrowing dulls the edge of husbandry.
Shakespeare, *Hamlet*, Act 1, Scene 3

With all wisdom and insight [God] has made known to us the mystery
of his will, according to his good pleasure that he set forth in Christ, as a
plan for the fullness of time . . .
Ephesians 1:8b–10a[1]

Political analyst Kevin Phillips links the problems of the last chapter to the problems we will encounter in this chapter. As he puts it, "Anglo-Saxon speculative capitalism . . . decided to celebrate the 'end of history' and the perceived vacuum of serious economic rivalry by staging the largest-ever orgy of debt and credit."[2] The global expansion and global bursting of the so-called housing bubble provides an instructive case study of deeper problems that we will explore in a moment. But on the personal level we should not consider ourselves exempt from problems of the global financial system. When it comes time to imagine improvisational practices, we

1. This text is always read when there is a second Sunday after Christmas.
2. Phillips, *Bad Money*, 181. Thanks to Jane Hoyt-Oliver for this reference.

must start at home, understanding how we all participate in a system of global money circulation that runs counter to the forgiveness at the heart of the Kingdom.

Not long ago, the *New York Times* ran a business story that started out this way: "The wide availability of automated teller machines, Web banking, and electronic payroll deposits has made banks almost an abstract concept. About the only time you need to visit a branch these days is to deposit a check."[3] But the story was about how you could now make deposits with digital images of paper checks, scanned into the computer. So much for the need to visit a branch, one of the last traces of physicality in banking. Forget a trip to the bank: you can scan in your checks and deposit them electronically, all from the comfort of your own desk. Yet this illustrates how global money and banking systems, accelerated by information technology systems, encourage us to disdain our earthiness, to ignore the real "flesh and blood" behind money and credit.[4] We have moved from coins to currency, from checks to electronic debits. However, when money becomes an electronic transfer it is less clear what it really is. Money and finance increasingly become abstractions that mediate the value even of human relationships.[5] "The problem with money is . . . that it substitutes for particularity instead of investing in it and affirming it."[6] We value particular things in terms of money rather than attending to their uniqueness, thus allowing the "money metric" to "flatten everything—and indeed everyone—onto a kind of level objective plane."[7]

Global money systems can then detach us from our particular communities and from human relationships.[8] Now when we pull up to a gas station to fuel up, we can pay merely by scanning a credit or debit card at the pump—and we never even need to talk with a gas station attendant.[9] Framed as a trend toward greater efficiency to speed up financial transactions, the technology discourages human connections: instead of chat-

---

3. Joachim, "Sparing Paper Checks." Even Friedman, *World is Flat*, 3rd ed., 515–18, notices the intrusion of technology into relationships, highlighted in a taxi ride from the airport to downtown Paris.

4. Goodchild, *Theology of Money*, 230, 238–39, 241, where he gives a fascinating reading of Shakespeare's *Merchant of Venice*.

5. Ibid., 65, 80, 82, 212–14.

6. Ibid., 214.

7. Gay, *Cash Values*, 83.

8. Goodchild, *Theology of Money*, 64–65, 178.

9. Thanks to Andrew and Lynn Rudd for this point.

ting about the weather, we charge it and go. Financial systems promoting this kind of mobility now extend around the world. Even when traveling outside our home country we can spend months or years abroad while relying on ATM machines. My own family did this while living in the Middle East for ten months, using a debit card to withdraw cash or spend debits out of our local credit union account back home in Ohio without ever having to open an account where we lived. We even traveled freely to other countries, all the while needing to carry only two pieces of plastic to pay for the rest of our journeys: our debit card and a credit card. Although such personal capital mobility facilitates travel (and allows Christians to move freely), it also detaches us from our neighbors and removes us from connecting with others in communities. Instead of getting to know people at the local bank, we used the ATM. Although we gained in mobility, we lost in human connection. Since we returned, we found more self-checkout systems at grocery stores and even libraries.

These systems of monetary mobility cultivate an attitude of arrogance, a sense of mastery that monetary and credit systems themselves tend to generate as they encourage us to pursue money for the sake of money and to value everything in terms of monetary value. As Philip Goodchild notes, "Money . . . expresses individual power as can nothing else."[10] Our ability to draw on credit while overseas allowed my family to move freely, making us into sovereign choosers who could do whatever we wanted to do when we could pay for it: "the one possessed of money appears to enjoy a sovereign freedom of self-determination over how money may be spent."[11] This remarkable power encourages all of us to live an "implicit theology" of money that makes money sovereign instead of God.[12] We are in danger of losing humility and dependence on God to the extent that we allow money to guide our priorities and habits. "Where God embodies the moral virtue of generosity or grace, money embodies the moral virtue of honoring one's contracts and paying one's dues."[13] It is difficult to humbly live in God's economy when one lives in a financial system that promotes sovereign independence rather than dependence on a gratuitous giver of gifts.

10. Goodchild, *Theology of Money*, 41.

11. Ibid., 219.

12. Ibid., 221.

13. Ibid., 215.

These three problems—abstraction, disconnection, and arrogance—are also reflected in the global financial crisis going on as I write this. After describing how these problems show up in the contemporary world, I will describe how re-enacting the story of Christmas helps the church live out of the fullness of the Incarnation and live into the richness of life. In an oft-read Christmas text, Paul writes that "when the fullness of time had come, God sent his Son, born of a woman, born under the law" (Gal 4:4). The story of the arrival of the fullness of God in the fullness of time helps the church re-imagine itself and improvise financial practices that flow from the earthiness, relationships, and humility modeled in the Christmas drama. In order to appreciate these virtues, we must first take stock of how globalized financial practices today tend to habituate us in abstraction, detachment, and arrogance. Each of these vices is demonstrated in abundance in the so-called subprime mortgage mess.

The Globalization of Finance in My Neighborhood

Glancing through a thicker-than-usual classifieds section of my local newspaper not long ago, I noticed that there were five pages of public notices. A quick glance showed that most of these notices were announcing foreclosures or public auctions of foreclosed properties, so I decided to investigate further. On this Thursday, December 6, 2007, there were eighty-four such notices, announcing public sales of properties with a modest median value of $75,000, which suggests that many of the people losing their homes were so-called subprime borrowers with poor credit histories.[14] I also noticed that the banks that were foreclosing or selling houses in our area were large national and global banks, including one called Deutsche Bank. It turned out that Deutsche Bank was foreclosing on ten of these properties, more than any other single bank mentioned in the notices. To some, this might appear to be a random story, but it illustrates the link between financial globalization and my own community in northeast Ohio. Like many cities, we had been hit by the "subprime

14. *Canton Repository.* On January 25, 2008, there were 177 such notices in this newspaper; on April 24, 2008, there were 190; and on October 2, 2008, there were 215. Thanks to my student, Mary Boosz, for this last count. The number of foreclosures in the county was a record-high 2,811 in 2007. Wang, "Panelists." The median home value in our county in the year 2000 according to the U.S. Census Bureau was $100,300, and many foreclosures were on homes below this value.

mortgage" mess, which is closely tied to the globalization of finance, specifically to this German global bank.

The expansion of global financial markets essentially created more money. Former Wall Street analyst Michael Pettis argues that "a sudden expansion of financial liquidity in the world's leading banking centers . . . has been the catalyst behind every period of globalization."[15] The main cause of contemporary globalization, on this view, is the expansion of capital through new financial practices that essentially create money, and the main effects are financial panics that subsequently shrink the amount of liquid capital (the major problem of 2008 and 2009). The financial boom-and-bust cycle is endemic to the global capitalist system. Indeed, the inherent instability of financial and currency markets led a leading economic historian to recount their history as a history of recurrent "manias, panics, and crashes."[16] The contemporary situation fits within this pattern. First, increased accumulations of capital since 1980 have driven lenders to push more money out the door in investments or loans, and this push led to more lending and borrowing and investing across national borders: "Cross-border transactions in bonds and equities in the United States . . . rose from 9 percent of GDP in 1980 to 89 percent in 1990. . . . By 1996, they came to 164 percent of American GDP."[17] In other words, more money was moving in and out of the United States in a year than was produced domestically in the real economy, with much of that money going toward speculative investment activity. Striving solely for financial gains, using money to make more money, such investment activity or "hot money" triggered financial crises, as it has done throughout modern times. Whether it was the great tulip mania of Holland in the 1630s, the Great Depression of the 1930s, the stock market crash of 1987, the crash of the Mexican peso in 1994, the Asian financial crisis of 1997–1999, the popping of the "Dot com" bubble in 2000, or the housing bubble in 2007–2008, the world has seen many sudden collapses of financial markets on the heels of euphoria about a future of unlimited growth; bubbles pop and real people suffer.[18]

Despite this unstable history, Thomas Friedman sees the global financial Electronic Herd as a major force advancing globalization and

15. Pettis, "Will Globalization Go Bankrupt?" 52, 54.

16. Kindleberger, *Manias, Panics, and Crashes*.

17. Solomon, *Money on the Move*, 110.

18. Kindleberger, *Manias, Panics, and Crashes*, 14–28.

extending its benefits. Friedman explains that the democratization of technology, finance, and information "gave birth to all the key elements in today's globalization system." They "created the networks which enable each of us to reach around the world . . . [creating] the links and the space for the Electronic Herd and the Supermarkets to really emerge."[19] Friedman uses the term Electronic Herd to refer to "a new power source in the world . . . made up of all the *faceless* stock, bond and currency traders sitting behind computer screens all over the globe, moving their money around from mutual funds to pension funds to emerging market funds, or trading on the Internet from their basements."[20] This rapid movement of capital around the world is a defining trait of the flat world. A trillion dollars a day changes hands in currency markets alone, and most of that activity is speculative, driven by profit motives.

Mortgage-backed bonds are another fast-moving part of the Electronic Herd, an innovation admired by Friedman as a symbol of this brave new world of globalization. For Friedman, the "securitization" of home mortgages illustrated the alleged benefits of money sloshing around the world in an increasingly deregulated environment of financial markets.[21] However, securitization, one of the newest techniques to make money out of money, is also the chief element that made foreclosures in Ohio part of a global crisis. Securitization refers to the practice of banks and investors turning home mortgages into commodities that secure bonds as collateral; thus, the mortgages are debts that back additional debts, creating borrowing upon borrowing. It is a technique that allowed investors from around the world to purchase pieces of mortgages in my town through global banks such as Deutsche Bank, a major player in the trade. It is a complicated trade, but Friedman quotes a bond trader friend to explain how it works:

> Suppose you are a home mortgage company in Minneapolis and you have a hundred home mortgages out in the local market. And those hundred home mortgages involve an outlay by the mortgage company of a hundred million dollars and they bring in one

19. Friedman, *Lexus and the Olive Tree*, 140.

20. Ibid., 109. Emphasis added.

21. On securitization, also see Solomon, *Money on the Move*, 109. For an illuminating typology of different types of capital flows—foreign aid, foreign direct investment, bank loans to governments, bank loans to the private sector, portfolio investment in government, and portfolio investment in private firms—and their implications for politics, see Armijo, "Mixed Blessing," 17–50. Many thanks to Dan McDowell for this and other references.

million dollars a month in interest and principal payments. That mortgage company can bundle all its home mortgages together and then issue them as bonds that you or I can buy for a thousand dollars each. The advantage for the mortgage company is that it can get its hundred million dollars back right away without having to wait for all these people to pay off their mortgages over thirty years. The advantage for the bondholders is that they are paid off by the cash flow from the interest and principal payments that come in each month, and the interest rate will be a few points higher than a money market or savings account would pay. . . . As long as what you are doing, manufacturing, or performing produces a cash flow that can be statistically predicted over a period of time, *we can turn it into a bond.*[22]

Friedman continues, "The more capital controls have fallen between countries, the more everyone is offering everything for sale as stocks, bonds or derivatives." The world is moving toward turning more and more things into financial instruments, toward "securitizing everything" and toward "offering everything for sale."[23] Thus bond markets that buy and sell mortgage-backed bonds are part of a web of interconnected financial institutions that are linked through global electronic transfers. The creation of ever-increasing amounts of capital through such innovative techniques helps to explain why bankers and finance houses are eager—even desperate—to invest money wherever it can bring returns—a process of reward-seeking that computer networks have sped up and globalized.[24]

It turns out that the story of these mortgage-backed bonds is central to the story of the globalization of finance today, as evidenced in the global financial crisis of 2007–2008. "The story has played itself out time and time again over the past 30 years," writes Paul Krugman of *The New York Times*:

> Global investors, disappointed with the returns they're getting, search for alternatives. They think they've found what they're looking for in some country or other, and money rushes in. But

22. Friedman, *Lexus and the Olive Tree,* 118–19. Emphasis added. Millman, *Vandals' Crown,* 241–43 also discusses mortgage securities. Additional forms of securitization are described in Aliber, *New International Money Game,* 284–86. For a postmortem on the industry, see Ashcraft and Schuermann, "Understanding the Securitization of Subprime Mortgage Credit."

23. Friedman, *Lexus and the Olive Tree,* 120.

24. Garson, *Money Makes the World Go Around,* 3, 26, 39–40, 320, notes her surprise at seeing banks "awash" in money and desperate to keep from paying interest on it.

eventually it becomes clear that the investment opportunity wasn't all it seemed to be, and the money rushes out again, with nasty consequences for the former financial favorite. That's the story of multiple financial crises in Latin America and Asia. And it's also the story of the U.S. combined housing and credit bubble.[25]

After the bubble popped, financial institutions were stuck paying out interest on bonds backed by mortgages. Many of the loans had artificially low "teaser" interest rates to start and balloon payments or interest-only payments that started low but increased substantially after a few years, making it impossible for low-income borrowers to keep up their house payments when the interest rates jumped up or they began paying on the principal of the loan. So the higher-risk borrowers of these mortgages began defaulting in large numbers as their payments increased. At the same time, property values began to drop as sales activity dropped off and speculators could no longer count on real estate prices increasing (the classic pop of a speculative bubble), but this put many people in the position of owing more money than their homes were worth. In response, banks raised mortgage interest rates, tightened lending requirements, and began to foreclose on increasing numbers of mortgages to subprime borrowers, thereby undermining the security of many bonds that depended on borrowers' steady repayments. Certainly there were some reckless borrowers who acted irresponsibly, but some of those losing their homes probably did not understand what they were getting themselves into when they signed up for these types of mortgages. In my own community, it is clear that many of the foreclosed loans in December 2007 were for people of modest means buying modest homes. How many of them truly understood what they were getting themselves into? Certainly, some were reckless or irresponsible but others were victims of a predatory system that harmed all but the top players.

At the global level, the foreclosures triggered a cross-border financial crisis. Private banks were hit with defaulted loans, and already by the end of 2007 several Wall Street firms had lost billions of dollars ($15 billion for Merrill Lynch, $275 million for American Express, $1.9 billion for Bear Stearns).[26] Both global banks and local communities suffered as foreclosures in neighborhoods like mine spread to create problems overseas, preventing banks from keeping up payments on bonds owned

25. Krugman, "Don't Cry for Me, America."
26. Grynbaum, "Stocks Drop Sharply." Clark, "Bear Stearns Chief Steps Down."

by German pensioners, Japanese investors, or sovereign wealth funds (government-owned investment funds), among others. By August 2007, the European Central Bank had to lend 100 million Euros to European banks in order to help prevent them from running out of liquid assets, and share prices in Asian stock markets began falling, due to fears of an economic slowdown in the United States.[27] In December 2007, the U.S. Federal Reserve needed to lend out $40 billion more to banks, while the central banks of Europe and Canada were to lend out $50 billion more in January 2008.[28] According to one estimate, foreigners owned at least $1 trillion of the mortgage-based debt that was backed by the quasi-government agencies of Fannie Mae and Freddie Mac, both of which needed massive government backing by mid-2008.[29] By the end of 2008, giant insurance firms, several global banks and most Wall Street investment firms needed bailouts.

All of this reflected the globalization of financial markets. Not only did problems in the U.S. radiate outward to the world, but world investors probably also contributed to the crisis to begin with, as economics columnist Robert Samuelson notes: "Surplus savings from Asia and the Middle East, funneled into U.S. financial markets, may have abetted the 'subprime' mortgage crisis by encouraging sloppy American credit practices. Too much money chased too few good investment opportunities."[30] There really is something strange at work here: the money to finance my next-door neighbor's mortgage comes from a bank who sells that mortgage (and many others) to a Wall Street investment firm who in turn sells those bonds to overseas investors from South America, Europe, the Middle East, or Asia. The global pool of money encourages lenders to be careless, giving out loans to just about anyone. And when my neighbors default on their mortgages, they bring down the banks, the Wall Street firms, and bondholders around the world. A German pensioner's retirement is at risk because Deutsche Bank sold mortgage-backed securities tied to houses in Ohio. Weird!

The resulting financial meltdown, occurring on a global scale, illustrates three problems of globalizing money and finance that we touched upon at the outset of this chapter. In a world where the Electronic Herd

27. Norris, "Credit Crisis"; Fackler, "Sharp Sell-Off Sweeps Asian Markets."

28. Bajaj and Norris, "Central Bankers."

29. Samuelson, "Baffling Global Economy."

30. Ibid.

of finance capital gallops freely around the world looking for the best returns on its investments, these problems seem inherent in the system.[31] First, a global monetary system can cut us off from our earthy roots, threatening to make us lose sight of our embodied existence and become detached from concrete practices of money. As Philip Goodchild puts it, with money, "humanity is already enslaved to the 'abstract machine.'" [32] The pursuit of the abstraction of profit without regard to real-world realities can lead to disastrous consequences.[33] To escape our physical limits of time and place and become like God is perhaps the oldest human dream—an ancient temptation. G. K. Chesterton spoofed this kind of desire for abstraction and escape from limits already in the 1930s, when he wrote the following little sketch:

> A stockbroker in one sense really is a very poetical figure. . . . He does deal to a great extent in what economists (in their poetical way) describe as imaginaries. When he exchanges two thousand Patagonian Pumpkins for one thousand shares in Alaskan Whale Blubber, he does not demand the sensual satisfaction of eating the pumpkin or need to behold the whale with the gross eye of flesh. It is quite possible that there are no pumpkins; and if there is somewhere such a thing as whale, it is very unlikely to obtrude itself upon the conversation in the Stock Exchange.[34]

Because finance abstracts itself from the concrete realities of "Patagonian pumpkins" and "Alaskan whale blubber," it risks schooling us in habits of abstraction. Instead of attending to tangible truths, it seeks out imaginary, abstract financial ones.

So, too, there was a great deal of abstraction in the run-up to the global housing problem. The abstract nature of securitization illustrates this problem quite clearly when we apply it to Northeast Ohio. An hour's drive north of my house is the city of Cleveland, where the BBC reported in early 2008 that "one in ten homes in Cleveland had been repossessed and Deutsche Bank Trust, acting on behalf of bondholders, was the largest property owner in the city."[35] The reader will recall that Deutsche

---

31. To his credit, Friedman admits some worries and challenges with this system. See *Lexus and the Olive Tree*, 142.

32. Goodchild, "Capital and Kingdom," 141.

33. Waalkes, "Money or Business?"

34. Chesterton, "The Outline of Sanity," 188–89.

35. BBC News, "The U.S. Sub-Prime Crisis."

Bank was a leading bank foreclosing in my area as well. It turns out to have been one of the leading global banks in the trade nationwide, but nearly a quarter of the mortgages backing Deutsche Bank-sold bonds in the United States were in default, and the bank expected to lose approximately $3 billion in 2007 and wrote off its mortgage-backed debts in 2008.[36] However, if you had read the public notices carefully, you would have noticed that Deutsche Bank was foreclosing on behalf of others, such as "HSI Asset Securitization Trust," holders of "Mortgage Loan Trust Asset-Backed Certificates," or holders of "Mortgage Pass-Through Certificates"—all names for groups of bondholders who owned mortgage-backed securities sold by Deutsche Bank. The point here is that that the bank itself no longer owned these mortgages: trusts or certificate holders, legal fictions, did. So here was a global bank originally based in Germany among those selling "trillions of dollars" of mortgage-backed bonds to investors all around the world, including some of those based on loans to people in my town, now trying to sell off properties that it claimed in the names of these faceless investors.[37] Yet instead of a local bank with a face, the owners were the bondholders who owned $1,000 or $10,000 chunks of mortgage bonds. And this legal fiction made the whole enterprise quite abstract. Interestingly, then, a federal district judge threw out fourteen foreclosure cases in Cleveland, ruling that Deutsche Bank did not own the properties because collections of bondholders did.[38] It seems the judge relied on rather concrete reasoning to rule that the bank did not own these houses. But how can a collection of bondholders own my house? Do they each own a tiny piece of it? The whole thing remains artificial and abstract.

Second, the Herd's globalized financial system breaks down relationships between real people. The strangeness of the subprime mortgage story also illustrates the problems with having a *faceless* global bank lending out mortgages and selling off bonds to faceless investors. The bank and the investors care little for cities or people in my neighborhood, or anywhere else for that matter; they care about profit. They turn the people in Ohio into transactions without faces, merely a means to greater profits. Yet this detachment is a key element encouraging finance

36. Landler, "Deutsche Bank's Hit." Anderson and Bajaj, "Wary of Risk." Landler, "Losses at Deutsche Bank."

37. Andrews, "Fed and Regulators."

38. Weiner, "Foreclosure-Proof."

capital to flow freely across the globe; it is central to the system. Investors seeking to earn interest are matched with borrowers seeking to obtain finance via interest rates, which are the primary vehicle for global lending. Unlike profit- and loss-sharing contracts, in which the lender agrees to assume risks for a right to the returns, contracts that lend at interest require little information; they are arms-length transactions. By contrast, investors who share risks with partners they know will be more likely to seek out information "on the trustworthiness of the borrower or the exact amount of profit being made with their funds . . . information that is most readily available at the local or regional level. Consequently, interest permits financial flows to occur on a far greater scale than would otherwise occur."[39] Financial globalization depends on *impersonal* lending based on interest rather than intimate knowledge of local partners. Requiring such intimate knowledge before borrowing or lending would slow down the movement of money around the globe.

That all the players in the mortgage business were practicing an impersonal facelessness driven by greed was clear in a concise description of the crisis by National Public Radio's Adam Davidson: "These people were making a lot of money. Homebuyers were getting more money than they could afford. Everyone at every step of the chain was making massive amounts of money."[40] And everyone must have known deep down that something was fishy:

> The mortgage brokers, many of them, clearly knew that they were extending loans to people who couldn't afford it, but they didn't mind because they were passing those loans very quickly on to the mortgage banks. The mortgage banks were taking on extreme risk, but they were passing on those loans to Wall Street. Wall Street was taking on extreme risk, and many knew it, but they were passing it on to global investors, now many of whom say they weren't paying enough attention, because they were just trusting the credit rating agencies.[41]

All were practicing facelessness and impersonality in the pursuit of money, rather than attending to how money would serve relationships and community.

39. Mills, "Ban on Interest."
40. Smith and Davidson, "Analysis."
41. Ibid.

Third, the Herd can make humans begin to live the dream of money making more money worldwide; it threatens to teach us that we can manage and control financial risks by pricing the future. Thus, it cultivates arrogance rather than humility. But as Philip Goodchild notes, our modern mystification of money and capital makes money into the "supreme value" and source of power. [42] When one enters the global capitalist system, one has little choice but to seek to make money, since credit, capital, and currency are the modes of participation in it. In so doing, one learns to do whatever is necessary to make money, whether in providing for one's household, in speculation, or in creating money through credit. It is these latter two areas—speculation and credit—that illustrate the problem of global finance, in which banks and financial institutions sought to escape the limits of the past and invent new financial techniques such as mortgage-backed bonds. These new techniques were especially attractive after the breakdown of the Bretton Woods monetary system in the 1970s, which led to the demise of state-controlled, fixed exchange rates between currencies and led to the creation of global currency markets to buy and sell currencies. The end of capital controls and fixed exchange rates created opportunities for investors to make profits (or losses) simply from speculating over future changes in exchange rates.[43] These new financial instruments—bought and sold by traders in faceless electronic trading— have contributed to highly volatile, unregulated financial markets that troubled even some free-market, pro-globalization economists, even before the global crash of 2008.[44]

The arrogance of this system is especially apparent in the contrasting effects of debt and credit upon the poor and the rich. Poorer communities suffered when houses were foreclosed or abandoned, evicting poor folks from neighborhoods, while top bank executives maintained their high compensation levels. It might seem irrational to make risky loans to poorer borrowers, but Sebastian Mallaby of the *Washington Post*

---

42. Goodchild, "Capital and Kingdom," 140.

43. For vivid descriptions of this process, see Millman, *Vandals' Crown*. Also see Solomon, *Money on the Move*; Aliber, *Money Game*; and Eichengreen, *Globalizing Capital*, 136–96.

44. Stiglitz, *Globalization and Its Discontents*; Bhagwati, *In Defense of Globalization*, 199–207; and Wolf, *Why Globalization Works*, 278–304. Eichengreen, "Financial Instability," 253, notes that "volatility is intrinsic to financial markets." Yet he takes a moderate view of capital flows as a necessary evil in his book *Capital Flows and Crises*, 289–306. For concrete descriptions of these new instruments, see Aliber, *New International*, 279–93.

describes why they were attractive: "Lenders figured out that households with a history of poverty or unreliability should be welcome to borrow for mortgages, *provided that they paid a premium* to reflect their high risk of default." Mallaby continues, without irony, to write, "The social consequences were marvelous."[45] The marvelous consequence Mallaby has in mind is an increase in the rate of homeownership from 65 percent to 69 percent of the national population. But how does this modest increase compare to the high price of recent foreclosures? And what kind of system makes the poor pay a premium while paying the top executives who sold mortgage securities a million dollars a year or more? "The average total compensation for managing directors in the mortgage divisions of investment banks was $2.52 million in 2006 . . . . This year [2007], mortgage officials will probably earn $1.01 million." [46] According to the Associated Press, the chief executive officer of the largest subprime lending company, Countrywide Financial, stood to walk away with nearly $66 million in compensation when the Bank of America planned to buy out his company; meanwhile, many of my neighbors are losing their modest homes.[47] The *Non Sequitur* cartoon of October 10, 2005, highlighted the problem of arrogance when it showed a group of six executives seated around a conference table containing a roulette wheel and stacks of chips. One of the executives says, "No, when it's *our* pensions at stake, then it becomes a serious problem." Who pays the premium and who takes on the risk? While elites walk away full, many of the poor walk away empty.

Arrogance also crept in as financiers began to imagine they could price the future and manage risks. "Finance isn't about taking risks *on*; it's about laying risks *off*," writes Barbara Garson.[48] In response to the inherent risks in speculating or hedging against currency changes or stock market drops, or bond market crashes, financial engineers have created a number of techniques to minimize risks while maximizing gains for those at the top of the system. Another financial reporter writes, "The world is volatile, and at its best the new financial system that replaced Bretton Woods transfers risks from those unwilling to bear it to those most able to take it on."[49] However, the problem of risk is clear when we

---

45. Mallaby, "Pain, and Gain." Emphasis added.

46. Anderson and Bajaj, "Wary of Risk."

47. Associated Press, "Countrywide Failed to Survive Slump."

48. Garson, *Money Makes the World Go Round*, 317.

49. Millman, *Vandal's Crown*, 270.

discover that many retirement pension funds are investing in risky hedge funds in order to gain higher returns, with up to $300 billion now being poured into such funds each year.[50] The financiers sitting around the conference table get to gamble with retirement pensions, always walking away with lucrative compensation, even if the pension savings of ordinary people disappear. The deepest spirit behind the current global financial system is aptly captured by the title of Peter Bernstein's history of risk management: *Against the Gods*. Bernstein argues that the definitive idea marking modern times is "the notion that the future is more than a whim of the gods and that men and women are not passive before nature."[51] Of course, humans should not give up efforts at responsible stewardship in the world, but they should remember their limits. Yet money and practices of capital encourage us to escape those limits and school us in the belief that we can control the future. Calculating future risks—pricing the future—is central to practices of modern global capitalism, and it relies upon a belief in "a humanly engineered future."[52] One engineers the future by putting a price tag on it.[53] But this pricing of the future threatens to school humans in the arrogant belief that they can manage the future, whereas only God is in control of time: "the earth is the Lord's, and the fullness thereof" (Ps 24:1). Humility requires recognition that one cannot put a price on things beyond human control, as the collapse of global financial markets reminds us.

Re-enacting the Christmas Story

In contrast to the arrogance, lack of relationships, and abstraction embodied in the global meltdown, we find material concreteness, relationship, and humility affirmed in the Christmas story. The story celebrates a person with a face who entered into time; it celebrates a relational, family community; and it celebrates a humble baby Jesus. Christmas is the church's re-enacting this major chapter of the fullness of the Christian story: the story that the Word of God became flesh in the womb of a

50. Atlas and Walsh, "Pension Officers."

51. Bernstein, *Against the Gods*, 1.

52. Giddens, *Runaway World*, 24–25. Thanks to Maria Lam for bringing this chapter on risk back to my attention.

53. Goodchild, "Capital and Kingdom," 140: "Money as speculation is based on a projection of the future as an imagined present."

Virgin, only to suffer and die an unjust death, before being raised to new life and ascending to heaven. This true story schools us in concreteness: we recall the baby in the manger in Bethlehem. It schools us in community and relationships: Jesus was born of a woman, born into an extended family, born into a neighborhood, born into a village, and born into friendships.[54] And it schools us in humility: the birth of our Lord was a modest birth, in the humble circumstances of a migrant family. Hence, the story of Christ's birth offers contrasting ways of imagining globalization that can lead to constructive improvisation and concrete action that is re-framed by the Christmas story. Re-enacting the Christmas drama helps us re-imagine alternative practices to the current system of global money and global capital circulation.

As a feast season celebrating the nativity of Jesus, Christmas stretches on for twelve days (hence the song, "The Twelve Days of Christmas"), a compromise arrangement between the Eastern and Western branches of the church that dates back to the fourth century.[55] But its present-day shape will help us re-imagine the globalization of finance in ways that respond creatively to its problems. First, many churches re-enact Christmas pageants during Advent (although liturgical purists would urge that they wait until Christmas Day and after). The urge to re-enact the story year after year in churches—in live nativity scenes, in children's musical pageants, or in dramatic re-readings of Matthew's and Luke's nativity narratives—suggests a similar attentiveness to the centrality of the Incarnation for Christian faith, life, and practice. Year after year, Christians enjoy listening again to recitations of the Christmas story from the gospels of Matthew and Luke. Even the *Charlie Brown Christmas* television special ends with Linus reciting Luke's account. Something draws us: whether the sentimentalized Christmas story of a baby in a manger, fond memories of Christmases past, or the sheer generosity of God's gifts. It is a truism in North American Christian circles that commercialization has distorted the feast season of Christmas into the "holiday buying season" that extends from October beyond Christmas Day. But attempts to reclaim Christmas by re-enacting the "reason for the season" demonstrate the importance of the concrete staging of the story. The nativity story is

54. Long, *Divine Economy*, 185, invokes Leo XIII's teaching on the Holy Family as applied to labor.

55. Dix, *Shape of the Liturgy*, 357; Cobb, "History," 466–67; Talley, "Constantine and Christmas."

not just a generic way of expressing a principle of incarnation. Instead, its shocking concreteness reminds the church of the specificity and particularity of Jesus' birth into history. As von Balthasar puts it, "The Incarnation is not the *n*th performance of a tragedy already lying in the archives of eternity. It is an event of total originality."[56] This is a story that demands participatory re-staging. The North American church already takes this event quite seriously and attends to its concreteness. Precisely because it is the story of Christ entering into time, the Christmas story is always rich with detail and color. It is always told in the "little town of Bethlehem" with a manger, angels, and shepherds. This will remind us to attend to concreteness with our money.

Second, the story is heavily embedded in a series of relationships that make it possible. This is especially clear in the context of the story, where so many people join Mary in the pageant, connecting this birth to the fulfillment of the hopes of Israel (as we saw in the last chapter): the angel Gabriel appears to Mary in Nazareth to tell her the good news that she would bear a savior for her people Israel and she should name him Jesus ("Yahweh saves"). Joseph is ready to disavow her, but the angel appears to him to persuade him to marry her and name the baby Jesus. The angel appears to Zechariah in the Holy of Holies in the Temple to tell him that his wife Elizabeth would have a son who should be named John. Mary visits Elizabeth, her cousin, whose baby (John the Baptist) kicks in her womb upon the sound of Mary's greeting. John the Baptist is born to Elizabeth and Zechariah. Zechariah speaks again, insisting that the boy be named John and sings out a song of deliverance. The Incarnation of Jesus enters into and affirms all these relationships. Hebrews 2 asserts that Jesus is our brother, sharing in our humanity: he is "like his brothers in every way" (Heb 2:17). As Paul tells the Galatians, God sent his son "so that we might receive adoption as children" (Gal 4:5). We in the church are in his family, adopted to become the brother of Jesus.

However, this family is not an end in itself. The Christmas story is about more than a sentimental "little Lord Jesus, no crying he makes" gathering of admirers. It is, thirdly, about the coming of a humble Kingdom of love that culminates in the cross. It is about how the family of Jesus is called to follow him in humility in order to help God reign. Thomas Merton writes, "If we accept this Infant as our God, then we accept our own obligation to grow with Him in a world of arrogant power

56. Von Balthasar, *Theology of History*, 39.

and travel with Him as He ascends to Jerusalem and to the Cross, which is the denial of power."[57]

The best way to illustrate this point within the Christmas season is to share an idea from a friend and colleague, Greg Miller, who imagined a Christmas pageant entitled "God on the Run." To start, it would be a traditional nativity play, focusing at first on the main event: Mary and Joseph would journey from Nazareth to Bethlehem, then Mary would deliver the child and lay him in a feeding trough, an angel would appear to shepherds outside Bethlehem, terrifying them, but the angel would share the gospel for all people: that a Savior and Messiah had been born in Bethlehem and that he would be wrapped in strips of cloth and lying in a manger. After that, some angels would come to praise God, and then the shepherds would journey to Bethlehem to find Mary and Joseph and the baby lying in the manger. Then the wise men from the East would come to King Herod and ask where they could find the new king of the Jews. Herod, after consulting with the chief priests and rabbis, would direct them to Bethlehem, with instructions to make a diligent search and to report back what they had found. The wise men would follow the star to the house where little Jesus lay, and they would bow down and worship him, presenting their gifts of gold and frankincense and myrrh, an angel would appear to them to warn them not to return to Herod, and they would return home another way.

But this is not the end of the story in Greg's pageant or in the gospel of Matthew. The next act ends the Christmas pageant with the second chapter of Matthew, the slaughter of the Holy Innocents and the flight of the holy family into Egypt. Imagine this happening as the end of a traditional nativity play in a typical North American church: The angel appears again to Joseph to warn him to get up and take the family to Egypt to escape from Herod. Joseph listens, waking up the family in the middle of the night to start the long journey to Egypt. Meanwhile, as we see the Holy Family trudging off into the distance, Herod's soldiers storm the stage, trashing the house where Jesus had just been sleeping. On stage, we see babies ripped from their parents' arms, and the parents start screaming. Bethlehem descends into chaos, and all the actors are crying. The soldiers then rush out into the aisles of the congregation, grabbing young children from their parents and taking them outside. The curtain drops, and the pageant is over.

57. Merton, *Love and Living*, 231.

Such an ending would be a real shocker. Parents of young children would probably sue the church for emotional distress. Yet this ending aligns with the liturgical observance of St. Stephen the Martyr on December 26 and the Feast of the Holy Innocents on December 28. The historical church at least recognizes that this slaughter was part of the Christmas story, as it sets aside a day to re-enact and remember these deaths as the earliest martyrs of the faith. Matthew's gospel reminds us not to sentimentalize the Christmas story but to see its gritty political point.[58] The gritty political point of the Christmas story is that it teaches us how the world reacts to a humble kingdom of love that threatens worldly systems of power. It thereby teaches us humility in an arrogant world. Joyce Zimmerman describes the placement of St. Stephen's Day and Holy Innocents Day as a way to "remind us that our taste of eschatological fulfillment is flavored by the exigencies of human existence."[59] There is, then, a positive and a negative edge to this part of the Christmas season. Positively, this is a story of the coming of God's loving Kingdom in humility, with God's love being shown even to the point of allowing his son and our King to be a refugee. Matthew's gospel story reminds us that the Kingdom of God was born on the run, an upside-down Kingdom, which promises to lift the humble and bring down the powerful. Matthew teaches us that God's reign works through the small, the weak, and the marginalized. God lifts up humble people like Mary and Joseph but therefore threatens rival kingdoms. Negatively, then, the coming of a loving Kingdom—even in the person of a tiny, helpless baby— threatens and provokes the Powers that Be.[60] Herod the Great was so paranoid about challenges to his rule that he killed a score of innocent babies preemptively. Herod expected a Kingdom that would put forward a rival King to topple him, a political Messiah who would seize power and impose a Jewish kingdom, so he does what any Machiavellian would do. We shouldn't single him out as uniquely horrible. As we know, the Powers often react to potential threats through violent action in our own day, through preemptive wars, assassinations, coups, and revolutions. Herod practices a conventional politics. But this is not the politics of

58. A colleague who lived in Kenya for six years tells me that a Kenyan church did in fact end with the slaughter of the innocents, suggesting that Christians elsewhere are better prepared to interpret the story correctly.

59. Zimmerman, *Liturgy as Living Faith*, 117.

60. On the theology of the Powers, see Berkhof, *Christ and the Powers*; Yoder, *Politics of Jesus*, 134–61; and Wink, *Powers That Be*.

humility embodied in Jesus and his family. While Herod was correct that a rival Kingdom threatened his kingdom, he mistook the nature of that rival Kingdom, just as we would have if we were in his shoes. That rival Kingdom works through weakness.

The King could have taken the easy way out, the way of power and force and domination, the way of run-of-the-mill human kingdoms. But he chose the difficult way of incarnation and the cross, the way of weakness, the way of self-sacrificing love, the way of suffering, and the way of dispossession. Instead of imposing his Kingdom upon the world, God allowed us humans to drive his Son into exile, to spit on him, to curse him, to whip him, and to crucify him. The Son was on the run from the beginning of his life on earth—a humble refugee king in flight with his family—and the Son ended up dying as a political criminal. Humility is not just a desirable character trait; it is the path at the beginning and the end of Christ's Kingdom.

Re-Imagining Globalization

Re-narrating the story of Christmas in the church year helps us re-imagine the ascendance of global finance capital by focusing attention on earthiness, community, and humility. Each of these elements of the drama helps us re-imagine a fuller world than the flat world of globalization.

First, God creates humans out of dust and in his image (Gen 1:26–27; 2:7; 3:19), a creational earthiness that Jesus' birth affirms and echoes. It is a scandalously particular story, claiming that God-in-the-flesh was born after nine months of gestation inside a young Jewish girl, in a little town called Bethlehem, in a Jewish province on the edge of the Roman Empire. But this story backs the claims of the Apostles' Creed: God is the creator of heaven and earth and his son Jesus Christ was "born of the virgin Mary." God valued the dust of humanity enough to enter the womb of the Virgin, and likewise he values us enough to send his Holy Spirit to blow into our frail frames of dust. God is attentive to human embodiment in ways that global money is not. In this story, our earthy status as creatures is something to be embraced. God created the first man and the first woman out of earth, and they were very good. God Incarnate was born in a stable, and it was good.

By contrast, the global financial system escapes particularity and inculcates habits of abstraction in ways that the ancient Greek philosopher

Aristotle anticipated in his critique of money.[61] In his *Politics*, Aristotle supports self-reliance in a non-monetary barter system. His ideal is that households or political communities should farm the land, fish the seas, and cultivate the animals that nature provides, only exchanging goods when necessary to supplement what is lacking. Thus he makes a sharp distinction in his *Politics* between the legitimate acquisition of goods for household use and the illegitimate pursuit of gain through exchange.[62] Aristotle contends that there is nothing wrong with barter trade, with households (or city-states) obtaining one type of useful goods by trading their own goods—for example, state A exchanging wheat for state B's corn. Such commerce seeks only "to re-establish nature's own equilibrium of self-sufficiency" and therefore fits the original goal and purpose (*telos*) of household management (economics).[63]

Unfortunately, in Aristotle's view, this rudimentary exchange brought about the need for currency, which quickly led to trade, in which people sought simply to gain wealth measured as currency. Such pursuit of monetary gain is contrary to nature, says Aristotle, because it seeks goals external to the production of goods for the welfare of the household or state and violates the purpose of money, which is to facilitate exchange. In his teleological (purpose-directed) view, one must always be attentive to the purposeful ends being pursued within the process of work itself, toward which the work is aiming. As Paul Wadell nicely puts it, "the telos is not so much something toward which we move, but something in which we participate." He continues, "True, the telos represents the goal, the fulsome meaning of life. While it can be said that we advance toward that end through the virtues, the movement implied is not a change of place but a change of person. To Aristotle, a person moves toward the telos by being changed according to it."[64] All of the process in achieving the end is part of the end, and the dispositions of character (the virtues or vices) formed along the way participate in achieving it.

Aristotle argues that the pursuit of monetary gain for its own sake as a telos can lead to some disturbing results: "And it will often happen

---

61. Goodchild, *Theology of Money*, 64: "Aristotle was prescient here: the use of money to make money, money that bears interest, or the quest for profits for their own sake, have no determinate value and so no place within the polis."

62. Aristotle, *Politics*, I.9–10, 81–85.

63. Ibid., 81.

64. Wadell, *Friendship*, 42–43.

that a man with wealth in the form of coined money will not have enough to eat; and what a ridiculous kind of wealth is that which even in abundance will not save you from dying with hunger!"[65] Holders of large amounts of Weimar German marks, Thai bahts, Indonesian rupiahs, Bolivian bolivianos, or Argentine pesos—or any other currency that has suffered rapid devaluation or hyperinflation—could relate to the absurd problem of money becoming meaningless paper. For that matter, holders of large amounts of now-worthless mortgage-backed bonds can also relate. Acquisition of credits or monetary gains can be wiped out easily by changes in the financial system that have little or nothing to do with tangible changes in the provision of household goods—an irrational but common outcome of the pursuit of money. Pursuing money for the sake of money means chasing an abstraction, a quantified value that no longer connects to concrete realities. The pursuit of money takes priority over the details of work itself:

> For where enjoyment consists in excess, men look for that which produces the excess that is enjoyed. And if they cannot procure it through money-making, they try to get it by some other means, using all their faculties for this purpose, which is contrary to nature: courage, for example, is to produce confidence, not goods; nor yet is it the job of military leadership and medicine to produce goods, but victory and health. But these people turn all skills into skills of acquiring goods, as though that were the end and everything had to serve that end.[66]

In Friedman's phrase, monetized societies run the risk of making "everything for sale," where even the provision of health care becomes seen as producing a good: doctors go into practice in order to make money as much as to heal.[67] When more and more skills are rewarded according to how well they help one obtain wealth (measured in currency), the true aim of work or other practices will tend to be amassing money, rather than cultivating virtuous habits intrinsic to the work itself.[68] Therefore, Aristotle worries that a monetized society will be concerned with gaining material wealth for its own sake, without attention to goods internal

---

65. Aristotle, *Politics*, I.9, 83.

66. Ibid., 85.

67. Also see Kuttner, *Everything for Sale*, 39–67.

68. Shawn Floyd reflects on this problem in education in "Morally Serious Pedagogy," 255–56.

to practices such as medicine. Such a society will reward the pursuit of extrinsic rather than intrinsic rewards, and money will be the measure of extrinsic reward. But this is chasing an abstraction rather than a tangible good.

Likewise, the investment of money to make money is chasing an abstraction. The Catholic philosopher Thomas Aquinas helps make this clear in his teaching on usury, which remains firmly rooted in tangible facts. Borrowing directly from Aristotle, Aquinas opposed the charging and payment of interest on the grounds that it likewise separated things themselves from payments to use those things. Following Aristotle he says, "Money was devised to facilitate exchange, so that the proper and principal use of money is its use or expenditure when exchanges are carried out."[69] If I loan someone money and expect them to pay back the principal and extra charges simply for its use, I would be "[selling] the same thing twice or [selling] what does not exist—a clear sin against justice."[70] I am doing something contrary to the nature and purpose of money, which is to be consumed in use. I transfer the ownership and use of money to the other person, at which point they take on the risk of loss. They could lose the money, spend it frivolously, or fail in the venture for which they had borrowed. If I as a lender simply let them "own" the risk and the money and yet also expect them to pay me a charge for the money I originally "owned" (regardless of what happens to it), then I am trying to charge them for something that now belongs to them. I am trying to obtain something for nothing. I am putting a price on something that is not mine to sell.

Aristotle and Aquinas thus offer a bracing critique of the impulse behind the subprime mortgage fiasco. Through their attention to the tangible practices in which money is embedded, their attention to embodiment, they remind us how abstract the whole thing became. In mortgage-backed bonds, the bank first sells the mortgage loan and then turns around to sell the mortgage-backed bonds, by which it recoups the principal of the loan all at once (selling the same thing twice). Likewise global investors are entranced by the prospect of a high-yield, low-risk investment in these bonds: selling their money to make more money. But both are trying to price something that is not theirs. Meanwhile, as Sebastian Mallaby said earlier, the poorer, subprime borrowers *paid a*

69. Aquinas, *Summa Theologiae*, II-II.78, 74–75.
70. Ibid., 74.

premium for the "privilege" of borrowing. They own the risk, and they are responsible for the payments, but the mortgage bank retains the property as security and can sell it again, thereby limiting their risk. Although the banks did have to write down their payments on the bonds when borrowers failed to keep up payments, they still walk away with assets in the form of real properties that can be re-sold and executives with millions of dollars in compensation. Bondholders around the world lost some of their investments, but they had amassed enough money to buy such investments in the first place and also participated in buying something that did not exist—a bond backed by the "security" of a mortgage. Both the banks and the investors failed to root their approach to money in tangible, earthy practices. By seeking to make money from money, they sought to detach themselves from earthly realities, but in the process they made some homeless. By attending to the earthiness of the Christmas story, its connection to Bethlehem and a homeless family there, we might learn to embed our money in concrete times and places.

The second virtue of Christmas is its reminder of the power of relationships and community. Money attracts us, according to Philip Goodchild, "because of the promises it offers to the individual: liberation from the control of nature and material need; liberation from social obligation and dependency on others; and freedom to pursue one's own desire."[71] Money means freedom, the freedom to flee communities and avoid relationships. At the gas station, when we pay at the pump with a credit card, we miss the hassle of needing cash on hand, telling the cashier our pump number, and waiting to receive change. But we also miss the possibility of having a conversation with a gas station attendant. Our world is a more efficient world, but it is also flatter in its loss of connectedness and rootedness. Our humble, embodied selves lose connection to others.

But the Christmas story helps us re-imagine how God values an embodiment that requires community and relationships oriented toward the good that must guide our employment of money. One point of Jesus entering into a web of relationships is to create a community of brothers and sisters who live closer to the original Creation in their worship of God. Being created in the image of the trinitarian God implies that the church—just as the Godhead of the Father, Son, and Holy Spirit—is a relational community of persons. Our worship in local churches is testimony

71. Goodchild, "Capital and Kingdom," 139.

to how we require flesh-and-blood relationships with others in order to worship God. We cannot worship as disembodied spirits. We need to worship as physical beings together.

A 1996 Doonesbury cartoon imagines a church that has lost its attention to embodiment and community, spoofing the fascination with money, efficiency, and technology that can break down face-to-face relationships. This particular comic strip pictured the Rev. Scott Sloane in his Little Church of Walden. Showing an old friend around the church building, Rev. Sloane says, "The old house is used for our spiritual wellness seminars and various 12-step recovery programs. In the new wings, we have a food court, a fitness center, and our interpretive dance studios."

His friend asks, "Um . . . where do people worship?"

"On our website. Keeps the heating bills down."[72]

One hopes that we can get the joke.[73] A real church can't worship in any meaningful way over a website. We must sing and break bread together in the flesh—the very flesh that the Word entered (and enters) at Christmas. We care enough about gathering to pay the heating bills.

D. Stephen Long suggests that the traditional ban on the charging of interest has a relational dimension: "The principle is quite simple: money does no work; people do. So when we assume our money to be working for us to make more money, we have not accurately described God's economy."[74] And yet by detaching money from relationships and communities in our spending or investments, we are putting our money to work for us—without bothering to figure out who our money is affecting or how it is affecting them, neglecting the relationships which ought to come before money. Thus, writes Long, "We lose the ability to describe how our lives are embedded in the narratives of others. The food that we eat, the clothes we wear, the transportation available to us, clean restrooms, floors, etc.—all these things are provided for us without any awareness on our part of the practices that make such external goods possible. We cannot name our debts; thus we cannot pray well."[75] Both churches and businesses ought to be places where we embed money

---

72. Trudeau, *Doonesbury.*

73. However, see the many online churches, including the "world's first online 3D church" at http://www.churchoffools.com, where you can create your own character and enter a virtual sanctuary. Thanks to Luke Thompson for reminding me that such "churches" do exist.

74. Long, *Divine Economy,* 239.

75. Ibid.

within relationships to real people rooted in time and place who bring us the food, the clothes, the transportation, the clean restrooms, and all the rest. A church that re-enacts the story of Christmas rightly will form people who try to have money serve the goods of community and relationship. It will care about what the community's money does for or to others. Thus the church ought to be attentive to the ends toward which their money and business activity is aimed. It will be concerned about the effects of global finance on neighborhoods and families.

The Christmas story also demonstrates a third truth: how God values an embodiment of humility and self-imposed limits. This is a story of great humility, of a forced *downward* mobility and an embrace of created limits—the story of the refugee king. Participation in Christ allows us to accept poverty as gain. If we travel with him the roads from Bethlehem to Egypt, from Egypt to Nazareth, and from Nazareth to Jerusalem, we are humbled. Thus the story fleshes out practices that work against the dream of capital growth without limits and control of financial risks. The Creator of the universe is willing to enter Mary's womb and be born as a human baby, to grow as a child, and to die as a young man—the ultimate mystery of self-imposed limitation. We are reminded here that we are called to humility and self-emptying, as Paul evokes these themes in Philippians, of God's self-emptying embrace of limitations in order to illustrate an attitude of humility in common life (Phil 2:1–4).[76] Aristotle worried that a monetized society would free itself from the limited purposes of commerce (material provision) and pursue monetary gain for its own sake, which would contribute to pride. Long describes how conventional financial practice sells "the *use* of a commodity, rather than the commodity itself, and in so doing it sells time."[77] This is arrogance in the face of God. But the church confesses that the fullness of time comes from God's humility in entering our time and embracing limits. Selling time as if we can control it violates our created limits. God the Creator is in control of the future while humans are not; God enters time, but humans cannot reach eternity in this life. When people are humble enough to know that God is still in control, they know that risks cannot be eliminated. They know their own limits, and they know how to limit

---

76. Fowl, *Philippians*, 77–88. For an attempt to ground humility theologically, see Moroney et al., "Cultivating Humility in Students."

77. Long, *Divine Economy*, 77.

the pursuit of money for its own sake, a pursuit that challenges our humility if not kept in check.

The Christian church has yet to live out compelling alternatives to the global financial system. Most of us depend on interest and insurance and practices that put price tags on the future. We like having our money earn more money, without having to be attentive to the relationships and communities in which our money is embedded. We are tempted toward the arrogance of thinking we can control our financial futures through risk management. We enjoy escaping our earthly limits with these abstractions called money or capital.

IMPROVISING PRACTICES

Yet I retain the hope that a church that still holds Christmas pageants might improvise. A church formed by the Christmas season can begin responding to the problems of abstraction, arrogance, and impersonality through creative improvisation. Re-enacting Christmas each year speaks directly to how concretely we think about money, to how we learn who owns our mortgage, to how we learn who benefits from or is harmed by our investments, or to how we learn to trusts in insurance more than our church community. What follows are a few thoughts on what improvisation might look like, offered in hope that others in the church can build upon these.

Practicing Concreteness with our Money

My father was a member of the board of our denominational ministers' pension fund for several years. Just before he took the position, some denominational agencies lost millions of dollars in a real estate investment scheme that crashed. Managers of these agencies' pension funds had trusted the executives of the investment firm without fully understanding the risks involved. If even one of the managers had been humble enough to ask, "What exactly are you doing with our money?" it might have connected the money to earthly practices. In the 1990s, a manager at the global ABN Amro bank in New York didn't understand how one of his traders kept reporting huge gains from currency options trading, and he didn't check the paperwork. Eventually, accountants discovered that the gains were really based on bogus paperwork that covered up a $50 million loss.[78] More recently, a trader at a French bank managed to lose approximately $7 billion of his bosses' money in one day in a similar fashion. We too quickly forget how money is embedded in our earthly lives. We fail to think about what our money is actually doing on earth while thinking that money can reproduce itself.[79] The Enron Corporation collapsed after its executives sought paper profits that were detached from concrete realities, as did many organizations trading mortgage-backed bonds.

Barbara Garson's story is an instructive one for the church to consider improvising upon. Garson decided to write a book on what happened to "her" money after it was invested, and she managed to convince a publisher to give her an advance based on this premise.[80] She took half of her book advance and invested it in a small local bank in upstate New York, which in turn invested some money with the global Chase Manhattan bank. She took the other half and invested it in an aggressive mutual fund. And then she tried to track some of the major investments made by each financial institution. Of course, she could not literally track "her" money, because as soon as she deposited it, it no longer "belonged" to her. It became part of large anonymous flows of "capital" invested all over the United States and the world. Still, Garson manages to meet the bank and mutual fund officials who took her original deposits, and then she travels to Singapore, Malaysia, and Thailand, as well as to Tennessee and Maine, to find out what happens to money invested in just a few projects by these financial institutions.

She shares many stories of ordinary people she encounters along the way. She is appalled at how "her" mutual fund supports a corporate takeover of Sunbeam Corporation that eventually leads to the closure of a plant in Maine. She is amazed to watch an oil refinery being built in Thailand with money invested through "her" account in Chase Manhattan bank. She is disturbed to see that "her" investments are contributing to the construction of shrimp ponds that destroy mangrove swamps in Malaysia. She is troubled to see that "her" money goes to another oil refinery under construction in Singapore that keeps tight control over its labor force.

78. Millman, *Vandals' Crown*, 259–69.

79. Long, *Divine Economy*, 77.

80. Garson, *Money Makes the World Go Round*.

Can the church improvise by emulating Garson's path? Few of us have the resources to travel after "our" money around the world as Garson did, but this impulse to re-embed money within flesh-and-blood realities can be a starting point that might provoke us to follow our money, to pay attention to the tangible ways it affects the world. This poses a personal challenge for professors. The New York firm TIAA-CREF manages the retirement portfolios of many college professors in the United States, including mine, and it is one of the largest investment funds in the United States. Money is transferred electronically from my paycheck into portfolios of bonds, stocks, real estate, or annuities, but what actually happens to the money after that? Few professors have much of an idea what TIAA-CREF does with the money, and in fact even the managers in New York likely have little idea what actually happens with their money once it is invested. Nor do they likely care. They are merely after financial returns; they are not interested in the nuts-and-bolts or flesh-and-blood of each enterprise that receives their investments. Still, it is possible to make a minimal human connection with this money, as one friend of mine did. He shifted all of his pension allocation into two funds that are more tangible than the rest: real estate and the Social Choice Fund. Reports on the real estate fund actually tell investors the addresses of properties bought or sold during that quarter of the year. Conceivably my friend could actually visit the places that "his" money purchased. Likewise, my friend can be assured that his investments in the Social Choice Fund will exclude shares in corporations that gain "revenues from alcohol, tobacco, gambling, weapons production or nuclear power." Any other investments are evaluated on a number of issues, including "environmental stewardship, human rights, community relations, employee relations, workforce diversity, product safety and quality, and corporate governance."[81] My friend's investment move has challenged me to do something similar.

However, such so-called "socially responsible investment" is no panacea, especially if it allows people to lapse back into habits of abstraction and alleviate their need to connect their money to relationships. It may be impossible to overcome the abstraction inherent in money and credit systems.[82] The limits are clear even within professors' pension funds. For instance, TIAA-CREF appears to have watered down its language about social choice investing in the last few years. An earlier

---

81. TIAA-CREF, "CREF Social Choice Account."

82. This appears to be the view of Goodchild, *Theology of Money*.

version of its prospectus contained more robust language in its criteria for investment, focusing on "respect for the natural environment; strong charitable giving and employee benefits programs; the presence of women and minorities in leadership positions; quality products and leadership in research and development; and the payment of fair wages and protection of the environment where they operate."[83] Yet even then, a group called "Make TIAA-CREF Ethical" protested the appearance of the Coca-Cola Corporation in the Social Choice fund in light of its environmental record, its human rights record, and its potential contributions to childhood obesity.[84] At the same time, the Mennonite Mutual Aid Society, a socially responsible investment group, invested in Wal-Mart. There are no simple solutions here.

It might be difficult to envision a world without money, but Bill McKibben suggests another improvisational tactic that the church might employ: the use of an alternative local currency that would only work in a given locality:

> Say I lived in Burlington, Vermont, and I had in my wallet, next to my federal greenbacks, a wad of "Burlington Bread," an alternative currency that could be spent only in the metropolitan area. Faced with the choice of buying local food at the farmers' market or food imported from California at the Stop & Shop, I'd be more likely to buy the local product, which I could pay for in Bread. ... And then the local famer would have Burlington Bread in her wallet, increasing the likelihood that her next purchase would be local, and so on.[85]

While such an idea might sound rather unusual, it is worth thinking concretely about alternative practices that help us reframe how money works concretely, both locally and globally. I know of one church in the Chicago suburbs that started an alternative currency that allowed people to trade babysitting or other favors with each other. If the community and its relationships take priority, then such techniques might avoid the problems of money becoming detached from community.

Yet another alternative practice is a barter network. Commercial barter services already exist, but these tend to value services in dollar

---

83. Brendan Coyne, "Investment Company Challenged on Social Responsibility." This statement is no longer on the TIAA-CREF website.

84. Ibid.

85. McKibben, *Deep Economy*, 162.

terms.[86] Still, these services could foster greater concreteness as networks of suppliers and service providers emerge to connect one need to another: An auto mechanic could exchange a three-hour car repair job for three hours of landscaping. Instead of allowing money to mediate community needs abstractly, it might be possible to match needs and thus foster relationships. As a start we can practice concreteness with our money, re-attaching it to earth. Who cares about the purposes toward which the money is put? Who cares about the relationship helped or harmed? Church people should care about such things, and they should especially care to build up relationships with their funds.

Re-embedding Money in Relationships, Attaching Loving Faces to Money

The Incarnation reminds us that the Son of God was born into a web of familial relationships. But the institutions of global finance create an ever-greater impersonality and estrangement between economic actors. For one thing, they create what economists call principal-agent problems.[87] Who is the principal actor and who is the agent? With whom does final legal authority reside? Simply put, it is not clear who is in control. Corporations are legal persons, but they do not appear to be responsible in any sense. Are shareholders, boards of directors, or managers running the corporation? Do the shareholders know one another or do they even know the board or the managers? Do workers have a say? As part of the system of publicly traded corporations, many pension funds and institutional investors take investors' money and place it in all kinds of investments, many of which the investors have no idea about. At some level these fund managers are responsible for managing our money, yet can they be held responsible for what the recipients of our money do with it?

As a place of authentic relationships, the church ought to be in the lead in pointing the way to alternative modes of financial practice with clear lines of responsibility and mutual care. The church might distinguish between lending and borrowing money in order to make more money versus lending to fellow Christians who are suffering. As Stanley Hauerwas asks, "is it appropriate for Christians who are pledged to care for one another to take advantage of others who are in economic

---

86. "Bartering Gains Steam."

87. Schluter, "Risk, Reward, and Responsibility," 72–73.

distress?"[88] Such "economic distress" could mean being forced to buy a brand-new furnace during the winter when you have little savings, as happened to my young family several years ago. When our furnace broke down, my wife mentioned it to Christian friends, who shortly thereafter offered to lend us money to help cover the costs. Many people borrow money from credit card companies in times like this, or they pay back an installment loan with interest. We accepted our friends' offer of tangible Christian love, which helped us to avoid being saddled with a large debt compounded by high interest rates. And we paid them back promptly even though they said nothing about repayment. It was a small glimpse of the kind of economic relations Christians ought to be practicing in their churches. The church already does live out such relational financial practices. The ethic of global finance puts money to work globally, following the Electronic Herd to find the highest returns on money.[89] A Christian ethic puts our money into tangible earthly uses that are humble and that build up relationships in love.

Churches are mainly made up of relationships. And a big part of even a small church is dealing with finances: paying the pastoral staff, maintaining the buildings, approving the budget, and so on. The more faithful churches are practicing "God's economy," which runs differently than the economy of disconnection promoted by global finance. By contrast, the church is a place where we are more likely to know the relationships rooted in tangible realities of time and place that bring us the food, the clothes, the transportation, the clean restrooms, and all the rest. God creates us to love him and our neighbors. Do church economic practices reinforce this love? Can we name the people to whom we are indebted for the potluck supper? Do we know the cleaning staff at the church? Do we know the people who staff the food pantry and those who use it? Do we volunteer to drive the church van and know the people who ride it? Do we have relationships with those who give and receive the money in the offering plate? Do we lend money to each other when we are in hard times? Churches that can answer these questions in the affirmative are closer to embodying the love and true charity to which Christians are called. As Long reminds us, "For Thomas [Aquinas] the heart of the matter is that the law should direct human actions to virtuous ends. The heart of his teaching was that our economic activity should be able to be directed to

88. Hauerwas, "Work as Co-Creation," 124.

89. Friedman, *Lexus and the Olive Tree*, 53–60, 112–42.

those virtues that assist us in our ultimate end—friendship with God. . . . [He] seek[s] to direct our lives in all their physical embodiment to that single end and to uphold charity as necessary for our journey."[90] So the real question is whether our financial activities promote charity in us and our neighbors. Do they build up or break down loving relationships with our neighbors as we all journey toward God?

Some have commended practices of relational tithing that connect peoples' needs via a website (http://www.relationaltithe.com), but one wonders whether a dispersed network that communicates electronically can overcome the flatness of globalized financial practices.[91] Still, there is no question that connecting members of communities together without the intrusion of money is a step in the right direction. Barbara Garson discovered that "her" money in Chase Manhattan Bank was not serving to love her Mexican neighbors when it entered and then quickly departed from Mexico in 1994. In the subsequent financial crisis, one in five workers had lost their jobs, the price of tortillas shot up 50 percent, calls to suicide hot lines increased tenfold, and people decided "to feed their children instead of their draft animals so hungry beasts [came] to town to forage in garbage pails."[92] Chase and other international banks pushed the International Monetary Fund and the U.S. government to lend to the Mexican and Thai governments so that they could continue paying back their debt obligations to the private banks. Perhaps half of the money lent to the Mexican government ended up in foreign banks, yet the entire nation was being squeezed to pay back the loans. Ordinary people suffered from a global financial crisis that they didn't choose. Meanwhile, the investors in Chase Manhattan were disconnected from the effects of their money on Mexican families. The church can do better.

Practicing Humility and Charity with our Money

Although contemporary financial practices reinforce arrogance, this runs directly counter to the coming of God's rule in the lowly, infant Jesus. A

---

90. Long, *Divine Economy*, 77.

91. Claiborne and Haw, *Jesus for President*, 302–3.

92. Garson, *Money Makes the World Go Round*, 300–302. Eichengreen, "Financial Instability," 225, adduces similar evidence from Indonesia, which saw an increase of the population in poverty from 7 to 8 percent to 18 to 20 percent, and South Korea, which saw an increase of total numbers in poverty from 6 million in 1997 to over 10 million in 1998, along with sharp increases in divorces, drug addiction, and suicides in 1998 and 1999.

Monty Python skit from 1970s *Flying Circus* television show captures the contrast perfectly. The skit involves a City of London banker and a certain Mr. Ford, who is collecting charitable donations for orphans with a tin can in hand. Their dialogue is hilariously revealing, since the banker, played by John Cleese, literally cannot comprehend the idea of charity, and Mr. Ford struggles to explain the practice of charity to a banker bent on making money out of money. When Mr. Ford asks the banker to donate a British pound, he is puzzled:

> BANKER. No, no, no, I don't follow this at all, I mean, I don't
>   want to seem stupid but it looks to me as though I'm a
>   pound down on the whole deal.
> MR. FORD. Well, yes you are.
> BANKER. I am! Well, what is my incentive to give you the pound?
> MR. FORD. Well the incentive is . . . to make the orphans happy.
> BANKER. *(Genuinely puzzled.)* Happy? You quite sure you've
>   got this right?
> MR. FORD. Yes, lots of people give me money.
> BANKER. What, just like that?
> MR. FORD. Yes.
> BANKER. Must be sick.[93]

The banker goes on to steal Mr. Ford's idea and then pulls a lever so that Mr. Ford disappears through a trap door. Practicing ruthless business, the banker demonstrates the stark contrast between the logic of business practices without scruple and the logic of giving-in-love without expecting a return. The lowly practices of charity seem ineffective when compared to the ruthless use of financial power. But Christians who emulate their King are called toward self-giving love more than financial success. They are called toward humility.

One of the problems of contemporary financial practice is the arrogance it instills when it puts a price tag on the future in insurance or risk management services. As a response to this danger, churches might consider alternatives to health insurance policies, policies that are based on actuarial predictions of the future. Christians have already started organizations that pool monthly contributions for medical expenses. Each month, those members who need help to pay medical bills draw on the fund, while the rest of the members contribute as usual. It

---

93. Thanks to Jay Case for first tipping me off to this episode. Rasmussen, *Monty Python's Flying Circus*, Episode 30.

is a more concrete way of meeting expenses after they happen, rather than planning for and predicting the future. One must trust that the group contributions will be enough and will be monitored well, instilling humility and fostering community. Humility recognizes that we are not God, and therefore there are always risks of the unknown. Despite all of our elaborate statistical techniques, our scientific knowledge, and our robust institutions, we cannot predict earthquakes, tsunamis, or financial downturns. Thus we should never fool ourselves into believing that our investments on earth are secure. Our financial practices should express the church's conviction that we are not in control and that God is. That is humility, which leads to community, the reliance on each other in the face of an uncertain world.

Christian charity, rooted in love of neighbor and of God, has usually involved the giving of aid without expectation of return. It practices an ethic of generosity and grace, and this ethic is perhaps most evident in the bursts of charitable activity that have occurred during the Christmas season for centuries.[94] By contrast, the ethic of financial globalization expects returns on investments. It charges the poor a premium while rewarding the rich handsomely and cannot comprehend an economy of gracious giving. Thus we have a stark contrast between the kingdom that expects returns and the Kingdom of self-giving love, and one is more attractive to the poor than the other. Yet the understanding of gracious Christian charity has motivated a number of Christian development agencies to demonstrate tangible love of neighbors in a global economy, including groups such as World Vision, Catholic Relief Services, Mennonite Central Committee, Samaritan's Purse, and so on. Even mainstream cultural elites like *New York Times* columnist Nicholas Kristof have taken notice of their work. In some of his columns and weblog commentaries, Kristof has commended Christian non-governmental organizations (NGOs) for their work in places that many other secular groups have abandoned.[95] By helping to empower people through local development aid, many of these organizations take a relational approach that views the people in targeted communities as whole human beings.[96] For these

94. Medieval English Christmas celebrations were a time for peasants to "bring harvested produce as gifts to the lords of their estate, and the lord in return would sponsor a feast." Forbes, *Christmas*, 113.

95. Kristof, "God on their Side." Kristof, "Following God Abroad."

96. Myers, *Walking with the Poor*, 137–97, outlines the shift in thinking at World Vision toward understanding relationships in community.

Christian groups, money fosters relationships of care for others, without expectation of return. That is true, sacrificial charity. It will not surprise us to discover that churches have already taken the lead in helping their neighbors deal with foreclosures.[97]

The global scale of the subprime mortgage meltdown might make this brief sketch of alternative practices to financial globalization appear puny by comparison. But, then again, the flight of the holy family to Egypt reminds us that the Kingdom ushered in at Christmas is a Kingdom of the helpless and weak, a Kingdom led by a refugee King. The story motivates us to put our money into the service of this Kingdom of love, so that it better cultivates earthly embodiment, communal relationships, and a gracious humility that serves the poor. It should also affect how we eat in a global food economy, helping us to receive the gift of Creation as a miracle.

97. Dobnik, "Churches Offer Help in Mortgage Crisis."

CHAPTER 4

Epiphany: Stewardship as Sacramental Participation

The whole earth is full of his glory.
Isaiah 6:3b

Life as a miracle is a gift to be accepted. Its acceptance implicates us in grati-
tude, and in a responsibility of care that is fearful, difficult, and yet pleasing.
This is the only antidote I know to the ideas of life as commodity, as property,
or as subject. . . . We need that word "miracle," honestly used . . . especially,
as a part of the language of sanctity that we have come so near to losing.
—Wendell Berry[1]

One summer day not long ago I pulled a Granny Smith apple out of the
refrigerator. As I walked to the sink to wash it, I peeled a thumbnail-sized
sticker off its waxy green skin—a sticker that said, "New Zealand, ENZA,
Granny Smith, #4017." "That's odd," I thought. New Zealand is thousands
of miles from my home in Ohio. I checked our receipt and found that
we paid 99 cents a pound for these apples at our local grocery chain—a
nice price, but how strange that they were shipped all the way across the
world to be eaten here in the Midwestern U.S. in the summer. Although
the price tag was cheap, what was the real cost? And, for that matter, are

1. Berry, "Is Life a Miracle?" 184–85.

short-term monetary costs and financial statements adequate measures of value in a world that is a gift from God? Our New Zealand apple became a commodity with a price tag rather than a gift.

That apple reflects the problem of sustainability inherent in the affluent world buying its food globally—the central problem I explore in this chapter. Of course, the apple itself was a global product, having been grown 9,800 miles away. Did the growers use pesticides or chemical fertilizers? How did they care for the land? I haven't managed to get to New Zealand to find out yet, and I'm not sure I ever will. Transporting my apple was the largest part of the problem, burning a fair amount of jet fuel, diesel fuel, and gasoline in its journey from the orchard through the air and on the road to the grocery store. The fuel problem extends to most of the food supply of affluent North Americans, since the average fresh produce or simply processed food item travels around 2,500 miles from the farm to our plates.[2] Many of our global neighbors are even more reliant on food imported from far away. And most North American foods consume copious amounts of fossil fuel: the process of raising a single steer for beef in the typical American fashion burns up the equivalent of thirty-five gallons of gas.[3] So how we eat raises serious ecological issues about long-term sustainability, about the depletion of fossil fuels, and about long-term climate changes due to the burning of these fuels. The Food and Agricultural Organization of the United Nations, for instance, estimates that livestock production for food accounts for around "18 percent of the global warming effect—an even larger contribution than the transportation sector worldwide."[4] "Whether driving our cars, heating our homes, or casually leaving the lights on, [or eating] we generate a quarter of the world's fossil fuel emissions with less than five percent of its population."[5] Much of this consumption is tied to our eating.

Meanwhile, people in the United States suffer from a glut of food while many worldwide can afford very little food: "As a nation, we spend fifty billion dollars a year on weight loss, about two hundred dollars apiece, roughly equivalent to the annual incomes of a billion of the earth's people. . . . we spend as much money to lose weight as a sixth of the world

2. Smith and McKinnon, *100-Mile Diet*, 30. Thanks to Allen Plug for sharing this book with me.

3. Pollan, *Omnivore's Dilemma*, 83–84.

4. Cited in Halteman, "Compassionate Eating as Care of Creation," 34.

5. Jackson, *Earth Remains*, xvi.

spends to survive. . . .">[6] North American and European beneficiaries of this global system are mostly unfamiliar with hunger. Because higher-technology food production has become globalized with high-speed shipping, they find a plethora of food produced through industrial methods. The Green Revolution of agricultural technology, combined with cuts in trade barriers, has increased food supplies faster than demand, leading to effective price cuts (in inflation-adjusted terms) for most basic foodstuffs. Wheat farms in Kansas grow grain that is exported around the world. Vineyards and orchards in Chile ship grapes and apples to North America and Europe in our winter, since it is summer in their opposite Southern Hemisphere growing season. Fishermen FedEx their fresh catches to the world. Anyone who eats and who can buy food in the markets experiences a seeming cornucopia of food choices. Instead of global food shortages, the last thirty years have led to larger food supplies, lower food prices (in real terms), and increased consumer choice—for those who can pay for it in the market. For those who cannot afford market prices for food, the system fails them if they become dependent upon it. Still, supporters of globalization, many of them well-meaning, argue that the sheer increase in the quantity of food produced on the industrial model will lower the prices of food, which will help the poor by making that food cheaper. These people do have evidence to support their views. In 2005, even the United States was expected to import more food than it exported for the first time since the 1950s.[7] Partly as a result, food prices remained relatively low as a percentage of total household spending in the United States. North Americans now "spend around 7 percent of their disposable income on food, down from 22 percent in 1950."[8]

Yet the globalization of food in this so-called Green Revolution mostly benefits the wealthy nations. As the food economy became a long-distance economy, recent oil price increases increased the costs of transporting food, with the worldwide impact falling more heavily on those with low incomes (for whom food costs are a larger percentage of their income). The system not only leaves out those poorer participants who cannot buy food in the markets, but it also participates in a "structural

6. Ibid.

7. Wilkins, "Think Globally, Eat Locally."

8. Smith and McKinnon, *100-Mile Diet*, 99. Also see Southgate, *World Food Economy*, chapter 1; and Johnson, "Food Security and World Trade Prospects."

evil" that benefits rich consumers while harming poorer producers.[9] It also contributes to the global ecological issues the world now faces: the loss of topsoil, the depletion of non-renewable fossil fuels, the destruction of watersheds, the extinction of species, and shifts in climate patterns—to name only a few ecological effects connected to how we buy groceries and prepare our meals. "Everyone wants to eat like an American on this globe," said one agricultural consultant, "but if they do, we're going to need another two or three globes to grow it all."[10] And we can't make up the difference by eating fish: a group of scientists project the disappearance of most seafood species by the year 2048, if consumption continues at its current rate.[11] We are pushing against the ecological limits of Creation. So where do we find hope for change in this situation?

This chapter argues that the celebration of Epiphany can help the church participate in the fullness of God in the world; it can help us imagine connections between our eating and our land and help us learn again to receive Creation as a gift. It can help the church improvise healthier practices of eating. The day I picked up that apple was the day that I had to start thinking seriously about my relationship to Creation and the global-industrial food economy in which I am immersed. It was, in fact, an epiphany. The Feast of the Epiphany on January 6 focuses on how the fullness of God's glory was revealed in Jesus—a story that ought to form us to love Creation and God's creatures. Of all the church's feasts, this one opens us the most up to the possibility to the sacramental dimension of life, to the possibility that life is a holy, miraculous gift, a revelation of God's loving glory. Thus, the Epiphany re-grounds practices of Christian stewardship in the terms of God's relationship to Creation a gift of glory that reveals his love for the world. In other words, living in sacramental relationship with Creation as an epiphany—actually seeing earthly matter as revealing God's love and glory—can eventually better ground and foster stewardship practices of simplicity and conservation in the church's members.

Such a sacramental vision of stewardship as participation in God, while most at home in Eastern Orthodoxy, is accessible to other Christian

---

9. Sider, *Christ and Violence*, 72–73, 76. Thanks to Josh Elek for sharing this reference.

10. Streitfield, "Global Need for Grain."

11. Dean, "Study Sees 'Global Collapse' of Fish Species"; Eilperin, "World's Fish Supply Running Out, Researchers Warn."

traditions.[12] Reading Wendell Berry's essays and poems, for instance, you find that his vision of life is surprisingly sacramental and surprisingly attuned to the epiphanic and theophanic (God-revealing) relationship between Creation and human beings. That is, he believes that we participate in the revelation of God's love and glory through our eating and its relationship to God's other creatures. With Berry, I assume that how we eat in this globalizing world is related to how we farm—or as he puts it, "eating is an agricultural act."[13] In a recent essay he says that we must begin to understand that the earth is holy, "for at present there is nothing, literally nothing, that is held sacred by proponents of so-called development."[14] It is easy to fall into despair over imagining alternatives to the present system, says Berry, because we are "helping to cause the problems we are helping to deplore and solve."[15] So how might the church's participation in the divine love and glory, celebrated in the Feast of the Epiphany, help us re-imagine and improvise constructive responses to the global food economy while recognizing global ecological limits?

THE DIFFICULTY OF MOVING FROM INDUSTRIAL TO SUSTAINABLE EATING

Critics of the global food economy must grant the point that globalizing the food supply meant increasing the quantity of food available, at least in the short run, even as fewer people worked the land and most of those in affluent countries lived in urban areas. Yet how do we measure cost and efficiency? Berry says, "If you can keep the context narrow enough (and the accounting period short enough), then the industrial criteria of labor saving and high productivity seem to work well." "But," he continues, "the old rules of ecological coherence and of community life have remained in effect. The costs of ignoring them have accumulated, until now the boundaries of our reductive and mechanical explanations have collapsed." He worries that we have learned "to think mechanically about

---

12. Both Wendell Berry and Orthodox theologians make this argument. See Guroian, *Ethics after Christendom*, 159–60; Sherrard, *Eclipse of Man and Nature*, 90–118; and Wesche, "ΘΕΩΣΙΣ [Theosis] in Freedom and Love," 118–28. Berry cites Sherrard in both "God and Country" and "Christianity and the Survival of Creation."

13. Berry, "Pleasures of Eating," 145.

14. Berry, "Purpose of a Coherent Community," 71–72.

15. Ibid., 74–75.

the land and its creatures."[16] We turn God's good gift of the earth into the "cash values" explored in the previous chapter.[17] Hence, the real costs of globalizing your food supply, according to Berry, fall outside a narrow calculus: "Is there, in reality, such a possibility as an 'economy of scale' or 'growth economy'? . . . And it is from agriculture that we receive the most immediate answer: only if we are willing to sacrifice everything but money value, and count that sacrifice as no loss."[18] The problem with my New Zealand apple and the shopping habits that brought it to my refrigerator is that I had become an "industrial eater," one "who no longer knows or imagines the connections between eating and the land."[19] When we become industrial eaters, we reduce agriculture to its productive yields; we define the meaning of food in terms of prices; and we flatten our world yet again.[20] It is simply not true that, in one Wal-Mart official's words, "the same principles of and value, price and quality that apply to things like television sets also apply to food."[21] By shopping and eating according to these principles, we have gotten ourselves into a mess.

Having posed this problem, I must now offer a confession. My family and I like industrial and fast-food eating, and we are finding it difficult to bring our habits into line with the journey that our experiences in the fullness of time provoke us to undertake. My point is that the globalization of food offers some tantalizing short-run benefits that most of us in the affluent world enjoy, and our family is no exception. Unschooling us from our food habits will take time. Although Berry articulates a positive vision of how we ought to live, we have only begun to journey toward his prescriptions: "in the long run the safest food supply is a local food supply, not a supply that is dependent on a global economy. Nations and regions within nations must be left free—and should be encouraged—to develop the local food economies that best suit local needs and local conditions."[22] My family has been more inclined to enjoy how we profit from a global food economy rather than to think about local solutions.

16. Berry, "Renewing Husbandry," 94–96.

17. Also see Goodchild, *Theology*, 84–89, on how monetary exchange systems fail to account for ecology.

18. Berry, *Gift of Good Land*, xi.

19. Berry, "Pleasures of Eating," 146.

20. Pollan, *Omnivore's Dilemma*, 214.

21. McKibben, *Deep Economy*, 53.

22. Berry, "Bad Big Idea," 50–51.

We participate selfishly with others in a global food economy all too much when we travel to the grocery store. I noticed how this problem affects others most clearly during the 2004–2005 academic year. We were living in the island state of Bahrain, in the Arab (Persian) Gulf, a place that attracted many people because it was an oil producer—although its petroleum has mostly run out. If Bahrain followed Berry's prescriptions to the letter—"the safest food supply is a local food supply"—then we and most other people would not have been there. Bahrain annually receives only a couple of inches of rain. With temperatures soaring into the 100s for the summer, most crops hardly stand a chance. Underground aquifers and extensive irrigation in the north have allowed lush date palm groves to flourish, but the southern part of the island is a desert. Most plants require daily watering. Local food, apart from date cultivation and fishing, is not a viable option. And, yet, today over 700,000 people live in Bahrain without starvation. Food imports from the world, combined with thriving retail grocery competition, allow residents to choose from thousands of food options, albeit with rising prices at present. The reality, however, is that the globalization of food has extended the possibility of life to more places.

But the question of sustainability is the great worry worldwide and in the microcosm of Bahrain; here is where the critics of globalization have a point. As the population of Bahrain has grown, drinking water from the aquifers has begun to run out. To keep up, the government built desalination plants to convert seawater into fresh water—with financing coming from petroleum dollars in our oil-hungry global economy. Today, however, Bahrain has mostly run out of oil and only exports a little. Its soil is increasingly salinated by irrigation water, making even date palm cultivation difficult. The country now depends on outside food sources, instead of the fish and dates that sustained the local diet for centuries. In addition, "reclaiming" land from the shallow sea is big business. Huge shopping malls and a Ritz Carlton resort now sit where the green waters of the Gulf once were. Pollution of the waters is a growing problem, and the Parliament is working to save a wildlife-rich mangrove habitat that has been destroyed by greedy landowners who fill in the water to sell brand-new real estate. Fishermen no longer gain their livelihood from the sea, with fishing a recreational pursuit at best. Coral reefs offshore are threatened by land reclamation, increasing water temperatures, and increasing salinity. While Bahrain might be an object lesson for the benefits of globalization, you also wonder seriously about its costs. How sustainable are the practices in Bahrain? How sustainable is a global food economy and a global oil economy?

Even Thomas Friedman, evangelist for the flat world, addresses such concerns.[23] As he wrote in the late 1990s, "in the next decade, if globalization continues to bring more and more people into this lifestyle, and if we cannot learn to do more things using less stuff, we are going to burn up, heat up, pave up, junk up, franchise up and smoke up our pristine areas, forests, rivers and wetlands at a pace never before seen in human history."[24] He also notes that around 1,000 new cars enter the transportation fleet in Beijing every day, and he has become a champion of oil conservation and a "geo-green" agenda.[25] However, Friedman's proposed solution to the problem of earth destruction is for the electronic herd of globalizers to see that "being green, being global and being greedy can go hand in hand."[26] He believes that problems such as global climate change or over-consumption can be solved while leaving greed intact. And perhaps this all boils down to good public relations, since Friedman writes that "Global companies are learning that by supporting conservation programs they can improve the image of their global brand among customers, who increasingly value the environment."[27] Without reforming the desires or limiting the appetites of affluent consumers, image rebranding hardly seems like a solution.

RE-ENACTING THE FEAST OF THE EPIPHANY

By contrast, living out of the church's celebrations of Epiphany—once the third most important feast day for the ancient church, after Easter and Pentecost—challenges the greed in our lives.[28] *Webster's Dictionary* defines the word "epiphany" in several ways: as "an appearance or manifestation especially of a divine being," "a usually sudden manifestation or perception of the essential nature or meaning of something," "an intui-

---

23. As this book was in its final stages, Friedman published *Hot, Flat, and Crowded*.

24. Friedman, *Lexus and the Olive Tree*, 280.

25. Friedman, *World Is Flat*, 407; Friedman, "Power of Green."

26. Friedman, *Lexus and the Olive Tree*, 282–83. This is essentially the thesis of *Hot, Flat, and Crowded*.

27. Friedman, *Lexu and the Olive Tree*, 290.

28. Kleinhans, *The Year of the Lord*, 58.

tive grasp of reality through something usually simple or striking," or "an illuminating discovery, a revealing scene or moment." The Feast of the Epiphany gives birth to and encompasses all these meanings and more. It celebrates the *appearance* of Christ to all, the *manifestation* of God's fullness in the baby, the *realization* of the eastern kings that a simple child was the king—all in a moment of *illumination* and *revelation* depicted lovingly in numerous paintings of the Adoration of the Magi.

On this day, the Western church celebrates with the kings from the East who have come to the light of Christ, the first of the Gentile converts. In some Catholic countries, the day is known as "three kings day," and families exchange gifts then, as do many Orthodox believers. Liturgically speaking, it is certainly a more appropriate day for gift exchange than Christmas, since gift exchanges are central to the story: the gift of Jesus to the Gentiles; the gifts of gold, incense, and myrrh to the holy family; the gift of the Incarnation to the world; and the gift of Creation. In the midst of all these gifts, the wise men from the East "bowed down and worshipped" the baby Jesus (Matt 2:11), a posture also imitated by the church, which is now mostly Gentiles. Through Israel and Jesus, non-Jews receive the messianic redemption of all Creation, implicating us in the divine exchange of gifts with humanity.[29]

In addition to reminding us of the gift, re-enacting this story can reform our imaginations to conceive of the fullness of God's economy on earth. The original feast was more significant for the Eastern church than Christmas (which was more significant in the Western, Roman church). Unlike the Western church, the Eastern church calls this feast Theophany (the revelation of God) and commemorates the baptism of Jesus, celebrating how "on this day Christ, by his baptism, had sanctified all the waters of the earth."[30] This global image conveys the importance of divine participation in the redemption of Creation as part of Epiphany. Here we glimpse a universality of vision that extends salvation to the Gentiles. The church is reminded of this theme every year when reading the first several verses of Ephesians 3, where Paul refers twice in this passage to the economy (*oikonomia*) of God, first to the economy of grace (v. 2) and later to the economy of "the mystery hidden for ages in God who created all things" (v. 9b). Epiphany celebrates the deepening and expanding

29. Milbank, "Can a Gift Be Given?"

30. Talley, *Origins of the Liturgical Year*, 125. Also see Dix, *Shape of the Liturgy*, 357; Cobb "History," 467–68; and Winkler, "Appearance of Light," 147.

revelation of *this* global economy that covers the whole earth. This is also clear in the royal Psalm 72, which is read every year at Epiphany and concludes with this praise of Yahweh: "Blessed be his glorious name forever; may his glory fill the whole earth" (v. 19).

Thus we glimpse the glory of God at Epiphany—the God who extends his economy of redemption beyond Israel to include the whole world. Every year on Epiphany the church also reads Isa 60:1–2: "Arise, shine; for your light has come and the glory of the Lord has risen upon you. For darkness shall cover the earth, and thick darkness the peoples; but the Lord will arise upon you, and his glory will appear over you. Nations shall come to your light, and kings to the brightness of your dawn." Here we learn to see the world as an emanation of the glorious light of God, and the people of God as the witness to that light. This becomes explicit in the prayer for Epiphany in the *Book of Common Prayer,* which says, "O God, by the leading of a star you manifested your only Son to the peoples of the earth: Lead us, who know you now by faith, to your presence, where we may see your glory face to face."[31] The prayer asks God to lead the church to his presence, just as the wise men were led. The church also asks to behold the glory of the Lord—a theme resonant with the biblical narrative. If we are led to God's presence, if we behold a glimpse of His glory, we are put in the posture of those who are ready to receive the created world, the first Incarnation of God's word, as a miraculous gift matched only by the second Incarnation of God, the birth of Jesus. At the very least, a proper response to the story of the Epiphany ought to be a higher appreciation for the world as a gift and a corresponding decrease in our own gluttonous habits. Yet North American society seems a long way from living out of the grace and gift of the Epiphany story in its eating habits.

This is surely in part because it has lost the sacramental understanding that the story proclaims—the understanding that the world is pointing to the Creator—and because it has participated in the "desanctification of nature," the "loss of the sense that the very stuff of the universe has a sacred quality."[32] Thus, how and what we eat, as Orthodox theologian Alexander Schmemann suggests, expresses our relationship to God.[33] By that standard, my family's relationship to God was in real trouble. We hardly thought about our daily bread as a gift participating

---

31. Episcopal Church, *Book of Common Prayer,* 214.

32. Sherrard, *Eclipse,* 90–91.

33. Schmemann, *For the Life of the World,* 11–22.

in divine holiness and glory. Building upon the images of gift, glory, and holy light, however, the Epiphany also reminds the church of its sacramental relationship with the Creator in ways that the Eastern Orthodox tradition best captures. Schmemann describes this sacramentality this way: "All that exists is God's gift to man, and it all exists to make God known to man, to make man's life communion with God. It is divine love made food, made life for man. God blesses everything He creates, and, in biblical language, this means that He makes all creation the sign and means of his presence and wisdom, love and revelation."[34] Greek Orthodox theologian Philip Sherrard defines sacramentality as "the idea that creation actually participates in the divine, and is an actual mode of existence or embodiment of the living, ever-present God . . . with the rider that all nature has therefore an intrinsically sacred character."[35] The epiphany of blessing helps us re-imagine our stewardship and our concern for ecology as our participation in the mystery of redemption, in God's economy, and in God's created glory. If God's glory is revealed in all that is and in our worship, then we should respond with changed lives—or else our lives diverge from the truth of our worship.

Re-Imagining Global Stewardship as a Sacramental Practice of Redemption

But what does this drama have to do with stewardship? That word was one of those Christian buzzwords that I heard a lot as a child. Growing up Dutch Reformed in the 1970s, I still heard a fair amount about stewardship in relation to the Creator. In my Christian school, for instance, we often sang the familiar hymn "This Is My Father's World," which is forever associated in my mind with stewardship, or what Reformed theologians call the Cultural Mandate in the Genesis stories. As the first story goes, when God created the first man and first woman, he "blessed them and said to them, 'Be fruitful and increase in number; fill the earth and subdue it. Rule over the fish of the sea and the birds of the air and over every living creature that moves on the ground'" (Gen 1:28). In case we missed the point, preachers and teachers would draw on the other creation story in Genesis 2, which says that God "took the man and put him in the Garden of Eden to work it and take care of it" (v. 15). And,

34. Ibid., 14.

35. Sherrard, *Eclipse*, 91–92.

our teachers said, Adam was also given the task of naming the animals (vv. 19–20). This set the precedent that human work must be to care for Creation. When God put the first humans in charge, on this account, he intended for all humans to follow these commands. We were to work in caring for the world, and that work was a good thing—not just part of the curse of sin. We needed to take care of the Creation for our Master. It was our job to be stewards, co-laborers in the garden.

Note the prominence of active verbs in this Reformed account. We were to fill, to subdue, to rule, to work, to care, to name, and thus to steward. Yet all our striving would be losing if we thought we could redeem Creation under our own power. Without divine initiation, without sharing in "divine love made food, made life" for humans (to quote Schmemann again), there is no Creation, and there is certainly no redemption. Without our participation in God's grace, we cannot hope to change. By contrast, the Reformed emphasis on stewardship as human action fails to account for the ways in which modern thinkers have treated Creation as mere "resources" for human exploitation rather than the very gifts of God. The political philosopher John Locke, for example, viewed the natural world as "almost worthless materials" that were made valuable only through human labor, which turns the resources into property.[36] The Protestant emphasis on work ends up playing into this de-sacralizing tendency of modern thought, and thus it has a hard time checking humanity's rapacious consumption of the earth.[37]

Still, the spirit of stewardship is going in the right direction. Behind stewardship is the idea that everything in this world belongs to God and we are only caretakers of these things, just as God is the caretaker of Creation. God not only created the world in six days, but he continued to care for it after that. God provided food in the form of plants and trees for both animals and humans (Gen 1:29–30; 2:8–9); even after humans sin, God promises to provide. On these theological grounds Christopher Barrett argues that the idea of stewardship could hold a key to promoting sustainability. As he puts it, "Stewardship holds that the possessor of a

36. Locke, *Second Treatise*, chapter 5, paragraph 43, p. 27; cf. Arendt, *Human Condition*, 133–46.

37. See the famous article by White, "The Historical Roots of Our Ecologic Crisis," and responses by Bouma-Prediger, *For the Beauty*, 67–86, and Guroian, *Ethics after Christendom*. White appears to let the Eastern church off the hook (1206), a point that Bouma-Prediger does not engage directly in his attempt to defend Christianity from the charge that it contributes to ecological crisis. Also see Sherrard, *Eclipse*, 116, for a harsh critique of Western science.

natural resource should behave as a custodian, using the resource wisely but enjoined from destruction or disposal. . . . Stewardship identifies possessors as managers, servants, and beneficiaries rather than as masters."[38] But the danger is that we are still too Lockean in our views of Creation. Are we still going to be "managers" and therefore seize power? How are we to overcome the temptation toward mastery and instead learn to become servants?

Here is where the Epiphany, read through Eastern Orthodox tradition, directs us to an understanding of Creation as participating in God's glory and God's redemption of all things. Epiphany, where we behold the glory of the Lord anew each year, puts the church on this journey to know what God desires of us. Separated from our communal participation in God's glory, the term "stewardship" may still tend to emphasize individual human management of resources and may tend to eclipse God and the community; therefore, it needs to be framed within the deeper sacramental narrative of the Epiphany.[39] Because Creation is not ours but a gift of love, the church must care for it in community with a light touch, learning to live in relation to it rather than possessing it as "natural resources" or "my property" or even "God's property that we manage for him." Rather, re-enacting Epiphany grounds our stewardship in a larger story of God redeeming Creation.

Living out of Epiphany, we learn that, in Berry's words, "the Creation is not in any sense independent of the Creator, the result of a primal act long over and done with, but is the continuous, constant participation of all creatures in the being of God. . . . Creation is thus God's presence in creatures."[40] Treating stewardship as the outgrowth of Epiphany infuses a sacramental dimension into stewardship and also re-embeds it in the gospel narrative, for there is a *christological* center to stewardship that frames it as part of the process of redemption. Kenneth Paul Wesche captures this christological center in this vivid passage of an essay on ecology:

> This [the mystery of the Incarnation] gives to our understanding of stewardship a metaphysical orientation that teaches us to treat the world with loving care, since its salvation—transformation through union with the divine—is inseparable from ours. It

38. Barrett, "Markets, Social Norms, and Governments," 440.

39. Guroian, *Ethics after Christendom*, 159–60.

40. Berry, "Christianity and the Survival of Creation," 97–98.

teaches us, I think, that the cause of our present ecological disasters is humanity's failure to pursue the capacity for the divine
that makes us to be what we are. . . . [W]e approach the world as
though asleep, consuming its resources in a blind compulsion to
satisfy the egoistic desires of our own narrowly constricted egoistic world. We consume and consume and consume some more,
treating the world as if it were made for us and the satisfactions
of our bodily and spiritual lusts. We fail to see that our desire and
the world's essence can never be fulfilled until we undertake the
journey in the Logos of our being—whom the church identifies
as Jesus Christ—toward full individuation, full personhood in
communion with the divine in the Divine Logos incarnate.[41]

At Epiphany that journey toward becoming united with God begins as
the church celebrates Jesus, that divine Logos and our only way of communing with God, manifesting his glory to the kings and peoples of the
earth. Our stewardship, to use evangelical terms, then becomes part of
our growing relationship with Christ and that relationship gives it meaning. Or to use a term that applies both in Anabaptist and Orthodox contexts, we begin a process of divinization, theosis, or sanctification, where
humans are called to become more holy, as God is holy.[42] This process
is part of the healing of our minds, bodies, souls, and our relationships
with the earth, which join God's redeeming of all things through Christ.
Epiphany thus reframes our stewardship and our eating as part of a journey toward communion with our redeemer.

When my family buys grapes from Chile and apples from New
Zealand and lettuce from California—only made possible by oil from
Nigeria, Saudi Arabia, Kazakhstan, or Venezuela—we participate in what
we might call one of the quasi-liturgies of globalization: the liturgy of
the grocery store as provider. We begin to thank God for our local Super
Wal-Mart, rather than for the sunshine, the rain, the bees that pollinated
crops, the photosynthesis process, the fertile soil that allows it all to grow,
or the men and women whose work made it all possible. We fail to live in
receiving God's good gifts of Creation. By contrast, the *Book of Common
Prayer* offers a prayer for the stewardship of creation that challenges us to
live in God's gift economy in ways that challenge the global food economy:
"O merciful Creator, your hand is open wide to satisfy the needs of every
living creature: Make us always thankful for your loving providence; and

41. Wesche, "ΘΕΩΣΙΣ [Theosis] in Freedom and Love," 127–28.

42. Finger, "An Anabaptist/Mennonite Theology of Creation."

grant that we, remembering the account that we must one day give, may be faithful stewards of your good gifts."[43] This prayer adds an element of eschatology to our sacramental relationship with Creation. It reminds us that we fail to live with an eye to the end of time, with an eye to "the account that we must one day give" to God for the gifts with which we were entrusted as stewards.

Wendell Berry draws attention to the eschatological dimensions of stewardship when he turns to Rev 4:11, which says, "You are worthy, our Lord and God, to receive glory and honor and power, for you created all things, and by your will they existed and were created." Berry comments, "our responsibility, then, as stewards, the responsibility that inescapably goes with our dominion over the other creatures . . . is to safeguard God's pleasure in His work. And we can do that, I think (I don't know how else we could do it) by safeguarding *our* pleasure in His work. . . ."[44] We must participate with God in this process, attending to his work of Creation, in the shadow of the end of the Christian story, after the first Advent and before the Second Advent of Christ. Part of "the account that we must one day give" has to do with how we have eaten, how we received the good gifts of food that sustain us. The thought that I will have to account for how I have eaten frankly scares me, because I still like fast food. But, thanks to the grace of God, I am learning to be satisfied with the simple gifts of daily bread and water.

We cannot save the earth or its people. However, the church serves God by taking pleasure in his gifted work of Creation and sharing that gift with the world. The sharing side of stewardship requires tangible care for the hungry, the prisoners, and the broken—notably those broken by our participation in an industrial food system. A church formed by Epiphany will desire all people to live in healthier relationships with the Creator and his living Creation. After all, the church's members need to remember that they must "one day give an account" for the gifts that God has entrusted to them, including the food they ate.

IMPROVISING PRACTICES

Living stewardship out of Epiphany suggests that our problem goes beyond the deterioration of resources to the root problem of a devaluation

43. Episcopal Church, *Book of Common Prayer*, 259.
44. Berry, "God and Country," 100. Emphasis in original.

of creation and a separation of humans from creation. We flatten the world when we seek to exploit earth's resources on a global basis merely to eat. We no longer view the world as a miraculous blessing of God, as a revealer of God's glory, as a gratuitous gift, or as a world destined to be reunited with God. But there is hope. "The practical point," says Wendell Berry, "is that *if* I believe life is a miracle, I will grant it a respect and deference that I would not grant it otherwise. If I believe it is a miracle, then I cannot believe that I am superior to it, or that I understand it, or that I own it."[45] God's loving glory, after all, radiates through all created gifts. As the Jesuit poet Gerard Manley Hopkins put it so well, creation is "charged with the grandeur of God."[46] Or as Berry says, "When one receives a divine gift, one must be glad of it; one must be grateful for it; one must take care of it."[47] By contrast, a modern person can hardly imagine what Berry means that by our eating "we are all now complicit in the murder of Creation."[48] We can barely perceive that "destruction of nature . . . is the most horrid blasphemy. It is flinging God's gifts into His face, as if they were of no worth beyond that assigned to them by our destruction of them."[49] Berry says, "You cannot know that life is holy if you are content to live from economic practices that daily destroy life and diminish its possibility."[50] So is it possible that the church will be able to embody a resonant healing of our relationship to the earth that daily promotes life and flourishing? "The task of healing," writes Berry, "is to respect oneself as a creature, no more and no less. A creature is not a creator, and cannot be. There is only one Creation, and we are its members."[51] As members, we praise God "from whom all blessings flow" with all of our actions, and if this praise has any traction in our lives it can only change how we eat so that we begin to live into practices that sustain and promote life rather than promote destruction of the earth.

45. Berry, "Is Life a Miracle?"

46. Hopkins, "God's Grandeur."

47. Berry, "Is Life a Miracle?"

48. Ibid., 136–37.

49. Berry, "Christianity and the Survival of Creation," 98. Bouma-Prediger's excellent book, *For the Beauty of the Earth*, 13–14, starts with some seminary students' reaction to this quote; their denial that blasphemy was involved suggests how far we have lost a sacramental relationship with Creation that the liturgical year and Epiphany help to recover.

50. Berry, "Christianity and the Survival of Creation," 99.

51. Berry, "Healing," 9.

Already there are plenty of people trying to live out this vision. One is a "self-described 'Christian-conservative-libertarian-environmentalist-lunatic farmer'" named Joel Salatin, who runs a small-scale organic farm in Virginia.[52] A writer who visited the farm describes it this way:

> Polyface Farm is built on the efficiencies that come from mimicking relationships found in nature, and layering one farm enterprise in time as well as in space—in four dimensions rather than three. He [Salatin] calls this intricate layering "stacking" and points out that "it is exactly the model God used in building nature." The idea is not to slavishly imitate nature, but to model a natural ecosystem in all its diversity and interdependence.[53]

It's hard to imagine such an effort being undertaken without serious respect for the Creation as a gift. Farmer Salatin also points out the contrast between industrial eating and stewardship: "We wouldn't for a minute say, Let's go to the cheapest church in town; let's hire the cheapest preacher we can get. We wouldn't say, Let's go to the cheapest brain surgeon. But we're very happy to put on the lowest respect level and honor level the stewards of our food system and the stewards of our landscape."[54] Salatin spots a gap between our religious convictions and our practices, between our belief that God is the loving Creator and our grocery-buying habits. We care little for good stewardship of land or food and a great deal about saving cash on our bottom line. Overcoming this gap requires that we reframe our world and change our own habits in the face of strong pressures from our society.

Four short examples can illustrate what sacramental stewardship flowing from Epiphany might begin to look like. First, our family began learning to receive creation as a gift when we bought shares in a Community Supported Agriculture farm for the first time in the summer of 2007, but only after we had discussed the problem with others in an adult education class and our church small group—and only after other members of those groups took the lead in organizing our participation. We began purchasing local food grown in sustainable ways that flowed from our participation in a community that saw God's glory in Creation. For the first time, we city-folk began to learn what produce was in season

---

52. Pollan, *Omnivore's Dilemma*, 125.

53. Ibid., 215.

54. Dreher, *Crunchy Cons*, 84.

throughout the year. We began to learn to receive the food as a surprising gift each week, rather than a commodity awaiting our plans. This has required some adjustments to our cooking and preservation habits, but we are slowly starting to enjoy the challenge. Although our church group did not change its habits as a direct *result* of celebrating the Feast of the Epiphany, the sacramentality we experienced in the season helped reframe our world and shape our habits to align with God's economy. In celebrating Epiphany the church re-enacts the veneration of God's greatest gift, thereby re-imagining globalization as a threat to those gifts and improvising globalization in ways consonant with the story of Epiphany and with the grain of Creation.

Second, participation in the sacramental vision of Epiphany helps us to find ourselves in a larger whole, within a larger story of the cosmos. Christians whose stewardship grows out of sacramental participation in God's Creation will want to know the whole story, and in a modern world of fragmentation, disconnection, and a globalized food supply, this is no small thing. G. K. Chesterton in *The Outline of Sanity* nicely describes the modern loss of the whole:

> It is nobody's business to note the whole of a process, to see where things come from and where they go. Nobody follows the whole winding course of the river of milk as it flows from the cow to the baby. Nobody who is in at the death of the pig is in the eating. . . . We need a social circle in which things constantly return to those that threw them; and men who know the end and the beginning and the round of our little life.[55]

As he puts it, "What is wrong with the man in the modern town is that he does not know the causes of things."[56] Wendell Berry also expresses our failure of sacramental stewardship in pungent moral terms:

> One of the primary results—and one of the primary needs—of industrialism is the separation of people and places and products from their histories. To the extent that we participate in the industrial economy, we do not know the histories of our meals or of our habitats or of our families. This is an economy, and in fact a culture, of the one-night stand. "I had a good time," says the industrial lover, "but don't ask me my last name." Just so, the industrial eater says to the svelte industrial hog, "We'll be together

55. Chesterton, *Outline of Sanity*, 140.

56. Ibid., 137.

at breakfast. I don't want to see you before then, and I won't care to remember you afterwards."[57]

Our failures of eating are thus failures of ethics, failures of imagination, and failures to love creatures properly. By contrast, sacramental stewardship encourage Christians to develop a social circle, a sense of wholeness, and a grasp of connections that Chesterton and Berry lament humans losing. Simply put, if Christians take sacramentality seriously—the idea that their eating either glorifies or blasphemes God—they need to know about the sources of their milk. In a similar way we ought to know where our chicken comes from. Farmer Joel Salatin, for example, "brought up a well-known chicken magnate who has a reputation for being a conservative evangelical Christian" but whose plants employed illegal aliens. "My point is that when I eat that brand of chicken I am supporting all that. People don't see that. See, that's the disconnect."[58] Seeking to overcome such disconnects is what sacramental stewardship starts in us. It is much easier not to know and not to care about from whence comes our food. But it may be blasphemy and desecration. It is certainly a failure to love creatures as we love God and as God loves us.[59] Instead, we should search for connections.

Third, we can find encouragement in small steps of improvisation that might have larger effects in God's economy. One small action taken by our church and the office in which I work was to purchase sustainably grown coffees. While it is easy to criticize such actions as motivated by guilt or as inadequate to the task or even as counter-productive because they reinforce global market exchanges, this move was a small, tangible gesture of care for small coffee farmers. And this local action has affected larger global trends. Some estimates put the number of people directly dependent on growing coffee at 100 million. From 1997 to 2001, coffee production increased around 3 percent per year while consumption grew only 1.5 percent, leading to a glut of coffee and lower wholesale prices for

57. Berry, "Whole Horse," 113.

58. Dreher, *Crunchy Cons*, 83–84.

59. Berry addresses all of us plant-eaters and meat-eaters with this deeply sacramental point: "This is not to suggest that we can live harmlessly, or strictly at our own expense; we depend upon other creatures and survive by their deaths. To live, we must daily break the body and shed the blood of Creation. When we do this knowingly, lovingly, skillfully, reverently, it is a sacrament. When we do it ignorantly, greedily, clumsily, destructively, it is a desecration." Berry, *Gift of Good Land*, 281.

coffee; mass quantity instead of care for land ruled the day.[60] As prices dropped, farmers and workers in some of the poorest countries of the world lost their livelihoods. In Guatemala alone, 250,000 people out of the 650,000 in the industry lost jobs. But in recent years, the coffee industry rebounded as coffee drinkers turned to higher quality beans grown organically on hillsides and under the shady canopy of trees.[61] Instead of seeking mass-produced robusta beans grown in lowland sun (as in Brazil and newcomer Vietnam), higher-quality coffee suppliers are seeking out arabica beans grown on small farms in the shady highlands. The shift to more sustainable coffees rewards quality, improves environmental stewardship, and provides meaningful work for small coffee farmers. This is only a small step in the right direction, toward a healthier respect for the gift of Creation, but it illustrates how a better stewardship can work to the advantage of many.

Fourth, Wendell Berry argues for a turn to local eating and healthier small-scale farming—practices that most mainstream agricultural economists consider naive, romantic notions, but practices that increasingly make sense for us today, even by narrow financial standards. A local economy does not require total isolationism: it is possible to imagine a worldwide community of healthy local communities, in which necessary exchange occurs. What the mainstream view fails to imagine is that actually caring for the land and its creatures—living in communion with them—turns out to be a way of connecting with the true universal of Creation rather than the false universality of cash values. These cash values do not just devalue Creation, but they fail economically. In fact, a recent report funded by the Pew Charitable Trusts found that "the 'economies of scale' used to justify factory farming practices are largely an illusion, perpetuated by a failure to account for associated costs. Among those costs are human illnesses caused by drug-resistant bacteria . . . and the degradation of land, water, and air quality caused by animal waste too intensely concentrated to be neutralized by natural processes."[62] Meanwhile, some in the agricultural research community are challenging the dominant cash value paradigm. Some in that community are troubled enough by the current state of their profession that they argue for a new agricultural revolution that "will look to enhance the produc-

---

60. Ramirez-Vallejo, "Break for Coffee," 26–27.

61. Jordan, "Cappucino Effect"; World Bank, "State of Sustainable Coffee."

62. Weiss, "Report Targets Costs of Factory Farming."

tivity of our croplands not through fossil fuel-based inputs, but through stewardship: of soils, water, and life."[63] Wendell Berry's view is moving closer to the mainstream. These agricultural experts have recovered a vision of the whole of Creation that is certainly closer to the sacramental understanding I am advancing, although the push for profits could sneak in to corrupt the rest of the process, as it did when organic foods became an industrial commodity.[64] Still, the church could certainly support policies that move in this direction. Its main calling is to worship God, to invite others to join it, and to align its members' lives with the truth of who God is. While we can support policies that extend by analogy from worship, our calling is to let worship inform how we live. Above all, that worship connects us to the cosmos so that we can see the world rightly. We escape being the broken people of industrialism and begin to figure out from whence our milk or our bacon comes. We learn to attend to the sources of our bread and wine. We learn to eat differently, in ways that connect us rightly to Creation. We already embody alternative eating in the church: it's called the Eucharist.

Many people resist challenges to the industrial food paradigm by insisting that we cannot roll the clock back and become Amish. Yet even by the all-too-narrow accounting standards of the industrial food paradigm, it turns out that caring for the land and people is "efficient" (even in conventional terms). Because the industrial model prizes efficiency, its long-term sustainability is doubtful; it threatens to consume the earth. But healthier ways of being in communion with the earth may offer some hope. Steven Stoll tells the story of an Amish family he visited in Holmes County, Ohio, named the Klines. He found that the Klines made a $2,000 profit per dairy cow "compared with the $200 or $300 profit [per cow] common on industrial farms." The Kline's story, as narrated by Stoll, is worth quoting extensively:

> When David [Kline] grew wheat, he harvested 75 bushels per acre. For comparison, I found two reports from different parts of the country. Michigan wheat farmers collected a record-setting 67 bushels per acre in 1999—an accomplishment that local people attributed to "prayers and technology." Kansas farmers brought in an average yield of only 46 bushels per acre in 2000, under good conditions. David's wheat cost him almost nothing to grow—just

63. Horne and McDermott, *Next Green Revolution*, 257.

64. For this story, see Pollan, *Omnivore's Dilemma*, 134–84.

> two bushels of seed per acre, selected from his own reserves. . . .
> His principal tool for reaping and binding is a simple mechanism
> with a rotating reel, manufactured by the McCormick-Deering
> company. Sitting in the shed next to an equally vintage plow, the
> reaper looks like the first one ever made.[65]

Stoll says that the average American farm had a per-acre value of $923, whereas Holmes County farms had a per-acre value of $2,862. He suggests that the secret to their success as dairy farmers is "wily agronomy." By letting their cows graze in their fields and letting them manure the ground where they stand, Amish farmers save the hassles of planting feed corn and collecting manure. They produce as much milk as—or more than—conventional dairies while operating a much lower-cost operation. Some Amish dairy farmers take in $12,000 a month, while their typical costs are around $1,000. Simple, sound stewardship seems to be paying off even in short-run financial terms.

Lest you think this story is an isolated anecdote by a sympathetic admirer, consider a more recent study done by researchers at one of Ohio State University's extension centers. According to a news report,

> The net profit per acre for an Amish farmer growing . . . wheat
> is $126, while the net profit for a conventional farmer growing
> a crop of oats with a comparable livestock nutritional value is
> $10. . . . Startup costs are much lower for the Amish. While an
> Amish farmer will spend about $5,500 on five draft horses, a
> conventional farmer will spend $94,200 on a 160-horsepower
> tractor. . . . "It costs $2.30 a day for the Amish to operate a horse,"
> James [the lead author of the study] said. "You can't start a tractor
> for $2.30." An Amish farmer spends about $20,000 equipping a
> 60-acre farm for grain harvest, while it costs around $350,000
> to mechanize a 1,000 acre farm, according to the study. But that
> works out to around $333 an acre for the Amish, compared to
> $350 an acre for the modern-day farmer.[66]

According to one of the study's authors, this last figure does not account for the expenses involved in maintaining complicated technologies and equipment, as opposed to the simple technologies of the Amish. Maybe simplicity really is simpler and more efficient. Meanwhile it is difficult to imagine alternatives to our oil-based global food economy, and yet the

65. Stoll, "Postmodern Farming, Quietly Flourishing."
66. Associated Press, "Amish Way." The lead researcher's name is Randy James.

Amish are already living out such alternatives. They may be better prepared than any of us in the industrial world for a post-oil world, and they offer compelling examples of holistic farming practice.[67] They remind us that God's fullness and abundance is not a product of human technological mastery but a gift to those who cooperate with Creation.

But is it possible for city-dwellers to experience this fullness that is tied more closely to the land? Shoppers in farmers' markets certainly think so. The 6,000 members of "farm-to-table" food clubs in New York City meet face-to-face each week with the farmers who bring fresh vegetables and fruits.[68] Many urbanites, such as my own family, are learning about growing seasons, harvests, and different varieties of fresh produce through farmers markets or through CSA farms, in which they pick or the farmer delivers a portion of each week's harvest. The most radical part of these practices is that they connect both farmers and eaters with each other through God's gifts of food and land. For instance, my family's produce, eggs, and chicken are now connected with Alex and his small Mud Run Farm in Navarre, Ohio. We get our beef from a local cattle farmer who is also a co-worker, so in both cases our food starts coming with a story. Shopping at local farmers' markets might appear more expensive on the surface, but it participates more richly in God's economy of Creation. One sociologist found that people who shopped at farmers' markets had ten times as many conversations as those who shopped in supermarkets.[69] As our shopping becomes more human, we may slow down and make our eating human again as well. Is it possible to imagine our meals as more akin to communion than to filling up a tank of gas?

Allowing Epiphany to help us re-imagine the world can lead to embodied alternatives to the current global food economy. And re-imagining stewardship is not some abstract notion divorced from Creation. It is working with the grain of reality, in constant relationship with the ever-blessed and ever-blessing Creator. To work as stewards is not only to live up to a high calling; it is a way of working out our salvation and participating in the redemption of the cosmos into the Kingdom. Although we might not be called to live like the Amish, we can learn from their example of good stewardship tied to the land. We can act upon our story that this earth is a gift of our Lord and that he will one day return to restore it fully. We can

67. Thanks to Chris Miller of Judson University in Illinois for this point.
68. Johnson, "Bringing in the Harvest."
69. McKibben, *Deep Economy*, 105.

work in anticipation of that day, knowing that we are accountable to God for how we've treated his creatures, from the greatest to the least. Out of gratitude for grace, we can steward creation in ways that give glory back to the giver of the gift of life, the giver of the gift of the Messiah to the Jews and the whole world—the carpenter of Nazareth.

CHAPTER 5

The Sundays after Epiphany and the Globalization of Work

Isn't this the carpenter?

Synagogue worshippers, hearing Jesus preach (Mark 6:3)

We want to change man's work; we want to make people question their work; is it on the way to heaven or hell?

—Dorothy Day[1]

The significance—and ultimately the quality—of the work we do is determined by our understanding of the story in which we are taking part.

—Wendell Berry[2]

While one hears a lot about the "outsourcing" of jobs and about sweatshops, few of us have the chance to visit a global garment factory and to place it in the larger "story in which we are taking part" (to quote Wendell Berry). Thanks to friends in the island state of Bahrain, however, my whole family had the chance to tour a factory that assembles cotton pants as a subcontractor for retailers such as Gap, Banana Republic,

1. Day, "Blood on our Coal," 250.
2. Berry, "Christianity and the Survival of Creation," 109.

115

Tommy Hilfiger, Old Navy, and Eddie Bauer. The name of the place was Gulf Garments, and it turned out be a collection of cinderblock buildings in a dusty industrial area on the island. The business employs over 1,000 people who labor there up to ten hours a day, producing up to 12,000 garments a day. These same items retail for $40 to $60 each in the malls of North America and Europe, but the average cost to produce them per unit is $12 to $13, including the profit for Gulf Garments. Yet the workers' wages are a few dollars per day, due to the fact that garment production is a labor-intensive industry. It requires constant human touch and human attention in running the sewing machines, so it requires hiring and paying hundreds of laborers, making garment production expensive and leading to constant pressure to pay workers as little as possible to produce as quickly and efficiently as possible. It is humbling—troubling—to realize that every seam on the clothes you are wearing was likely sewn by a young woman bending over a sewing machine, in conditions unknown. It turns out that the workers at Gulf Garments, like many garment workers, are part of a system of flexible wage labor that is spreading worldwide. According to geographer David Harvey's reckoning in the year 2000, the number of workers working for wages "more than doubled in less than twenty years," partly through population growth but mainly through women going to work for money.[3] We were witnessing part of that trend in our tour. Even Thomas Friedman worries about this trend, as he writes: "Quite simply, for many workers around the world, oppression by the unchecked commisars has been replaced with oppression by the unregulated capitalists, who move their manufacturing from country to country, constantly in search of those who will work for the lowest wages and lowest standards."[4]

As we toured the plant, it became clear that a quest for efficiency permeated Gulf Garments' production process. While they once produced shirts, they now specialize only in jeans, pants, skirts, and shorts; according to the manager, it was "more profitable" to specialize. The management chooses and orders all fabrics, using computers to create patterns that will get as many panels as possible out of each bolt to minimize waste. It is up to Gulf Garments as the subcontractor to create all the designs; after receiving a general sketch of what the U.S. retailer wants, they create samples, and they hope that their bid for the item wins out. If the retailer

3. Harvey, *Spaces of Hope*, 41, 64.

4. Friedman, *Lexus and the Olive Tree*, 206–7.

is happy with the design samples and the price, they hire Gulf Garments as the subcontractor; often they are one of many firms competing for the contract. Automated machines using computerized designs do the actual cutting of the huge bolts of fabric. The production facilities are classic assembly lines, with up to twenty stations in each of the ten lines. Each station has a digital counter keeping track of the units, and there are four lines of a newer, automated system that tracks each worker's output in real time with microchips embedded in the hangers carrying each garment. Surveillance of individual output in order to increase efficiency is the point of the system. The pressure to produce is obvious and intense, a tangible presence on the shop floor. Doing the same small task hundreds or thousands of times a day looked painful. We wondered about repetitive stress injuries, and we also noticed that some workers wore masks (presumably to prevent inhalation of fabric dust). It was clear that their jobs were difficult, low-paying, pressure-packed, and boring.

However, it didn't appear that workers were *imprisoned* in a "sweatshop" all day. Many of the workers, especially the women, gave bright smiles when they saw our kids—so much so that we worried about distracting them from their work and hurting their production levels. Every room was either air-conditioned or well-ventilated, and all were brightly lit. Even the pressing room, where all the garments were steam-pressed by machine or ironed by hand, was relatively cool. The facility was generally clean. In the thread-cutting and tagging areas, women were working doing trimming garments and attaching price tags while listening to a recording of the Qur'an being recited and while conversing a little. One woman even said hello to us. At noon a bell sounded, and several women headed out for a break. We didn't have a chance to ask how many breaks they get in their workday, and just a part of me wondered if this was all managed for us.

But firsthand observation suggests that the problems go deeper than sweatshop labor. These garment workers' jobs are typical of the flexible system of the globalization of human work—in an Asian-owned firm contracting with an American clothing retailer employing Asian and Arab workers in a small island nation in the Arab Gulf—and they raise deep questions of how Christians should react to the effects of such globalization on traditional understandings of work. Often these questions are raised narrowly, as in: Do we buy more Gap clothes or boycott the Gap until they pay their workers more? But, however pressing, such questions are too narrow and pragmatic, since they miss the deeper problems that will require us to attend to the larger story of the Sundays after Epiphany in order to re-imagine alternatives and improvise responses.

These deeper problems became clearer when I toured another Bahraini garment factory on my own. As at Gulf Garments, the majority of the workers in this facility were young women from South Asia (especially Sri Lanka and India). When I asked the chief financial officer about his workforce, he said that wages in Bahrain were actually thirty percent higher than in India, yet there was still a benefit to being in their current location. He claimed that an average of between ten and fifteen percent of the workforce was usually absent on any workday in India, which made for a kind of "hidden tax." In Bahrain, by contrast, he said, the "controlled environment" made for less absenteeism and thus higher productivity. Because the workers were almost entirely brought in from outside and were away from their families, they had no diversions, and absenteeism was much lower.[5] Unlike in India, where the workers live in their villages near their families and commute to work, here they are living in company-owned housing and are bused into the plants. If a child gets sick at the factory in India, a mother might miss a workday. While here, her sick kids live well over a thousand miles away. By taking the women far from the distractions of home and family, the company obtained a more reliable workforce and greater efficiency, but at the cost of rupturing family ties. It is possible to argue that some of these young women were savvy and freely chose to leave their home countries in order to work eleven-hour days in this alien Arab country and benefit their own self-interest and the interest of their families.[6] But there is no denying that such choices are severely constrained. While North Americans or Europeans walk around in pants that cost $60, a week's worth of these young women's wages, the young women send their paychecks back to Sri Lanka or India to help their families eat. Work for them has become a means to an end, but it has little intrinsic worth. Meanwhile, their cost-conscious managers employ "controlled environments" to increase profits. Squeezing labor is at the heart of the globalization of work and outsourcing.

5. V. Muthukumar (chief financial officer, Ambattur Clothing, Sitra Island, Bahrain), in interview with the author, April 7, 2005.

6. Rivoli, *Travels of a T-Shirt*, 90–97, makes this argument, not entirely convincingly, for young women in China.

So, too, worries about the *quality* of daily work environments—and the worry that rich-country consumers might be unwittingly contributing to inhumane work conditions for poor workers in sweatshops—are backed up with stories. In 1997, media reports showed that some Nike athletic shoes were produced in Vietnam by young women working sixty-five hours per week for around fifteen cents per hour, while being exposed to cancer-causing agents at levels 177 times greater than the law permitted.[7] In 2003, reports emerged that a factory producing for the rapper P. Diddy's clothing line was reported to be employing workers in shifts up to twelve hours, requiring pregnancy tests for women (a positive test meant dismissal), and paying workers twenty-four cents for each sweatshirt sewn—sweatshirts that retail for fifty dollars.[8] The documentary film *China Blue* shows Chinese girls as young as fourteen working seven days a week for six cents an hour, sometimes for seventeen-hour shifts, with no overtime pay, stitching together blue jeans at a total cost per pair of $1.45—jeans that retail for at least twenty times that much.[9] These may be abusive extremes, but any item that requires extensive human work is liable to be produced by corporations that are trying to cut labor costs through global outsourcing, and so it is logical to worry that more and more workplaces will relocate in a "race to the bottom" to places with low wages and harsh working conditions.[10] Yet because we buyers are separated from the workers who make our clothes or other goods, we have little idea how to respond constructively.

For help, this chapter looks to the Sundays after the Epiphany in the church year, which focus on the work and ministry of Christ. God the Father authorizes this work of liberation, which the church joins through the Spirit, allowing it to listen for the voice of God and enter the fullness of divine glory.

---

7. Greenhouse, "Nike Shoe Plant."

8. Gray, "P. Diddy's Clothing Line."

9. *China Blue*, 2005.

10. Galeano, *Upside Down*, 163, 174–75. For a not-very-convincing response to the "race to the bottom" charge, see Larsson, *Race to the Top*, 49. Also see Drezner, "Bottom Feeders," 64–70; and Drezner, "Globalization and Policy Convergence," 53–78.

Problems with Globalized Work

Before revisiting stories of the season that reveal these themes, though, we need to specify five ways that globalization alters work, as illustrated at Gulf Garments. First, at least since Frederick Winslow Taylor, the modern workplace has been highly regimented, controlled, and rationalized to make production more efficient and thereby increase profits.[11] Surveillance of a worker's output is nothing new, but information technology makes it possible to gather and process more information more quickly and to scrutinize individual workers' outputs more closely. Thus the workplace has been flattened in Friedman's sense, as the process of rationalization has sped up and workers have become interchangeable across the globe. We can get a glimpse of this process at any local fast food restaurant, as Eric Schlosser notes in his book *Fast Food Nation*: "The strict regimentation at fast food restaurants creates standardized products. It increases the throughput. And it gives fast food companies an enormous amount of power over their employees."[12] Global outsourcing simply extends such systems across the world, making workers interchangeable between continents—a process that Friedman celebrates in *The World Is Flat*. For instance, he gets excited about software "that can chop up any piece of work and send one part to Boston, one to Bangalore, and one part to Beijing, making it easy for anyone to do remote development."[13] But while Friedman contends that technologies such as personal computers and work flow software empower individuals, he also admits that manual laborers face constant downward pressure on their wages—and he overlooks the quality of their workplaces entirely (as opposed to the workplaces of people in high-technology sectors).[14] Hence our worry here is over the condition of human work and human workers under increasing globalization. Dorothy Sayers' lament is as relevant now as when she wrote it in 1941: "It is, by the way, singularly unfortunate that much of our social machinery, including the material machines themselves, has in these days been given over into the hands

---

11. Chandler, *Visible Hand*, 274–82; Hardy, *Fabric of This World*, 128–40; Kanigel, *One Best Way*; and Gill, *Holy Tradition of Working*, 117.

12. Schlosser, *Fast Food Nation*, 70.

13. Friedman, *World Is Flat*, 6–7.

14. Ibid., 10–11, 268, 271, 282–83.

of the unghosted."[15] For Sayers, the unghosted are those lacking feeling or wisdom, lacking the Holy Spirit. They fail to consider the *spirit* of the globalized workplace and threaten to subordinate the workers to the machines; they lack a concern for the quality of the work experience.

Second, the workers at Gulf Garments, like most industrial laborers, are separated from the results of their labor and from the people who will actually use the products of their work. The clothes they sew all day are not for them to wear; they are for the rich "consumers" in North America and Europe. They are alienated in Marx's sense, unable to enjoy the fruits of their labor, therefore cut off from what, Marx claims, makes them human, their "species-being."[16] Unlike God the Creator, it seems, they have little chance to survey their work and proclaim it good; the items to be sewn, or the burgers to be flipped, keep coming down the line. Sayers asks, "But what of the factory hand, endlessly pushing a pin into a slot? How far does he feel of the far-off end-product of his task, 'This thing is mine?' And if he does, how often does the contemplation of it afford food for the soul?"[17] It is the separation of work from results which leads to a loss of responsibility for workers on the line.[18] Commentators like Friedman fail to consider alienating effects of working in a globalizing environment in which one is separated from the results of one's work.

Third, however, the work done by young people at sewing machines or burger grills has been turned into a commodity defined by monetary value; it is only meaningful to the business in terms of hourly wages and labor costs. This quantification of labor's value has coincided with a greater marginalization of workers' power, at least in the United States. According to the *New York Times*, "wages and salaries now make up the lowest share of the nation's gross domestic product since the government began recording the data in 1947, while corporate profits have climbed to their highest share since the 1960's."[19] In addition, job tenures have declined, at least for men between the ages of forty-five and fifty-four, and the prospects for low-skilled male laborers have dimmed.[20] But the worry here goes deeper than shoring up workers' wages or job security. As a

---

15. Sayers, *Mind of the Maker*, 143.

16. Marx, "Economic and Philosophic Manuscripts of 1844," 70–81.

17. Sayers, *Mind of the Maker*, 181.

18. Gill, *Holy Tradition of Working*, 118.

19. Greenhouse and Leonhardt, "Real Wages Fail to Match a Rise in Productivity."

20. Gross, "Behind that Sense of Job Insecurity"; Glynn, *Capitalism Unleashed*, 126.

host of commentators have noted over the years, the intrinsic meaning of work for humans is hard to discern when work becomes a commodity bought by employers bidding to pay the lowest wages possible and sold by workers bidding to obtain the highest wages possible.[21] We attend to the price of labor while losing attention to the intrinsic quality of the work itself—its process and its final products. To quote Wendell Berry, we must "safeguard God's pleasure in His work . . . and *our* pleasure in His work, and our pleasure in our own work."[22] It is hard to do that when reducing work to a monetary value per hour.

Fourth, and most importantly, the loss of intrinsic meaning in the work suggests a loss of the sense in which work is, in Dorothy Sayers' words, "in itself a sacrament and manifestation of man's creative energy."[23] Human labor loses its sacramental character, its being a form of participation with God and an offering to God, which contributes to careless and wasteful work.[24] As Berry describes this loss, "To work without pleasure or affection, to make a product that is not both useful and beautiful is to dishonor God, nature, the thing that is made, and whomever it is made for. This is blasphemy: to make shoddy work of the work of God."[25] By this standard, the workplaces we saw in Bahrain or that we see in a fast food joint appear to be dedicated more to the bottom line than to honoring God. Although we will see how it is possible to recapture in workplaces a trace of work as joyful participation in divine love—one can imagine a well-crafted pair of pants sewn by the young women we saw—it is also clear that a harsh, high-speed, efficiency-driven workplace makes such an approach to work more difficult to comprehend in any meaningful sense. Many workplaces thus inculcate blasphemy.

Of course, all of these problems are hardly unique to the current era of globalization. They have been live issues about work since the Industrial Revolution; indeed, reflection upon such problems has been central to many reform projects and to Catholic social teaching at least

---

21. Gay, *Cash Values*; Gill, *Holy Tradition of Working*; and John Paul II's papal encyclicals *Laborem Exercens* and *Centesimus Annus*. McCarraher, "Me, Myself, and Inc.," 185–231. Thanks to Jay Case for sharing this article with me.

22. Berry, "God and Country," 100.

23. Sayers, *Mind of the Maker*, 178.

24. McCarraher, "Me, Myself, and Inc.," 203–8.

25. Berry, "Christianity and the Survival of Creation," 104.

since the 1890s.[26] What is new, however, is that these problems are now spreading rapidly across the globe as the search for cheaper labor in garment production or other labor-intensive industries continues, and that they are happening more quickly. As Friedman reminds us, workplaces are being flattened and reconstructed on an almost-daily basis across multiple continents. The garment factories I observed in Bahrain were hardly permanent fixtures; they could well be gone by the time you read this.[27] This system of flexible, mobile production makes the industrial system from the days of Henry Ford look top-heavy, stable, and static (even though it was highly disruptive of earlier work patterns in its day). The point here is that an intensified, speedier version of industrialism that some call "post-Fordism" has been exported worldwide in the last few decades.[28] Friedman contends that this more flexible system liberates work from spatial constraints and empowers workers, but it seems more accurate to describe the trend as empowering those with mobile capital and mobile skills while weakening those who can only offer stationary labor. As this trend continues, even the white-collar workforce is being speeded up. One symbol of this flattening in the office workplace is the use of mobile electronic devices that allow workers to check email while away from their desks. Workers are expected to reply to messages all the time, even while at home. In Washington DC, I heard young staffers refer to their BlackBerrys as "leashes," since their boss could contact them at any time by phone, text message, or email. Even Friedman is forced to concede that mobile technology can intrude upon human relationships and human work; he tells a story of being picked up at the airport in Paris by a taxi driver who "was driving, talking on his phone, and watching a movie [while driving!]. I [Friedman] was riding, working on my laptop, and listening to my iPod. There was only one thing we never did: talk to each other."[29] Even as labor-saving technology connects regions of the world, it speeds up workplaces, disconnects people from each other, and simultaneously expands work so that people can escape it less.

26. McCarraher, "Me, Myself"; Gill, *Holy Tradition of Working*; Pope John Paul II, *Laborem Exercens*; *Centesimus Annus*.

27. In fact, many Indian and Pakistani firms moved to Bahrain to evade the quotas on textile products from those two countries, but the global quota system ended in January 2005, making it likely that such firms would return to these countries. Rivoli, *Travels*, 121.

28. On this system of "flexible accumulation," see Harvey, *Condition of Postmodernity*, 141–97; also see Budde, *Kingdom of God*, 18–27.

29. Friedman, *World Is Flat*, 3rd ed., 516.

A corporate leader in outsourcing from India recently summed up the goal of the new global outsourcing system in words that echo Friedman: "to take the work from any part of the world and do it in any part of the world."[30] By breaking work into pieces and shipping those pieces all around the world, it is possible to generate profit, but at a potentially high cost to laborers and our sense of the integrity of the whole of work. The potentially costly meaning of globalized *labor* took on a whole new dimension when I read recently in my local paper the headline "Giving Birth is Latest Job Outsourced to India." The story went on to describe how over fifty women in the town of Anand, India, were presently engaged in the entirely legal practice of "commercial surrogacy," after being "impregnated in vitro with the egg and sperm of couples unable to conceive on their own."[31] Quite literally, they were renting out their wombs to overseas couples for around $10,000 a birth, of which the Indian women receive $6,250 for their "labor." Other reports suggested that this was a booming industry elsewhere in India, driven by the low prices of outsourcing such *labor*. One American couple told a national television audience that they would have spent around $80,000 in the United States for a surrogate mother, but their total costs in going to India were $30,000. As the wife said, "Truthfully, we just looked at the price of what it would cost."[32] By outsourcing the work of pregnancy and childbirth to India, it was possible to save serious money. But that takes outsourcing to a nearly-absurd, troubling extreme. How might the church improvise a healthier way of work in a global world? By turning to the story re-enacted in the Sundays after Epiphany, it is possible to sketch out improvisations in work practices that affirm the whole human person under God's control, that resist commodification, that champion work as sacramental, and that promote greater stability.

30. Giridharadas, "Outsourcing Works." Friedman, *World Is Flat*, 3rd ed., says similar things on 6–8, 91–92.

31. Dolnick, "Giving Birth." Gentleman, "Surrogate Motherhood." The latter story quotes a medical technician who complains that only doctors, lawyers, and accountants could afford surrogacy before. So surrogacy in India empowers the middle class in the United States? Outsourcing benefits us all again!

32. Celizic, "Couples Finding Surrogates."

RE-ENACTING THE SUNDAYS AFTER EPIPHANY

It turns out that the Sundays after Epiphany help focus the church on Jesus' work in Galilee, and we will discern several paths toward reimagining work as we re-encounter the stories told in this season. Although current Roman Catholic practice labels this period a period of Ordinary Time preceding Lent, the readings are largely the same for both the Revised Common Lectionary and the Catholic lectionary, and they highlight the work of Jesus in relation to the revelation of the Father's glory.

The season begins every year with Baptism of the Lord Sunday, in which the church reprises an early drama of the synoptic gospels. In Matthew, Mark, and Luke, Jesus' baptism marks a turning point in the narrative, the transition toward Jesus' work and ministry and away from the work of John the Baptist. Because the baptism stories offer several distinct clues for reframing the globalization of work, we will attend to each one. We start by revisiting the story of Jesus' baptism in Matthew (Matt 3:13–17). In this account, we see the theme of fullness evoked. Jesus tells John the Baptist that the baptism will "fulfill all righteousness" (v. 15), and the divine voice announces to the audience the identity of Jesus as the beloved Son who pleases the Father (v. 17)—an epiphany of the full trinitarian glory of God that we will not see again until the end of the season, in Transfiguration Sunday. At least one commentator has noted the parallels of this divine announcement to the royal decree in Ps 2:7 and the word to the suffering servant in Isa 42:1, suggesting that "sovereignty is joined to sacrificial service."[33] The mark of God's reign is the divine work of humble, self-giving love between the persons of the Trinity, marked in the baptism as a *kairos* moment that reminds us that the divine word initiates the work.

Mark's account of the baptism has the divine voice speaking directly in the first person to Jesus: "You are my Son, the Beloved; with you I am well pleased" (Mark 1:11). This is a personal, audible call at the beginning of the earthly work of Jesus, suggesting that one important way of discerning our calling in work is not merely to seek to divine God's will but to listen for God's voice—the voice first heard in our own baptism.[34] As disciples, it is important for us to hear God affirming his pleasure in us, his creatures and followers. Can we hear him say to us, "With you I

---

33. Craddock et al., *Preaching Through the Christian Year*, 82.
34. Hansen, "Finding God's Will," 14.

am well pleased"?[35] In our own work, we must live out of this divine affirmation in our own baptism, which is a gift of grace. And in light of such grace, we can continue to listen for God's affirmations in our daily work. Work and vocation are of course closely related in the English language, while the Latin root of vocation and voice is the same. To find a vocation, one must listen for the voice.

Unlike Matthew and Mark, Luke describes the descending dove in the narrator's voice, as if everyone can see it. As he puts it, "the Holy Spirit descended upon him in bodily form like a dove" (Luke 3:22a). Luke reminds us, among other things, of how the Spirit's presence makes the work of the Son (and his disciples) possible. The Holy Spirit is not just revealed privately between the Father and the Son but is revealed to all of us as participants in the drama. And it is clear from all the narratives that the Father's voice and the Spirit's descent are central to inaugurating the work of Jesus.

The themes of participation in the fullness of trinitarian glory, of discerning the divine voice, and of the Spirit's empowering of work overshadow the following Sundays, culminating in Transfiguration Sunday. The second Sunday after Epiphany stresses the glory of the Lord each year, as evidenced in the prayer for that day from *The Book of Common Prayer*, which asks, "Grant that your people, illumined by your Word and Sacraments, may shine with the radiance of Christ's glory, that he may be known, worshiped, and obeyed to the ends of the earth." [36] Flowing from this glory to the work of mission, the prayer anticipates themes that emerge in the following Sundays and themes that flow from the Gospel of John, which offers the assigned readings each year on this Sunday. The link between this glory and the work of Jesus is clearest in the story of Jesus changing water into wine at Cana, which John says was the first time that Jesus "revealed his glory" (John 2:11). The sharing of divine glory between Father and Son is a central motif in John's Gospel, linked to Jesus' escalating ministry: "the glory as of a father's only son, full of grace and truth" (John 1:14), a motif that appears at least five more times in John's Gospel.[37] As the Cana story indicates, the work of Jesus would be to point to the blessings of an abundant life to come and to grow into the fullness

---

35. This way of framing the story comes from N. T. Wright, by way of Harry Winters.

36. Episcopal Church, *Book of Common Prayer*, 215.

37. John 8:39, 11:4, 12:16, 12:23, 13:31–32.

of this grace and truth. It seems logical that disciples of Jesus are also called to this participation in the revelation of glory in their own work.

When reading Mark in the Sundays after Epiphany, the church immediately jumps into stories of a newly baptized Jesus who heals, calls disciples, prays alone, and who proclaims the Son of Man lord of the Sabbath (Mark 1:14—2:28). One commentator on this season's lectionary texts discerns these major themes in Mark: "In the coming weeks we shall read of Jesus' words and deeds, culminating in his transfiguration, and then, after the move to Jerusalem, in his passion. . . . The liturgical pilgrimage with Jesus from Galilee to Jerusalem is a paradigm of our whole Christian life of discipleship, which was inaugurated for us at our baptism."[38] These same themes are evident in abundance when the church listens to Luke in the following year. In the third Sunday after Epiphany, we hear Jesus telling the synagogue in Nazareth that he is the fulfillment of Isaiah's prophecy that God's anointed would "preach good news to the poor . . . proclaim freedom for the prisoners and recovery of sight for the blind, to release the oppressed," and to proclaim the Jubilee year (Luke 4:18–20).[39] From this point on, his work was to preach, to converse, to tell stories, and to perform miraculous signs that would free even the Gentiles.[40] The work of the church is to do the same, especially in a world of globalized work. It is a work of discipleship, a discipleship of liberation. Work for Christians is always connected to the mission of extending Jubilee.

However, the church is not alone, just as Jesus was not alone. Divine presence helps empower the mission. Transfiguration Sunday—the final Sunday of the season before Ash Wednesday—reminds us that the full glory of God shines through Jesus in the power of the Spirit. In all three synoptic gospels the story of the transfiguration is preceded by Jesus telling his disciples they must deny themselves, take up their crosses, and follow him if they want to come after him. He also tells them that

---

38. Fuller, *Preaching the Lectionary*, 229.

39. Yoder, *Politics of Jesus*, 2nd ed., 28–33.

40. The stories from Luke in the fourth Sundays after the Epiphany and beyond emphasize the beginnings of his work: Jesus is driven from Nazareth (4:21–30); Jesus calls the first disciples (Luke 5:1–11); Jesus forgives the sins of a paralyzed man and heals him as a sign to the Pharisees (Luke 6:17–26); Jesus calls Matthew and answers a question about fasting (Luke 6:27–38); Jesus tells three stories about the Kingdom (Luke 6:39–49); and Jesus heals the servant of a Roman centurion (Luke 7:1–10).

some of them will not die before seeing the Kingdom of God.[41] Then the Transfiguration—the radiant shining of divine glory in the person of Jesus—immediately follows. We hear the divine voice, saying again that this person is his Son.[42] We can infer that Peter, James, and John saw the Kingdom come with power when they saw the radiance of the divine glory shine through Jesus and heard the voice on the mountain. We are reminded that the early and late work of Jesus is sustained by participation in the glory of the divine Trinity, which is the Kingdom.

Likewise, we can conclude that our work as disciples of the King is also sustained by participation in divine glory, by the approval of the Father through the Son and the Spirit. This link is made explicit in the prayer for the last Sunday after Epiphany in the *Book of Common Prayer*, which reads: "O God, who before the passion of your only-begotten Son revealed his glory upon the holy mountain: Grant to us that we, beholding by faith the light of his countenance, may be strengthened to bear our cross, and be changed into his likeness from glory to glory."[43] We are not alone in our work as disciples of the King. Our work of self-sacrificing love participates in the fullness of God's glory, shining out through the Spirit, helping us re-imagine the work of others, even as the work requires a turn toward Jerusalem and Holy Week, toward bearing the cross, and toward bearing the likeness of Jesus.

RE-IMAGINING THE GLOBALIZATION OF LABOR

Thus far we have identified five focal points from the gospel dramas after Epiphany. I want to argue that each of these can help us re-imagine global labor: the divine work of the Father works against technological determinism, the mission work of humble liberation offers hope for alienated laborers, the empowerment of the Holy Spirit helps us counter the commodification of persons, the calling of the divine voice helps us rediscover work as vocation, and the fullness of divine glory helps us rest in God's sufficiency, over against the increased pace of our fast, flat world. Each of these focal points therefore suggests an antidote to the problems with globalized work described earlier. To reiterate those problems, they are increasing technological control and "de-skilling" of workers, alien-

41. Matt 17:1–9; Mark 9:2–9; Luke 9:28–36.

42. Matt 17:5, Mark 9:7, Luke 9:35.

43. Episcopal Church, *Book of Common Prayer*, 217.

ation from the results of work, the commodification of work, the loss of work as a sacrament, and the speeding up of changes to workplaces globally. In response to each of these, the Sundays after Epiphany help the church re-imagine and reframe the practices of globalization so that it can improvise new practices that respond to the problems with the globalization of work.

First, the process of flattening that Thomas Friedman celebrates increasingly puts the control over work into the hands of technologies that chop up the work process into ever-smaller pieces, shipping that work out around the world. At the extreme, one can outsource pregnancy and let someone else bear your child. After nine months of work, the baby can be shipped back to the parents—and all very cheaply. By contrast, the church contends that the divine Father is truly in control of the whole of our work. Turning matters of reproduction over to technology and the market may be an extreme example, but the use of information technology to split work into ever-smaller pieces is a pervasive concern. Therefore, as even Friedman admits, manual industrial laborers are losing control of their lives, not unlike the rest of us who have been "de-skilled." Skilled craftsmanship—creating from the beginning to the end of a process—is increasingly rare in the world. Few of us grow grain, grind it into flour, and make the flour into bread. Instead, we depend upon specialization, technology, and a division of labor—upon the grower, the miller, the baker, and the grocery store.[44] Yet the challenge is how to improvise practices of craftsmanship that attend to the whole of work, whether from conception to birth, from seed to table, or from idea to final product.

From the baptism of Jesus onward, we disciples learn that the Father authorizes the work of the Son. God the Father, the master Creator and Craftsman, is ultimately in control of our lives. Yet we allow technology to usurp this Creator, to take control of our work, allowing technology to replace God. Like Friedman, we are tempted to embrace a progressivist belief that the autonomous evolution of technology is liberating humans. Yet that technology might just as easily be enchaining workers in garment factories, fast food restaurants, and elsewhere. Here the divine affirmation of the human Son reminds us that the Father affirms the whole human person. Human dignity in work is affirmed as a form of participation in the fullness of divine glory. Dorothy Sayers grasped this when she wrote, "If the common man is to enjoy the divinity of his humanity, he can come

---

44. Heilbroner, *Making of Economic Society*, 3.

to it only in virtue and right of his making."[45] Rather than being flattened, work for the disciple is always being expanded into fullness, as one discovers that one is walking on the path first laid out at baptism—living out of the grace of the affirmation that God the Creator is fully pleased with us and that he calls us to take up work that helps demonstrate God's reign. A blind evolutionary process of technology does not control our work. Rather, we learn to emulate the Son and work after our baptism until we are united again with the fullness of the Father's glory. Since the Father is in control, we need never fear that powers of economic change will take control. Instead, we are empowered to understand these powers as capable of falling under God's redemption. We are empowered to model alternative ways of work that embrace the wholeness of the task and that glorify God.

A second problem is that workers in many globalized workplaces are alienated, cut off from the products of their work. But the Sundays after Epiphany plunge us into the meaning of the great work of the Son in extending the good news of jubilee, including to the workplace. Thus the work of the church is not only to do the work of preaching, but to continue to embody liberation in the larger story from baptism to transfiguration—the story of the revelation of the Father's glory. Freeing alienated workers is not an end in itself, and the church is not called to impose a new regime of liberation for its own sake. Rather, the church is called to walk this road from the Jordan to the mountain of Transfiguration. On the way, the church necessarily proclaims Jesus' good news that God's glory is revealed right in the midst of the liberation of the poor, the prisoners, the ill, and the oppressed. These are not merely metaphors for people trapped in sin; they are meant to suggest that the gospel is to liberate God's creatures from physical forms of bondage as well. And it is the church's job to proclaim and embody this gospel. Therefore, our concern will certainly extend to the wages and working conditions of our neighbors. Yet none of this activity is to bring glory to anyone; it is simply the way in which the church participates in the full glory of the Father. God is doing a new thing, not us (Isa 43:19). Hence, the liberation of alienated workers in our own day would be a sign that the church is participating in that glory.

But do we see signs of the church working to help those alienated in their workplaces? It may depend if we are talking about members of

45. Sayers, *Mind of the Maker*, 174.

the church or those outside it. Speaking of those within the church, I recently had the chance to talk at a Mennonite church's adult education class where one of the members poured out his heart about his own workplace. He said that he worked in an engineering firm where he faced increasingly intense pressure to get in projects by deadlines. He felt that his workplace was speeding up and that the timeframes for deadlines were getting shorter. He would hustle to get projects in before deadlines, only to wait on people at other businesses who took their time. My response was to say that our church groups need to be talking about just these sorts of problems. We need to be able to listen to such concerns and help our members discern God's call in the midst of such circumstances and advocate changes in workplaces. For those outside the church, the work of liberation will be different. The way in which the Father is glorified is the way of attending to the concrete needs of our neighbors in nearby engineering offices, in India, or at the closest fast food joint. We should care about the workplaces of those inside and outside the church.[46]

A third problem is that work is in danger of being reduced to an hourly or yearly commodity to be supplied in a bargain between employers and workers. And thus we are in danger of commodifying the value of persons according to how well they can supply such labor.[47] In contrast to this spirit of quantification, the Holy Spirit works in and through our work. The descent of the dove at the baptism of Jesus reminds us that he is the one who has authority to assess the value of work, since the Spirit clearly gives such authority. Not only does Jesus teach with authority (Mark 1:22, 27) and forgive sins with authority (Mark 2:10), but he also has the kind of authority that only a Roman centurion can understand (Luke 7:7–10). Yet this authoritative teacher and preacher was "moved with pity" for a man with leprosy (Mark 1:41). It is this Spirit-given care for others that we will need. With the help of the descending dove, we are to see our co-workers—especially those not yet on the path of discipleship—with new eyes of compassion through the power of the Spirit. We are to treat all those we meet as whole persons, bodies, souls, and spirits. Our care and compassion should extend to suffering workers nearby or far from us. It is not enough to fight for better wages or benefits for them; we must learn to promote cultures of care and compassion in workplaces.

46. See Bakke, *Joy at Work*, 167–75.

47. Arendt, *Human Condition*, 137–38.

A fourth problem is that we have lost the sense that work is a sacrament signifying the active presence of God in the thick of daily life. Work loses its sense of purpose, and we wonder why we work—apart from earning money to buy the stuff we want. Yet, as Wendell Berry says, "If we think of ourselves as living souls, immortal creatures, living in the midst of a Creation that is mostly mysterious, and if we see that everything we make or do cannot help but have an everlasting significance for ourselves, for others, and for the world, then we see why some religious teachers have understood work as a form of prayer."[48] A central element of prayer is attentive listening, and it is here that we discover the importance of hearing the divine voice as a source for the work of discipleship, with discipleship defining the Christian's work in the world. Central to the first and last Sundays after the Epiphany is the voice of the Father claiming the Son, and announcing his pleasure in this child. Yet we disciples must also listen for the voice of God in the middle of the story, for it helps to reveal the purposes of work and the ways in which that work participates in divine glory. It is not just a matter of obtaining some mystical sense of enchantment, but it is about listening for the proper divine words to frame our daily activities of work, right in the midst of that work, so that we not only have a sense of direction but also so that we have a sense of God's pleasure in our work. Hearing the voice of God is not a means to escape the world, but it is precisely a way to find direction more deeply within it, by listening for God's voice right in the middle of the messy, here-and-now, nitty-gritty, daily grind. If Christ is the fullness of God in time, then we should be able to hear the divine voice right in the middle of our workday.

A lovely example of this kind of workaday divine speech in the Sundays after Epiphany comes when the disciples are out fishing, making their living. After a night of catching nothing, Jesus tells Peter to head out for the deep water and lower the nets. To his credit, Peter does listen and act on Jesus' words, albeit grudgingly, with an "if you say so" (Luke 5:5). Once the disciples do act on the divine voice, they are overwhelmed with a bulging catch that begins to break their nets and sink their boats. Peter falls down in the sinking boat at Jesus' knees and says "Go away from me, Lord, for I am a sinful man" (Luke 5:8)! At that moment, Peter realizes that God the Creator—the divine voice—is in the boat with him. Yet, Jesus says to Peter, "Do not be afraid; from now on you will be catching people" (Luke 5:10). And it is at this point in Luke's gospel that the

48. Berry, "Christianity and the Survival of Creation," 110–11.

disciples leave everything and follow Jesus, so it is at this point that they have received their calling, right in the midst of their daily work world, in the language of their daily work world, of fishing. They obtain their sense of purpose by hearing from the Son. Likewise, we must hear the divine voice in the midst of our work, whether it is calling us to leave it behind or to keep at it (or sometimes both). Jesus tells Peter not to be afraid, and we might also be called to face our fears of the deep waters in our own work. Whether one stays at one's job or leaves it all behind, one has to wonder what it means to fish for people, to be a disciple who seeks to invite others onto the path of discipleship. Certainly part of it can be to help one's co-workers not be afraid. But toward what end are we working? What are we trying to accomplish in our work? Our work is to participate in the fullness of God's Kingdom and to help bring others into it. We are to catch people in the nets of God's grace.

But a final problem with work is that most workplaces lack grace and exist more in the flat world than in the fullness of God. They are a part of a system that operates by its own profit-driven rules and makes little space for those who would structure their workplaces to look more like God's Kingdom. Instead, workplaces have sped up on a global basis. With the increased use of fast-paced information technology comes more intense pressure to produce results quickly, to outsource work processes, and to foster mobility whenever it is profitable to do so. By contrast, we can understand the revelation of God's glory in Jesus to be a slow process unfolding in the Galilee region. Although the fullness of the Father's glory shone out from the person of Jesus, he revealed it only bit-by-bit. He seems to be in no hurry to rush into his work. In Matthew, he takes his time teaching his followers a new law of love in the Sermon on the Mount. In Mark, after healing the leper, he told the man not to tell anyone (Mark 1:44). At Cana, he resisted his mother's invitation to do something about the shortage of wine, saying "My time has not yet come" (John 2:4). Instead of quickly revealing the glory of the Father, Jesus slowly does so across this season. After seeing the full glory of God revealed at his baptism, we see small bursts of divine activity that stretch out until the Transfiguration, at which point, God's full glory shines through again—but only for a moment and only to a select few disciples. This suggests that we must learn to see the divine glory in the midst of work; we cannot expect every day to be like that day in the Jordan or that day on the mountain. We must find God's glory right in the middle of the slowness of our ordinary times of work. The Orthodox theologian Father

Alexander Schmemann touches on such ordinary work in a dense yet brilliant passage about time and mission:

> We Christians have too often forgotten that God has redeemed the world. For centuries we have preached to the hurrying people: your daily rush has no meaning, yet accept it—and you will be rewarded in *another* world by an eternal rest. But God revealed and offers us eternal Life and not eternal rest. And God revealed this eternal Life in the midst of time—and of its *rush*—as its secret meaning and goal. And thus he made time, and our work in it, into the *sacrament of the world to come*, the liturgy of fulfillment and ascension. It is when we have reached the very end of the world's self-sufficiency that it *begins* again for us as the material of the sacrament that we are to fulfill in Christ.[49]

Schmemann is arguing, I think, that our participation in Christ transforms how we live in time by connecting us to the eternal Life of Christ, right in the thick of time—the Life that redeems time and the world. Already now, as we participate in that Life in our worship, we participate in "the liturgy of fulfillment and ascension." When eternity steps down into time, when the dove descends on the man, when Jesus tells us to fish for people, when the voice calls out, "This is my Son," both on the riverbank and the mountaintop, we become part of a drama that we must "fulfill in Christ." His work of service, of proclamation, and of invitation has become our work. We, like Jesus after Epiphany, are somewhere between our baptism and our ascension. We are on the road toward loving God and our neighbors, after receiving the grace of baptism and before we experience the grace of God's voice again. To imagine how treading this road of love might affect our work, we might consider Dorothy Sayers' description of work motivated by love: "When a job is undertaken from necessity, or from a grim sense of disagreeable duty, the worker is self-consciously aware of the toils and pains he undergoes, and will say: 'I have made such and such sacrifices for this.' But when the job is a labor of love, the sacrifices will present themselves to the worker—strange as it may seem—in the guise of enjoyment."[50] But the question remains: how might it be possible to promote workplaces that allow the practice of such love? It is not up to individuals alone to discover this love on their own, but it is the task of Christian communities to help advance such love in

49. Schmemann, *For the Life of the World*, 65. Emphasis in original.

50. Sayers, *Mind of the Maker*, 107–8.

communities of work. Could we help others discover the possibility of work as something to love and enjoy? The Sundays after Epiphany present us with the model of a person engaged in just this kind of work.

It is precisely because the fullness of time enters into our own time that we are able to understand our own mission as the church during this season. It is not the case that we replace Christ in the work of making disciples, but it is the case that we are to do that work while participating in Christ, who continues to enter into our time in the drama of daily worship through the liturgical year. By entering into the fullness of Christ, we find that our work becomes more and not less meaningful, because we are always seeking to hear the divine voice right in the midst of our lives. We then start seeking to catch people in a labor of love. And as we do so, part of our mission of catching people will certainly entail attention to oppressive work practices and the technological domination of work environments. But unlike the workers scurrying around us, workers in the church can rest in God's fullness and slowness as they seek to reveal God's glory through their sacrificial service of witnessing to God's reign of liberation and redemption.

IMPROVISATIONAL PRACTICES FOR THE CHURCH?

All this leads to an improvisational theology of work rooted in the Sundays after Epiphany. Such a theology is not content to rail against the problems of the globalized workplace, but it seeks to help us begin to imagine constructive alternative possibilities for work. What follows are a few suggestions to illustrate how a church living out of the season after Epiphany will offer hopeful possibilities to a world where growing numbers of workers are in the situation of the young women we met in the Bahraini garment factory.

First, we learn through the season that the divine Father who approves of the Son is in control of our story. A deep assurance of divine control can help challenge the technological determinism that threatens to take over the workplace at times. If we truly live in the fullness of the Father's approval, we can restore a sense that God is in control. Sometimes during this season, the church reads the passage in the Sermon on the Mount about worry: "Therefore do not worry, saying, 'What will we eat?' or 'What will we drink?' or 'What will we wear?' For it is the Gentiles who strive for all these things; and indeed your heavenly Father knows that you need all these things. But strive first for the kingdom of God and his righteousness, and all these things will be given to you as well" (Matt 6:31–33). Our basis for not worrying here is the sufficient fullness of the provision of the Father, who feeds the birds of the air and clothes the grasses of the fields in great beauty. This seems like naïve advice to modern people, and yet it goes to the heart of seeking the Kingdom of God by trusting the Father. Schmemann may well have had such advice in mind when he wrote (as we saw earlier): "It is when we have reached the very end of the world's self-sufficiency that it *begins* again for us as the material of the sacrament that we are to fulfill in Christ."[51] We give up the notion that we control our own provision, and we learn to receive it as a gift of God, to trust God's abundance. When the community of the church sees that the human and technological management of work cannot work, since it assumes the world's self-sufficiency, it learns to trusts in the fullness of the Father. The church learns that time is not a precious commodity to be hoarded in the work process, but rather that trusting God gives us enough time to complete the work to which we are called. We learn that a more humane work environment, driven less by the assumption of scarcity, hence less by the need to maximize "throughput," and more by trust in God's plenteous provision, might actually be more productive and fulfilling in the long run.

This is something that church members can already experience when they carry out the work of worship together. This work, one hopes, is not driven by the bottom line but by communal attentiveness to the tasks at hand. The work of cleaning the church building, maintaining the landscaping, teaching Sunday School, leading the youth group, staffing the nursery, making up the bulletin, copying liturgies, rehearsing the music, and preparing the sermon is not typically outsourced. Instead, the community organizes itself to complete the tasks each week and then performs the work of worship all together. Such work might look like a "royal waste of time" and appear to be highly inefficient on a cost-benefit calculus.[52] It would be more efficient to outsource the whole business. But to those participating in the activities it might well be the fullest part of their lives. It might seem frivolous in a world of economic injustice to spend a couple of hours on a Sunday (or weeknight) preparing to give praise and glory to God, and then doing so, but it is the most important

---

51. Schmemann, *For the Life of the World*, 65. Emphasis in original.

52. Dawn, *Royal "Waste" of Time*.

work of all of the church.[53] Yet many churches, like all of us, may be tempted to worship the false gods of Productivity, Efficiency, and Success. These false gods rely on the assumption that in a self-sufficient world it is all up to us to carefully marshal scarce resources to accomplish results in the world. Yet the Sundays after the Epiphany re-enact for us the reality that, as with Jesus, our work can only proceed if we are bathed in the radiant glory of the Father and are constantly attending to the divine voice that alone can sustain our work.

A second problem with work is the problem of alienated and disempowered workers. This is not just a problem of wages and job security, although those issues are part of the deeper problem. That deeper problem is our collective failure to attend to the wholeness of work. Friedman celebrates the corporate leader in the outsourcing of accounting services, who said, "we are taking apart each task, [standardizing it,] and sending it around to whoever can do it best, and because we are doing it in a virtual environment, people need not be physically adjacent to each other, and then we are reassembling all the pieces back together at headquarters."[54] However, it seems likely that the power in this situation resides with those who are at headquarters and not the workers. It is also likely that those workers will be unable to participate in the whole of the work and will be separated from the results of their labors. Our care for the whole of work could express itself in campaigning against sweatshop labor or in campaigning to eradicate mold from an office building ventilation system. It could express itself in work at an office furniture manufacturer to reduce repetitive stress injuries from heavy computer usage. It could lead us to develop new technologies for garment production. It could help workers design their own daily work environments. Or it could start with a targeted campaign to raise workers' wages in a particular area.

Although there can be problems with such actions—especially if we take them to avoid the deeper questions about work raised here—the church could also mobilize the buying power of members to help victimized workers. As Larry Reed argues, we live in a system based on individual choices in the market, so changing those choices would shape the system.[55] If Christians sought to promote products and work practices that promote human flourishing, they could have a significant impact,

53. Wolterstorff, *Until Justice and Peace Embrace*, 146–61.

54. Friedman, *World Is Flat*, 3rd ed., 91. Brackets in original.

55. Reed, "Ten-Trillion-Dollar Stewardship," 72.

since Ron Sider estimates that Christians annually spend $10 trillion on consumption.[56] Some churches already have used their consumption power to effect change. Not long ago, the United Methodists and the Presbyterian Church (USA) stated their support for a boycott of Taco Bell—a boycott aimed at raising the wages and improving the working conditions of Mexican migrants who pick tomatoes for Taco Bell suppliers in Florida, where conditions amounted to "indentured servitude" (in Taco Bell's own words). A Taco Bell executive initially resisted meddling in "another company's [its supplier's] labor dispute," and said that the labor abuses were "heinous, but I don't think it has anything to do with us." Eventually, however, Taco Bell agreed to help improve conditions in Florida, pledging to pay one additional cent per pound, money that the growers promised to pass on to the pickers. This would "nearly double" pickers' wages at an estimated annual cost of "a few hundred thousand dollars a year—not a huge sum for a fast food company with annual sales of $9 billion worldwide."[57] Helping liberate workers who are being exploited is one part of the mission of discipleship. At the same time, however, the church must go beyond mere wage increases. It must be willing to do the harder work of helping construct alternatives for those at the bottom of the wage system. And it must not lose sight of the quality of the workplace and the primary calling to be the church, even when that looks like a waste of time. If the Sundays after Epiphany teach us anything, it is that the Holy Spirit's presence, now made manifest in the church, makes the work of compassion and participation in the fullness of God possible. With the Spirit's permission, the creative, compassionate work of the church in response to abuses of labor will continue. Already parachurch groups such as the International Justice Mission (IJM) have helped to free young girls trapped in the most egregious forms of child labor in the sex trade by working through the domestic legal systems of the countries concerned. Child labor is illegal even in countries where the practice is widespread, so IJM holds governments accountable to their own standards.[58] Such work will no doubt continue around the world, thanks to an improvising church.

56. Ibid., 67.

57. Schlosser, "Side Order of Human Rights."

58. Gary Haugen, the founder of this nongovernmental organization and ministry, explains the goals behind IJM's work in his book *Good News about Injustice.*

For those who are called to engage in public policy debates and influence government policy—and not all churches are called to this work, which at times might be a distraction from the real tasks at home—there are concrete options. The story of reactions to Myanmar's labor abuses is instructive here. Myanmar (formerly called Burma) has had a repressive military regime for many years that has forced villagers into doing construction work for no pay. In November of 2000, the International Labor Organization (ILO), the multilateral organization of over 175 member-states devoted to enforcing better labor standards, responded by calling for trade sanctions. However, no nations responded, and European and U.S. trade with Myanmar actually increased—despite knowledge of worker abuses. According to the *New York Times*, this was partly due to the fact that a trade ban on textile exports from Myanmar would violate free-trade rules of the World Trade Organization (WTO), of which Myanmar is a member.[59] So will efforts to enforce labor standards be undercut by the rules of the WTO? A recent book published by the pro-globalization Institute for International Economics in Washington DC argues that the WTO could and should allow countries to ban imports of products produced in violation of the ILO's labor practice standards. If the WTO allowed countries to penalize goods produced by abusive countries, and to support goods promoted by non-abusive countries, that might prevent another Myanmar story. International economists are often skeptical of governmental "meddling" with "market forces," but this study by leading economists makes the case that better labor practices contribute to sustainable economic success.[60] A basic regulatory framework of international labor standards is already in place, but enforcement will help provide incentives for governments to foster better work practices that will make for more productive workers. Workers paid a just wage will be happier workers. But this is hard to see without the Spirit's presence to help one trust the Father's care and provision.

The presence of the Spirit also helps to counter the reduction of work and workers to a mere commodity to be bought and sold—a third problem in the current globalized workplace. Here I want to point to two Christian corporate leaders who felt the nudge of the Spirit enough to challenge this trend in their workplaces and promote alternative practices of work. One example comes from Christian businessman Dennis

59. Olson, "Myanmar Tests Resolve."

60. Elliott and Freeman, *Can Labor Standards Improve Under Globalization?* Also see Barry and Reddy, *International Trade and Labor Standards*.

Bakke, who tried to instill a corporate ethos at the AES energy company that made work fun, seeking to empower workers at all levels in the company.[61] Although the effort floundered when Bakke was forced to leave the company in 2002, for a time it seems that it was possible to counter the spirit of treating workers as disposable expenses on the corporate balance sheet. Instead, Bakke sought to break down barriers between labor and management by empowering worker teams to make important decisions across all areas of the company. He was committed to reversing this part of the Industrial Revolution, even to the point where most workers were brought on as salaried members of the company rather than hourly workers, allowing "everyone in the plant to be trusted as a business person."[62] He expands on this idea by saying that "the key to a great workplace is the freedom to make important decisions and take responsibility for their results. Other elements of the work environment contribute to the joy of work, but none . . . compares with being treated as an important and trusted decision-maker."[63] Bakke tells the story of visiting one plant and hearing about one older maintenance technician who had passed up a lucrative severance package when AES bought his plant, thereby choosing to stay even though it was financially less lucrative. When Bakke visited on the night of the company Christmas party, he found that this senior worker, who normally worked days, was working in the plant. When Bakke met him that night, the worker said, "After 40 years, I finally feel like I have responsibility and control over my work, including responsibility for contractors. Under the old system, I was never given the opportunity."[64] Another worker in a cleanup team said that he found that "I am free to learn new things and make decisions. I'm not a cog in the wheel. I'm not just a worker. I love my colleagues, supervisors, the values, and the entire approach to work."[65] Bakke claims that he could "think of no instance at AES when taking the steps needed to create a fun workplace had a long-term negative effect on the economics of the

61. Bakke, *Joy at Work*.

62. Ibid., 172–73. To illustrate empowerment, he quotes a story from the *Wall Street Journal* about maintenance technicians managing a $33 million plant investment fund (231–32).

63. Ibid., 196.

64. Ibid., 230.

65. Ibid., 234.

company."[66] Christians committed to recovering the Holy Spirit in work ought to promote such empowering opportunities.

Similarly, Max DePree led the office furniture maker Herman Miller as CEO, and during his tenure he also sought to put into practice a philosophy of "touch," which entailed greater care and attention to making workplaces more humane and which he has outlined in his books.[67] As DePree noted, those who defined the standards of "effectiveness and productivity" usually did so from the manager's viewpoint rather than considering the front-line worker's experiences.[68] By contrast, viewing work with a sense of touch is part of a holistic and integrative understanding of work.[69] Attention to the larger social and physical context of work means that DePree regularly criticizes a narrow focus on financial measures only in understanding work. The key, in DePree's view, is to view workers as persons, and not as quantities to be manipulated for the bottom line. "In addition to all of the ratios and goals and parameters and bottom lines," says DePree, "it is fundamental that leaders endorse a concept of persons. This begins with an understanding of the diversity of people's gifts and talents and skills."[70] DePree points out that "a short-term look at the financial status of a corporation or a dependence on immediate financial results will lead to a partial and perhaps twisted view of the whole picture. A crucial element may be missing. We may not be running the entire race."[71] DePree has another view of the corporate race that sounds a tinge heretical in American business: "Profit, the hoped-for result . . . is normal and essential. Those results, however, are only a way to measure our resourcefulness at a point in time, mile markers on a long road. Why we get those results is more important."[72] He says, "profit gives us the chance to make a difference in the world, but profit is never more than a by-product."[73] And here is the most heretical-sounding aphorism

66. Ibid., 174.

67. DePree, *Leadership Jazz*, 3. DePree *Leadership Is an Art*, 76. For further analysis see Waalkes, "Money or Business?"

68. DePree, *Leadership Is an Art*, 27–28.

69. Ibid., 34. Also 76, 113–14.

70. Ibid., 7. Also see DePree, *Leadership Jazz*, 89.

71. Ibid., 130–31.

72. Ibid., 2.

73. DePree, *Leadership Jazz*, 191, also 137. See also DePree *Leadership Is an Art*, 47, 63, 83, 99–100, and 129–32.

in DePree's arsenal: "Being faithful is more important than being successful. If we are successful in the world's eyes but unfaithful in terms of what we believe, then we fail"[74]—a statement at least vaguely reminiscent of seeking Christ's Kingdom first and finding material sufficiency added to it. Another heretical tenet of DePree's leadership was his promotion of employee stock ownership plans and a willingness to abide by a policy of limiting his annual cash compensation to no more than twenty times the average pay of a factory worker.[75] By contrast, the average chief executive in the United States made *270 times* what the average full-time worker made in 2007.[76] DePree argued that workers were co-owners and partners in the collective work of the company. As DePree puts it, "There is a certain morality in connecting shared accountability as employees with shared ownership. This lends a rightness and a permanence to the relationship of each of us to our work and to each other."[77] Hence he argues for the priority of long-term, high-quality covenantal relationships over short-term contractual relationships as the heart of his business.[78] Although neither Dennis Bakke nor Max DePree was perfect or perfectly successful, both give us a glimpse of the direction that Christians nurtured in the church have already taken to champion good work that treats co-workers gracefully as whole persons.

A fourth problem with work is the loss of a sacramental understanding of work and the loss of the divine voice in the midst of work. This is perhaps the deepest and most difficult problem in which to imagine the church improvising constructive responses. How might we imagine ways of promoting work as a form of prayer and attention to God's voice? A friend who is a nurse shared one small but significant practice. When she started working part-time at a Catholic hospital operated by the Sisters of Charity, she and all other new employees had their hands anointed with holy oil—even the maintenance staff. In a small but tangible way, each worker was reminded that they were called to serve in a ministry of

74. DePree, *Leadership Is an Art*, 61.

75. DePree, *Leadership Jazz*, 131. Cynics attentive to current practice will wonder about stock options beyond cash compensation, a loophole for executive pay. However, this practice only became widespread in the 1990s, after DePree's tenure.

76. Sahadi, "CEO Pay." When including part-time workers, it rises to 364 times.

77. DePree, *Leadership Is an Art*, 85.

78. Ibid., 25, 32–33, 50–53.

healing. One hopes that more workplaces could express their mission in such significant gestures that reframe work.

At a minimum, it is impossible to promote work as sacramental activity in participation with Creation if one never takes breaks. A constant, uninterrupted stream of work—24 hours a day, 7 days a week, 365 days a year—is a picture of the very flatness that God's fullness interrupts. And here is where the practice of Sabbath-keeping is a reminder of how God's fullness invades and affirms human life in order to liberate humans from work alone.[79] Whereas the Exodus account of the Ten Commandments explains the Sabbath as the day that God rested from Creation, the account in Deuteronomy—often read during Epiphany—explains it as a day to remember when we were slaves in Egypt and God brought us out of slavery, a reminder of liberation (Deut 5:15).[80] Just as the Israelites recalled their liberation on the seventh day, we are to recall our salvation and the baptism that signifies our dying to sin and rising with Christ in our "eighth day" observance of a Sabbath festival that also liberates us from work for a day. As someone who grew up in a strict Sabbath-keeping form of Dutch Calvinism, I recall the days in which we rested from all public activity on Sundays, and I learned to relish those breaks from work. Thus I still rue the day when restaurant chains, malls, and big-box retail stores started opening on Sundays. That is why I find the actions of the fast-food restaurant chain Chick-fil-A so interesting. Unlike every other fast-food franchise, this privately held, family owned company requires that all its stores close on Sundays. Such a move is not enough on its own to counter the erosion of work as a sacramental activity, but it helps stem the tide of the 24/7/365 culture of work that has emerged in the last few decades in North America. With the eclipse of so-called Blue Laws that required businesses to close on Sundays, it is much harder for any retail business to risk the loss of sales and profits by closing one day a week. And yet such a move opens up space for all employees to rest. The founder of the company, Truett Cathy, connects the Sunday-closing policy to Chick-fil-A's corporate mission: "To glorify God by being a faithful steward to all that is entrusted to us [and] to have a positive influence on all who come

---

79. On this theme, see Pieper, *In Tune With the World*, 18–19, 26–28, 38–40, 82–83. Also see Pieper, *Leisure, The Basis of Culture*, 53–54. Thanks for turning me to Pieper go to Bill Cavanaugh and participants in the Calvin College Seminar in Christian Scholarship, "Liturgy and Politics: Is the Church a *Polis*?" July 2006.

80. Bass, *Receiving the Day*, 48.

in contact with Chick-fil-A."[81] Should the company ever go public on the stock exchange, it is hard to imagine such a corporate mission lasting very long. But surely the Christian church ought to be nurturing those who would lead businesses in similar directions, resisting the flattening pressures of the public corporations, and championing those who stand against the busy rat race of the 7-days-a-week flat world.

The larger question, however, is whether it will be possible to nurture practices of work that allow workers to find the calling of God and participate in work as a sacrament in the midst of their concrete activity. Surely this is where the church can continue to challenge its members to listen for the voice of God within their daily activities, to challenge them to find whether their work (paraphrasing Dorothy Day) is on the way to heaven or hell. Dennis Bakke argues that churches should commission members to carry out their vocations in their workplaces. While church employees or missionaries face scrutiny and accountability, few pastors ever visit people in their workplaces. And yet people spend forty hours or more at their work and only a couple of hours at most in the church building.[82] The point is to help church members discern God's voice right in the midst of their daily work environments. If they cannot hear God's voice calling them to do the work they do, perhaps they need to leave that work. Churches will need to support those who challenge the system and get fired for it.[83]

Finally, then, how might the church improvise practices that respond to the speeding up and splitting into pieces of work across the world? How might our resting in the fullness of divine glory help us rest in God's sufficiency, over against the faster pace of the flattening world? The German philosopher Josef Pieper suggests that Christian worship offers the world a hopeful contrast. "In the very midstream of worship and only from there," he writes, "comes a supply that cannot be consumed by the world of work, a space of unaccountable giving, untouched by the ever-turning wheel of buying and selling, an overflow released from all purpose, and an authentic wealth: it is festival-time."[84] As a people who

81. Cathy, "Chick-fil-A's Closed-on-Sunday Policy."

82. Bakke, *Joy at Work*, 267–75.

83. Claiborne and Haw, *Jesus for President*, 242, quote Brian Walsh: "A Christian can hold any job. But if they act as Christians, they will simply need to be ready to fired within a few weeks."

84. Pieper, *Leisure*, 53–54.

live out of that "space of unaccountable giving" in the "festival-time" of worship we have the opportunity to help the world rediscover the meaning of work—even in conditions of greater globalization. It is precisely because we find the fullness of God at the center of time in worship that we are able even to imagine constructive alternatives to globalized work. As we saw above, this fullness of God is not imposed through Christ in a hurry; it is a slow process by which the glory of God is revealed through the Son in the Spirit over time. As Sam Wells says, "God gives his people everything they need to worship him, to be his friends, and to eat with him." [85] That is, God has given us an abundance of what we need to live in this world, even if it is not always immediately apparent. This suggests that the most important contribution we can make is not to panic about globalization's impact on work and workers, but to live deliberately in loving service, to live out the abundant time and abundant life we receive as gifts in worship. The fullness of the divine glory is behind all the stories after Epiphany. As with Jesus, that glory is the source of whatever power we might have as a church of disciples. And the presence of that glory in the church should also free us to act in faith, to love our neighbors.

As Wells points out, Christians can rest in the knowledge that it is not up to them to make the world turn out a certain way.[86] Since we already know that the church is literally on the road to glory in its mission of love, the only question is then how we are to act in this drama. How are we to bear witness to the glory of God now in such a way that the busy globalized workplace might know the sufficiency of God? One direction might be to help build communities that craft workplaces into environments where work would become more of a labor of love that would breed enjoyment (something Dorothy Sayers mentioned above). Instead of treating work as a hoop to get through or a means to make money, work would be oriented toward sacrificial service to others, giving glory to God for any successes. This would mean helping guide members of the church into such work and discouraging work that could not be a labor of love. It would also mean sustaining communities where such work could be found, where attention to the whole process of work from start to finish could be sustained, where excellent craftsmanship would be prized, where communities of workers attending to common ends would

---

85. Wells, *God's Companions*, 1.

86. Wells, *Transforming Fate*, 177–79.

be forged, where the glory of God would be revealed from beginning to end in common work.

I think we get a glimpse of what this might look like from time to time when we slow down enough to make time for conversations with our co-workers about our work in the midst of the workday, when we carry out even the smallest details of our work to the glory of God, when we grow our own food and harvest it, when we raise children from conception to their adulthood, when we create a piece of art, or when we volunteer at church—to mention only a few activities. We learn to get in on the beginnings of a slow work and we see it through toward its end. Precisely because we get to see the wholeness and slowness of a process, we learn to give glory to God. Instead of chopping up work into smaller pieces and shipping it around the world, we are present through the whole business and we share the ups and downs of the work. This is the joy of Creation.

One day we are fishing and we are overwhelmed by the power and glory of the Father, and we fall to our knees. For weeks or months or years we work through the daily grind, occasionally glimpsing why we do what we do. Later we are on a mountaintop seeing God's glory shining out. And the next day we are journeying toward Jerusalem and the suffering that awaits us.

CHAPTER 6

Lent and Global Consumption: Re-Directing Sacramentality

Jesus, full of the Holy Spirit, returned from the Jordan and was led by the Spirit in the wilderness, where for forty days he was tempted by the devil.

Luke 4:1–2a

An old *New Yorker* magazine cartoon shows two anti-globalization activists passing out leaflets to passers-by on the sidewalk of what looks like Michigan Avenue in Chicago. One young man—sporting a ponytail, baseball cap, stylish sandals, baggy shorts, t-shirt, and backpack—has stopped to read their leaflet. "I totally agree with you about capitalism, neo-colonialism, and globalization," he says to one of the activists, "but I think you come down too hard on shopping." After all, the stylish young man likes shopping: his cap, sandals, shorts, t-shirt, and backpack were all likely assembled overseas, probably by garment workers in "controlled environments." And it's a real downer to have to change your own comfortable habits.

Like many commentators, then, the cartoonist has seen through the hypocrisy of anti-globalization protesters wearing the latest and hippest global fashions. Yet like both the young man in the cartoon and young women at the sewing machines overseas, we North American shoppers are also unable to escape the contradictions of globalization. We may have concerns about globalization, but we enjoy shopping for global

147

products. We cannot easily imagine a world without these products. We cannot easily imagine a world without shopping and we cannot easily imagine ourselves as anything other than global "consumers." Yet this chapter argues that we can re-imagine global consumerism and our part in it by journeying through the re-enacted gospel of the Lenten season. By entering into these forty days of fasting and prayer, we can improvise alternative practices that can help free us from our bondage to the current system of global consumption.

As the last chapter showed, the globalization of consumption is the other side of the globalization of production: outsourcing the production of goods to the places with the cheapest labor makes it possible for us to enjoy an abundance of cheap consumer goods—whether clothing, washing machines, toys, tools, or anything else that can be bought at Wal-Mart, Target, Kmart, Costco, or Sears. Just by shopping at such retail chains, we are going global, because in many cases workers in China produce the goods sold there, instead of workers closer to home; in fact, an estimated 80 percent of the factories that supply Wal-Mart are in China.[1] Although imports from China account for around 7.5 percent of U.S. consumer spending or 15 percent of total imports, they amount to approximately "80 percent of toys, 85 percent of footwear, and 40 percent of clothing."[2] So a trip to the store to buy these items is really often a trip to China. And while the last chapter studied how globalization affects work, in this chapter we focus on the consequences of our participation in the global system of "flexible accumulation" as consumers.[3]

When we buy cheap Chinese-made shoes, we participate in global consumption, which connects our ability to consume ever-cheaper stuff to the outsourcing of production to lower-wage locations. The low wages for workers equal low prices for us and high profits for the retailers. Thus, as consumers, we benefit from the system, as do retailers. But as workers we and our neighbors suffer. We like the fact that we can buy lots of stuff, yet we worry about job security. We feel divided. Even Thomas Friedman recognizes that Wal-Mart, functioning here as a symbol for any globalized American retail chain, divides the human person into different sides:

1. Fishman, *China, Inc.*, 154, citing Goodman and Pan, "Chinese Workers."
2. Barboza, "China Inflation," A–1; Naroff, "Foreword," x.
3. Harvey, *Condition of Postmodernity*, 141–97; Budde, *(Magic) Kingdom of God*, 18–27.

> The Wal-Mart shopper in all of us wants the lowest price possible, with all the middlemen, fat, and friction removed. And the Wal-Mart shareholder in us wants Wal-Mart to be relentless about removing the fat and friction in its supply chain and in its employee benefits packages, in order to fatten the company's profits. But the Wal-Mart worker in us hates the benefits and pay packages that Wal-Mart offers its starting employees.[4]

However, Friedman fails to mention the workers at the Chinese or other companies that supply Wal-Mart—companies that might not even offer benefits or even have "pay packages." He admits that these workers' low wages help bring us cheaper stuff, yet cheaper stuff also creates a contradiction for families with tight budgets. On the one hand, these families can afford to purchase more stuff with less money. On the other hand, Wal-Mart drives the cycle of cutting "labor costs" for workers, creating insecurity for families who depend on work in the retail or service sector, where pay is low. They are therefore split between their shopper and worker selves, between their consumer and producer sides. In other words, we all benefit from this system as shoppers but loathe it as workers. We enjoy global consumerism but we detest outsourcing. So how can we restore wholeness to our lives in relation to globalization? How can we (to take up Friedman's question) "sort out and weigh [our] multiple identities— consumer, employee, citizen, taxpayer, shareholder . . . ?"[5] How can we overcome the disease of "affluenza" that brings both material abundance and spiritual impoverishment, both comfort and a restless pace of life?[6] How can we avoid the danger of being reduced to global consumers?

Liturgical rhythms are implicated here when we realize that the rhythms of consumption have displaced the liturgical rhythms of the Christian year, most notably at Christmas and Easter. As Leigh Eric Schmidt puts it, "The marketplace serves . . . as an obvious arena of holiday preparation, observance, and enthrallment—a central location for the commemoration of Christianity's most important holy days as well as

---

4. Friedman, *World Is Flat*, 215. Interestingly, in the later edition, this quote was altered to tone down the language about shareholders. The relevant passage reads: "So the Wal-Mart shareholder and shopper in us wants Wal-Mart to be relentless about removing the fat and friction in its supply chain and in its employee benefits packages in order to fatten the company's profits—and keep its prices low." Instead of singling out shareholders, he lumps them in with consumers. *World Is Flat*, 3rd ed., 251.

5. Friedman, *World Is Flat*, 3rd ed., 252.

6. De Graaf et al., *Affluenza*.

for the enactment of America's most prominent civic holidays."[7] And all are commemorated through shopping. North American Christians even live by a different liturgical calendar that has mimicked and displaced the authentic one by subtly turning their Christian festivities into buying seasons fitting in the rhythms of American retailers: Halloween is the retail Advent, a season of transition that prepares us for Thanksgiving and Christmas, the center of the retail year. Valentine's Day is retail Epiphany, a brief burst of activity before the retail Easter, which is less important than retail Christmas. Mother's Day and Memorial Day form a retail Ascension, feasting before the retail Pentecost called the Fourth of July, which promotes a small burst of spending spirit. We then enter an ordinary time of summer relaxation, back to school shopping, Labor Day, and the transition into the fall, looking toward Halloween. The Puritans helped clear the way for this calendar of capitalism by cutting down on the old Catholic fasts and feasts and promoting a flatter sense of time: "The sooner such festivals and holy days were brought under control and reduced in number, the better for commerce, civic prosperity, and genuine piety."[8] Yet we ended up with a cycle of seasons after all, one that promoted steadier consumption than seasons of fits and starts, highs and lows, fasts and feasts—and one that is speeding up and pushing Christmas ever earlier.[9] But how might we learn to live differently and slow down?

Lent gives us the space to begin finding and living out answers to this question so that we can enter the fullness of God in time. By fasting from the temptations of the world for a season we develop the disciplines to live with openness and receptivity toward grace. By journeying through Lent in the practices of resting, prayer, fasting, and confession, it is possible to discover true repentance, a real turn-around of thoughts and actions through habits of decreased consumption and greater reflection. Entering into the story of Lent each year can even help the church improvise constructive ethical responses to problems inherent in global consumption.

7. Schmidt, *Consumer Rites*, 3.

8. Ibid., 23; also see Robinson, *Work, Leisure, and the Environment*, 109.

9. Thanks to Amy Milnes for this last point.

CONNECTING THE DOTS AND SLOWING DOWN

Chief among the problems of global consumerism is how it embodies fragmentation, disconnection, and a lack of wholeness for those of us who are serious shoppers. We shoppers rarely connect the dots between our own habits, global economic practices, and the rest of Creation. We are like that modern person who, in G. K. Chesterton's words, says that she likes "milk out of a clean shop and not a dirty cow."[10] Thus, as Chesterton lamented, "It is nobody's business to note the whole of a process, to see where things come from and where they go."[11] His contemporary, Eric Gill, wrote that "the fundamental trouble with industrialism is that it provides unlimited goods for consumption but provides, of its own nature, no education for consumers."[12] This trouble is even greater in consumption that has gone global. We do not see the total process by which consumer goods come to us from people around the world. Yet living through Lent could help us see things whole and see how our own desires (to consume stuff at ever-cheaper prices) contribute to insecure workplaces and an insecure world. A season of fasting from consumption helps us break this cycle and reconnect to the wholeness of life. We find the space to think about where things come from and where they go.

But this will be difficult, as several writers remind us, because the system of consumerism has shaped the very way we live our daily lives.[13] Wendell Berry, for example, has written about how the global industrial economy inculcates the habit of not connecting the dots. As he put it, "The industrial economy requires the extreme specialization of work, the separation of work from its results, because it subsists upon divisions of interest and must deny the fundamental kinships of producer and consumer, seller and buyer, owner and worker, and work and product, parent material and product, nature and artifice, thoughts and words and deeds."[14] The Lenten season can help us to see these "fundamental kinships" again, by helping us to see how we have contributed to these divisions by our own participation in the system of global consumption.

10. Chesterton, "Outline of Sanity," 137.

11. Ibid., 140.

12. Gill, *Holy Tradition of Working*, 117.

13. For a history of twentieth-century commentary on consumerism, see Cross, *Time and Money*.

14. Berry, "Two Economies," 836.

Connecting the dots is something that I have slowly learned. Having lived and worked in Northeast Ohio for most of the last decade, I have seen the connections between our appetite for cheap stuff and job losses at home. In our area, a number of corporations made the decision to outsource, thereby forcing dislocation on our communities. Yet we benefited as shoppers. In 1998, the Huffy Corporation decided to shut its production plant in Celina, Ohio. Six hundred and fifty workers lost their jobs, and soon the county in which Celina was located had the highest unemployment rate in the state of Ohio. Huffy soon decided to shift all of its remaining production to Asia where labor costs were lower. However, bicycles remained inexpensive. Ohio Art, the maker of the famous red Etch-a-Sketch toys, decided to stop producing the toys at their plant in Bryan, Ohio. Instead, they shifted their production to China. One hundred workers lost their jobs. But toy prices remained low. In launching a new model of vacuum cleaner in the mid-1990s, the Hoover Company, headquartered in Ohio, asked its labor union to accept concessions that would require new workers hired on the new model lines to start out at lower wages. When the union rejected the deal, Hoover built plants in Mexico and Texas to produce the new vacuums. By 2008, the Hoover Company had ceased operations in our area, laying off over 1,000 local workers. But vacuum cleaners were cheaper than ever. GE Capital, a credit-card division of General Electric, runs a customer service phone bank center near my house and office. Yet one student who worked there told me that managers were gradually cutting back in her area as more work was being outsourced to India. The chairman of India's National Association of Software and Services Companies says that as many as 400 out of the Fortune 500 companies now have operations in India.[15] Wages are said to be one-tenth the level in America, and companies are eager to save money on labor-intensive phone banks, customer service desks, and "back office" services. Workers in my area lost jobs, but the cost of services was cheaper than ever.

Although imports accounted for just over twenty percent of the total share of manufactured goods sold in the United States in 2006, the stories from my local area help us see the economic link between our desire to consume ever-cheaper goods and services and our sadness at disappearing jobs in many communities.[16] And this leaves the question

15. Bray, "New Faces of Outsourcing."
16. Uchitelle, "Goodbye, Production."

of the quality of products entirely aside.[17] Our desire to get the best prices in our national binge of consumption helps to create the "global supply chains" catering to our appetites. Lower wages, lower prices, and new jobs in places such as Mexico, China, or India are all connected. But we fail to see this, because our consumption is detached from production. So we must recognize that we are facing down powerful practices that already cut us off from how commodities—items without connections—come to us. Theologian Vincent Miller illustrates the power of our system of commodification in an eloquent passage in his book *Consuming Religion*:

> A trip to the supermarket trains us in the mental habits of commodification. We choose our food from a vast array of items that compete with each other for our attention. They call us with their appearance and packaging. Glistening meats and colorful produce are arrayed in a spectacle of plenty. Deeper into the store, manufactured items call out from the shelves with their carefully designed packaging. No salesperson explains their quality and origins; they speak for themselves. There is a profound rhetoric of things here. The commodities offer themselves up to our credulous gaze. But like all seductions, they veil as much as they reveal. The meat in the counter, a paradigm of reduction to passive objectivity, refuses to tell of its origins. Glistening, boneless, skinless chicken breasts say nothing of the dangerous production lines on which they are processed. Gleaming filet mignons say nothing of the cow whose loins they were, of the slaughter that was necessary to remove them or the food and space it took to raise the cow. Was it a high-plains feedlot or a field recently slashed and burned from the rainforest in the Amazon basin? Simply gazing at the meat counter trains us in abstraction, in valuing things without asking such questions. How many times do we repeat this practice during our shopping trip? Fifty, a hundred, a thousand times?[18]

We shoppers need to move from consuming commodities toward a sacramental appreciation of material things that connect us to the Creator. But that will require that we seek to know from whence things come.

Instead, the modern desire to be liberated from the facts of production has led to the phenomenon of "paradigmatic consumption" described by philosopher Albert Borgmann. As Borgmann argues, thanks

---

17. Thanks to Becky Albertson for raising this question.
18. Miller, *Consuming Religion*, 38.

to technology, consumption has become "unencumbered enjoyment." He argues that we have become used to obtaining maximal pleasures with minimal work. We thus get in the habit of enjoying things without having to work for them. "Thus, we demand lean and healthy bodies without the pain of running, gourmet meals without the bother of cooking, entertainment without the labor of staging and deciphering it."[19] We enjoy consuming without all the burdens of producing. By contrast, observing a Lenten fast may help us re-imagine ourselves as members of the people of God on the way toward Jerusalem. Lent can help us reconnect to the struggle that accompanies any journey; it can remind us of the need to suffer through any good work.

We must recognize here that consumerism forms an alternative spiritual, liturgical, and economic system that subtly distorts healthy impulses toward the consumption of material things by promising us less work. After all, "There is no question about whether or not to be a consumer. Everyone must consume to live."[20] It is normal to consume material goods, and all of us do so. We all need food, clothing, shelter, and water. We are embodied creatures, and there is nothing wrong with matter, which is God's Creation. The problem is "not an inordinate attachment to material things, but an irony and detachment from all things."[21] As a result of our detachment from production, we fall prey to the attractions of "unencumbered enjoyment," in which we don't have to work as hard to get the things we need in daily life. This suggests that the problem is partly in us, the people in the pews, who enjoy the ease of consumption. Churches bear some responsibility as communities of faith who are called to cling to the true sacrament of communion rather than the false communion that occurs with consumerism. If church members are caught up in consumerism, it suggests that the church is failing to nourish them in their desire for identity and material satisfaction. The church that promises the bread of life seems to be allowing its members to sate their hunger elsewhere.

Consumerism, after all, turns us into spiritual shoppers: "it is not simply *buying* but *shopping* that is at the heart of consumerism," writes Bill Cavanaugh, because shopping breeds a "restlessness" that is all about

---

19. Borgmann, "Consumption," 420.

20. Cavanaugh, *Being Consumed*, 53.

21. Ibid., 91.

"the pleasure of stoking desire itself. . . ."[22] It is all about the thrill of the hunt for bargains or that just-right article of clothing, which becomes a substitute for a genuine quest for God, the source and end point of our affections (as Jonathan Edwards might put it). Consumerism thus becomes a substitute path to the fulfillment of what are really deep spiritual longings. Father John Kavanaugh, SJ, describes the path this way: "Friendship, intimacy, love, pride, happiness, and joy are actually the *objects* we buy and consume, much more so than the tubes, liquor bottles, Cadillacs, and Buicks that promise them and bear their names. And since none of these deepest human hopes can be fulfilled in any product, the mere consumption of them is never enough."[23] We are *global* consumers, accustomed to choosing from many brands that promise us good news. We can buy imports from all over the world. Besides Cadillacs and Buicks, we can satisfy our longings by buying Audis, BMWs, Fiats, Hondas, Hyundais, Kias, Mazdas, Mercedes, Nissans, Renaults, Toyotas, Volkswagens, or Volvos. Each type of car promises us good news and great joy. But we are actually chasing abstractions such as "*number, status, coolness, youth, beauty, fashion growth.* The things themselves—cars, cosmetics, companies, songs—are just means to the end, which is an abstraction that is by nature unattainable."[24] Our longings are actually for something deeper.

Our consumption becomes a form of misdirected sacramental activity, a substitute for fulfilling participation in the church. In a little book published in 2003, Tom Beaudoin argues that global branding mimics a kind of spiritual discipline. It works through the "schooling of imagination." "It works in part," he writes "because of its unique dynamic: branding offers a consistent, coherent identity, in which you are told about your true self; it offers membership in a community; it issues an invitation to unconditional trust; it offers the promise of conversion and new life. Thus, there is a way of life, an identity, that can be had by participating in the logo-centric economy. These are, after all, worthwhile ends and even deep human needs."[25] The problem is that our own human desires are implicated here. We search for identity and find it, at least temporarily, in our consumption. Vincent Miller suggests that this may be because consumerism is a "misdirected form of sacramentality"

---

22. Ibid., 35, 91.

23. Kavanaugh, *Following Christ in a Consumer Society*, 34. Emphasis in original.

24. McLaren, *Everything Must Change*, 212. Emphasis in original.

25. Beaudoin, *Consuming Faith*, 44–45.

that detaches material things from God.[26] While it is healthy to seek God and our identity in the material stuff of everyday life, in bread and wine and water and clothes, that stuff ought to be mediating the divine and pointing as a sign back to the signifier, the Creator. But the pernicious aspect of global consumerism is that it promises much, demands little, and delivers even less. We are offered a glimpse of communion with something deeper, but that something deeper never quite comes along in the cars, electronic gadgets, or food that we buy, all of which typically fail to connect us more deeply to our Creator, because we cannot see how they emerge from Creation. Yet the purchase of such stuff may be more exciting on the surface than the offerings of the church. Who needs baptism or the Eucharist when you've got thirty-one flavors of ice cream down the street, hundreds of shops down at the mall, and billions of products on the Internet? For many people, shopping replaces worship.

We must also recognize powerful economic forces that support globalized malls and electronic commerce. Domestic consumption and global production benefit the economy, and outsourcing allows an increase in the standard of living even with little increase in wages. This is the economic reason why consumerism is so powerful. Because over two-thirds of the annual output of the U.S. economy ends up being consumed (rather than invested or saved or going to government spending), anything that affects consumption significantly affects the overall standard of living. As prices drop in real terms, due to lower labor costs, workers can afford to buy goods and services even if their wages fail to increase. In other words, even if Wal-Mart employees are paid lower wages in real terms, they can afford many of the items sold in their stores as the prices of goods stay steady in nominal terms (meaning they are falling in inflation-adjusted terms). In fact, a recent study sponsored by Wal-Mart and conducted by eighteen economists found that Wal-Mart caused a decline in nominal wages (not inflation-adjusted) of 2.2 percent between 1985 and 2004 in the United States, but this was offset by decreasing prices for consumer goods, which led to a 0.9 percent increase in real disposable income.[27] There are real—albeit small, short-term, and material—advantages in consuming cheap stuff from China. We can get more stuff for less money, and lower-income consumers should be

26. Miller, *Consuming Religion*, 189.
27. D'Innocenzio, "Wal-Mart Session Addresses Critics."

happy with that—or so defenders of globalization would argue.[28] Yet the number of manufacturing jobs in the United States declined nearly 18 percent from the year 2000 to the year 2005, while the average size of single-family houses increased from 1,095 square feet in 1990 to 2,227 in 2005.[29] Economists see both trends as good news. For them, outsourcing to more efficient producers allows displaced workers to shift to more efficient uses of their time and labor. Thus, outsourcing should allow Americans to enjoy leisure and a higher standard of living more than ever, even as jobs are lost in the manufacturing sector but gained in other, supposedly higher-paying sectors where the U.S. is more efficient and productive.

But, as Juliet Schor shows in her book *The Overworked American*, we are busier than ever, even as we produce more goods and services per hour of work.[30] Her research indicates that Americans spent on average about nine hours more each year at their jobs in 1990 than they did in 1970.[31] Schor describes our consumer system as a cycle of "work-and-spend" to keep up with our neighbors—a system rooted in the notion that time is money.[32] "Where time is money, it's hard to protect time for those who—such as low-wage workers, children, aged parents, or community organizations—can't pay for it. And it's hard to protect time for ourselves, for relaxation, hobbies, or sleep."[33] We can forget about long vacations, too. Despite outsourcing production and adding "labor-saving" devices, Americans work more of the year than Europeans, who take longer vacations. One economic study found that fully employed French workers received an average of seven weeks annual paid vacation, whereas fully

---

28. Naroff, "Foreword," x–xi. The chairman of President George W. Bush's Council of Economic Advisers, Harvard professor N. Gregory Mankiw, got into political trouble in February 2004 when he issued a report approving of outsourcing on just these grounds. He also went on the "Ask the White House" page of the White House website and told one online questioner that "Outsourcing is the latest manifestation of the forces of free trade and increasing international specialization in production." See "Ask the White House," and Kiker, "Bush Econ Adviser."

29. "Characteristics of New Privately Owned One-Family Houses Complete: 1990 to 2005."

30. Schor, *Overworked American*.

31. For a discussion of different statistical measures of time spent at work, see Schor, "Civic Engagement and Working Hours."

32. Schor, *Overworked American*, 112–14.

33. Ibid., 141.

employed Americans received less than four weeks.[34] Yet however busy we are, this system is fairly productive—at least in the sense of making a larger amount of cheap stuff, including larger houses (on average, anyway). To say that that Americans live in a cornucopia of material affluence is a cliché. Schor notes that the level of productivity—the amount of goods and services produced per each hour worked—has steadily risen in the post-World War II era, but "between 1948 and the present we did not use any of the productivity dividend to reduce hours."[35] Instead of taking the free time that labor-saving productivity growth gave us, Schor argues, that time has been filled by our appetite for consumer products. We kept working, but spent the benefits of increased productivity buying more stuff; we may be efficient producers, but we are also voracious consumers. Hence, we are swimming in new goods, and most of us have trouble keeping track of all our stuff. The United States exported nearly 7 billion pounds of *used* clothing from 1990 to 2003.[36] When our castoffs number in the billions of pounds, it may be an indicator that we suffer from the disease of "affluenza," defined as "a painful, contagious, socially transmitted condition of overload, debt, anxiety, and waste resulting from the dogged pursuit of more."[37] Lest this sound like the hand-wringing of cultural critics informed only by anecdotes, Australian economist Tim Robinson recently documented the statistical trend toward increased work and decreased leisure time in the United States, a trend linked to what he called a "fundamental flaw" in the market system that causes workers to overestimate the benefits and underestimate the costs of spending additional time at work.[38] The Gross Domestic Product rises as we work and spend on consumption, yet we are no happier: we work too hard, and we worry about the sustainability of this rat race. We need to see how acting on our desires is helping to create a flexible service economy in which worker security is threatened, in which many people are expected to be on call twenty-four hours a day, seven days a week. Businesses imbued with the rhetoric of global competition threaten "downsizing," "outsourcing," "flexibility," or "contingent" work arrangements.[39] If people don't

34. Krugman, "French Family Values."

35. Schor, *Overworked American*, 2.

36. Rivoli, *Travels of a T-Shirt*, 176.

37. De Graaf et al., *Affluenza*, 2.

38. Robinson, *Work, Leisure and the Environment*.

39. For a helpful review of increasing worker insecurity, see Rubin, *Shifts in the Social Contract*.

perform, and even if they do, they live with the fear that their job will be outsourced.

Yet, at the same time, we are swimming in stuff. Many of us have more stuff than we need. We have a substantial portion of our population taking antidepressants or facing the deadly disease of . . . obesity.[40] We seem to have every tangible good we could want, yet many of our neighbors are unhappy, insecure, restless, stressed, and busy. It becomes more difficult to imagine other ways of living, so many have asked: How do we slow down? How do we begin to and find a rightly directed participation in material things? How do we live into a healthier relationship with material stuff? To which I would add: How might we re-imagine and re-direct our relationship to material things so that we can re-connect to the fullness of God? By fasting for a season, we might learn to see things whole, and we might begin to connect the dots between our globalized production, our globalized consumption, our busy-ness, and our unhappiness. We need to re-enter the gospel stories of Lent.

RE-ENACTING THE SEASON OF LENT

Observing Lent can help us enter the fullness of God. In the broadest sense, Lent re-enacts Jesus' turn toward Jerusalem and his turn toward the suffering that culminates at the cross. It is a season of preparation for Holy Week and Easter, and in the early church it was a time to prepare catechumens before their baptisms on Easter. The observance of a forty-day fast (excluding Sundays) apparently began to emerge under the influence of the bishop Athanasius of Alexandria (ca. 296–373).[41] While practices of fasting immediately before the Triduum (Holy Thursday, Good Friday, and Easter Sunday) had emerged early in church history, Athanasius deepened and extended these practices by advising his charges to abstain from sexual activity and eating, to practice charity, and to study scripture

---

40. Remember that people in the United States spend $50 billion a year on weight loss products. Jackson, *Earth Remains*, xvi. Schor, *Born to Buy*, 141–75, reports on her survey of 300 children, which found a statistically significant relationship between participation in consumer culture and "depression, anxiety, low self-esteem, and psychosomatic complaints" (167).

41. Dix, *Shape of the Liturgy*, 355; Cobb, "History of the Christian Year," 465–66; Nardone, *Story of the Christian Year*, 46–49; Regan, "Three Days and the Forty Days"; Johnson, "Preparation for Pascha?"

more intensively during the several weeks preceding Easter.[42] Ascetic discipline thus became integral to Lent.

In the West, the season begins on Ash Wednesday, and the traditional texts for that service help to frame the purpose of the fast from the start. If we are tempted to think that our fasting can extract change from the divine through what evangelicals call "works righteousness," we are sadly mistaken. Isaiah 58, which is read every year on Ash Wednesday, reminds the congregation that God is not impressed with mere rituals of piety. When we fast and then oppress those who work for us (v. 3), when we "fast only to quarrel and to fight," when we fast only "to strike with a wicked fist" (v. 4), then we are rather missing the point. When we only bow our heads and put on sackcloth and ashes but go on living the same way (v. 5), we are merely going through the external motions. But this is not to say that the fast is merely for private spiritual devotion. It is about practicing justice. As the text says, "Is not this the fast that I choose: to loose the bonds of injustice, to undo the thongs of the yoke, to let the oppressed go free, and to break every yoke? Is it not to share your bread with the hungry, and bring the homeless poor into your house; when you see the naked, to cover them, and not to hide yourself from your own kin" (Isa 58:6–7)? Embodying a community of justice and care for the poor will allow the true healing for a return to Yahweh. "Then your light shall break forth like the dawn, and your healing shall spring up quickly" (v. 8). By breaking our old habits that harm the oppressed, the hungry, the homeless, and the naked, we can open ourselves to becoming the community of hope that God calls his people to be. That is the true meaning of fasting in this prophetic text. Jesus himself confirms this impression on Ash Wednesday, when we hear the same passage from the Sermon on the Mount each year: we should not make a public display of our fasting, but we should fast and pray in ways that are unseen, secret, and quiet (Matt 6:1–6, 16–18). We are to practice a kind of detachment that re-orients us away from earthly treasure and toward heavenly treasure (Matt 6:19–21). But this does not imply an escape from the world; rather, it implies that we are to live toward the Kingdom right in the midst of our daily lives, as we fast quietly and see the kingdom in the small, everyday things we do.

Robert Webber describes his first Ash Wednesday service as deeply meaningful because it was "an *experience* of the death and resurrection

---

42. Brakke, *Athanasius and Asceticism*, 182–200.

of Christ, not a mere cognitive assent to a fact that didn't touch me in the core of my very being."[43] In facing up to the reality of our own death, we enter experientially into the death of Christ on this day. The traditional practice of imposing ashes on worshipers' foreheads reminds us that we are dust and "to dust we shall return" (Gen 3:19). We begin the fast with a somber reminder that we are headed to Holy Week, to the passion and death of Jesus, to emptiness and grief, to sackcloth and ashes, to our own death. But this creates another opening for *kairos* time, preparing us to receive grace anew as we face up to both Christ's and our own suffering and mortality. This should help us re-imagine our relationship to the pursuit of commodities.

The first Sunday of Lent turns to the temptation of Jesus and helps us see the deep roots of our mis-directed desires. Although the story of the temptation comes immediately after the baptism of Jesus in Matthew, Mark, and Luke, the lectionary makes this story into the start of an entirely new chapter of the church's gospel story. Apart from the fact that the forty days of Jesus' wilderness wanderings evoke memories of Noah's time on the ark, of Moses' time on Mount Sinai, and of the forty years of wilderness wandering for the people of Israel, each gospel emphasizes a different theme.

Matthew emphasizes the overcoming of temptation by the second Adam (Jesus) that undoes the failures of the first Adam. When the first man and woman were tempted, they failed to resist. The allure of being like God, of knowing good and evil, was too much. Reading Genesis 3 alongside the temptation story in Matthew 4, as the church does every third year in the lectionary, shows that Jesus managed to succeed where the man and woman failed. They "saw that the fruit of the tree was good for food" (Gen 3:6) and succumbed, but Jesus overcame the real temptation to turn stones into bread (Matt 4:3–4). They saw that the fruit was "a delight to the eyes" (Gen 3:6) and succumbed, but Jesus resisted the temptation to demonstrate his power with a visible spectacle (Matt 4:5–7). They saw that the fruit was "to be desired to make one wise" and succumbed, but Jesus resisted the temptation to take worldly power (Matt 4:8–10). Hence, the epistle reading in Romans concludes for us: "For just as by the one man's disobedience the many were made sinners, so by the one man's obedience the many will be made righteous" (Rom 5:19). Drawing on the temptation story to start the season shows that the overcoming of sin by the new

---

43. Webber, *Ancient-Future Time*, 106. Emphasis in original.

Adam begins well before he gets to the cross. Yet this overcoming flows from the power of God, and we can participate in it, as the prayer for the First Sunday in Lent from *The Book of Common Prayer* reminds us. The petition in the prayer says, "Come quickly to help us who are assaulted by many temptations [at the mall?]; and as you know the weaknesses of each of us, let each one find you mighty to save."[44] As with the first woman and first man, we must turn to the one who is "mighty to save" if we have any hope of turning from temptation. This one has already resisted such temptation. If we are tempted to buy things to satisfy our deepest longings, we can lean on one who resisted.

He resisted temptation because he was already ushering in God's reign. Mark's much shorter account places the temptation on the heels of Jesus' baptism and reads in its entirety this way: "And the Spirit immediately drove him out into the wilderness. He was in the wilderness for forty days, tempted by Satan; and he was with the wild beasts; and the angels waited on him" (Mark 1:12–13). Right after this Mark tells us that "Jesus came to Galilee, proclaiming the good news of God, and saying, 'The time is fulfilled, and the kingdom of God has come near; repent, and believe in the good news'" (v. 14–15). If we listen to Mark carefully, the baptism and the overcoming of temptation together lead to the fulfillment of the times and the proclamation of the Kingdom.[45] Hence, the temptation story is a major turning point for Mark, worth a separate Sunday because it marks the first step toward the Kingdom.[46] Again we are reminded that we are being incorporated into this kingdom. When we resist the temptations of global consumerism, we are allowing God's reign to begin through the Spirit.

Luke's narrative interposes the genealogy of Jesus in between the baptism and the temptation stories, thereby stressing that Jesus is a true son of Israel, who was not only "full of the Holy Spirit," but also tied to the Hebrew ancestors and the land.[47] Jesus overcomes temptation in the

---

44. Episcopal Church, *Book of Common Prayer*, 218.

45. The Old Testament reading on Noah (Gen 9:8–17) and the epistle reading on Noah's ark as a prefiguration of baptism (1 Pet 3:18–22) also reinforce these themes.

46. In the Revised Common Lectionary, this theme is followed up the next week in Year B with Mark 8:31–38 and its depiction of the journey to the cross.

47. These themes are reinforced in the lectionary's parallel reading from Deuteronomy 26, in which Moses, on the east side of the Jordan river, advises the people to bring the first fruits of their produce to the priest when they enter the land they were promised. Moses also advises the people to give a short re-telling of the Exodus that ends with how Yahweh

Judean desert, the first part of the land one encounters upon crossing the Jordan valley from the east, and thus can now lay claim to the land. The overcoming of temptation is therefore the first fruit in the victory of God, Jesus moving into Canaan. When the people of Israel entered, they fell prey to temptations and went astray. But when the embodiment of the new Israel enters the land, he overcomes sin. Already on the first Sunday of Lent, we find one who is "mighty to save" and who brings us across the river of our baptism and into the new land of redemption. Thus, as we respond to the global consumer system, we lean on this divine power that redeems the hopes of Israel.

As the season winds down, Episcopalians recite a memorable prayer in *The Book of Common Prayer* that sums up the journey that a careful participant embarks upon in Lent: "Almighty God, you alone can bring into order the unruly wills and affections of sinners: Grant your people grace to love what you command and desire what you promise; that, among the swift and varied changes of the world, our hearts may surely there be fixed where true joys are to be found."[48]

We can find the central Lenten themes in this prayer. First, the prayer is for those who have been on the Lenten journey of wearing ashes, singing somber songs, fasting together, praying and meditating, and feasting on Sundays (which are not part of Lent but remain as feast days celebrating the Lord's Day of resurrection). We learn on this quiet journey of repentance, suffering, dispossession, and downward mobility that we are all sinners who require grace and that our community is more like the one criticized by Isaiah than the coming of the Kingdom. We fail to resist temptations—at the mall or elsewhere.

The prayer also reminds us that it is Almighty God alone who can help us to bear fruit through grace. Repentance does not depend upon our efforts but is merely a prelude to the gracious saving power of the one who is and who will be lifted up. The one who is "mighty to save" alone can help us. Faith and trust in this Lord, it seems, is good enough. This is part of what it means to re-direct our sacramentality: with faith in the resurrection, we are restored to a proper relationship with material things so that they point us back to the resurrecting God. We trust that there will be abundant provision, healthy relationship, and fulfillment.

"brought us into this place and gave us this land, a land flowing with milk and honey" (Exod 26:9).

48. Episcopal Church, *Book of Common Prayer*, 219.

We trust that we will receive the gifts we need to walk on the journey of discipleship. We walk into death, but we also walk in faith in the promise of the resurrection—the promise of the new covenant.

The prayer furthermore reminds us that God must "grant us grace" as we prepare to enter the metaphorical land of plenty across the Jordan (the fulfillment of the longed-for redemption of Israel). Like the Israelites, we are also in the wilderness of dispossession, but only the water of baptism—no product we consume—can slake our thirst. "Everyone who thirsts, come to the waters," says Isaiah (55:1). This call invites us to enter into genuine repentance and redemption, rather than to buy the latest products on offer from soft drink manufacturers and purveyors of bottled water. Paul tells the Corinthian church that "our ancestors . . . drank from the spiritual rock that followed them, and the rock was Christ. Nevertheless, God was not pleased with most of them, and they were struck down in the wilderness" (1 Cor 10:1, 5). Our fasting, after Christ, prepares us to receive the abundant waters of resurrected life in the same way as the church at Corinth. Lent is a season for us to re-orient and re-direct how we live with material stuff—with water, with food, with habits, and with practices—so that we can live in joyful communion with them. Our "unruly wills and affections" will tend to attach themselves to the earthly materials that surround our embodied selves, but this is a season to detach from those things that take us away from true joy and to re-attach our hearts to those things in which "true joys are to be found." Instead of gobbling down food for ourselves, we might break our addiction to mindless eating and drinking so that we might learn to eat slowly, to truly enjoy feasting, and to extend hospitality to others at our table. In order to receive the abundance of salvation, we must prepare to taste it; we must enter the wilderness and the death of baptism in the Jordan.

The Lenten prayer also anticipates the healing and restoring of Easter during this time of repentance and desert pain. Although Lent is primarily a season of preparation, it is also a time to taste a bit of the Kingdom, in which we trust God to bring about *re-directed sacramentality*. Re-direction implies that we would "love what you command and desire what you promise," seeking Christ's Kingdom first, which means true feasting on the living bread and water, and not merely escaping from the world of stuff. It means a sense of deep fullness in the material realm and not of restless "consuming" activity in this world of "swift and varied changes." But this kind of relationship to the creation requires the hope of God's new creation coming into our time. Lent offers glimpses of this hope in stories on the fourth and fifth Sundays of the season. On the fourth Sunday, the church often hears the story of the Israelites being attacked by snakes and being healed by gazing upon a bronze image of a snake nailed to a high pole (Num 21:4–9). The raising of the snake on the pole is really then a pre-figuration of the raising of the dead to life and of the ascension of Jesus to heaven. Jesus confirms this impression when he speaks with Nicodemus, telling him that no one has ascended into heaven but that "just as Moses lifted up the serpent in the wilderness, so must the Son of Man be lifted up" (John 3:14)—lifted up on the cross, lifted up out of the grave, and lifted up to heaven. As we suffer from material privation or deadly attacks during Lent, we are to turn to this one who loves us so much that he sends his own Son to be raised up to die, to be raised up in coming back to life, and to be raised up to heaven in the Ascension. We need to gaze up at the one who was lifted up in order to turn from the temptations of the consumer gospel. On the fifth Sunday of Lent, the church gets a foretaste of the paschal mystery of this rising again. Each year, it reads prophecies that foretell the new covenant: first, Ezekiel's vision of dry bones coming to life (Ezek 37:1–14), next, Jeremiah's vision of a new covenant that will be written on our hearts (Jer 31:31–34), and, last, Isaiah's vision of Yahweh saying that he will do a new thing (Isa 43:19). Even before Easter, the lectionary texts offer a glimpse of the resurrection that is to come, both at Easter and at the end of time.

And this prayer asks God to direct our hearts so that they may be "fixed where true joys are to be found." This suggests that we are to love our neighbors as much as we love God, and to seek out the Kingdom that God promises, where true joy awaits us. While we loosen unhealthy attachments to material things during this season, we are being prepared to *re-direct* our earthly attachments toward the loving purposes of the community of disciples under God's reign. Thus, if we are to journey toward God's kingdom of justice, love, and mercy, the material stuff in our lives should serve that journey. As Isaiah 58 reminds us on Ash Wednesday, the kind of fasting that Yahweh desires is the kind that leads to a Kingdom of care for the oppressed, the hungry, the homeless, and the naked. Do the material possessions that we purchase help to make that Kingdom more tangible each day? That is the kind of Lenten question we can share with our neighbors and take to the mall or the grocery store to reframe our purchasing decisions. Instead of living to shop, we might learn to shop in order to advance the Kingdom of life and joy and love.

Re-Imagining the Globalization of Consumption

The problems of global consumption take on a new dimension when we re-imagine them in light of the Lenten season. Our description of the re-enacted story contains several suggestive hints to re-form and re-direct our consumerism; here I focus on five of these hints to show how they positively reframe the problems with which this chapter started.

First, by entering experientially into the hunger and thirst of Jesus, we remind ourselves that we are unable to resist temptation in the same way that the new Adam did—including the temptation to satisfy our deepest wants with the purchase of material things, through bread and water. In Lent we enter a season of confession and repentance where we are forced to come face to face with our own sin and brokenness. Unlike Jesus, though, we will fall prey to seeking satisfaction in tangible things rather than "every word that comes from the mouth of God" (Matt 4:4), and this realization should prompt repentance in us. Robert Webber puts it nicely when he writes, "Lent is a time to intentionally confront all the ways in which the first Adam continues to control our lives, to carry these ways to the cross, to let them be crucified with Jesus, and to bury them in the tomb never to rise again."[49] We enter into the suffering of Jesus, and we re-discover that we are sinners and that we are dust. These brute facts should at least slow us down on our trip to the mall. They may even prompt us to begin practicing alternatives to restless shopping.

This journey into the wilderness could prove to be a powerful anti-dote to the problem of "unencumbered enjoyment" so ably identified by Albert Borgmann. It can do so by helping to break us of habits of such easy enjoyment. For instance, I recently experienced an entire Lent of giving up National Public Radio in the mornings and while driving in the car (a benign addiction, but an addiction nonetheless). This discipline helped make me more attentive to the ease with which I am entertained and distracted by something that I can find with the click of a button. Instead of having to work to find news and to wait until I could read a newspaper, the radio was there for me at any moment. My habit of switching on the radio was broken for a season, and thus a small space

49. Webber, *Ancient-Future Time*, 107.

for the divine opened up. Engaging in more traditional ascetic disciplines can also help one become more attentive to the sheer ease with which it is possible to consume things that bring one pleasure. For those addicted to coffee, giving it up for the season can be a powerful disruption to established habits of easy enjoyment. Lenten fasting thus can break the addictive behavior that starts the cycle of mindless consuming.

Second, as we seek to live in repentance, we learn to turn to the one who is "mighty to save" us during this time. If the first step is a break with our standard habits of eating, drinking, shopping, and buying, then the next step is constant prayer and attention to beg help from the second Adam who overcame temptation. Fasting from consumption might then heal the divide between our consuming and producing selves. We may learn to find identity in light of Christ's own suffering and privation, rather than in the global corporate brands that overwhelm North Americans with too many consumption choices. But God's power will be necessary if we are to bear fruit in living into this new identity. Successfully breaking our old habits of consumption will depend on divine initiative and grace, just as sustaining alternatives will depend upon divine sustenance. It is not up to us alone, for we can turn to the one who was lifted up. Here is where we can experience the beginning of a restoration toward wholeness, a beginning of the overcoming of the divisions that the global system exacerbates between people and within them. Like Jesus, we can withdraw into a wilderness space that takes us out of the existing power structures and systems. Yet even if we would become desert monks we would find temptation right there with us. We would begin to learn that the system of global consumption plays upon human desires and affections. Even if we could withdraw entirely from the global economy, which is impossible in any case, we would still find that we consumed things. We cannot give up eating and drinking. Like the desert fathers and mothers who went out into the caves of Egypt, then, we would discover that withdrawal from society does not solve our problems; it only makes clearer that our problems ultimately stem from within ourselves and our own unruly desires. For instance, it turns out that the divisions between our worker and producer selves find their source in our desires to have cheap stuff and yet also have good jobs. We all desire to have everything without facing tradeoffs. So in prayer we turn to the one who already suffered privation yet resisted temptation. To break the cycle of global consumerism and heal our division, we need to discover our whole selves in the silence of the wilderness. The global consumer system is not merely an external system foisted upon us by greedy corporations, it is a system that subtly caters to and distorts natural human desires for its own ends. Hence, only a return to the second Adam who overcomes temptation can help us to allow our unruly will and affections to be directed rightly. We have to cut the problem down at its roots, which are inside us.

Third, however, Lenten fasting also helps us rediscover the power of true feasting and to confront the problem of increasingly restless activity. Instead of working longer hours to afford more stuff, we discover in the Sundays of Lent that we can enter the land and find some measure of rest in this life—even in the midst of scarcity. Like the people of Israel sharing the firstfruits of the first harvest from the land of Canaan, we can begin to celebrate the overcoming of temptation and the homecoming of finding our true rest in the land. As feast days, the Sundays in Lent evoke Sabbath practice, which Marva Dawn helpfully describes as a movement from ceasing to resting to feasting and embracing.[50] Beginning with Saturday evenings, we can begin by ceasing from our normal activities and resting from busy lives. In that ceasing from commerce, from consumption and production, we are already being liberated. Herein lies the power of Lenten fasting. By detaching us from the consumption of goods we normally enjoy, it opens us to find our pleasure in gifts of God rather than in things detached from God, not unlike those Eastern Orthodox and Catholic Christians who fast before taking the Eucharist. By doing so, they cease their normal ways of eating and drinking before partaking of the great memorial meal at the center of worship. After ceasing and resting, they feast on the Body and Blood of the Lamb, a celebration of the love of God that can liberate us and take us into the land of new birth. After such feasting, we might well be "full of the Holy Spirit" as Jesus was upon entering the wilderness. We can then embrace the world in love and live with great joy, even as we are detached from mindless consumption. Living with joy will help us transform how we live with the material things around us. We will learn to embrace material things as gifts from God, just as the day of rest and worship is a gift of God. Restoring a sense of Sunday worship as a restful Sabbath practice is therefore central to Lenten fasting. On this note, the German philosopher Josef Pieper argues that in the true day of rest, humans freely and voluntarily "renounce the yield of a day's labor" and make time exclusively for God as an essential

50. Dawn, *Keeping the Sabbath Wholly*.

starting point, giving up their time as a sacrifice.[51] He continues, "Even in conditions of extreme material scarcity, the withholding from work, in the midst of a life normally governed by work, creates an area of free surplus."[52] From God, we receive the gift of "the superhuman abundance of life" in the "day that the Lord has made" (Ps 118:24).[53] On the Lord's Day, then, we find glimpses of the ultimate rest promised to us when we eat and drink in paradise, at the banquet of the Lamb. By feasting here and now, we obtain a foretaste of the great joy of eating at this banquet. All of this suggests that a recovery of a deep sense of feasting on the Lord's Day will help us appreciate the food, drink, and other items that can truly satisfy us. If we are fasting throughout the week, we can experience the Eucharist and rich meals afterward as true feasts. By recovering the observance of Sundays as feast days in Lent, we might well challenge the flatness of a world in which every day is the same and every meal is merely fuel for us to go on working. If a person is abstaining from alcohol throughout Lent, for example, the taste of wine on Sunday morning could be a moment of feasting and savoring the abundant grace of God. Feasting requires resting from the busy world of consumption before consuming rightly.

This suggests another point where we can re-imagine the practices of global consumerism. By observing a holy Lent, we can begin to find how to re-direct our desires and find a deeper gospel than the gospel of consumerism. Because consumerism comes to us as a kind of gospel of *misdirected sacramentality* (to evoke Miller's term again), and because we are thoroughly earthly creatures, the problem of consumerism cannot be eradicated by escaping from the material world, which is impossible anyway. Rather, we must learn to affirm our materiality while re-directing our consumption of material things to become part of a journey of discipleship for the Kingdom of love. If churches are following Jesus on a shared journey of discipleship, it should change the way whole church communities shop. Jesus says to potential disciples: "If any want to become my followers, let them deny themselves and take up their cross and follow me. For those who want to save their life will lose it, and those who lose their life for my sake, and for the sake of the gospel, will save

51. Pieper, *In Tune With the World*, 18–19; also see Pieper, *Leisure, The Basis of Culture*, 53–54.

52. Pieper, *In Tune With the World*, 19.

53. Ibid., 39–40.

it. For what will it profit them to gain the whole world and forfeit their life?" (Mark 8:34–36). In a small way, the self-denial of fasting starts the follower on the road to discipleship. By taking the tangible step of faith in giving up something, one begins to step into this re-directed sacramentality, in which every material thing is either part of the journey or something to leave behind. One can gain material life and possessions but lose one's life. Or one can lose one's material life and possessions but gain life. By giving up possessions and consumption, one gains a rightly directed relationship to things that can re-direct them to become part of one's discipleship journey. Whereas the gospel of consumerism requires nothing more than cash or credit, the gospel of Jesus requires that we be willing to forsake all and walk with him down dangerous pathways that could get us killed.

Fifth, then, as we found in the Isaiah reading for Ash Wednesday, the proper Lenten fast is one that fosters a community of justice that cares for the poor—a source of hope in a world of worker insecurity. While the recovery of fasting, of repentance, of Sabbath feasting, and of discipleship are immensely helpful in leading us, it will also be necessary for the church to practice works of mercy and social justice that help address a world full of anxious and busy workers and shoppers. All of our fasting will amount to little more than religious game-playing if there is not attention to those in our community who suffer from burdens of stress, overwork, credit card debt, unemployment, or job insecurity. Here is an important place where the church can learn to improvise practical responses in the wilderness it finds itself in.

IMPROVISING PRACTICES

The Onion, a satirical newspaper, recently published a fake magazine cover that captures the dilemma of anyone who proposes to counter consumerism within our global system. The cover photo is of a white paper shopping bag against a white background. On the bag in bold print are these words: "Top 10 Products to Battle Consumerism."[54] Note the rich irony. The picture mocks the idea that one can challenge consumerism by buying the right consumer products. Even purchasing fair-trade, organic, green-friendly products still reinforces the existence of a global-

---

54. "Top Ten Products to Battle Consumerism." Many thanks to Greg Miller for first posting a printout of this cover on his office door.

ized consumer system. So it is clear that any challenge to consumerism that reinforces the power of the consumer market system might undercut itself. That is why alternative rhythms of life stemming from Lent can help us so much. They not only encourage us to abstain from consumption, but they also root Christian action in an alternative story that helps the church live differently. We need to enter the wilderness space of Lent to begin to be formed by the journey of faithful walking with Jesus. Those wilderness spaces will vary for different communities and diverse persons, but I want to offer a few thoughts for further reflection and action.

First, fasting from consumption is an obvious outgrowth of Lenten practice, which can start with weekly observation of the Sabbath. On this issue, historian Dorothy Bass tells a story about an invitation that her twelve-year-old daughter got to spend a Sunday afternoon at the mall. When Bass told her daughter that she couldn't go, the daughter was angry at first, but then got into a rich conversation with her mom. After that, Bass hoped that when she and her daughter did visit the mall they would be "equipped with a degree of spiritual independence from its gaudy promises."[55] This is precisely when Lenten fasting can offer—not an escape from the evils of the world but a detachment from sensual pleasure that puts the world in its rightful place and reminds us that the deepest pleasures are not found in the mall but in true feasting. As Bass and her daughter discovered, staying home from the mall on Sunday can be liberating.

The Friday after the American Thanksgiving holiday is a day that is increasingly known as Black Friday, because it is a day crucial to retailers who hope to avoid red ink, "stay in the black," and make a profit. However, the writers of *Affluenza* counsel participation in the yearly Buy Nothing Day on this same day, as a gesture of resistance to the commercialization inherent in the Christmas season.[56] While this practice of resistance makes sense for Christians to take up, it falls short in a few ways. It is purely negative, rather than being balanced by a sense that one's fast is preparing one for true feasting or life in a Kingdom of love. Perhaps a better alternative is to serve the poor on this day and hold alternative feasts. The day is also a one-time event, rather than being part of a larger journey toward a destination. A single day is easy to dismiss as a short-term tactic, and it fails to convey the larger reasons why one might

55. Bass, *Receiving the Day*, 64.

56. De Graaf et al., *Affluenza*, 217–18.

need to attend to one's longer-term patterns of consumption behavior. The Lenten season restores to adherents a sense of participation in a journey of ascetic discipline and self-emptying as preparation for greater things to come. It would frame Christian abstention from consumption as a positive call toward discipleship, toward trust and faith in the Jesus who is leading us. By contrast, weekly observance of a Sabbath and yearly observance of Lent goes further in time and deeper in attacking the root of consumptive behavior. If one fasted from all retail purchases on all Sundays and all days of Lent, that would amount to ninety-two days a year (fifty-two Sundays plus the forty days' fast). Now, such a literal interpretation of the demands of fasting seems unduly narrow, but perhaps a dose of literalism would bring greater rigor to efforts to alter deeply rooted habits and practices. A Lenten focus on changing consumer behavior would re-connect us to liturgical time rather than the rituals of a national calendar. Thanksgiving, after all, is not part of the Christian calendar but a feast day in the nationalist liturgical year. If we take our cues from the Christian year, we are being incorporated into an ancient, gospel-centered calendar that brings us closer to the fullness of God rather than a retail shopping calendar. Instead of reacting against consumerist excess, the church could reframe resistance from within Lent.

A second improvisation that might flow from Lent is prayerful, intensive study of the Bible so that we can draw on its passages in moments of weakness. If we take Jesus and the desert fathers and mothers as inspiration, we will find that a change of location would not be enough to help us escape the temptations of our society. It will not be enough to say no to consumption. We can flee from mainstream society to the desert for a time, but even if we do find a true wilderness place, we still cannot flee from ourselves or find our help within. Instead we will need to be filled with something that sustains our fasting. So we will find that we need to turn to the one "who is mighty to save." And to find that one, we can cling to the scriptures, ancient liturgies, and constant prayer. When the desert fathers and mothers faced temptation they would often quote the scriptures that were engrained in them through monastic discipline. Similarly, as many preachers have noted, knowledge of the scriptures helped sustain Jesus in his response to the temptations. In fact, both Matthew and Luke have Jesus quoting passages from the Torah back to Satan in steadfast resistance. When tempted to turn stones into bread, Jesus falls back upon Deut 8:3, saying: "One does not live by bread alone, but by every word that comes from the mouth of God" (Matt 4:4; Luke 4:4). Having memorized this text in rabbinic fashion, Jesus was prepared to resist. But many North American Christians will be hard-pressed to draw on such resources at moments of temptation. It certainly could not hurt to drill such biblical narratives and texts into working memory. One of the most striking things I encountered in dialogue with Muslims in Bahrain was their ability to quote stories and sayings of the prophet Muhammad on issues of ethics. Cultivating such a memory of biblical narratives and sayings would be worthwhile for Christians as well. One might even find oneself reciting such passages to oneself at the mall or the superstore. Prayerful attention to the promises of scripture in the style of *lectio divina* (monastic-style "divine reading" that meditates deeply on short passages) would help breed powerful resistance to the false promises of the consumer gospel.

A third way of improvising alternatives to global consumerism will be to restore feasting to its proper place by making preparatory fasting a central Christian discipline, including fasting from shopping and mindless consumption. But we will need to recover liturgical rhythms in community to help organize our lives. My own church treats the Sundays during Lent as feast days, which heightens the contrast between the bleakness and flatness of six days of fasting by interrupting with a day of joyful feasting. One friend of ours at church gave up hot showers during Lent and limited himself to sponge baths that used no more than a bucket of water. But on Sundays he relished the chance to have a hot shower. The point of such ascetic discipline in Lent is to interrupt our rhythms of comfort so that we can relish small pleasures as gifts of grace, thereby opening up space for the divine grace that is much larger than hot showers. Once we break open that space by disrupting our habits, we can truly feast on new modes of grace. One can only imagine the space created if whole churches gave up mindless purchases of global goods for a season. Could we imagine fasting from shopping for all of Lent?

Sara Bongiorni's family gave up purchasing all goods made in China for a year as an experiment with globalization, and she tells about the results in her funny book, *A Year Without "Made in China."* She notes the positive side to her family ban early in the year when she describes how her husband resisted the impulse to buy a cheap whoopee cushion or "pointy plastic dinosaurs, inch-tall construction workers, or neon-colored pool toys" in the sale rack, because he checked the labels: all of the cheap stuff was made in China.[57] However, the family ran into trouble with receiving gifts from others, and they decided not to extend the ban that far, which left a large loophole that Bongiorni described as "a crucial pipeline of Chinese products pouring into our house."[58] They also ran into trouble when their young son had outgrown his old shoes. After a two-week search for shoes not made in China, they spent $68 for a catalog pair made in Italy (or so they thought at the time; later, they found that they might have been made in China).[59] Should the ban extend to individual components, such as a small part of a lamp that was mostly made in the United States? They decide that it should not, only this one part was made in China.[60] Purchasing non-China toys at the local Target turned out to be nearly impossible, apart from Legos. The family had already been practicing a boycott of Wal-Mart, but Bongiorni paid a surreptitious visit to one Wal-Mart store to sample 106 items of general merchandise, and she found that 49 percent of the items in her sample were indeed made in China.[61] In their pre-boycott Christmas, the family had given and received twenty-five gifts made in China and fourteen from the rest of the world, but in their post-boycott Christmas, they had only eleven items made in China and forty-two from the rest of the world.[62] Although Bongiorni's husband had grumbled about the boycott during the year, by the end both he and his wife found that their experiment had made them more thoughtful in how they spent their money. As Bongiorni put it, "The boycott made us stop and think before tossing something else in the shopping cart. . . . It made us thoughtful, and that can't be a bad thing."[63] Still, one of the most troubling things in Bongiorni's story is the puzzlement and outright resistance the family encountered from friends, co-workers, and family. It seems that becoming more thoughtful about consumption makes others uncomfortable. We will return to this point in a moment.

For now, Bongiorni's story makes me wonder if the church could help sustain patterns of discipline that would not only make Christians

---

57. Bongiorni, *Year Without "Made in China,"* 26.

58. Ibid., 26.

59. Ibid., 38–41, 168.

60. Ibid., 58–61.

61. Ibid., 91.

62. Ibid., 212.

63. Ibid., 216.

more thoughtful in how they spend their money but would also make them more attentive to simple joys that are inexpensive and creative. Perhaps church groups could undertake a similar abstention of some type during Lent, while re-directing one's attention and money to the service of others during that time. They might find joy in the process, as Bongiorni's family did when they traveled to San Diego for a family visit and beach vacation. Bongiorni's husband needed flip-flops for the beach, but the family was unable to find any that were not made in China. So her mother dug out some old flip flops from an attic or basement, but they were a mismatched pair. The husband continued to wear these mismatched flip flops around as a kind of badge of dishonor, but in the end it became a family joke. The ban also made it impossible to purchase plastic beach toys for the children, but the family picked up toys that had been left by other children at the end of the day. Bongiorni writes, "True, we never found non-Chinese squirt guns or water balloons, and the kids didn't get their hands on beach toys until the final days of our vacation, but in the end we've done all right. Better than all right. Tonight we helped clear the beach of debris, something that wouldn't have occurred to us if we'd acquired beach toys through the traditional route, by buying them."[64] This family discovered how fasting can help one to feast on simple joys, turning deprivation into an opportunity for creative adventure. Can the church reframe fasting as preparation for true feasting in the place where "true joys are to be found"?

A fourth practice of improvisation is for churches to re-direct their members' consumption behavior by reframing it as part of their discipleship journeys. Interestingly, Bongiorni resists framing her family's experience as anything other than a kind of science experiment, eschewing those who would infuse her story with patriotic or religious meaning.[65] She was indulging her curiosity, not trying to save America or embark on a spiritual quest. However, a more significantly Lenten or Christian narrative could reframe our purchasing behaviors in relation to Jesus' journey through baptism, temptation, and suffering—and even death, resurrection, ascension, and return. Instead of viewing changes to consumption behavior at the big-box retailer or the mall as science or a

---

64. Ibid., 133.

65. Ibid., 196–98. She registers her discomfort with a conservative Christian letter-writer who complained about how "our enemy, communist 'Red' China" was taking over Christmas at the same time that Americans neglected the religious meaning of Christmas.

matter of patriotic duty, we might see them as part of traveling with Jesus through Lent and beyond, finding the fullness of God before we get to the mall. And that way of reframing our consumption activity might just be the best way to help constitute Christian communities of support and encouragement that would help sustain healthier ways of buying global products.

A final improvisational practice is the fostering of communities of sharing and social peace. Stronger church communities might help us avoid the mockery, disbelief, and second-guessing that Bongiorni's family encountered when they embarked on their year-long journey of boycotting Chinese goods. Instead of finding discouragement when we attempt to change how we participate in the global consumer economy, with such communities we might find groups to share habit-altering practices, to scale back consumption, to slow down our lives, to brainstorm creative ways of living differently, and to offer support to those facing dislocation or uncertainty in the global consumption system. Small communities can also help model practices of simplicity and decreased consumption.[66] Several Mennonites that live near us on the same block share garden tools so that not everyone has to own a hedge trimmer. They all live near the college where we teach, as does my family, so we can all walk to work. Two of the families own only one car, despite having children in multiple activities. Along with another family from our church, we often give each other rides. Such small acts of sharing improvise resistance to consumerism.

On a larger scale, the fostering of community will form a crucial part of ameliorating the negative effects of current consumption practices, as well as the effects of any changes. Churches will need to form communities of social justice to help embody alternatives to current practices. For example, readers might be wondering about the fate of Chinese workers who might lose work if more people emulated Bongiorni's boycott. Here is where the global church and the Chinese church will have to be part of the discussion of problems and solutions. But we can start from the proposition that all parties in an oppressive system need to be liberated. Not just Chinese laborers but also North American consumers are trapped in a system that is difficult to imagine escaping. In a Lenten journal, English professor John Leax reflects on the political implications of the season: "Love requires me to see . . . that we are all enslaved, that we are all in

---

66. For more on this, see Schut, *Simpler Living, Compassionate Life*.

need of the liberating gospel."[67] Even people who were planning to locate a toxic waste dump in his area were in need of this love. Lent, it seems, helps us to see that we are all dust and that we will all return to being dust, thereby opening a space for us to see our neighbors as fellow sinners in need of love just like us. In other words, the community that is fostered is not just the church community clustered around fasting and feasting. It extends to the ends of the earth in love, and it liberates all of us.

On Ash Wednesday we are reminded that the only fast pleasing to God is one that fosters justice and wholeness for the community and the oppressed. The church must become a community of justice that cares for the poor, for dislocated workers, and for unhappy "consumers" if it is to have any hope of pointing the world to the wholeness and fullness that sustain our hope. We should not count on the coercive power of the U.S. military, the current global enforcer. We need to point the way to love and joy through our fasting, not force people into the way.

---

67. Leax, "Lent," 91–92. Thanks also to Sarah Moore who emphasized this same point in a summer book group.

CHAPTER 7

Holy Week and American Hegemony

This world is ruled by violence,
But I guess that's better left unsaid.

—Bob Dylan, 1983[1]

Nothing could conceal the God of the universe more completely than a
half-naked man being tortured to death. And yet the Christian claim is
that it is precisely here, in this self-emptying, that the very fullness of
God's inner life is revealed, for the Father is only the Father in his complete
self-giving to the Son, which is returned by the Son as the Gift, which
is the Holy Spirit. Therefore the ugliness of the cross itself paradoxically is
pure glory.

—Bill Cavanaugh[2]

My favorite recent book cover comes on a tome by a leading historian
of globalization at Princeton University. It shows a bust of President
George W. Bush clad in a toga and wearing a garland of olive leaves on
his head that makes him look like Caesar. And that is the point, since
the title of Harold James' work is *The Roman Predicament: How the Rules*

1. Dylan, "Union Sundown," *Infidels.*
2. Cavanaugh, *Being Consumed*, 80. Emphasis in original.

of International Order Create the Politics of Empire. His cover designer playfully portrays what many critics have said about the United States: we have become an empire in the Roman mold, the keeper of the *Pax Americana* that parallels the *Pax Romana* of the first century or the *Pax Britannica* of the nineteenth century.[3]

Empires, after all, do claim to bring the benefits of peace, as even the American empire does. A colleague of mine helped me notice this after the United States' invasion and occupation of Iraq.[4] He teaches modern world history and for years has had students read and discuss Rudyard Kipling's famous poem "The White Man's Burden" in class. The poem, an unabashed defense of imperial intervention by white men, was published in 1899, at the time of the Boer war and the Spanish-American war, the latter of which led to the U.S. invasion of the Philippines. To most non-Victorian ears, to most professors, and to most people in the developing world today, the poem will provoke cringes and disdain. Likewise, for years my friend observed his students reacting against Kipling and following a standard American line that is rhetorically committed to freedom, anti-imperialism, and multicultural tolerance. How dare Kipling be so arrogant as to impose his own definition of what is good for others! But around the time of the Iraq War, a number of students started coming to Kipling's defense. After all, these college students hear in Kipling that the White Man is bringing peace, ending sickness, liberating captives, reducing terror, calling on Freedom (if also testing his masculinity). For many well-meaning students, what we were doing in Iraq was helping people, even bringing the gospel to them. We had this "burden" of trying to help the people of Iraq. Isn't that the Christian thing to do? As young people schooled in the narrative of American civil religion, which says that America stands for freedom and has a duty to spread it, these students espoused a common view of the national narrative, equating the spread of freedom with the advance of the gospel. From the side of the weak, of course, this all sounds like imperialism. But there is also a benign, if naïve, intent.

By contrast, the advance of the gospel and the Kingdom—peace in the Christian sense—is not the imperial peace that spreads political goods through war. Whereas political leaders promise peace through quashing of violence by violence, Christian peace comes through rec-

---

3. James, *Roman Predicament.* Interestingly, a more recent edition has a new cover.
4. Thanks again to Greg Miller for sharing another insight.

onciliation and self-giving. As Frederick Buechner puts it, "For Jesus peace seems to have meant not the absence of struggle, but the presence of love."[5] And that love is demonstrated in the good news of the gospel. But the gospel narratives of Holy Week suggest that the gospel spreads through weakness, marginality, and martyrdom—not through the force of Caesar's arms but through death at Caesar's hands. At this focal point of the Christian Year, our pilgrimage through the Passion re-enacts the true politics of the Kingdom, by overcoming violence through nonresistance, challenging our acceptance of the politics of empire, and demonstrating love. The dramas of Holy Week—Palm Sunday, Maundy Thursday, and Good Friday—all suggest that resisting the temptation to violence by maintaining steadfast love of enemies is at the heart of the Christian story. Contrary to Bob Dylan's line, the world is ruled by the sharing of the Father's self-giving love, not violence. And yet violence (or the threat of violence) from American military forces undergirds the current global system.

Informal Empire = Hegemony

While that last sentence may sound like a radical, anti-American claim, even the 2002 version of *The National Security Strategy of the United States* document started from the premise that "today, the United States enjoys a position of unparalleled military strength and great economic and political influence."[6] Thomas Friedman says that the U.S. "today is the world's great geopolitical shaper."[7] American hegemony in a unipolar world is a truism among sober-minded political scientists who seek to understand the dynamics of the current global order more through an empirical, value-free approach than through partisan rants.[8] They offer a great deal of evidence to demonstrate that the globalization processes that we experience today reflect the globalization of U.S. military power after World War II, just as the previous wave of globalization in the nineteenth century reflected the dominance of British military power on a global

---

5. Buechner, *Wishful Thinking*, 83.

6. *National Security Strategy of the United States*.

7. Friedman, *Lexus and the Olive Tree*, 204.

8. Thayer and Layne, *American Empire*; Nexon and Wright, "What's at Stake in the American Empire Debate"; Bacevich, *American Empire*.

scale.[9] "These power relations and exercises of statecraft," writes Robert Hunter Wade, "are obscured in the current talk about globalization."[10] It turns out that the age of American hegemonic dominance, especially its unipolar dominance since the end of the Cold War, is similar to the age of the British Empire, in which the power of the British Navy put down all rivals.[11] Recently, the description of the United States as an Empire has gone public, with mainstream publications such as *U.S. News and World Report* picking up the theme as a cover story and popular authors drawing parallels to Rome.[12] Conservative authors such as Niall Ferguson, Michael Mandelbaum, and Deepak Lal have now openly advanced the argument that American imperialism benefits the world, along with liberal internationalists such as Michael Ignatieff.[13] Their views interestingly converge, then, with the views of radical critics such as Noam Chomsky or Michael Hardt and Antoni Negri.[14] It seems we can all agree that U.S. military power—its ability to inflict or threaten deadly force across the globe—is a central element in today's globalization system.

But we need to consider two disputes about how to interpret this central element of agreement. The first dispute is about whether this military and political dominance is truly an empire or a form of hegemonic dominance. Defining my terms carefully, I argue that U.S. dominance is mostly the latter. A formal empire directly controls other political units while hegemony or informal empire exerts domination by pervasively shaping the system in which those units operate. Therefore, the degree of control over the subordinate units is greater in an empire, whereas hegemony allows those units some freedom of maneuver to ally with others, although within a larger power structure that is dominated by the hegemonic power.[15] While empire is more open in its control, hegemony

9. Keohane and Nye, "Globalization," point out that World War II and the Cold War were high points of military globalization, defined as transcontinental contact between militaries.

10. Wade, "America's Empire Rules an Unbalanced World," 131.

11. Friedman, *Lexus and the Olive Tree*, xvi–13, starts with the end of the Cold War as the rise of globalization as the new metaphor governing foreign policy.

12. Tolson, "New American Empire?" 35–40; Ricks, "Empire or Not?"; Murphy, *Are We Rome?*

13. Ferguson, "Empire Slinks Bank"; Ferguson, *Colossus*; Mandelbaum, *Case for Goliath*; Lal, *In Praise of Empires*, 205–16; and Ignatieff, "Burden," 23ff.

14. Chomsky, *Hegemony or Survival*; Hardt and Negri, *Empire*.

15. These distinctions are honed by Nexon and Wright, "What's at Stake." Also see Watson, *Evolution of International Society*, 15–16; Ferguson, *Colossus*, 9–13.

is more veiled. Empire constitutes others' very existence while hegemony manipulates existing others within a system structured in line with the power of the hegemon. Empire dictates the cultural and political options, whereas hegemony leaves small spaces for alternatives. Empire controls both the domestic and foreign policy of the smaller units, while hegemony is content to dominate foreign policy.[16] But make no mistake: hegemony is a form of informal empire that does dominate others through coercion. Slavoj Žižek says, "The problem with today's America is not that it is a new global empire but that it is not one. That is, while pretending to be an empire, it continues to act like a nation-state, ruthlessly pursuing its interests."[17] This behavior is fully compatible with hegemony.

In general, then, informal empire or hegemony describes most of the United States' role in globalization, whereas the term empire applies better in those places where the United States maintains military occupation and the control of local politics within those places (e.g., Japan and South Korea in the past or Iraq until recently).[18] Indeed, British historian Niall Ferguson's stated concern is that Americans are too weak-willed to practice empire in Iraq or elsewhere in the British style.[19] But most political scientists who advance the "hegemonic stability theory" easily accept the term hegemony, arguing that the U.S. created an "open" trading system after World War II to serve its own security and economic interests.[20] In other words, like the Roman and British empires before it, the *Pax Americana* hinges on its military power being globalized in a hegemonic form, and a decline in that power presages a decline of the system.[21] Unlike those empires, however, the United States has fewer imperial clients or territories, and it often exercises a subtler form of hegemonic control. Few serious students of globalization question that the global system is backed up by U.S. military power, by far the most

16. Lal, *In Praise*, 205.

17. Žižek, "Denying the Facts," 17.

18. Johnson, *Blowback*, makes a strong historical case for the past existence of an American empire in East Asia.

19. Ferguson, "Empire Slinks Back"; Ferguson, *Colossus*, 288–89, also mentions reluctance in North Korea and Liberia.

20. Among others, see Krasner, "State Power," 317–47; Gilpin, *War and Change*; Gilpin, *Global Political Economy*, 93–102; and Ikenberry, *After Victory*, 163–214.

21. Ikenberry, "Globalization as American Hegemony." Also see Friedman, *Lexus and the Olive Tree*, 381–82, 463–68.

powerful military force on the globe.[22] Friedman reveals the true colors of this hegemonic globalization system when he writes,

> Sustainable globalization requires a stable power structure, and no country is more essential than the United States. . . . The hidden hand of the market will never work without a hidden fist. Markets function and flourish only when property rights are secure and can be enforced, which, in turn, requires a political framework protected and backed by military power. . . . Indeed, McDonald's cannot flourish without McDonnell Douglas, the designer of the U.S. Air Force F-15. And the hidden fist that keeps the world safe for Silicon Valley's technologies to flourish is called the U.S. Army, Navy, and Marine Corps.[23]

Friedman unashamedly brings this fist out into the open so we can all see it. It's no longer hidden.

But this raises another dispute over the military-backed hegemonic power of the United States in the system: Is it a benign force? Friedman asserts that "America truly is the ultimate benign hegemon and reluctant enforcer."[24] There is *some* truth to the idea of "benign" leadership. After all, since World War II, the United States understood its longer-run self interest and thus helped reconstruct the devastated lands of Germany and Japan, while creating collaborative institutions with its allies that promoted growing economies and fostered stability.[25] Yet these same institutions—notably the International Monetary Fund, the World Bank, and the World Trade Organization—not only solidified U.S. power but also contributed to violent change in the developing world, as we will see in the next chapter.[26] From the standpoint of Holy Week and the love at the heart of the Christian story, we must question whether domination can ever be "benign" and whether violence can ever be justified. American hegemony may also be less selfless than Friedman wants it to sound. One scholar notes that the current system—based on free capital mobility and the dollar as the international reserve currency—"frees the

---

22. In addition to Ikenberry, "Globalization," see Harvey, *Spaces of Hope*, 68–69.

23. Friedman, *Lexus and the Olive Tree*, 464.

24. Ibid., 467.

25. Ikenberry, *After Victory*; Ikenberry, "Globalization as American Hegemony;" Gilpin, *Global Political Economy*, 93–102.

26. On the mixed picture for these institutions, see Woods, *Globalizers*. On violence, see Harder, "Violence of Global Marketization"; and McGrew, "Organized Violence."

American government of constraints while constraining everyone else."[27] The U.S. government, for instance, has been able print dollars freely without suffering from exchange rate depreciation, since so many people hold the dollar as a reserve currency and so many people invest in the United States. (Other countries would suffer as foreigners would abandon their currencies when inflation would set in.) And "reluctant" seems an odd characterization for a state whose intelligence or security forces intervened in Korea in 1950, Iran in 1953, Guatemala in 1954, Lebanon in 1958, Cuba in 1961, the Dominican Republic in 1965, Laos, Cambodia, and Vietnam from 1954 to 1973, Chile in 1973, Nicaragua and Afghanistan throughout the 1980s, Lebanon in 1983, Grenada in 1983, Libya in 1985, Panama in 1989, Somalia in 1992, Haiti in 1994, Bosnia in 1995, Serbia and Kosovo in 1999, Afghanistan again in 2001, and Iraq from 1991 to the present—to name only a sampling of the best-known interventions.[28]

To take this last case, conservative Christians often defend the Iraq war as an exercise of power for the good, for the spread of freedom. But there is a clash between the politics of Jesus and the politics of empire. This becomes clear if we look at a rousing defense of American imperialism in August 2005 offered by a professor of humanities at Liberty University:

> Imperialism has received bad press for most of the last hundred years. We think of pith helmets when we hear the word, and tiger hunts, and pathetic little bands in remote Indian provinces playing "God Save the King." We think of a stiff upper lip that looks, over time, more like foolish bravado than noble resolve. We think of colonial hubris and the blind assertion of cultural superiority. But ancient Rome—always the brand name in empires—is the better model.[29]

Ah yes, the good old days of Rome, such a good example for early Christians of "political stability, the rule of law, political enfranchisement, preservation of learning and the arts, respect for other cultures and religions"![30] Because the United States is fighting in Iraq for "ideals of freedom and dignity," contends this professor, we should defend this

---

27. Wade, "America's Empire," 131.

28. On Iran, Guatemala, Vietnam, Chile, Grenada, Panama, Afghanistan, and Iraq, see Kinzer, *Overthrow*, 111–299.

29. Babcock, "If This Be Imperialism."

30. Ibid.

kind of imperialism.[31] While the morality of the war is a worthy subject of debate, an argument for the benign effects of imperialism at the very least creates some cognitive dissonance with the story of Holy Week. If this story is indeed at the center of the Christian story and the gospel narratives, we should at least pause before following an argument that leans on Rome as a positive example, since Jesus was executed under the power and authority of Rome. Yet he overcame Rome's violence through a non-resistance that should challenge our acceptance of the politics of Empire and hegemony—the very politics of the "hidden fist" that Friedman embraces so openly. Not surprisingly, Friedman supported breaking Iraq's "regime open, like a walnut" in order to induce "regime change," "regime transformation," and democratization.[32]

But Holy Week demonstrates that the most significant political transformation in history occurred through the holy absorption of violence by the chosen one, the suffering servant. Instead of inflicting violence out of (misdirected) love, he was the afflicted one who suffered for the sake of love. And thus the Kingdom is the kingdom of the donkey, the wash-basin, the crown of thorns, and open, nail-scarred hands. Although the main point of Jesus' politics was with "the reauthorizing of Israel rather than with the deauthorizing of Rome," "the dawning rule of God" came through the suffering King.[33] Challenging Rome's empire was not the purpose of the Kingdom, but the politics of suffering love necessarily drew a contrast between the military dominance of Rome and the dawning Kingdom. The new Kingdom was framed outside the "imperial framing narrative," to show another way of politics, the true way.[34]

Re-Enacting the Drama of Holy Week

Palm Sunday marks both the end of Lent and the beginning of the Passion Week. For the purposes of this book, it fits well in the latter role, despite the day's absence from the earliest liturgies of the church. In fact,

31. Ibid.

32. Friedman, *Longitudes and Attitudes*, 215, 272.

33. O'Donovan, *Desire of the Nations*, 117. O'Donovan steers a path between Horsley, *Jesus and Empire*, 55–127, who is in danger of reducing Jesus to an anti-Roman, non-violent insurgent, and Bryan, *Render to Caesar*, 39–64, who is in danger of making Jesus apolitical.

34. McLaren, *Everything Must Change*, 83–86, 158–59. Also see O'Donovan, *Desire of the Nations*, 119.

the establishment of a week-long pilgrimage to Jerusalem dates from the fourth century onward, whereas the three days of Holy (or Maundy) Thursday, Good Friday, and Easter Sunday were always at the center of the Christian calendar, paralleling the significance of the Passover setting in a new paschal mystery.[35] As the *Catechism of the Catholic Church* puts it, the Passion-Easter mystery of these three days (called the Triduum) is the "most solemn of all feasts," the center of the Christian year.[36] But in choosing to focus on the week, I hew more closely to Eastern Orthodox tradition, which tends to treat Holy Week as a coherent unit beginning with Palm Sunday or even Lazarus Saturday the day before. Interestingly, most of the services in Orthodox Passion Week are evening services, prayed in advance of the day they are to commemorate, leading one Orthodox co-worker of mine to suggest that the rhythm of the services —praying matins services, which are normally sung in the morning, in the evening—reverses the normal patterns of worship during this week. Quite literally, time is turned upside-down for those who keep these vigils throughout the week.[37] This feast moves around in the solar calendar. The paschal cycle is the only major Christian holiday without a fixed date in the Gregorian and Julian calendars, instead depending upon the Jewish lunar calendar—a constant reminder of the Passover context for these events. As with Passover, the entire week re-enacts a story of liberation and deliverance that calls us out from under the politics of power, hegemony, and empire—just as the Hebrew slaves were called out of the Egyptian empire and called to cross the Red Sea.[38] Although the liberation and deliverance from sin and bondage is a richer, deeper mystery than just this political liberation, there is no question that the political liberation of the faithful community is an important part of what Jesus enacted in this week, part of understanding the story of redemption as a parallel to the Exodus. The church is the covenant community liberated to serve a new politics centered in this week.

35. Nardone, *Story of the Christian Year*, 21–27; Cobb, "History," 459–63; Dix, *Shape of the Liturgy*, 337–60.

36. Catholic Church, *Catechism of the Catholic Church*, section 1163, p. 329.

37. Thanks to Barb Moginot for this comment.

38. For Old Testament parallels, see Brueggemann, "Always in the Shadow of Empire."

Palm Sunday: Humility Leads to Exaltation

In the traditional liturgical churches in the West, the day is marked with a processional that begins outside the church building, while in evangelical churches it is often marked by children re-enacting the palm-waving crowds watching Jesus march into Jerusalem on a donkey. As anyone retelling the story of Palm Sunday knows, the key to understanding it is its apocalyptic political context at the edge of the Roman Empire, amid heightened expectations on the part of Jesus' Jewish followers that the revolution against Roman oppression will now begin. All four gospels quote the crowds Jerusalem reciting the messianic passage from Psalm 118: "Blessed is the one who comes in the name of the Lord" (v. 26). In the liturgical processional, portions of this Psalm are read and the people wave palm branches while one of the synoptic accounts of the march into Jerusalem is read. But this action puts churchgoers in an awkward place, the position of those followers who praised Jesus because they thought of him as a conventional liberator. Although some that day in Jerusalem must have experienced dissonance, since this King entered on a donkey, and not a glorious white horse, the text suggests the crowd is not being ironic. Like those followers, though, we often sing on this day the words of the famous hymn, "All Glory, Laud, and Honor to Thee, Redeemer King." Yet we re-enactors know that this King is entering Jerusalem to meet his death at the hands of those threatened by this new Kingdom. We know, as preachers have long pointed out, that the political domain Jesus is establishing in Jerusalem is not the conventional one that his followers imagined. We also know that many of those in the original crowd were surprised by the Kingdom that did come. We know that he was founding a new Kingdom in Zion, but it was a Kingdom built on marginalized communities rooted in humility, self-sacrifice, and love. These are strange materials on which to found a Kingdom, but they were intended to be the basis for a new community of Zion centered on the Temple that Jesus promised to rebuild in three days—the body of the broken Christ. If we re-enact the story rightly and embody it, we will experience some of this dissonance—this gap between the kind of politics that the world expects and the kind of politics practiced in the Kingdom. This week calls us to attend to the embodiment of this politics, and right at the start, re-enacting the Palm Sunday story ushers us into the mystery of the founding of this strange domain.[39] As Joyce Ann Zimmerman puts it, in Palm Sunday "we are beckoned to enter into the passion events; Jesus acts and we are saved. Only by giving ourselves over to the Cross can we enter with him into glory."[40] Only by joining Jesus on this journey of humility that brings glory can we begin to grasp the paradox of the "upside-down kingdom" that is God's Kingdom.[41]

The journey is one of loneliness and self-emptying, but this journey of sacrifice is precisely what brings glory to the King. We can see the loneliness in the Orthodox icon of Palm Sunday, in which Jesus sits forlornly on the donkey, looking back at his disciples who are on the left side of the icon. On the right side of the icon is the crowd, while a tiny child ducks directly underneath the donkey to lay down a palm branch and a cloak. We can already see the betrayal in the air; the disciples will soon turn away and so will the crowds and the children. This image of loneliness also reflects the readings for the day in the Western lectionary —readings which point us forward to the events to come, in which God will paradoxically be humiliated and therefore glorified. Framing the entry into Jerusalem, the servant song in Isa 50:4–9 is read every year, including the powerful image of one who faced disgrace and dishonor: "I gave my back to those who struck me, and my cheeks to those who pulled out the beard; I did not hide my face from insult and spitting . . . I have set my face like flint. . . ." (v. 6–7a). We listeners instinctively apply these images to Jesus on the lowly donkey, thinking ahead to the events of the coming week.

But these images are given fuller meaning by the Christology of Paul in Phil 2:5–11, which the Western liturgical church also reads every year on this day. Paul, of course, encourages the church at Philippi to think in the same way as Jesus, "who, though he was in the form of God, did not regard equality with God as something to be exploited, but emptied himself, taking the form of a slave, being born in human likeness" (v. 6–7). Stephen Fowl, in his commentary on Philippians, interprets these profound verses to mean that "in refusing to use his participation in the glory of the God of Israel to his own advantage and adopting, instead, the disposition of self-emptying, which includes incarnation, obedience,

39. The influence of Yoder, *Politics of Jesus*, is evident in this framing.

40. Zimmerman, *Liturgy as Living Faith*, 119.

41. Kraybill, *Upside-Down Kingdom*. Although Kraybill does not dwell on the significance of the Palm Sunday story (only mentioning it on 59), it fits his larger thesis.

crucifixion, and ultimately exaltation, Christ is actually displaying the form of God, making God's glory manifest to humans."[42] Therefore, "the best way to think of Christ's manifestation of the glory of God is in terms of Christ's beautiful body, a beauty that is not diminished but enhanced by taking on the 'form' of a slave."[43] We experience God's fullness, then, through participation in his self-emptying love; we observe his beauty through the ugliness of his appearance as a stricken, smitten, and downtrodden slave; we glimpse his exalted Kingdom through his abject humiliation. An upside-down Kingdom is already coming through the emptying of God-in-Christ. As John Howard Yoder puts it, "[Our] willingness to suffer is . . . not merely a test of our patience or a dead space of waiting; it is itself a participation in the character of God's victorious patience with the rebellious powers of creation."[44] Palm Sunday gives us a glimpse of the pain and humiliation that is to come, but it is pain that we must enter. "Mercifully grant that we may walk in the way of his suffering," goes the *Book of Common Prayer* collect for the day.[45]

The Neglected Days: Weakness and Shame Bring Exaltation

The Monday, Tuesday, and Wednesday of Holy Week are largely neglected in the Western church. Public worship services are rare on these days. However, the lectionary does prescribe the public reading of several texts that reinforce this theme of humiliation bringing glory and exaltation. Typically the church reads two of the servant songs of Isaiah (Isa 42:1–9 on Monday, and Isa 49:1–7 on Tuesday) before returning to Isa 50:4–9 again on Wednesday. Read along with the epistle and gospel texts, these images of a suffering messiah suggest that the heart of God's kingdom is found in a suffering love that looks contemptible by conventional human standards. For this reason, Paul identifies the cross as a "stumbling block to Jews and foolishness to Gentiles" (1 Cor 1:23). It is frankly embarrassing to think that God suffered from so much human mockery, and yet that seems to be the key to the inauguration of the glory of the Kingdom. As Paul puts it, "God chose what is foolish in the world to shame the wise; God chose what is weak in the world to shame the strong; God

---

42. Fowl, *Philippians*, 96.

43. Ibid., 94.

44. Yoder, *Politics of Jesus*, 209.

45. Episcopal Church, *Book of Common Prayer*, 219.

chose what is low and despised in the world, things that are not, to reduce to nothing things that are, so that no one might boast in the presence of God. (1 Cor 1:27–29). As the author of Hebrews says, Jesus not only endured the shame of the cross but even endured the shame of "hostility against himself from sinners" (Heb 12:3).

How can such shame bring glory to the divine? The assigned gospel readings from John suggest that in the passion story there is a close connection between self-giving shame and ascendant glory. The first scandalous and shameful event is to be re-enacted on Monday, when Mary the sister of Martha anoints the feet of Jesus with perfume and tears.[46] In first century Palestine, a woman who uncovered her hair was making a sexually provocative gesture, perhaps offering additional context for Judas' hostile reaction.[47] But Jesus redeemed this moment of shame by labeling it a pre-figuration of his being anointed at his burial (John 12:1–8). On Tuesday, we hear Jesus' strange response to some Greeks who were in Jerusalem for Passover. Told of their request to meet him, Jesus says, "The hour has come for the Son of Man to be glorified. Very truly, I tell you, unless a grain of wheat falls into the earth and dies, it remains just a single grain; but if it dies, it bears much fruit" (John 12:23–24). Death is looming. Right in the midst of the subsequent discourse on losing one's life, Jesus is glorified, as John tells it: "Then a voice came from heaven, 'I have glorified it, and I will glorify it again'" (John 12:28). In case we have missed the point, Jesus goes on to say, "and I, when I am lifted up from the earth, will draw all people to myself" (v. 32). John editorializes that Jesus said this "to indicate the kind of death he was to die" (v. 33). However, it is also a pre-figuration of the Ascension and a reminder that we cannot separate "Christ in his humiliation and Christ in his exaltation."[48] Abject humiliation is the way to the glory of the Father's Kingdom—a pattern that continues to the cross.[49]

46. Interestingly, on Tuesday evening, the Eastern church celebrates Luke's account of the sinful woman anointing Jesus' feet at Simon the Pharisee's house (Luke 7:36–50).

47. I owe this insight to Kenneth Bailey's commentary on the parallel story of Luke 7:36–50 in its cultural context. See Bailey, *Jesus Through Middle Eastern Eyes*, 248–50.

48. Farrow, *Ascension and Ecclesia*, 222. After I wrote this section, I discovered through Farrow that Kierkegaard concludes his book *Practice in Christianity* "with a series of seven expositions of John 12:32" (222) on the humiliation-exaltation link.

49. The pattern is also evident in the collects for these days in the *Book of Common Prayer*, 220. On Monday, we address the Son who "went not up to joy but first he suffered pain, and entered not into glory before he was crucified." On Tuesday, we pray, "Grant

Holy Thursday: Footwashing, Not Swords

On this day, writes Robert Webber, "we pass with Jesus into the darkness of his last night, a darkness that will tremble with evil forces—the betrayal, the arrest, the scourging, and his ultimate death on the cross." Webber continues, "This is a difficult night, a dark night of the soul in which the determination of Jesus to go to the cross is set in vivid contrast to the powers of evil against which he must struggle. We must walk that path with him."[50] If the pattern holds, we must enter into this darkness in order to experience glorification. We must experience the loss of power that is the path to true power in order to find the true politics of the Kingdom that re-imagines hegemony.

Observances on this day cluster around three events in the gospel narratives. First is the Last Supper meal, set in a Passover context by the reading from Exodus 12 which institutes the practices of recalling the liberation from Egypt. We also read Paul's words of institution from 1 Corinthians 11 on Holy Thursday: "The Lord Jesus on the night when he was betrayed took a loaf of bread, and when he had given thanks, he broke it and said, 'This is my body that is for you. Do this in remembrance of me.' In the same way he took the cup also, after supper, saying, 'This cup is the new covenant in my blood'" (v. 23–25). We are thus reminded of how the meal that embodies the glory of God comes on this dark night, "the night when he was betrayed." While we might experience great joy in the meal during the year, partaking on this night puts us in the position of Judas and the rest of the disciples, who abandoned him. We re-experience a taste of our distance from Jesus and we imagine how lonely it must have been to sup with sinners like us—not to mention wash their feet—when they are about to abandon him.

Foot washing is the second Maundy Thursday event (with "Maundy" coming from the Latin *mandatum* or command, referring to the command that Jesus gave to his disciples to wash feet and love each other).[51] John says that during the supper Jesus got up, took off his robe, tied a towel around his waist, poured water into a basin, and washed his disci-

---

us so to glory in the cross of Christ that we may gladly suffer shame and loss. . . ." On Wednesday, "Give us grace to accept joyfully the sufferings of the present time, confident of the glory that shall be revealed."

50. Webber, *Ancient-Future Time*, 126.

51. Both York, "Dirty Basins, Dirty Disciples, and Beautiful Crosses," 11–18, and Nation, "Washing Feet," make strong cases for footwashing as a binding liturgical practice.

ples' feet. Jesus undertakes a culturally humiliating action, but John again frames it as part of Jesus' participation in the Father, placing these words immediately before Jesus rises to start the washing: "Jesus, knowing that the Father had given all things into his hands, and that he had come from God and was going to God" (13:3). Because Jesus knew the Father, he undertook this calling of love. And it is clear that this practice, rooted in divine participation, is not merely a metaphor or a parable for how to live ethically. "Instead," writes Tripp York, "it is a practice required of all disciples if we are to be followers of Jesus."[52] York elaborates: "Following the lead of its king, Christianity, as a political culture, operates on a politics characterized by love of one's enemies, forgiveness of sins and, among other things, the humbling act of washing one another's feet."[53] Not only does Jesus humiliate himself, invading a personal space that our own culture resists violating, but he also washes the feet of Judas, the enemy who is about to betray him and the disciples who will soon abandon him. Furthermore, he takes on the "tools of a slave" by doing work only women and servants would normally do, and he constitutes a new community when he says to his disciples that "you also ought to wash one another's feet" (John 13:14).[54] He is calling all disciples to a life of service in a community without hierarchy, a life of downward mobility and service to each other that brings glory to the ones who serve, suffer, and give their lives for others in imitation of their king.

This call to service through an alternative community is the call to the Kingdom, but it also causes a clash with the powers that be. "That God's kingdom has come near threatens those powers that refuse God's authority. Such powers (what are essentially rival kingdoms) tend to respond disapprovingly. Kingdoms of the earth demand complete and total allegiance."[55] Donald Kraybill suggests that there were four alternative approaches to politics in Jesus' time: a Sadduceean option that "cooperated extensively with the Roman occupation," a Pharisaical option of "proper religion," an Essene option of monastic withdrawal, and "the righteous revolutionary violence of the Zealots." By practicing "the politics of the basin," Jesus takes a rather unusual approach: a fifth political

52. York, "Dirty Basins," 13.

53. Ibid., 14.

54. Ibid.

55. Ibid., 15.

option.[56] This option helps land Jesus in trouble, just as it might land the church in trouble when it challenges the self-serving power politics of hegemony. "Such politics is not at home in this world and we should not expect it to be publicly acceptable—though this makes it no less public. . . . We also must remember what happened to our king: Jesus, because he washed our feet, became a slaughtered Lamb."[57] The nascent disciple-ship community is about to be crushed and dispersed by force and in-timidation, the chosen tools of dominant powers. Will it survive? Can it survive today?

A third Holy Thursday event is often re-enacted in private devotion or during vigils, and it is also central to understanding the politics of Jesus. John's narrative, the focus of the lectionary, glosses over the agony in Gethsemane, but the synoptic accounts heighten the drama, in which Jesus suffers great anguish while his closest disciples sleep in the garden near him (Matt 26:36–36; Mark 14:32–42; Luke 22:39–46). What is the anguish all about? What was so tempting (besides the obvious desire to avoid suffering)? Yoder suggests that Jesus' own will was to take the easy way out—the zealot way of grasping power with the sword. "Once more Jesus sees this option as a real temptation."[58] When Peter pulls out a sword and cuts off the ear of the high priestly delegation, Jesus rebukes him and denies that he is leading a rebellion (Matt 26:52–55; Mark 14:43–51; Luke 22:47–53; John 18:11). Instead, Jesus overcame the temptation to grasp power and willingly took on the roles of suffering servant and Passover lamb. And if disciples are to emulate Jesus, they too are called to follow their savior, servant, and lamb. The church is to decline the easy solutions of power and coercion in its journey toward being glorified by God. Its members are to die to the temptations to achieve their goals with power and to rise to the new life of practicing love, service, and reconciliation. To learn this, we need to walk the dark path with Jesus.

Good Friday: The King Abandoned

Good Friday is the darkest day of the Christian calendar, yet we also glimpse some joy in "knowing that his death was the death of death, the

---

56. Kraybill, *Upside-Down Kingdom*, 291.

57. York, "Dirty Basins," 15.

58. Yoder, *Politics of Jesus*, 45–48, quote at 48.

ruination of the powers of evil."[59] By entering into the depth of the suffering and the death of the Suffering Servant, however, we re-experience our own baptismal sinking into death. In order to appreciate being raised to life, we must experience death and grief ourselves. Joyce Ann Zimmerman points out that on this day we enter "a soteriological moment without an eschatological counterpart." [60] That is, we experience the saving death but without the joy of its ultimate meaning for history; we experience the humiliation without tasting the glorification. Or, as Zimmerman puts it, "Good Friday is a prolonged entry into the 'not yet' of redemption. This liturgy leaves us hungry for the hope that only life can bring. Death has its sting."[61]

However, the lectionary reading from John hints that death does not have the final word; Jesus is still King, even in disgrace—giving us a glimpse of the hope that we will find in the cross, the hope that the Lamb who is slain will still be worthy to take the throne of the Lion of Judah. Pilate asks Jesus if he is the King of the Jews, and Jesus replies: "My kingdom is not from this world. If my kingdom were from this world, my followers would be fighting to keep me from being handed over to the Jews. But as it is, my kingdom is not from here." Pilate asks Jesus if he is a king and Jesus answers, "You say that I am a king. For this I was born, and for this I came into the world, to testify to the truth" (John 18:36–37). When the soldiers humiliate him with a crown of thorns and a purple cloak, we see this king humiliated by the power of imperial Rome. Yet Roman power and authority, vested in Pilate, is challenged by Jesus. Pilate asks him, "Where are you from?" (John 19:9). But Jesus does not answer.

"Do you refuse to speak to me?" asks Pilate. "Do you not know that I have power to release you, and power to crucify you?" Jesus answers him, "You would have no power over me unless it had been given you from above" (John 19:10–11). In this contest of power and authority, John makes a political statement, making it clear that political authority is in the hand of the true King. Pilate then says to the crowd outside, "Here is your King" (v. 14b). But the crowd rejects him and calls for him to be crucified. "Pilate asked them, 'Shall I crucify your King?' The chief priests answered, 'We have no king but the emperor'" (v. 15). The contrast with the politics of Jesus could not be clearer, since he is a king who lays claim

59. Webber, *Ancient-Future Time*, 130.

60. Zimmerman, *Liturgy as Living Faith*, 121.

61. Ibid.

to that office through the politics of gentle firmness rather than the politics of accommodation with the emperor. At this moment, John shows the bankruptcy of leaders who would ally with the hegemonic power to advance their agendas. Yet Pilate is also a vehicle for the divine agenda, since he ironically insists again that Jesus is a king, posting a sign on the cross proclaiming Jesus as the King of the Jews and enigmatically telling the protesting Jewish leaders that "What I have written I have written" (v. 22). Jesus is a king. Thus, as Jesus goes through the process of being crucified, he goes as a lamb to the slaughter who is also crowned a king, the model for all martyrs who follow in his path. As such martyrs suffer, they are called to say also, as Jesus did on the cross: "Father, forgive them; for they do not know what they are doing" (Luke 23:34). Jesus might have called down the force of heaven to escape and coerce his Kingdom into being, but he chooses to die as a political rebel against Roman authority.

This yields a profound political lesson at the heart of Good Friday, about love for enemies even when they are killing you. David Augsburger summarizes it when he writes, "Nonviolence is right not because it works but because it is the way of Jesus. It anticipates the triumph of the Lamb that was slain. It reveals the heart of God."[62] But Good Friday does not merely provide a salutary ethical model. It also re-enacts the profound mystery of exaltation coming through love that goes through humiliation. Yoder suggests that the cross fulfills the promise of the glory of the kingdom coming, precisely in its suffering love. "Here at the cross is the man who loves his enemies, the man whose righteousness is greater than that of the Pharisees, who being rich became poor, who gives his robe to those who took his cloak, who prays for those who despitefully use him. The cross is not a detour or a hurdle on the way to the kingdom, nor is it even the way to the kingdom; it is the kingdom come."[63] In such divine love, we find the hope of a new Kingdom and thus the ability to live an alternative politics to the politics of hegemony. As Buechner puts it, "Jesus didn't forgive his executioners on principle but because in some unimaginable way he was able to love them."[64]

We re-enactors know that the Resurrection is coming, so we are not trapped on the dark path. We also know that the hope of the Kingdom is found not merely in the practices of footwashing, nonviolence, and love

62. Augsburger, *Dissident Discipleship*, 138.

63. Yoder, *Politics of Jesus*, 51.

64. Buecher, *Wishful Thinking*, 88.

of enemies. These practices must be completed in the larger economy of divine love and thus an alternative politics does not depend upon our power. Rather, we must see the cross in the larger story of God's activity, into which we are called to participate, the story of God's love, which moves from humiliation to exaltation. Douglas Knight writes, "The resurrection demonstrated the cross to be the enthronement and exaltation of the God of Israel over his enemies." [65] The cross is thus "the true beginning of time. The reconciliation of God and humankind in this event is the beginning that corresponds to the end God has prepared."[66] Or as N. T. Wright puts it: "Good Friday is the point at which God enters into our chaos, to be there with us in the middle of it and to bring his new creation."[67]

The ultimate mystery of the cross comes when Jesus says "it is finished" and gives up his last breath, the point of abandonment and utter emptiness (John 19:30). Yet that mystery challenges the church to live differently, to re-tell this story through its witness and martyrdom (the root word in the Greek is the same). As York writes,

> Precisely in the moment of rejection, martyrs are at their best because they imitate Christ in his moment of rejection. In this moment of rejection, of a feeling of abandonment that even Jesus weathers, the ultimate gift is given: the redemption of creation through the slaughtered lamb. The martyrs retell this story with their deaths, placing themselves out of any narrative that would call them victims, for they are blessed with the opportunity to participate in the perpetual gift-giving exchange that occurs between God and God's creation.[68]

Can we imagine such gift-giving and the retelling of Good Friday happening in our own day? Could the church nurture martyrs who retell the story of Good Friday? They would certainly help us re-imagine hegemony by witnessing to an alternative politics of self-sacrificing love that transcends the politics of coercion and fear.

---

65. Knight, *Eschatalogical Economy*, 135.
66. Ibid., 136.
67. Wright, *Christians at the Cross*, 58.
68. York, *Purple Crown*, 148.

Re-imagining U.S. Global Hegemony

The story of Holy Week helps us re-imagine the politics of global hegemony in four ways. First, we learn that Jesus and his followers are to practice an unconventional politics of an upside-down Kingdom, a surprising politics of humility and self-giving, a politics that might appear upside-down in conventional political terms but that is revealing the grain of history in reality. After all, the church claims to find the center of history in the events of this week. On Palm Sunday, we recall Jesus riding on a humble donkey. On the next three days, we recall how humiliation leads to exaltation. On Holy Thursday, we recall the politics of the washbasin and towel. On Friday, we enter darkness and death. On Saturday we wait (more on this later). These days demand the specific community-forming practices of self-emptying (riding donkeys rather than white horses), accepting shame and humiliation as the path to glorification (seeing abandonment and betrayal as a way to glory), practicing selfless service (washing feet), sacrificing one's life (even to the point of death), and waiting expectantly even when hope has vanished. All these practices constitute the politics of Jesus and the politics of the church, communal signs that bear witness to the social reality of the Kingdom and that require social embodiment in groups of disciples who are willing, literally, to wash each other's feet. As the Mennonite historian John Roth has put it, such practices of communal service are "parables of the kingdom," pointing the way toward its final triumph while participating in its anticipation already.

When the church practices this kind of politics, it is telling the world of the Powers, "This is the direction that the world is headed someday, even though our work looks tiny and futile right now." It may look tiny and futile now, but the church is living with an eye to how the story of this week fits in the larger story of God, in which the church plays a far more significant role than the state. "The meaning of history—and therefore the significance of the state—lies in the creation and the work of the church," writes John Howard Yoder.[69] As Yoder puts it, specifically discussing the cross, "God's intervention, not human progress, is the vindication of human obedience."[70] Thus, a Christian political ethic requires "being longsighted, not shortsighted; it means trusting God to triumph

69. Yoder, *Christian Witness to the State*, 13.

70. Yoder, *Original Revolution*, 66.

through the cross."[71] So while it may be unclear how a politics of foot washing, sacrifice, and love of enemies can ever work in a world dominated by coercive military power, the storyline trusted by the church is that obedience, even to the point of death on a cross is the way to exaltation (Phil 2:8–9). Such a storyline empowers the church to act without fear, expecting downward mobility.

Second, then, we learn to re-imagine the politics of hegemony from the perspective of a lonely politics that means "setting one's face like flint" (Isa 50:7) toward the suffering ahead, walking through loneliness, facing shame, entering darkness, and suffering great pain. Yet, as the story has it, all this suffering brings glory. Jesus is still a king through it all, indeed he is King *because* of it all. From the story we learn to walk through pain and suffering inflicted upon us by the Powers in order to arrive at the glorification that comes from God.[72] It will not be popular to dissent from the politics of hegemony, but unpopularity will be necessary if witness to the Holy Week story is to be sustained. Here we might recall that the "ladder of the Beatitudes" starts with internal dispositions but culminates in outward manifestations of faithful activity that bring the disciple into conflict with the kingdoms of this world: those who make peace and those who are unjustly persecuted for pursuing justice are blessed (Matt 5:9–12). The further one progresses in living out the commitment to the new kingdom, the more one is called into actions that bring conflict with the old kingdoms of power and domination.[73] Disciples are called to seek peace and to face persecution for the sake of witnessing to Jesus' reign, and in this there is blessing and glory.

Thankfully, however, it is not up to heroic individuals alone to imitate Christ; the church forms communities that can alleviate some of the loneliness of resistance to hegemony. At the same time, we must be attentive to the ways in which even the church can be co-opted by power, as the Anabaptist critique of Constantinianism has reminded us. The danger is that the church will lose sight of the loneliness promised to anyone who follows in the footsteps of Jesus and will instead become a chaplain

71. Ibid., 67.

72. This is the central point of Wright, *Christians at the Cross*, which reprints a series of talks given during Holy Week in the depressed ex-coal mining town of Easington Colliery. As he puts it, "But I am convinced that when we bring our own griefs and sorrows within the story of God's own grief and sorrow, and allow them to be held there, God is able to bring healing to us and new possibilities to our lives" (xv).

73. Forest, *Ladder of the Beatitudes*.

to Constantine, Theodosius, or any emperor who promises to put political power at the service of the church. We cannot forget that Jesus refused political power throughout his ministry, but most importantly through his passion.[74] The loneliness of Holy Week offers an analogy for the church's own political path: not cozying up to the power of Rome or Washington but setting one's face toward Jerusalem. At the same time, though, we are called to be a community of disciples that learns not to betray the suffering one.

Third, then, we learn to re-imagine hegemony from a perspective that sees violence as a temptation even for Jesus, and nonviolence as a difficult way that leads to the cross and the forgiveness of those who slaughter the lamb of God. Nonviolence for the church is central to a consistent witness out of the story of Holy Week and central to any challenge to the politics of hegemony and military globalization. Note that this is a question for the Christian community, not an issue of Christian obligations toward the state, nor of the state's proper role. In other words, nonviolence is a central practice of the faith community, but states are understood as "powers and principalities" in this fallen world that will continue to use coercive power.[75] The nettlesome ethical question is about Christian duties toward the political community of the state. Can we serve in the army? Should we pay taxes if we are troubled by the huge amount of government spending on the military? Needless to say, these are crucial and specific ethical questions that flow from our re-imagination of hegemony, but my goal here is not to provide a blueprint toward easy answers on questions that have kept Christian ethicists busy for two millennia now, but rather to help us re-imagine ourselves within the story of Holy Week. We will touch on the edges of such questions in a moment. For now, I want to insist that journeying through Holy Week teaches us that nonviolent witness is central to the witness of the church to a globalized world. The unique role of the church is as a witness to a difficult way: the way of Jesus, the way of the Lamb, the way of love. And this witnessing role necessarily calls us to question our support for the hegemonic power of the United States through a consistent and faithful witness to the divine love that is at the center of the mystery of the cross.

74. Yoder, *Original Revolution*, 59.

75. See Yoder, *Politics of Jesus*, 134–61; Yoder, *Christian Witness to the State*; and Wink, *Powers That Be*.

Fourth, we are reminded that the politics embodied in Holy Week ultimately depends on divine work, on God's economy. If we seek the work of peace or face persecution for the sake of the Kingdom, we do not bless ourselves, but we do receive divine blessing. Likewise, the role of the cross in the divine economy of salvation suggests that success is not up to us and that it is not the mission of the church to succeed in defeating global hegemony. Indeed, the story of the cross is a story of failure from the human perspective: the death of Jesus was not the way the disciples imagined the Kingdom coming. Yet the political Powers failed to crush and disperse the budding community of the church. Both failures were redeemed and woven into the story of God's plan. The disciples abandon Jesus and flee when the Son of God himself is killed. They lose hope, scatter, and go into hiding on Holy Saturday. Yet they would soon find out on the third day that God could redeem even this dead end. This suggests that the church is freed from having always to succeed, since it is not up to us to achieve results. Like Jesus, we are to be faithful even unto death, and we trust that the Father can redeem even our failures. Although we may be called to be martyrs like Archbishop Oscar Romero of El Salvador, we must realize that a successful outcome to the drama is not up to us. It is not our political action that advances the kingdom but only the work of God's love through the church, including its martyrs.

IMPROVISATIONAL RESPONSES TO HEGEMONY

"Often times . . . a resilient basin ministry will . . . land us on a cross," writes York.[76] As footwashing Christians are called into the story enacted in Holy Week, they may challenge those who find U.S. military hegemony as the key to peace. However, because the response of hegemonic power is often to try and crush challenging alternatives, Christians can expect resistance when they seek to live out this story of the Kingdom. They may even be called to the point of martyrdom. At a minimum, however, re-imagining global hegemony through the re-enacted Holy Week story entails taking the risk of challenging the Empire with the good news of a kingdom of reconciliation that is the ultimate meaning of history. What might such improvisational practices look like, especially in relation to the most recent locus of American global hegemony in Iraq?

76. York, "Dirty Basins," 15.

Those practices flow from the four main ways in which the story helps us re-imagine hegemony. First, such a politics will always appear upside-down in the eyes of the world. It will never appear effective to the dominant narratives of hegemonic powers. Yet, in faith, the church nurtures small, mustard seed-style actions of truth-telling and hopeful resistance to hegemony.[77] The dominant narrative of the Iraq War is a story of regime change carried out for greater security for the United States and the promotion of freedom in Iraq. Yet the subsequent occupation suggests that more was happening than this story admits. *Washington Post* reporter Rajiv Chandrasekaran reports that the U.S. occupation authorities' plan for "a fundamental economic restructuring—abandoning Saddam's centrally planned, social-welfare state for a globalized, free-market system—had little resonance on Iraqi streets."[78] Unsurprisingly, U.S. contractors such as the Bechtel Group, Halliburton, KBR, and Blackwater were well-positioned to enter this newly opened system. Meanwhile, the Iraqi government faced U.S. pressure as late as 2008 to pass a law that would open up the Iraqi oil industry to foreign investors. According to a February 2008 UPI report, BP, Chevron, ExxonMobil and Shell were already discussing the first steps of contracts with the Iraqi Oil Ministry, even before the law was passed.[79] By June 2008, even the mainstream media were reporting that unusual no-bid contracts for two years would go to these oil giants, along with the French company Total.[80] This might have been troubling and surprising to me, but not after my students in Bahrain told me a disturbing story about the looting in Baghdad after the fall of Saddam's government that I had never heard before living in the region. Although most public buildings were devastated in the capital, the Oil Ministry was largely untouched. Why? It turned out that troops from the 101st Airborne Division were guarding it closely. But this story was never prominently carried in the American news media, most likely since it didn't fit with the master-storyline of the war, which framed it in terms of "freedom" for the Iraqi people, and it would have posed an uncomfortable truth to those families whose children had died

---

77. I prefer this humbler metaphor from Matt 17:20 to the "moving mountains" metaphor favored by McLaren, *Everything Must Change*, 300–301.

78. Chandrasekaran, *Imperial Life in the Emerald City*, 110.

79. United Press International, "Exxon, Shell."

80. Kramer, "Deals with Iraq."

in service to the cause.[81] The fact that Iraq's oil reserves might amount to 300 billion barrels, "one quarter of the world's oil resources," and that this might have affected U.S. strategy, is an inconvenient fact for the story of freedom, better left omitted.[82]

Because of the master storyline of freedom, the work of the Christian Peacemaker Teams (CPT) in Iraq hardly registered in American media. Yet CPT offers an example of a parable of the upside-down Kingdom, a small effort that looks quixotic through the eyes of the world's Powers. CPT sent a delegation of Christian pacifists into Iraq in 2002 and maintained a presence on the ground throughout the bombing of Baghdad. As with their efforts elsewhere, the CPTers lived out the organization's motto: "getting in the way." This motto does not convey the impression that this work will be effective on the grand scale, and no one is claiming that they will bring peace. Rather, the image "denotes the practice of stepping between aggressors and victims, the practice of challenging structural violence and domination, and the practice of active nonviolence as taught by Jesus."[83] CPT's mission statement says in part that the group seeks "to enlist the response of the whole church in conscientious objection to war, and in the development of nonviolent institutions, skills and training for intervention in conflict situations."[84] Such work seems tiny when compared with the global problems inherent in the U.S. invasion and occupation of Iraq. A dozen or so Westerners "getting in the way" by living daily life within Iraq? Hardly the sort of thing that would set the Powers quaking in their boots. Indeed, most people ignore them.

And yet the formation of CPT offers a small parable of the Kingdom and a model for the kinds of practices that the church can use to improvise in response to global hegemony. CPT started in response to a challenge from Ron Sider at an international conference of Mennonites in France in 1984. While grounding a nonviolent ethic in a theology of Holy Week, he challenged his affluent listeners to actually act upon their pacifist convictions and be willing to die as martyrs for peace. This passage must have helped sparked the imagination of those present:

81. Agence France, "Oil Ministry." For a detailed chronology of western press coverage, see Riedlmayer, "Yes, the Oil Ministry Was Guarded!" Riedlmayer is a bibliographer of Islamic art and architecture at Harvard University's Fine Art Library.

82. Holt, "It's the Oil."

83. Brown, "Christian Peacemaker Teams," 14.

84. CPT Founding Conference, "Mission Statement."

What would happen if we in the Christian church developed a new nonviolent peacekeeping force of 100,000 persons ready to move into violent conflicts and stand peacefully between warring parties in Central America, Northern Ireland, Poland, Southern Africa, the Middle East, and Afghanistan? Frequently we would get killed by the thousands. But everyone assumes that for the sake of peace it is moral and just for soldiers to get killed by the hundreds of thousands, even millions. Do we not have as much courage and faith as soldiers?[85]

To translate the thrust of Sider's call into the language of Shane Claiborne and Stanley Hauerwas, is it possible to be an "extremist for love" or a "fanatic" for peace?[86] A modest effort emerged a few years later and today CPT has dozens of Christians a year who volunteer to enter dangerous conflict zones in places such as Iraq, suggesting that it is possible to find people who will risk their lives to witness to the love of Christ.

One of those team members is Peggy Gish, who recounts her experiences of three different extended stays in Iraq from 2002 through 2004 in a telling memoir that makes a number of important points about the war and occupation of Iraq from the perspective of a pacifist Christian living among ordinary Iraqis. As the bombing started in Baghdad in March 2003, Gish entered a time of darkness that reminds us of Holy Week: "At a time like this, all the right, religiously correct answers fall away, and for a time, you feel only the helplessness, anguish, and pain. Is God still here in this darkness?"[87] After experiencing the terrors of living in Baghdad through the Shock and Awe campaign, she and some fellow team members were expelled from the country while the war was still going on. When they returned, they were appalled, she says, by the CNN television coverage of the war which was entirely "from the US military perspective, celebrating every successful maneuver. There was no mention of the victims of all the strikes or images of their casualties."[88] Just a week earlier, she had seen a young boy injured by shrapnel with "a hole in his abdomen about the size of a grapefruit, through which we could see his intestines."[89] After returning in June 2003, during the occupation, she

---

85. Sider, "God's People Reconciling."

86. Claiborne, *Irresistible Revolution*, 208; Hauerwas, "Nonviolent Terrorist."

87. Gish, *Iraq*, 118.

88. Ibid., 141.

89. Ibid., 125.

notes the sad irony of so much reconstruction work going to American companies: "Something also seemed wrong with destroying the infra-structure and creating a need for reconstruction that would mostly profit the country that destroyed it."[90] Unlike many American experts, she and her team heard of problems with the occupation early on. In fact, the CPT team heard Iraqi families' complaints about problems at Abu Ghraib and other U.S.-run prisons and advocated on behalf of prisoners and their families well before most of us had even heard of Abu Ghraib. In February 2004, Gish and her teammates were forced to face up to their own potential deaths when they were visited by two men who claimed to be on a suicide bombing mission but who later left with all their money. Whether the men were robbers or truly suicide bombers who were talked out of it by the team was never clear. But the team reacted calmly and talked to the visitors throughout the ordeal.[91] Throughout Gish's entire story, common worship times are helpful in sustaining the group and her own personal faith. She frames the last parts of her narrative in Christocentric terms:

> Jesus . . . realized that his was a path of humility, of servanthood, not of winning the admiration of others. . . . He called others to join him in living in a new order, but doing that challenged the old systems of injustice and oppression. So we want to follow this path in Iraq or anywhere we are. It involves compassion, humil-ity, and servanthood while challenging the powers of evil, living under different loyalties, and not accepting the commonly held myths of power and violence.[92]

She goes on a few pages later: "We chose to see things through the worldview of Jesus and the prophets, so we believe that the only way to solve the problems in Iraq is through turning around, changing direc-tions (repentance), and establishing justice. But that means giving up US domination in Iraq." And she immediately follows up this thought with a set of questions: "Is it possible to walk, live, and work in a system of horrendous, overt structural violence without being overcome by it? How can we do that today here in Iraq, the US, or any other nation?"[93] She asks a series of questions that can help us continue to improvise the

90. Ibid., 161.
91. Ibid., 223–26.
92. Ibid., 292.
93. Ibid., 298.

politics of the Kingdom: "What, if any, risks are we willing to take? Will we be willing to take on suffering or give our lives out of this love? And knowing how weak we each are, will we give up, or will we seek and allow God to give us the strength and hope we need to act in love?"[94] Instead of imposing a triumphal end on the story—an impossible task when dealing with Iraq today, anyway—Gish simply ends with questions that bring us back to the mystery of Holy Week. Can we emulate Jesus?

This is an important question, because any challenge to hegemonic politics guarantees one a lonely place if that challenge entails suffering, deprivation, or death, as we found in our second point of re-imagining. Thus Christians who take on the challenge will often be misunderstood and maligned. A prime example of this lesson is the story of a later CPT team member named Tom Fox, a Quaker from Northern Virginia who was one of four members of a CPT team that were kidnapped in Iraq in November 2005. According to the *Washington Post*, "Fox was born in Chattanooga and graduated with a double degree in music performance and education from George Peabody College for Teachers, now part of Vanderbilt University, in Nashville. An accomplished clarinetist, he spent 20 years playing with the Marine Corps Band." He was also "the father of two college-age children and was an assistant manager at a Whole Foods supermarket in Springfield before quitting to join Christian Peacemaker Teams."[95] Yet he chose to go to Iraq in September 2004, only to be killed by his captors in March 2006. In response to his death, the co-directors of CPT released a statement that said, among other things: "Even as we grieve the loss of our beloved colleague, we stand in the light of his strong witness to the power of love and the courage of nonviolence. That light reveals the way out of fear and grief and war."[96] Tom Fox, it seems, died well for the sake of Jesus. It was sad enough that mainstream media coverage marginalized Fox's story as a curiosity and a human-interest story, making it a lonely death. But it was far sadder, making the death even lonelier, when some identified with the Christian cause attacked such work in terms that showed an inability to understand the Holy Week story and thereby rightly understand martyrdom and witness. If we take

94. Ibid., 307–8.

95. Weil and Chandler, "Virginian Taken Hostage in Iraq Is Found Dead."

96. Christian Peacemaker Teams, "CPT Release: We Mourn the Loss of Tom Fox."

Thomas Aquinas' definition of martyrdom, which "requires that a man suffer death for Christ's sake," then applying the label to Fox is apt.[97]

However, Fox's story suggests the difficulty that some American Christians have in rightly seeing martyrdom because of their commitment to the hegemony of the United States. For example, just days after Fox's death was discovered, columnist Cal Thomas, a favorite of conservative Christians, argued that it was tragic but not a case of martyrdom.

> It is tragic whenever an innocent person is murdered. It is also tragic because the likelihood that the presence of Fox and his colleagues would change the attitude or behavior of their captors was zero to none. That the "peace activists" believed their brand of Christianity would trump the fanatical Muslims who regarded them as infidels and worthy of death meant that Fox and the others would either be used for propaganda purposes by the enemies of freedom, or made to sacrifice their lives like animals on an ancient altar in the furtherance of the fanatics' dream of a theocratic state. In this instance they were used for both.[98]

So the sacrifice was in vain, says Thomas, because it could never achieve results and crush evil. But this misunderstands the point of witnessing. The lonely witness is to point the way to the Kingdom in such a way that her death can help shock others into seeing the love of the Kingdom embodied. We must agree with Thomas that being crucified is hardly a logical recipe for political success.

But we must see that Thomas also misunderstands this transnational, global Kingdom that far transcends the American effort to bring "freedom" to the world. He blames "these peace movements" for rarely criticizing dictators, writing that "it is only when their own country attempts to end the oppression that the activists become active against America, not the initiators of evil."[99] This conveniently neglects the fact that CPT was a global group that had arrived before 2003, debated about the limits on its movement due to the restrictions of Saddam's regime, and suffered from a partial expulsion when some team members disobeyed orders.[100] The belief that CPT is an American antiwar

97. Aquinas, *Summa Theologica*, II–II, Q. 124, Art. 4. See also Wicker, "Introduction."

98. Thomas, "Tom Fox Tragedy."

99. Ibid.

100. See Gish, *Iraq*, 64–65, 124–32. Gish and others were expelled from Iraq for venturing too freely outside their hotel to observe the site of a bombing on March 25, 2003. One of the three vehicles in their caravan to Jordan blew a tire and crashed, forcing some

operation fails to recognize that it sends multinational teams—including Canadians, British citizens, and others—to conflict zones in Colombia, Palestine, the Great Lakes region of Africa, the U.S.-Mexican border, and Canada. Members of a CPT team that included the evangelical activist Shane Claiborne connected with the Christian community in Baghdad, where Claiborne met many Christians, including a bishop. When told that many American Christians supported the war, the Iraqi bishop told Claiborne that he would be "praying for the church in the US . . . to be the church."[101] Are we in the American church capable of imagining Iraqi Christians as brothers and sisters? Claiborne and Gish encountered the transnational church, suffered with it, and yet found it ministering to *them*. Thomas cannot imagine a church this large. His church is the hegemonic state.

The theological problem here—the failure to see the heart of the Christian story—is a grave one. Thomas writes, "Peace, like happiness, is a byproduct, not a goal that can be unilaterally attained. Peace happens when evil is vanquished."[102] But evil was vanquished in Holy Week, not through coercion, but through suffering love. Thomas returns to the theme of evil in his conclusion: "Peace 'activism' may make its practitioners feel good, or validate their belief that they are doing the will of God, but evil cannot be accommodated. Evil must be defeated if peace on earth is to exist. That Fox and his colleagues could not, or would not see this, is most tragic of all."[103] Again, one must ask, how was evil defeated in Holy Week? The martyrdom of the suffering servant defeated evil. Everything else is commentary. And while there is a serious argument to be made for careful reflections on just war or pacifism for Christians facing serious evil, this piece was not that. Instead, it is an attempt to construct a theology for the defeat of "evil" (or at least dictators who no longer serve the interests of the United States) by the U.S. military. By repudiating Fox just days after his death, Thomas dishonors a martyr who died for the Kingdom. Thomas thereby fails to recognize the Christian narrative for the defeat of evil within which Fox's efforts were framed. He is missing

---

of the team members to get medical attention in the western town of Ar-Rutbah. See Gish, *Iraq*, 133–41; and Claiborne, *Irresistible Revolution*, 214–16.

101. Claiborne, *Irresistible Revolution*, 212–13.

102. Thomas, "Tom Fox Tragedy."

103. Ibid.

not only how evil was defeated in Holy Week but also how martyrs seek to emulate Jesus on the lonely road.

Can soldiers in Iraq emulate Jesus? This would seem to be a question toward which the argument is heading: encouraging Christians to leave the military.[104] But that raises a third improvisation, relating to the centrality of nonviolent witness and the questions this might raise for non-pacifist Christians. Both sides agree that faith makes one ready to die well, but there is a fundamental distinction between killing others and dying for others, a distinction that clarifies the difference between martyrdom for Muslims and Christians. While suicide bombers are hailed as martyrs, Christians reserve the label of witness/martyr for those who witness nonviolently and then die for the sake of Christ—not those who kill for Christ (if such a category can exist in truth).[105] Unless Christians can prove that killing others is a way of loving them, they will have a hard time supporting violence in the name of Jesus.

Not unlike Cal Thomas, I once thought that nonviolence was a half-baked, utopian ideal that was grafted onto Christian theology by liberals who didn't really take the gospel seriously, who failed to do justice to the stern Father God, and who weren't all that loyal to their country. But living through Holy Week—the central mystery of the Christian year—has convinced me that emulating Jesus' nonviolent stance is central to reframing our entire lives as participating in the Kingdom. Not only does Jesus, God in the flesh, preach the message to love your enemies and turn the other cheek, but he also practices these teachings when he faces his accusers in the garden, when he faces the Sanhedrin, when he faces Pilate, when he faces Rome's cruel soldiers, and when he faces his executioners on the cross. He doesn't merely endure injustice, torture, and pain, but he forgives his tormentors out of love. Thus I have concluded that Christians who accept the Gospels as authoritative and yet reject a nonviolent stance toward enemies have the greater interpretive burden. They must explain how and why we are not to emulate Jesus' teaching and his lived example during Holy Week. If our standard is that we should read the entire Bible with Jesus Christ as the center of the Christian story and thus as an authoritative model, then we will be hard-pressed to defend violence as a strategy for the Christian community. Overturning a few

104. Claiborne and Haw, *Jesus for President*, 212: "If it appears as though we are encouraging folks to leave the military, that's because we are."

105. Wicker, "Introduction," 4–5.

tables in the temple courts is hardly a solid basis for justifying violence in Jesus' name.

However, I am absolutely willing to grant the point that, even if Christians should not kill for the sake of the Kingdom, the state retains the legitimate authority to use violence in this age in which the Kingdom is not yet fully manifest.[106] The question is whether Christians should participate in supporting this violence without questioning. Romans 13, which explicitly refers to the sword, does not command blind obedience to the state and in the Roman imperial context of Nero's regime seemed to suggest the opposite meaning: Christians were to submit themselves to a government that oppressed them.[107] At a minimum, Christians who support the theory of the just war (which, sadly, many Christians ignore) should support the possibility of selective conscientious objection as an option for Christian service-members who find themselves serving the military arm of a global military power like the United States, although pacifists of course would avoid such service in the first place. Yet currently the United States military justice system does not allow service-members to object to service in a particular conflict that fails to meet the criteria for a just war (e.g., Iraq). Instead, they must follow orders, or else they must file for a generalized conscientious objector status that would exempt them from all combat service. Recently a young Army Lieutenant named Ehren Watada became the first commissioned officer to refuse a deployment to Iraq because he believed it was an unjust conflict. Because no other options were available apart from complying with orders or refusing orders, Lt. Watada was forced to face charges of "missing movement" and "conduct unbecoming an officer." However, his trial ended in a mistrial and the charges quietly disappeared.[108] Christians who support just war theory should agree that an individual like Lt. Watada who becomes convinced of the injustice of a conflict should have the option of not being coerced into serving in a war that they are convinced would be unjust to enter.[109]

106. Yoder, *Original Revolution*, 62–67, discusses the two aeons; the state is part of the order that is passing away, while the church is participating in the growing reign of God. Also see Yoder, *Christian Witness to the State*; Yoder, *Politics of Jesus*; O'Donovan, *Desire of the Nations*; and Cavanaugh, *Theopolitical Imagination*.

107. Yoder, *Politics of Jesus*, 193–211.

108. Barber, "Mistrial Ends Watada Court-Martial."

109. Westmoreland-White, "Watada Case and Just War Theory."

The governing body of my own denomination, the Christian Reformed Church, recently approved a report advocating selective conscientious objection, making a sensible distinction in practice: "Current policies protect the conscience only of those who, after volunteering for military service, are converted to a position of principled pacifism. The situations of those who cannot in good conscience participate in the nation's current military operations but who believe that military force is justified under other circumstances deserve equal respect."[110] Although some Christians might be called to emulate Tom Fox, others might also improvise practices such as selective conscientious objection to put a check on the unquestioned hegemony of U.S. military power and to make the just war tradition more operative. For instance, if all the Catholics in the U.S. military had followed Pope John Paul II in his opposition to the Iraq War and exercised the (non-existent) selective objection option, a significant portion of the forces being deployed would have stayed home, thereby putting a check of conscience on that military power. It's hard to imagine what might have happened if the 375,000 Catholics in the military (around 27 percent of the total manpower of the U.S. armed forces) had refused to deploy to Iraq.[111] It is hard to imagine such loyalty to the Kingdom challenging the state.

However, we are reminded that God is in control of the drama and the success of the story is not up to us. Although we are called to participate in living for the reality of the Kingdom now, we will not succeed in achieving peace on earth or calling hegemony to task on our own. Only a God of resurrection and ascension can give us true hope. A theology of the cross alone is incomplete without a theology of Easter.[112] This is the fourth improvisation in the face of hegemony, the place where we can hope that God, who turned the crucifixion into exaltation, will somehow weave in the current situation in Iraq and the current global system dominated by U.S. military hegemony into the larger narrative of the Kingdom. In classes where I have discussed how the Iraq War does not meet the criteria for a just war, students have mentioned friends and relatives serving in Iraq. They are concerned that I am personally

110. Committee to Study War and Peace, "Report from the Committee to Study War and Peace to Synod 2006," 30.

111. For the numbers, see Lorge, "New Archbishop Pledges to Find More Chaplains." Thanks to Bill Cavanaugh who raised this point in our Summer 2006 seminar at Calvin College.

112. See Wright, *Surprised by Hope.*

condemning them for volunteering to serve in the armed forces and for deploying there, and they suggested that there was some good coming of those efforts: Iraqis were being exposed to Christianity, stability was being brought to another land. In the story of God's Kingdom, none of us knows fully how God can use all of us, including these young people in Iraq. If God can redeem his people through the death and resurrection of the Son, then he can somehow turn the efforts of these Americans into part of his story, just as he can weave a constructive alternative out of the current mess that American hegemony has wrought. It is encouraging to hear of stories of soldiers being moved to tears in discussions with Gish or Claiborne. Both of their accounts stress that young men and women have little agency and are caught in systems of domination.[113] No one is labeling individuals as evil here. That would violate Christian charity and show a real lack of grace.

But all Christians are called to be faithful in witness, and that witness might include martyrdom for the sake of love. "Martyrdom," writes York, "like any other form of witness, is praiseworthy only because it points to Jesus. It is one act of fidelity alongside many others that displays a person's belief in God."[114] We should not romanticize martyrdom or prioritize it over other ways of pointing to the Kingdom. "The nun who spends her entire life bathing the unwanted leper and then dies silently in her convent, without making headlines on the nightly news, makes Jesus just as visible as the highly dramatic tortured death of the martyr."[115] But we must see how "the martyr's death mimics the death of Jesus, but only because her life also mimics the life of Jesus. . . . Martyrdom is only a final sign or confirmation of one's holiness. It is a testament to a life well lived—a life that is blessed to show Christ not only in life but also in death."[116] Martyrs "take the gospel at its word," and seek to live in the Kingdom proclaimed in the gospels today, even though that gets them killed.[117] One prays that such martyrs are unnecessary for the American church to wake up and see the global military hegemony of the United States for what it is, but the death of Tom Fox seems to have had little

113. Gish, *Iraq*, 166, 266; Claiborne, *Irresistible Revolution*, 220–21.

114. York, *Purple Crown*, 154.

115. Ibid.

116. Ibid.

117. Ibid., 155.

impact in exposing the conflict between hegemony and the gospel of self-sacrificing love.

The church would do well to wonder why the United States has more than 725 military bases overseas, "234 military golf courses [that] it operates worldwide, not to mention the seventy-one Lear jets, thirteen Gulfstream IIIs, and seventeen Cessna Citation luxury jets used to fly admirals and generals. . . . At a cost of $50 million apiece, each Gulfstream accommodates twelve passengers plus two pilots, one flight engineer, a communications system operator, and a flight attendant."[118] The United States government spent nearly $530 billion on its military in 2007, including money spent for such luxuries as these golf courses and jets, with the total amount roughly equal to that spent by all other militaries in the world combined.[119] Friedman argues that the United States has to "manage globalization," and perhaps this is the cost of that task.[120] We can debate whether such a global military complex serves the spread of "freedom" worldwide, but there should be little debate that it also encourages the perpetuation of domination and violence worldwide. The military may keep order in the short run through the suppression of violence by violence, but this is only a temporary Roman peace, rather than the peace of Jesus rooted in love. The American church is in danger of becoming accommodating toward this system of hegemony. If the church equates the American "peace through freedom" with the spread of the gospel, then perhaps more martyrs like Tom Fox will be needed. The story of the resurrection suggests that God turns the death of Jesus into the turning point of history, and Christians witness to that hope, trusting that God can turn the Iraq tragedy and the hegemonic efforts of the globally stretched United States military into something properly hopeful. But that will require a proper understanding of the fullness of hope in Easter, to which we turn in the next chapter, after ending with the mystery of Holy Saturday.

The day between Good Friday and Easter may be the strangest of the entire Christian year, since here we re-imagine the body of Jesus lying in the tomb. Like the disciples, we are waiting, marking time, still thinking

---

118. Johnson, "Sorrows of Empire," 333.

119. Office of Management and Budget, *Budget of the U.S. Government, Fiscal Year 2009*, 49; "World Wide Military Expenditures."

120. Friedman, *Lexus and the Olive Tree*, 437.

about the anguish of yesterday, still wondering about death and burial.[121] We are puzzled, just like the disciples on the road to Emmaus. "That sense of puzzlement," says N. T. Wright, "is the classic Holy Saturday place to be. We have expressed our sorrow and our anger, and we have brought it to the cross and we will leave it there. Now we must wait quietly to see what God will do."[122] But unlike the disciples, we also know the end of the story. As Tony Campolo says, we know that Sunday is a-comin'. The collect in the *Book of Common Prayer* for Holy Saturday summarizes our plight: "O God, Creator of heaven and earth: Grant that, as the crucified body of your dear son was laid in the tomb and rested on this holy Sabbath, so we may await with him the coming of the third day, and rise with him to newness of life."[123] As we rest in anticipation, we must wait, since the enactment of the Kingdom is not up to us but to the one who has the power to raise the dead.

121. The Old Testament lectionary readings for the day focus on death: Job 14:1–14; Lam 3:1–9, 19–29; and Ps 31:1–4, 15–16.

122. Wright, *Christians at the Cross*, 65.

123. Episcopal Church, *Book of Common Prayer*, 221.

CHAPTER 8

The Gospel of Easter and the Gospel of Free Trade

Free Trade is God's diplomacy, and there is no other certain way
of uniting people in the bonds of peace.

—Richard Cobden, 1857[1]

We've kept the Forty Days of Lent; we've walked the Holy Week path; we've
been attentive to Jesus' story for the last three days in particular. And now
what we really should do is to have a forty-day party.

—N. T. Wright[2]

Although current college students are now too young to remember the
Battle in Seattle in December 1999, it was a time when labor activists,
environmental protestors, and young anarchists staged massive protests,
triggering downtown riots that shut down the city and ended a global
conference of trade ministers discussing a new round of negotiations to
"liberate" trade in goods and services for the WTO. Immediately afterward, the conservative columnist George Will responded sarcastically
to their efforts, writing that "the protestors oppose the most progressive
force of the past two centuries. Trade that drives economic development—

1. Hobson, *Richard Cobden*, 246, quoted in Terry, review of *Richard Cobden*, 257.
2. Wright, *Christians at the Cross*, 73.

and better nutrition and health—has been, strictly speaking, progressive because the poor have gained the most."[3] So free trade equals progress for the poor. Who could argue with that—apart from crazy anarchists, energetic environmentalists, and self-interested labor activists?

When the question is framed in terms of progress, few Christians who are concerned for the poor can easily challenge or reframe this discourse. Instead, many of them affirm Cobden's epigraph or Will's conclusion, seeing the advance of free trade and economic reform as divinely appointed good news for the poor. As we saw in chapter 2, a progressive development model of history is often behind an embrace of globalization. To the extent that evangelicals embrace such a model, they are in danger of embracing free trade capitalism as Richard Cobden did: as the inevitable hand of God's providence, part of a grand design to benefit all through mutual exchange. One Christian ethicist alludes to "the great benefits provided by the next stage of global capitalism."[4] A Christian executive writes that "the forces of globalization are inevitable and of potentially positive benefit to both the developed and the developing worlds."[5] A theology professor describes global capitalism as "the greatest liberating power in human history."[6] Although Jesus never mentioned free markets, one evangelical retorts, "But Jesus was in the 1st century . . . and we're in the 21st century."[7] Another evangelical surmises that globalization is part of the process of spreading the good news.[8] Each of these writers affirms at some level that "free trade is God's diplomacy." Although free and mutual exchange is highly desirable, the belief that we must therefore promote free trade to spread the good news is highly problematic. The danger here is that opening to the global economy replaces the true gospel hope of resurrection with modern progressivism's alleged good news. But, as we will see, that progressive vision in practice often entails bad news for the poor; it is a recipe for their being flattened. Leaving aside the philosophy of history behind this gospel, the first section of this chapter argues that the gospel of free trade fails on its

---

3. Will, "Seattle Mounts Its Own Version."

4. Sedgwick, *Market Economy and Christian Ethics*, 272–73.

5. Mather, "Combining Principle with Profit," 34.

6. Schneider, *Good of Affluence*, 2.

7. Stafford, "Evangelicals!" 41–45, quote at 44.

8. Lott, "Is Globalization Christian?" 32–33.

own terms. I then turn to the liturgical year to re-imagine free trade and describe alternative practices.

Is Free Trade Good News for the World's Poor?

"If Cobden had an obsession," writes a reviewer of his biography, "it was in his confidence in free trade as a panacea for the world's ills."[9] Friedman would agree, as he cites the "irrefutable fact that more open and competitive markets are the only sustainable vehicle for growing a nation out of poverty."[10] Likewise, freeing up the market has come to be the panacea of choice for many well-meaning Christians and economic writers who genuinely seem to wish for healthier lives for the poor. For instance, *Wall Street Journal* editorial writer and Catholic thinker William McGurn provocatively charges that "our economists and businessmen . . . preach a message for the world's poor that is charged with greater hope than what it is typically taught by many of our leading theologians and preachers."[11] Leaving aside this provocation, I focus here on McGurn's statement that "one measure of solidarity is the creation of structures that give the poor the ability to sell the fruits of their labors to all the world—and to buy from that world what it can give them."[12] This is a laudable way of framing free exchange—mutual trading that brings greater dignity than foreign aid handouts, trading that treats the poor as full partners. When I talk about "the poor" in this chapter, I am thinking of the roughly 2.2 billion people on the planet who work and live on farms of less than five acres, and especially the roughly 800 million people who earn less than a dollar a day by working on even smaller farms.[13] I agree with McGurn that such people ought to be able to share their labor with the world in ways that give them dignity. Only the most extreme advocates of "total self-reliance" would suggest total withdrawal from all trading, especially when it might be possible for the poor developing countries to gain by selling their crops or wares.[14] By McGurn's measure, however, the gospel of global free trade as currently practiced is not good news for the poor.

9. Terry, review of *Richard Cobden*, 257.

10. Friedman, *World Is Flat*, 3rd ed., 409.

11. McGurn, "Pulpit Economics," 21–25, quote at 21.

12. Ibid., 25.

13. Polak, *Out of Poverty*, 119–20.

14. Brown, *Fair Trade*, 158–59.

Precisely because the world's current "free trade" prescription imposes structures that do *not* allow many poor farmers to sell their goods and services to the world as full partners, we must hesitate to advocate this prescription as a liberating gospel. Instead of seeking to incorporate small farmers into a global economy, we might wish for them to find small-scale local markets. Instead of preaching an abstract gospel to their leaders, we must understand how the gospel of economic reform brings ill tidings, so that we can distinguish between genuine global help for the poor and the reality of the current global system. We must understand the true gospel of Easter as more liberating than the gospel of global economic integration. Only then can we re-imagine improvisational alternatives that live hopefully and constructively out of the Easter story.

A number of seemingly well-meaning advocates for the poor support free trade. They contend that opening up to the world economy allows countries to specialize in producing for export while benefiting from cheaper imports.[15] They argue that the shock of opening up to global markets, including global financial markets, stimulates general economic growth that allegedly benefits all, including the poor. If the economy is not growing, there will be less to go around, say these experts. They say that opening a country to import and export trade offers a wider range of consumer choice; that trade fosters specialization based on comparative advantage; that higher incomes create a rising tide of economic growth that will lift the boats of the poor; and that foreign capital flows will help countries privatize state-run enterprises and finance new ones.[16] If only stagnant, closed economies can open up, declare these free-trade advocates, incomes will grow and the benefits will trickle down to their citizens. Hence Friedman says that "the spread of capitalism has raised living standards higher, faster and for more people than at any time in history. It has also brought more poor people into the middle class more quickly than at any time in human history. So while the gap between rich and poor is getting wider . . . the floor under the poor has been rising steadily in many parts of the world."[17] Good news for anyone who cares about the poor, no?

15. Wolf, *Why Globalization Works*, 173–219; Mandle, *Globalization and the Poor*, 9–23; Larsson, *Race to the Top*, 53–60; and Bhagwati, *In Defense of Globalization*, 122–34 and 228–29.

16. Dollar and Kraay, "Growth is Good for the Poor." However, income inequality also increases. See Weller and Hersh, "Free Markets and Poverty."

17. Friedman, *Lexus and the Olive Tree*, 350.

Bolstered by such confidence in the results of economic globalization, Friedman bluntly offers the details of the free-market prescription, which he calls the "Golden Straitjacket." "If your country has not yet been fitted for one," he says ominously, "it will be soon. . . . It is not always pretty or gentle or comfortable. But it's here and it's the only model on the rack this historical season."[18] Among the dozen or so policies that a government must adopt in taking on this straitjacket, according to Friedman, are: "eliminating and lowering tariffs on imported goods, removing restrictions on foreign investment, getting rid of quotas and domestic monopolies, increasing exports, privatizing state-owned industries and utilities, deregulating capital markets, making its currency convertible, [and] opening its industries, stock and bond markets to direct foreign ownership and investment . . ."[19] These prescribed policies are hardly unique to Friedman. Throughout the 1990s, the International Monetary Fund and the U.S. Treasury Department required governments that borrowed from them to enact an identical set of reforms called the Washington Consensus—a set of policies that included liberalizing financial systems, adjusting the exchange rate to encourage new exports, reducing tariffs on imports, removing all barriers to foreign direct investment, forcing foreign domestic businesses to compete with foreign ones, and privatizing state enterprises.[20] One veteran scholar says that this approach "bulldozed over" previous approaches "to create the impossible: a 'level field' on which experienced and inexperienced firms were supposed to complete."[21] In our terms, the powers-that-be in Washington flattened the world to expand trade and global markets, the very process that Friedman applauds as good news.

In order to understand the surprising appeal of this flattening process, we need to recognize the power of the discourse of free trade-as-liberation, to see how it is a *religious* discourse.[22] It parallels the true good news in hoping for a better world, but it contradicts it in prescribing violence to get results. The religious character of the advice to embrace

18. Friedman, *Lexus and the Olive Tree*, 104, 105.

19. Ibid., 105. Also see Friedman, *World Is Flat*, 3rd ed., 409.

20. For the complete list of ten policies, see Henry and Springborg, *Globalization and the Politics of Development*, 13. For a brief history of the Washington Consensus, see Woods, *Globalizers*, 47–64.

21. Amsden, *Escape from Empire*, 127.

22. This is no surprise. See Nelson, *Economics as Religion*; and Nelson, "What Is 'Economic Theology'?" 58–79.

globalization is apparent to others: one political scientist compared the Washington Consensus to "fatwas" and a "gospel" pushed by conservative economists, *Foreign Policy* magazine labeled the advice of free traders such as Tony Blair as "spreading the faith," and a leading economist pointed out that the U.S. "preached the virtues of competitive markets" while failing to practice what it preached.[23] *New York Times* columnist David Brooks penned a column entitled "Good News about Poverty." Brooks says, "Write this on your forehead: Free trade reduces world suffering."[24] He then cites a World Bank report that described "spectacular" decline in poverty in Asia and asks, "What explains all this good news? The short answer is this thing we call globalization."[25] Brooks makes a point that is well-worn in the globalization discourse. William McGurn made an identical point in 2001 when he wrote that "half of those who moved out of poverty within these past two decades were in East Asia—again, in those countries that have been more open to trade and globalization. By contrast, the countries whose poor have done the worst are those that have closed themselves off to globalization, most notably Sub-Saharan Africa."[26] Here, too, the contrast between Asia and Africa is an old theme in economic development discussions.[27] Both of these gentlemen are preaching, you might say, to the elite converted choir: their affluent readers in the affluent North, who identify with neither the Ohio factory worker displaced by global outsourcing nor the poor Mexican peasant displaced by cheap American corn. To their elite audience, they are preaching the truth, telling a story of good news, and offering glad tidings to the poor: open up to the global economy and you will prosper. In order to appreciate Easter's alternative, we need to unpack this discourse on the virtues of economic openness.

Friedman argues that the Golden Straitjacket thrusts states onto the playing field of the global economy. It "pinches certain groups, squeezes others and keeps a society under pressure to constantly streamline its economic institutions and upgrade its performance . . . through more trade,

---

23. Amsden, *Escape from Empire*, 127–28, 135; Rodrik, "Trading in Illusions," 57 (see sidebar "Spreading the Faith"); Stiglitz, *Globalization and Its Discontents*, 244.

24. Brooks, "Good News About Poverty."

25. Ibid.

26. McGurn, "Pulpit Economics," 23–24. Friedman, *World Is Flat*, 3rd ed., 410, makes a similar point.

27. Also see Griffiths, "Trade, Aid, and Domestic Reform in the Fight Against Global Poverty," 22–23.

foreign investment, privatization and more efficient use of resources under the pressure of global competition."[28] Seeing the alleged benefits, ordinary people who desire increased material prosperity should therefore be clamoring for the chance to have their economies globalized. Thus, said Friedman in 2001, "Africans themselves will tell you that their problem with globalization is not that they are getting too much of it, but too little."[29] Or, as an entire chapter in *The Lexus and the Olive Tree* attempts to demonstrate, there is a "groundswell of people demanding the benefits of globalization," because it raises living standards.[30] He thus claims that "globalization emerges from below, from street level, from people's very souls and from their very deepest aspirations." What drives globalization is "the basic human desire for a better life."[31] Yet a foundation in this simple desire is difficult to reconcile with the coercive element of globalization that Friedman also admits. "As harsh as the globalization system can be," he writes, "it also gives those brutalized by it a greater ability to tell people about their pain or get organized to do something about it . . . [and] help the poor confront poverty in some unique ways."[32] Specifically, Friedman believes that mobile telephones and the Internet can unleash entrepreneurs in countries like Bangladesh.[33] However, because Friedman admits that workers get "knocked around" by globalization, which causes "churning" and is even "painful," his argument hinges on whether or not adoption of the Golden Straitjacket will bring material benefits to ordinary people, since it assumes that such material benefits are what people truly desire.[34] The question remains, however, whether ordinary humans truly desire to participate in a system that is so coercive. If the Golden Straitjacket is the only option and it is a painful option, then do ordinary people really want the system forced upon them? Can we imagine a fuller, richer way of global exchange? Must communities that help the poor be forged in pain? With Augustine, we might say that our hearts will not rest until they rest in God, our truest desire—a deeper

28. Friedman, *Lexus*, 105–6.

29. Friedman, "Protesting for Whom?"

30. Friedman, *Lexus*, 350, chapter 16.

31. Ibid., 348.

32. Ibid., 357, 359.

33. Ibid., 362.

34. Ibid., 349, 350, 357, 362.

desire than the desire for unfettered economic freedom.[35] Can global communities of exchange bear witness to and participate in a gentle love of God and neighbor?

The classic theory of free trade based on comparative advantage, upon which Friedman depends, not only fails to foster gentle love but it also *requires* pain and dislocation to work. Typically the pain and dislocation is euphemized as "adjustment costs," but the pain of these adjustments will fall more heavily on the poor in the global south than the rich in the global north. It is one thing to preach the gospel of comparative advantage to an audience in the industrialized world, but it is quite another to preach it to one in the so-called developing world, where the pain of globalization is rarely mitigated by institutions that cushion ordinary people from the effects of harsh competition. Key to the entire theory of comparative advantage is the notion that opening up to foreign competition forces people out of business when they are unable to compete with foreign competitors who can produce more cheaply. Now, the classical theory does not stop there. It goes on to say that these "inefficient" producers will be "freed up" to move to higher-productivity, more-efficient sectors of the economy which presumably will be able to produce exports.[36] Explaining the classical theory in a nutshell, one economist describes "the basic problem caused by globalization: the damage that is done to some as a result of change that is beneficial to most."[37] For every job lost in an Ohio manufacturing plant due to imports or outsourcing, there should be plenty of export-driven jobs in Silicon Valley—or so the theory goes.

But this theory, as explained by a popular economist, openly admits to coercion. "Smart governments know that by allowing trade," writes Todd Buchholz, "nations *gently coerce their citizens* to shift precious resources from low-productivity to high-productivity industries."[38] Was the fifty-year-old father of three who lost his assembly-line job in Ohio due to imports free or gently coerced? Like many people who have been "displaced," he will probably find another position, perhaps even in a more productive enterprise that exports products to the rest of the world, but he will certainly feel forced to do so. Yet, unlike the poor in most countries, the Ohio worker also has a safety net of social services to fall back

---

35. See Cavanaugh, "Unfreedom of the Free Market."

36. For a clear exposition of this logic, see Burtless et al., *Globaphobia*, 1–88.

37. Mandle, *Globalization*, 125.

38. Buchholz, *From Here to Economy*, 124. Emphasis added.

upon. He can collect unemployment and possibly also what economists call trade adjustment assistance—aid that is targeted to workers who lose their jobs because of import competition. But the poor in most countries have no safety net to fall back upon when globalization renders them "inefficient." The peasant farmer who can no longer grow corn or cotton because of a flood of U.S. imports has little recourse but to "adjust" on her own. Wrenching competition is thus often bad news for the poor. The playing field on which they are to compete, as we will see, is decidedly tilted in favor of the rich world.

A more significant problem with the discourse of globalization as good news is that it falsely portrays what happened in East Asia. While there is no disputing a simultaneous opening to international trade and an increase in economic growth in Asia, there is still a vigorous debate over whether globalization or free trade alone caused the so-called Asian Miracle—a "miracle" of rapid industrialization that lifted the incomes of millions of workers in Asian countries. Many scholars dispute the simple equation of globalization with success and suggest that state intervention rather than the free market was the key to Asian economic growth.[39] Even the World Bank, which helped to start this discourse with its famous *East Asian Miracle* report in 1993, admitted that Asian governments intervened heavily in their economies.[40] The preachers of globalization who praise Asia fail to recognize the complexities of this debate and the wider set of policies that help to explain the economic growth of China, Indonesia, Malaysia, Singapore, South Korea, Taiwan, Thailand, and Vietnam (among others). We can start with Paul Kennedy by admitting that there *is* a stark contrast between Asian and African economic results: "Nothing better illustrates the growing differences among developing countries than the fact that in the 1960s, South Korea had a per capita GNP [Gross National Product] exactly the same as Ghana's ($230), whereas today it is ten to twelve times more prosperous."[41] To explain this

39. See, among others, Haggard, *Pathways from the Periphery*, 67–75, 97–99, 113–15, 123–60. Wade, *Governing the Market*; Wade, "What Can Economics Learn from East Asian Success?" 68–79; Jomo, "Rethinking the Role of Government Policy in Southeast Asia."; Cumings, "The Origins and Development of the Northeast Asian Political Economy," 1–40; Amsden, *Rise of the "The Rest"*; Johnson, "Developmental State"; and Kohli, *State–Directed Development*, 24–123.

40. World Bank, *The East Asian Miracle*, 325–26, 352–68.

41. Kennedy, *Preparing for the Twenty-First Century*, 193. Friedman, *World Is Flat*, 3rd ed., 410, makes a similar comparison.

gap between Africa and Asia, however, simple openness to globalization is hardly sufficient, and Kennedy credits several factors "taken together" to explain Asia's economic increase: an emphasis on education, a high national savings rate, a strong state role in the economy, a commitment to exports (rather than domestic self-sufficiency or import-fueled consumption), and a local model of success (emulating Japan).[42] To repeat, simple adoption of the Golden Straitjacket or Washington Consensus does not explain industrialization and economic growth in Asian states. In fact, just the opposite: the strong and pervasive role of government in promoting education, fostering private savings, picking export industries to promote through favorable credit, controlling exchange rates and financial systems, discouraging consumer spending, and carrying out long-range planning suggests that the Asian states gained wealth because they selectively resisted the pressures of the global market.[43] "China's economic policies," for example, "have violated virtually every rule by which the proselytizers of globalization would like the game to be played."[44] China "has achieved integration with the world economy *despite* having ignored these rules—and indeed because it did so."[45] China was not alone: most of the Asian governments slowly opened up to trade and international finance over time, only selectively participated in the global economic system, and regularly followed their own "homegrown business plan."[46]

By contrast, governments that adopt the Washington Consensus open themselves to becoming dependent upon the global economy. And while it is a desirable thing to offer material improvement to the poor, the evidence from Asia suggests that keeping the Golden Straitjacket in storage was their way to "liberating" their peasants and workers through industrialization. Furthermore, many other differences between Africa and Asia—including historical, cultural, political, geographic ones—help to account for their economic divergence. Crediting globalization for the differences in measurable economic output between the two is singling

42. Ibid., 197–200. Also see World Bank, *East Asian Miracle*. In fairness to Friedman, he does briefly mention infrastructure, education, governance, and the environment as necessary factors for development. See *World is Flat*, 3rd ed., 408.

43. Even the pro-liberalism authors Yergin and Stanislaw admit this in *Commanding Heights*, 151–77.

44. Rodrik, *One Economics*, 238–39; also see "Trading in Illusions," 59.

45. Rodrik, *One Economics*, 239. Emphasis in original.

46. Rodrik, "Trading in Illusions," 62; Rodrik, *One Economics*, 239.

out one factor among many; it flattens out the rich contrasting histories of two continents and reduces both to case studies of economic policy and technique. Yet this simple comparison of Asia and Africa continues to drive much of the globalization and development discourse.[47]

Fortunately, a growing number of scholars working within that discourse have begun to challenge the simplistic explanation of development drawn from the simplistic comparison of Africa and Asia.[48] Chief among them is the Harvard economist Dani Rodrik, who contrasts Haiti and Vietnam to illustrate the contrary point: Haiti, "a WTO member, has slashed import tariffs to a maximum of 15 percent" and earned a commendation from the U.S. State Department for having few obstacles to U.S. exports, while Vietnam "engages in state trading, maintains import monopolies . . . and is not a member of the WTO."[49] But Vietnam's economy grew and poverty was reduced, while Haiti remained mired in destitution. Clearly, free trade alone is not enough. Yet, as Rodrik writes, "Global integration has become, for all practical purposes, a substitute for a development strategy. This trend is bad news for the world's poor."[50] With people like George Will, Thomas Friedman, William McGurn, and David Brooks clearly in mind, Rodrik makes a sarcastic point: "Openness to trade and investment flows is no longer viewed simply as a component of a country's development strategy; it has mutated into the most potent catalyst for economic growth known to humanity."[51] However, the evidence suggests that both open financial flows and open trade flows can actually harm the poor.[52] Many African and Latin American states borrowed heavily from the World Bank or International Monetary Fund and adopted parts of the Washington Consensus or Golden Straitjacket, but this openness was not good news for them; it actually lowered their

---

47. For a slightly more sophisticated version that still credits globalization for Asia's growth, see Mandle, *Globalization*, 13–20.

48. Toppen, "Fixing Globalization," 379–90.

49. Rodrik, *One Economics*, 216.

50. Rodrik, "Trading in Illusions," 55.

51. Ibid.

52. Rodrik carried out a careful study of correlations between tariff rates and economic growth rates across the world, finding "no systematic relationship between a country's average level of tariff and nontariff restrictions and its subsequent economic growth rate." This study challenges "the ubiquitous claim that trade liberalization promotes higher growth." Rodrik, *One Economics*, 217; "Trading in Illusions," 60.

economic growth rates.[53] According to one review of the evidence, "Since 1980, the world's poorest countries have done worse economically than the richest."[54] Opening up capital markets "has been at the heart of many of the crises in the developing world since the 1980s. Even when capital flows were not the direct cause of the crises, they played a central role in their propagation."[55] Careful students have drawn similar conclusions about the impact of free trade on poor countries. A recent Carnegie Endowment for International Peace study predicts that current proposals for opening up global agricultural trade (in the so-called Doha Round of WTO talks) would "overwhelmingly" benefit developed countries "while developing countries actually suffer slight losses as a group."[56] Under "almost every scenario" currently being discussed, "Bangladesh, East Africa, and the rest of Sub-Saharan Africa are adversely affected."[57] Using a different model, another group concluded that "the gains [from proposed trade scenarios] are much greater for high-income OECD [Organization of Economic Cooperation and Development, or rich-world] countries than for other countries" and that "the gains are likely to be skewed toward high-income OECD countries."[58] We can find a regional precedent for this dating back to 1994: since signing the North American Free Trade Agreement (NAFTA) with the United States and Canada, Mexico has found the percentage of its population in poverty remaining the same.[59]

With such evidence in mind, Rodrik challenges the WTO to shift away from its current priorities and return to one of its stated purposes of raising living standards around the world. "Instead of asking, 'How do we maximize trade and market access?' negotiators would ask 'How do we enable countries to grow out of poverty?'"[60] Unfortunately, all too often, the latter question is much less important to the powerful countries than the former one. Since the powerful countries largely drive the WTO's negotiating agenda, much of it has been dictated by the priorities of the

53. Przeworski and Vreeland, "Effect of IMF Programs."

54. Milner, "Globalization, Development, and International Institutions," 833–54, quote at 837.

55. Ocampo et al., "Capital Market Liberalization and Development," 1.

56. Polanski, *Winners and Losers*, viii.

57. Ibid., ix.

58. Hoekman and Olarreaga, "Challenges to Reducing Poverty," 17, 18.

59. Jordan and Sullivan, "Very Little Trickles Down," 15.

60. Rodrik, *One Economics*, 214. Also see Hoekman, "Development and Trade Agreements."

United States and the European Union.[61] Instead of focusing on ways for trade to help the poor, for instance, the WTO was used to protect the "intellectual property rights" of U.S.-based software and pharmaceutical companies. Even when the enforcement of patents caused the cost of anti-AIDS drugs to stay high in Africa, the regime held, until the U.S. and Europe finally backed away from such strict enforcement under pressure in late 2001.[62] The WTO's globalization agenda is less about bringing good news to the poor and more about reflecting the power and priorities of its strongest members.

The theory of comparative advantage fails to align with reality. It suggests that poorer countries should have an advantage in low-technology, labor-intensive production such as agriculture. If trade in agricultural products were truly freed, it seems, sub-Saharan African farmers should be able to sell their goods to the U.S. and European markets. But the reality is that the playing field onto which the sub-Saharan farmers step is tilted against them in at least four ways.

One problem is subsidies, government payments to rich-country farmers that give them an advantage over others. For instance, "cotton production costs 73 cents per pound in the United States and only 21 cents per pound in West Africa," and there are 18 million cotton farmers in West Africa and only 25,000 in the U.S.[63] Yet these 25,000 American farmers received around $4 billion in annual subsidies in the year 2000, an amount that surpassed "the entire GNP of a number of the world's poorest cotton-producing countries, as well as the United States' entire USAID budget for the continent of Africa."[64] African cotton farmers who are freed to enter the playing field of global cotton production find their competitors are on government steroids.

Second, even if there are no tariffs or subsidies on a product, the infrastructure of roads, farm machines, trucks, ports, and government regulations is often underdeveloped and more difficult to navigate in non-industrialized states, whereas governments in the wealthy countries sustain a web of institutions to support export producers.[65] Cotton

---

61. Milner, "Globalization," 842–44, 848.

62. Stiglitz, *Making Globalization Work*, 103–32; Drezner, *All Politics Is Global*, 176–203.

63. Carter, "Subsidies' Harvest of Misery"; Rivoli, *Travels of a T-Shirt*, 51.

64. Rivoli, *Travels*, 51.

65. Ibid., 53–57; Bradsher, "Ending Tariffs Is Only the Start," C1; Harford, "Yes, We Have Bananas."

producers in the United States receive assistance from the United States Department of Agriculture and state university agricultural programs, as well as cooperative associations and electronic exchanges that helps them market their cotton products in new ways and makes their production into a high-technology endeavor.[66] Cotton producers in Africa are mostly alone, farming by hand.

Third, even if developing country farmers can get their products to market in the rich world, they often face what economists call "non-tariff barriers," such as regulations on "quality, safety, compatibility, and health" that block their products from being sold.[67] Farmers in Jamaica, for example, found that American companies rejected their tomatoes because they didn't meet packaging and appearance standards.[68]

Fourth, because of state support for exports in the developed world, when trade is "freed," the effects are often devastating for the weaker side. For instance, after the signing of the NAFTA agreement, "imports of corn to Mexico from the United States have increased nearly eighteenfold," while Mexican corn production began to drop.[69] Not only was a traditional staple crop for Mexican families threatened, but also the genetic diversity of distinct breeds of corn was lost as the standardized breeds of American agribusiness flowed south. Once the borders were open, Mexican farmers could not "compete against the mechanized, subsidized giants of American agriculture."[70] Because so many Mexican producers were small farmers (about 90 percent on five or fewer acres)[71] who lost their livelihoods, many of them began to migrate to the crowded cities of Mexico, or to the United States. The cold logic of comparative advantage would tell these farmers to adjust and find work in sectors that were competitive, but what if those sectors are in the United States? Do the advocates of comparative advantage also favor free immigration? To be fair to their own logic, they should.[72]

66. Rivoli, *Travels of a T-Shirt*, 47–49.

67. De la Dehesa, *What Do We Know?* 161.

68. Chapters 7–8, *Life and Debt*.

69. Weiner, "In Corn's Cradle."

70. Ibid.

71. Ibid.

72. De la Dehesa, *What Do We Know?* 305–6. It is significant that this strong advocate of the benefits of globalization for the poor warns here of "very grave consequences for all" if uneven economic development continues because of unfair trade but the industrialized countries continue to block migration of the poor. The logic of comparative advantage requires open borders for migration.

The inability of poor farmers to compete—the fact that many of them have suffered in opening up to global competition—suggests that the poor will be unable to buy and sell on fair terms under the current rules. It turns out that the displacement of small farmers was a logical and predictable outcome of a WTO regime that prioritizes the interests of the powerful states and thus makes less powerful states less self-sufficient, more dependent on giant food exporters with excess cheap food to sell.[73] Thus, "developing countries are yet to receive the promised benefits from agricultural trade liberalization."[74] Worse yet, however, many of their people are paying the costs of the "freedom" promised under current global trade rules. When food prices sharply increased recently, the poor began to suffer from hunger. As the *Washington Post* recently reported, "globalization was supposed to eliminate" food shortages, "but it turned out that globalization did not really work for food," because countries that previously exported their surplus now held back their exports to feed their own people, leaving importing countries with higher bills for food.[75] Thus Wendell Berry's question stands for countries that no longer grow their own food and depend on food imports: "If people lose their ability to feed themselves, how can they be said to be free?"[76]

Using William McGurn's reasonable measure of solidarity quoted at the beginning of this section—"the creation of structures that give the poor the ability to sell the fruits of their labors to all the world and to buy from that world what it can give them"—the coercive, WTO-, IMF-, and World Bank-driven globalization process fails the test.[77] In fact, "the poorest region in the world, Sub-Saharan Africa, was actually made worse off as a result of the last round of trade negotiations."[78] So where might the church locate hope for the poor? The story of Easter, after all, suggests that true hope is found in the accounts of the resurrection of the Son of God from the dead.

73. Bello, "Building an Iron Cage"; and Shiva, "War Against Nature and the People of the South."

74. Dowlah, *Backwaters of Global Prosperity*, 132.

75. Faiola, "Where Every Meal is a Sacrifice," A1.

76. Berry, *Sex, Economy, Freedom*, 49.

77. McGurn, "Pulpit," 25.

78. Stiglitz, *Globalization and Its Discontents*, 245.

Re-Enacting the Easter Story

We hear the heart of the Easter gospel in the verses of a praise song from the 1970s that dates back to ancient Christian liturgies: "His resurrection sets us free. Therefore we celebrate the feast."[79] We recall that the good news celebrated in the Easter feast flows directly from the work of the cross—the humiliation that brings exaltation—that we saw in the last chapter.[80] Paul revisits this language in 1 Cor 15:43: "[The body] is sown in dishonor, it is raised in glory. It is sown in weakness, it is raised in power." So the resurrection confirms that the suffering, humiliation, and death of Jesus is integral to the story, which Karl Barth suggests means that *humanity* is exalted when "Jesus is the Victor."[81] His victory over death, in fact, sets humanity free, redeems us, and reconciles us with God. The suffering and resurrected Jesus is the firstfruits of the new creation. He is risen.

Easter is at the center of the Christian year, the church's greatest feast. Jesus' passion, death, and resurrection take up the bulk of each of the four gospels (Matt 21:1–28:15; Mark 11:1–16:8; Luke 19:28–24:49; John 12:12–20:31). As many have said, these books are in many ways "passion narratives with extended introductions."[82] Taking their cues from the texts, Christians also believe that the paschal mystery is the center of history, "the source event of all the events of the Christian year . . . like the neck of the hourglass."[83] Because the Easter story not only forms the center of the gospel narratives but also the center of time, it reconfigures the way that we mark time. As the *Catechism of the Catholic Church* puts it: "the new age of the Resurrection fills the whole liturgical year with its brilliance . . . The mystery of the Resurrection, in which Christ crushed death, permeates with its powerful energy our old time, until all is subjected to him."[84] From this mystery, according to N. T. Wright,

79. The original one-verse song by Linda Stassen, "Lift Up Your Hearts Unto the Lord," was written in 1974, but stanzas 3 and 4, which I quoted, were added by oral tradition and incorporated in some hymnals. See Calvin Institute of Christian Worship, "Psalter Hymnal #309."

80. Barth, *Dogmatics in Outline*, 121.

81. Ibid., 121–23.

82. McClendon, *Doctrine*, 198, 228.

83. Webber, *Ancient-Future*, 143; Catholic Church, *Catechism of the Catholic Church*, section 1163, p. 329, section 1169, p. 331.

84. Catholic Church, *Catechism of the Catholic Church*, sections 1168 and 1169, pp. 331–32.

we see the new creation: "the resurrection of Jesus offers itself . . . not as an odd event within the world as it is but as the utterly characteristic, prototypical, and foundational event with the world as it has begun to be. . . . Jesus of Nazareth ushers in not simply a new religious possibility, not simply a new ethic or a new way of salvation, but a new creation."[85] Time is reconfigured in the paschal event, as *kairos* has now fully come: "God has brought his future, his putting-the-world-to-rights future, into the present in Jesus of Nazareth, and he wants that future to be implicated more and more in the present."[86] Wright therefore links the time-shattering reality of Jesus' resurrection to the worldwide mission of the church: "God's future has arrived in the present in the person of the risen Jesus, summoning everybody to become people of the future, people in Christ, people remade in the present to share the life of God's future."[87] As Wright emphatically and succinctly puts it, "resurrection doesn't mean *escaping from* the world; it means *mission to* the world based on Jesus' *lordship over* the world."[88] In the next chapter, we will see the importance of the forty days after Easter up to the Ascension in framing the political mission of the church under the lordship of Jesus, but here we focus on the day the empty tomb was discovered, the day of the good news—news that reframes the church's hope for itself and the poor worldwide.

Unfortunately, Christian liturgical practice has not always corresponded with the sweeping statements in the previous paragraph. Although the resurrection is truly good news for the church, good news for the poor, and good news for the entire world, you would not always know it by observing churches in the week after Easter. Despite being the very earliest liturgical season for all branches of the church, the paschal season typically lasts one day for most Christians. On Monday, it's back to work. Although the *Book of Common Prayer* has prayers listed for each weekday in the week after Easter, few churches hold services on any of these days in which these collects would be recited.[89] "Is it any wonder the world doesn't take much notice if Easter is celebrated as simply the one-day happy ending tacked on to forty days of fasting and gloom?"

---

85. Wright, *Surprised by Hope*, 67; see also Barth, *Dogmatics in Outline*, 122.

86. Wright, *Surprised by Hope*, 215; see also Wright, *Christians at the Cross*, 75–76.

87. Wright, *Surprised by Hope*, 287.

88. Ibid., 235. See also Wright, *Resurrection of the Son of God*, 603, 649, for the prominence of the theme of mission ("meet me in Galilee") in Matthew, Luke, and John.

89. Episcopal Church, *Book of Common Prayer*, 222–24.

asks Wright.[90] "Is it any wonder we find it hard to *live* the resurrection if we don't do it exuberantly in our liturgies?"[91] If Easter is truly the center of the Christian year, Easter feasts and celebrations should extend far longer, at least as long as Christmas. Yet, sadly, the Easter feast has been largely displaced in the United States by Thanksgiving and Christmas meals. In practice, *these* are the most important (perhaps the only) celebratory feasts in the average American's year. While the Christmas season in North American secular practice (where Advent is not practiced) lasts a full month, few Christians keep the paschal feast for a month. With this and English practice in mind, Bishop Wright suggests that Easter ought to give us eight days of feasting and festivity, if not a forty day party (to recall his epigraph to this chapter).[92] One cannot draw a direct correlation between the recovery of feasting and the promulgation of the true gospel, but certainly it would not hurt the church to follow Wright's advice. I favor the forty-day party myself. On a more serious note, the prophetic texts assigned for this day (Jer 31:1–6, Isa 25:6–9, Isa 65:17–25), all emphasize that this is a day of feasting and joy in the holy city. Portions of Psalm 118, read every year, also evoke the festive theme: "The stone that the builders rejected has become the chief cornerstone. This is the Lord's doing; it is marvelous in our eyes. This is the day that the Lord has made; let us rejoice and be glad in it" (Ps 118:22–24). As Wright suggests, it would be nice to put these texts into practice within the worshiping community, rejoicing not just on the day but for the whole season.

Why celebrate? We can find in the texts for this day the core message of good news (the evangel) that the church proclaimed and preached from the start: Jesus the Messiah died, rose again, and appeared to his disciples—just as he will someday appear again. This message is echoed in Peter's sermon in Joppa from Acts 10 (typically read every year on Easter Sunday): "They put him to death by hanging him on a tree; but God raised him on the third day and allowed him to appear, not to all the people but to us who were chosen by God as witnesses, and who ate and drank with him after he rose from the dead" (vv. 39b–41). Paul tells a similar story about the good news he received: "that Christ died for our sins in accordance with the scriptures, and that he was buried, and that he was raised on the third day in accordance with the scriptures, and that

90. Wright, *Surprised by Hope*, 256.

91. Ibid.

92. Ibid., 256–57.

he appeared to Cephas, then to the twelve" (1 Cor 15:3–5). Following in the footsteps of the apostles, then, we are also witnesses to the resurrection, and we want to share the good news that the tomb is empty, Christ is risen, he is on the loose, some of us ate and drank with him, and we expect to be with him more fully some day.

The Gospel accounts all share this good news, but each in different ways. In Mark's Gospel, the briefest narrative, the women come to the tomb with spices to anoint the body, but they encounter a young man dressed in white who tells them that Jesus has been raised and they should tell Peter and the disciples to meet Jesus in Galilee (Mark 16:1–8). Wright offers a helpful analysis of this story, arguing that it is highly unusual in its "narrative grammar": "The story we find in these verses only works as part of a different, larger one; the women are summoned to be helpers *in someone else's drama*. . . .When we enquire what larger story this might be, the answer is obvious: it is the story in which the 'subject' is, at one level, Jesus, and at another level, Israel's god. The women are to be 'helpers' in this drama."[93] As Mark puts it, "So they went out and fled from the tomb, for terror and amazement had seized them; and they said nothing to anyone, for they were afraid" (v. 8). This was probably the original ending of Mark's gospel, a genuine cliffhanger. Interestingly, the lectionary passage from Luke also emulates Mark's cliffhanger effect by leaving off with the story of Peter dashing into the tomb: "stooping and looking in, he saw the linen cloths by themselves; then he went home, amazed at what had happened" (Luke 24:12b). The breathless tone here is key to re-enacting the Easter tidings: we end with the shocking news that the tomb is empty.

But this is only half of the shocking, good news.[94] The other half of the news comes in the appearances of Jesus himself. Not only has Jesus risen, but people encounter him; he appears in his resurrected body. Both Matthew and John place Jesus right at the tomb where he speaks first to the women. Matthew emphasizes the women's encounter with the feet of Jesus: "Suddenly Jesus met them and said, 'Greetings!' And they came to him, took hold of his feet, and worshiped him. Then Jesus said to them, 'Do not be afraid; go and tell my brothers to go to Galilee; there they will see me'" (Matt 28:9–10). John's vivid, moving account places Mary Magdalene alone in the garden, weeping outside the empty tomb, where

93. Wright, *Resurrection*, 629–30. Emphasis in original.

94. Ibid., 629, 680, 686–93.

Jesus comforts her. And both Mary and the women in Luke encounter the transformed physical body of Jesus. They have literally touched him.

This retelling of the Easter gospel story helps us re-imagine the news of coercive free trade prescribed by the Golden Straitjacket—a re-imagining that is necessary in order to begin discussing alternative practices.

RE-IMAGINING THE FREE TRADE GOSPEL

While free trade might generate economic growth—and this can be good for the poor—the enacting of such a message cannot match the full gospel which is enacted in the Easter story. Thus we need to re-imagine free trade in light of the true gospel of Easter. I want to highlight four ways in which the story helps us reframe the message of the Golden Straitjacket.

First, Easter is the full gospel in time; it is shockingly good news that gives us the standpoint from which to view all the rest of time in hope. In re-enacting Easter, we need to hear this news afresh for ourselves: the tomb is empty, some have touched him, and he wants us to join him in Galilee, where the mission began. As we saw, the resurrection saves us and liberates us by ushering in the firstfruits of the new creation, which causes any other saving or liberation promised by humans, including the Golden Straitjacket, to pale in comparison. This gives us true hope—a theme well captured in a lovely Easter sermon by Frederick Buechner:

> Anxiety and fear are what we know best in this fantastic century of ours. Wars and rumors of wars. . . . We have heard so much tragic news that when the news is good we cannot hear it. But the proclamation of Easter Day is that all is well. . . . In the end, his will, not ours, is done. Love is the victor. Death is not the end. The end is life. His life and our lives through him, in him. Existence has greater depths of beauty, mystery, and benediction than the wildest visionary has ever dared to dream. Christ our Lord has risen.[95]

At this point, Christians in liturgical traditions would respond, "He is risen, indeed: Alleluia!" Like Buechner, the church finds its true hope in the good news that the loving redemption of life and not destruction is

---

95. Buechner, *Magnificent Defeat*, 80–81. Thanks to Harry Winters and Debbie Romesberg for first drawing my attention to this quote by printing it in our church newsletter a few years ago.

the true end. A joyful dénouement—not a tragic, unhappy, or pointless death—is the true end of the story. With this knowledge that the true ending is already partially here, and it is a joyful one, we know that our labor of "building for the Kingdom" is not in vain and that coercion is no longer necessary.[96] We are freed to work, fearless until the end, since death has lost its sting. That is very good news.

The fullness of the Easter gospel therefore gives us a starting point from which to compare proposals for saving others through coercion. When we start with a more skeptical approach toward the claims of the world, rooted in a firm confidence of the truth of Easter, we gain a critical distance. Thus, if we listen carefully we find even staunch free traders admitting that free trade alone is not enough: "Simply liberalizing poor economies," writes The Economist magazine, "without giving them support during the transition, can be a recipe for economic instability."[97] Free trade by itself is not enough to save people. However, the hope of Easter suggests that good news for the poor is not simply wishful thinking or something to put off until the afterlife. Rather, the redemption of all things must include the sharing of concrete steps that bring justice to our poor neighbors. If the redemption that breaks into time at Easter has any meaning, it will transform the way the church shares hope for the poor here and now. The good news is not that someday when we die we will all go to heaven. Rather it is the news that the world is beginning to be put back on track via the firstfruits of the Kingdom of God and that disciples of the King are working to help build and point the way to that Kingdom. The true liberation of Easter is thus the liberation of all things from bondage to sin and death and the redemption of all things, including our bodies. This is good news to anyone who lives in a body and especially to a person trapped in deathly bondage. It frees that person up to give or receive embodied hope.

Second, then, there is a fullness to the Easter gospel in its recognition of Jesus' and our embodiment. The women in the Gospel accounts touch Jesus, just as Peter sees the bandages lying in the tomb. Jesus is the first to be resurrected, giving us a glimpse of what it is like to be his disciple at the dawn of this new creation. "With Jesus, the future hope has come forward into the present."[98] We can see where the world is headed,

96. Wright, Surprised by Hope, 208; 1 Cor 15:58, also Isa 65:23.

97. "Not by Their Bootstraps Alone."

98. Wright, Surprised, 151.

as the new creation bursts forth at Easter, which transforms how we live now, even transforms what we do with our bodies here and now. The next chapter picks up this story to focus on the positive political mission of the church, but here we must note that our position is the same as that of the disciples. We have heard the news, and some of us have touched him, but we must all figure out how to live faithfully with our bodies in response to his resurrection.

One implication of full embodiment—an implication of the resurrection of Jesus' *body*—is that we must be concerned for present, embodied life, including the lives of the poor. If we are concerned for our fellow creatures' bodies, minds, and spirits we must see the ways in which free trade is at best a single government policy that must be part of a larger, holistic context in "economic development." Indeed, we must challenge those who contend, as we saw in chapter 2, that "development" is the sole goal of life (although both might be woven into the purposes of God in ways that we might not understand). Easter reminds us that the real goal of life is that our resurrected bodies will be part of the new heaven and new earth that will be the Kingdom of God. Thus all our work now will in some way participate in God's designs later.[99] This is a strong affirmation of our embodied existence now, suggesting that the church needs to care about doing justice now, while understanding that the ultimate achievement of justice is up to God.[100] At a minimum, the fully embodied Easter gospel suggests that those who desire flourishing for the poor should understand justice and true economic development to be a holistic approach that includes cultural, educational, technological, political, communal-religious measures of careful discernment that consider carefully what "development" and "economic growth" mean for any given group.[101] Instead of assuming that free trade brings economic growth from the outside, Christians and the church would need to work closely from the inside: to collaborate closely with the poor in every nation at their level to understand what they need in order to be truly liberated in mind, spirit, and body. We need to be fully present and listen to the poor just as Jesus was present in bodily form to give hope to his disciples. Instead of relating to the poor from a distance, we must come to share with them in body.

99. Wright, *Surprised*, 211.

100. Ibid., 213–22.

101. Thomas, *Global Resurgence of Religion*, 238–42.

Third, we must recall that Easter is a season of feasting and great joy rather than of grim competition under conditions of scarcity. Christians who live out the gospel of Easter hope are quite unlike those who prescribe the pain and suffering of wrenching "economic adjustment." Instead, the church feasts freely at Easter on the abundance of the good news of true liberation—the liberation from "the bondage to decay" (Rom 8:21) that comes from the triumph of love and life in the fullness of God. The church contends that this abundance is the center of history, the standard by which the rest of life is judged. God's plentiful love and grace—not the sin-filled misery of dominance and coercion—is the true origination and destination of the world, even though sin often makes it difficult to see this reality.

Thus true liberation for the poor does not come from following a set of harsh and burdensome rules but in the setting free of the whole world in the new creation. Starting with a small band of followers who are to meet him in Galilee to get their calling to a mission—the same place where it all began with the declaration of a jubilee and the liberation of the poor—the church shares the news to all the world that this Jesus who was crucified is now alive, that sin and death are now defeated, and that anyone who seeks true hope for living will want to turn to this Jesus and seek this abundant life among his followers in the church. Instead of settling for the Golden Straitjacket as good news for the poor, then, we need to be finding ways to embody the good news that God has already given the church "everything they need to worship him, to be his friends, and to eat with him."[102] At a minimum, this suggests that we need to eat with the poor, having them join us in eating with God, both in the Eucharist and in other meals. It implies that we need to share the tangible abundance of the hope of the resurrection here and now. We need to share our abundance of food, both literal and spiritual food.

Fourth, the Easter accounts are stories of gentle love rather than harsh coercion for the followers of Jesus. Whether the women encounter angels or Jesus himself, the good news is broken to them gently, since they are terrified. John's account of Mary Magdalene is paradigmatic: "She turned round and saw Jesus standing there, but she did not know that it was Jesus. Jesus said to her, 'Woman, why are you weeping? For whom are you looking?' Supposing him to be the gardener, she said to him, 'Sir, if you have carried him away, tell me where you have laid him, and I will

102. Wells, *God's Companions*, 1.

take him away.' Jesus said to her, 'Mary!' She turned and said to him in Hebrew, 'Rabbouni!' (which means Teacher)" (John 20:14b–16). Evident in this tender account is the divine love that urges us not to be afraid. These gentle Easter morning scenes form a stark contrast to the immediately preceding scenes of the violence of the cross, which expose the crucifixion as an attempt to crush the divine messenger through force.

Not unlike those accounts, as we have seen, the classical theory of free trade depends upon harsh coercion to work. A brief return to that theory sharpens the contrast for us. To use the language of economics, free trade's benefits are at the macroeconomic level—the level of the national economy—and the expectation is that its benefits will be spread across the country to consumers. But typically not everyone truly experiences the benefits. At the microeconomic level of households, small businesses, and small farmers, there are no guarantees of benefits, only hypothetical ones, whereas the costs of "adjustment" to competition are all too clear for those households, businesses, and farmers that cannot compete with foreign competition. To use the technical terms of economists, an opening to trade can be defended as optimal if the gains to the winners from trade are so great that they would allow the winners to compensate the losers (presumably for lost income) and still be better off. The problem is that in the real world this never happens fully.[103] The losers are guaranteed to lose but the winners are not guaranteed to compensate them. In any case, that compensation rarely occurs in poorer countries. Industrialized countries with strong governments can afford and administer trade displacement assistance to aid those harmed by trade, but workers, families, small business owners, and farmers displaced by trade in countries without social safety nets are on their own. Even on its own terms, the theory of free trade promises that it will hurt some members of a society. Not only does it fail to save everyone but it also may make the poor more miserable.

By contrast, the Easter story reminds us of the tender divine love for all the poor followers of Jesus. Easter is the fullness of the gospel enacted for all who accept it and live under it. It is shockingly good news that offers us the hope of a new life now and in the new creation that is to come. It is a fully embodied hope that anticipates the resurrection of our bodies, and which therefore heightens the importance of the work for justice that disciples do now. It is a time of joyful feasting—the kind of

103. Kapstein, "Winners and Losers," 364.

feasting in abundance that the church wants to share with the world. And it is a story of gentle divine love that strikingly contrasts with the harsh dictates of the Golden Straitjacket.

IMPROVISING PRACTICES

Is there a better way than the way of the Golden Straitjacket? The documentary film *The Yes-Men* humorously suggests that there is.[104] A group of filmmaking pranksters, the Yes-Men posed as fake representatives of the World Trade Organization (WTO) and showed up at a conference of Australian accountants in 2002 to "announce" that the WTO in its present form would no longer exist. Instead of serving business interests, they said, the newly reformed organization would serve human interests. The new charter of the group would be based upon the Universal Declaration of Human Rights. Interviewed for her reaction on camera afterward, one unsuspecting conference-goer found this to be a positive step in a world in which "the strong are getting stronger and the weak are getting weaker." Another duped conference participant applauded the announcement as a "brave move" and a "terrific sign of hope" that we could have a global economy that truly benefitted everyone. These Australian accountants recognized that the system of free trade was not always serving the people it claimed to liberate. They were surprised and relieved when hearing of the supposed new WTO. Deep down, it seems, these accountants recognized that such organizations might fail to serve the poor after all. Although the announcement turned out to be bogus, these accountants' reactions suggest that many of us have a deep unease with the current system of trade. But, apart from pulling pranks, how might the church improvise alternative practices that embody hope?

Early in this chapter, we heard the allegation that economists and businessmen "preach a message for the world's poor that is charged with greater hope than what it is typically taught by many of our leading theologians and preachers."[105] Yet the message of Easter is far more hopeful than the message of free trade. Therefore, Christians inspired by Easter ought to be in the forefront of spurring innovations that offer a deeper and truer hope for the poor that will actually help them rather than

---

104. Bonanno and Bichlbaum, *Yes Men*. Thanks to Graeme Dunkley for recommending this film.

105. McGurn, "Pulpit Economics," 21.

coerce them. I want to describe three sets of reflective practices that flow from the re-imagining of the free-trade gospel just undertaken.

First, the practice of fair trade helps overcome fear through loving action. The Easter stories in the Gospels calm our fears and encourage us to live out of gentle love, just as the angel and Jesus calm the fears of the women who arrive at the tomb.[106] Christian academics often fear that in challenging the dominant discourse of capitalist globalization they are advocating socialism or failing to provide alternatives, but this chapter suggests that the policies of capitalist globalization fail on their own terms. They fail to deliver what they promise. Therefore we should not be afraid to challenge a system that fails, especially because we can point to alternative ways of promoting free exchange with the poor that are rooted in the gentle love that Jesus embodies toward Mary Magdalene outside the tomb. Instead of promoting a coercive process that forces adjustment at the macroeconomic level in the hopes that benefits would trickle down to individuals, Christians were early leaders in fair trade movements that promoted exchanges that directly benefited small business owners, poor families, villages, and small-scale farmers. Precisely because they loved the poor and hoped to embody good news to the poor, these Christians hoped to find ways that would offer tangible benefits at the microeconomic level.

Alternative trading methods are one way in which the church showed the world another way of trading that would bring benefits directly to the poor. It is significant that the movement to sell fair trade handicrafts started in humble peace churches before it mushroomed into a significant global movement that has increasingly detached itself from its churchly roots.[107] The movement, in its North American version at least, started in two churches, the Mennonites and the Brethren, after World War II. In 1946, "Mennonite Central Committee (MCC) worker Edna Ruth Byler of Akron, PA, visited MCC volunteers who taught sewing classes in Puerto Rico" named Mary Lauver and Olga Martens.[108] The women in the sewing classes were poor, and the volunteers hoped to help

106. The "young man" in Mark 16:6: "Do not be alarmed"; the angel to the women in Matt 28:5: "Do not be afraid"; Jesus to Mary Magdalene in John 20: a calming presence.

107. For scholarly reviews of the fair trade movement, see Nicholls and Opal, *Fair Trade*; Raynolds et al., *Fair Trade*; Brown, *Fair Trade*; Littrell and Dickson, *Social Responsibility in the Global Market*.

108. Nicholls and Opal, *Fair Trade*, 65; Littrell and Dickson, *Social Responsibility*, 63.

them. So Edna invested $500 of her own money[109] and "brought several pieces of embroidery home to sell to friends and neighbors. In the early 1970s, the flourishing project moved out of Byler's basement and car trunk and became an official MCC program."[110] In the 1950s, MCC volunteer Ruth Lederach added to such efforts by selling needlework by Palestinian refugees in Jordan.[111] These combined efforts became the roots of the Ten Thousand Villages organization that emerged in the 1970s. In 1949, members of the Church of the Brethren who were concerned with the condition of German refugees after World War II arranged to sell cuckoo clocks in the United States that were crafted by the refugees, with the proceeds going directly to the refugee artisans.[112] This Sales Exchange for Refugee Rehabilitation and Vocation (SERRV) program grew into one of the largest alternative trade organizations in the world. Since its humble beginnings with handicrafts, the mushrooming fair trade movement has become well known as it moved into certifying sales of coffee, bananas, and chocolate as fair trade goods. The fair trade labeling and certification approach is by no means a panacea, however. Since it works both with and against global markets, it may be co-opted or mainstreamed by those in the market eager to profit from it while well watering down the distinct practices of fair trading.[113] Unless all trade is fair trade, there is a danger that the dominant unfair practices will drive out fair practices, which will look like luxuries.[114] Thus I would not argue that fair trade is God's diplomacy. But several of its distinct practices, originally dreamed up by innovative Christians such as Edna Ruth Byler, Mary Lauver, or Olga Martens, directly addressed trade's benefits for the poor.

Using Ethiopian coffee growers as a reference point, I can highlight four ways in which fair trading practices actually aid the poor more directly than free trade policies. First, fair trade guarantees producers fair minimum prices that meet their cost of production, even when the world price drops below that cost. Merely to feed and clothe their families, buy clean water, and send their children to school, small Ethiopian farmers estimated in 2005 that they needed to receive a price of $1.10 per kilo for

109. DeCarlo, *Fair Trade*, 66.

110. Nicholls and Opal, 65.

111. Littrell and Dickson, *Social Responsibility*, 63

112. SERRV International, "Our History."

113. Nicholls and Opal, *Fair Trade*, 52–54; Raynolds and Murray, "Fair Trade," 223–34.

114. Jaffee, *Brewing Justice*, 35.

their raw coffee cherries, but the world price was around one-tenth of that.[115] This world price is the logical outcome of competition to provide coffee in a perfectly competitive market, which operates by pitting developing world farmers against each other to produce ever-more-cheaply until profits evaporate. Instead, fair trade pricing guarantees that participating farmers who are heavily invested in one kind of production (e.g., coffee trees, which take five years after planting before they produce for harvest) will not be forced out of business by low prices but will be able to survive, thereby stemming the coercion of the market.[116] Second, fair trading organizations often pay "an agreed social premium" and require small farmers, farm workers, or crafters to organize into cooperatives that decide how to spend this additional development money—making the cooperatives a crucial element in empowering local communities.[117] Such cooperatives typically work by consensus and encourage farmers to work together to use the social premium for community purposes (such as clean water or a new school). Thus, fair trading approaches work directly to support community development, as opposed to the Golden Straitjacket method that hopes for the trickle-down effects of increased income after the macroeconomic shock of opening up the world. Third, fair trade approaches strive to purchase directly from producers on a long-term, cooperative basis. This helps "to lessen the influence of brokers, consolidators, and other agents in global supply chains."[118] In other words, it helps to cut out profit-driven corporate "middlemen" along the line from the producer to the purchaser.[119] Instead of up to six intermediaries between Ethiopian coffee farmers and the coffee drinker, for instance, fair trade cuts that down to a few. This more direct purchasing not only connects farmers to purchasers at the other end, but it also allows more of the profit to flow to farmers. A single cup of coffee might retail at Starbucks for $2.90, while a kilo of roasted coffee can brew eighty cups of coffee. Multiplying eighty cups by the retail price would make the kilo of coffee worth $232. But Ethiopian farmers in 2005 received twenty-three

---

115. "Chapter 2," *Black Gold*.

116. For a critique of fair trade "interventionist schemes," see Brink Lindsey, "Grounds for Complaint?" Nicholls and Opal, *Fair Trade*, 37–38.

117. Ibid., 6–7, 45–52. DeCarlo, *Fair Trade*, 39, 90–91.

118. Ibid., 7.

119. Brown, *Fair Trade*, 64–76, highlights this problem.

cents per kilo, reflecting the bottom end of a markup of 1,000 percent.[120] Profits came all along the way between the grower and the drinker of coffee; but those profits did not trickle down to enrich the farmers. Fair trade helps return some of that value to the growers, something that a free trade regime typically fails to do. Fourth, fair trade offers direct assistance to small farmers or handicraft producers, allowing them actually to enter markets and effectively sell their goods. Fair trade organizations often provide advance credit or payment to farmers or crafters, allowing them a steadier income and reducing the risk of their planting and harvesting or buying materials but then losing their up-front investment if prices drop.[121] In addition, fair trade organizations help "keep producers informed about market movements."[122] They can give feedback to what works and what doesn't work to meet demand in North American or European markets—information that isolated small farmers or handicrafters will be hard-pressed to gather. Thus fair trade actually helps fulfill the standard of equal exchange. Even in narrow financial terms, for every dollar spent, participating farmers were estimated to receive $2.80 in increased income.[123] Thus, it helps poor farmers or handicrafters sell their goods to the rich world rather than wait upon foreign aid (the very thing that William McGurn judged to be good news for the poor).

However, the fair trade approach will be in danger of devolving into yet another system of economics reinforcing the status quo—becoming merely a certification system that is open to being corrupted while merely making consumers "feel good" about their purchases while losing touch with poor rural farmers—if it loses a second key element of Christian practice flowing from Easter: the practice of embodiment.[124] Christians who love the poor will need to join those like Edna Ruth Byler to live with and listen to the poor. The exciting part of the fair trade approach is that it moves in the direction of "de-commodification" (converting products into relationships) by encouraging rich-world purchasers to connect with

120. "Chapter 2," *Black Gold.*

121. Nicholls and Opal, *Fair Trade*, 33–38.

122. Ibid., 7, 33–36.

123. Ibid., 216.

124. Raynolds and Wilkinson, "Fair Trade in the Agriculture and Food Sector," 33–47, point made at 42. Developing states are pushing for fair trade practices in international negotiations: Wilkinson and Mascharenas, "Southern Social Movements and Fair Trade," 125–37.

those who labor to provide them with crafts or certain food products.[125] Such a return to embodiment points in the direction of a healthier alternative globalization that encourages citizens of the richer countries to visit and live among small farmers or villagers making handicrafts—and that encourages small farmers or villagers to visit and live among us. Even short-term service trips by Christians can help them encounter the reality of situations in which the poor live. They can begin the process of establishing partnerships between churches in which the benefits flow both ways and embodiment helps us share news with our neighbors. Not all of us can visit the coffee farmers who grow coffee beans under fair trade systems, but a church friend named Nicole has visited El Salvador and spent time with coffee farmers and their families. Not all of us can visit villages where fair trade crafters work, but a development worker supported by my church has. In fact, this worker, Ben, spent a couple of years working in poor villages in Cambodia with Ten Thousand Villages to help connect handicapped crafters to sell fair trade handicrafts for export to the United States. These crafters not only paid off significant debts or bought animals with their income, but they also found rewarding work that kept them busy during the half year when they were unable to work in their rice paddies. Ben estimated that households were able to increase their income between $100 and $400 a month because of this activity. To get to this point took years of slow work. There were no panaceas, apart from showing up in person, listening carefully, and doing the work to develop partnerships and embody hope. Much of Ben's work was simply being there, giving feedback to the villagers on which of their crafts would sell or not sell in the U.S. For that kind of feedback, an embodied presence at the village level was necessary. And from that embodied presence, Ben shared his own presence with us to tell this story of hope. We are reminded that the Easter witnesses touched Jesus' body.

Another story of embodied presence comes from Paul Polak, the founder of International Development Enterprises. Polak passionately advocates listening to poor farming families in the non-western world who work on plots of one acre or less by hand. He thus promotes an embodied approach that works by listening to those at the bottom of the society, rather than forcing a country to open up to the global economy

---

125. Fridell, *Fair Trade Coffee*, 16, 96, 281–83, argues that such de-commodification is limited and fails to stop the deeper entrenchment of market mechanisms, a helpful cautionary note.

at the top of society. He says, "Many people have become so used to being poor that they have lost hope about changing anything."[126] This loss of hope is exactly where the re-enacted Easter story can break in to inform a constructive response. But the best way to communicate the Easter hope is through embodied actions framed by the Easter narrative. While Polak himself does not explicitly live out of that narrative—he comes from a Jewish family that fled Nazi-occupied Europe—he personally spends time with poor families in order to listen carefully to what they need. In fact, he says that he learned this need to enter into the world of the poor as a psychiatrist assigned to care for a homeless, mentally ill man named Joe. After spending a whole day going through Joe's daily routines and filming him, Polak realized that he learned a great deal from Joe.[127] Drawing on this experience, Polak's first three pieces of advice to those who want to help the poor are to "go to where the action is," "talk to the people who have the problem and listen to what they have to say," and "learn everything you can about the problem's specific context."[128] Unlike the development experts who prescribe one-size-fits-all solutions for every developing country from the comfort of their offices in the District of Columbia, Boston, or New York, Polak makes the rather obvious suggestion that one should actually start by visiting with the poor one is aiming to help—and not just for a short-term visit that confirms how sad their situation is.[129] Rather, one must listen to what people actually need. In Polak's case, he found that affordable drip irrigation systems or treadle pumps were critical to helping farmers grow and sell more of their produce at profitable times when non-irrigated produce is unavailable. But solutions will certainly vary depending on the situation. The point here is that one must be part of the situation in body and not just in mind or spirit. If economic practices become a panacea without encouraging us actually to spend time with poor farmers, then they will miss the mark.

126. Polak, *Out of Poverty*, 142.

127. Ibid., 5–9.

128. Ibid., 14–15.

129. Easterly, *The Elusive Quest for Growth*, 5–8, starts out describing such a short visit to the village of Gulvera in Pakistan; and he ends the book, 285–89, with a similar vignette. The main point seems to be that these people are desperately poor, which then sets the tone for a search for proposed macro-solutions. To his credit, however, he does avoid panaceas and appreciates complexity. Still, I would like to see Easterly live in Gulvera for a year and then write a book.

Embodiment is necessary to help model the hope of Easter in constructive and winning ways.

Finally, Easter is all about abundance and feasting—an abundance that is to be shared. Christians believe that they have received the full gospel at Easter, and they celebrate it, although perhaps not heartily enough. As we noted, for many churches the extended joy of Easter feasting is missing. But churches that celebrate forty-day parties can bring in others to share in the abundance they have received. If we recovered an ability to feast and celebrate abundance, this could transform how we share the good news of Easter. Instead of treating efforts to relieve poverty in the world as grim and dull work, we might invite neighbors near or far to join in the feast with us. (Our own church decided to start once-a-month fellowship lunches when we realized that the two main groups of people we were attracting were refugees and students.) At the level of eschatology, this means sharing the good news that one day the new heaven and the new earth will be inaugurated with a giant banquet, the feast of the Lamb. We want people to know that all our stories and the world's story, are headed to this banquet. At the level of ecclesiology (the study of the church), this feast is present in our churches in the Eucharist. We want people to know that they can get a foretaste of the giant banquet in our humbler suppers of the lamb. But at the level of our social mission, rich and poor need to eat together. We need to invite others to meals and to share our food.[130] We need to learn how to feast in order to learn better how to share.

Most church groups already participate in international relief and development efforts, and Christian non-governmental organizations have also helped to share monetary resources. But the challenge is to move beyond monetary donations to church charities that relieve our guilt and toward genuine sharing and mutual presence in not just mind and spirit but in bodily presence. Such genuine sharing can move us from aid programs that can perpetuate dependence through handouts toward mutual exchanges that empower the less well-off to share their labors with those who have more, which in turn allows those blessed with more to share their labors. The fullness of the Easter hope is, to repeat, all about the fact that we also will receive resurrected bodies in the new creation at the end of time. Without the resurrection of the body, we cannot truly

130. Yoder, *Body Politics*, 14–27, argues that the common meal is an economic act of sharing.

celebrate. As St. Paul puts it, "If there is no resurrection of the dead then Christ has not been raised; and if Christ has not been raised, then our proclamation has been in vain and your faith has been in vain" (1 Cor 15:13–14). But the Easter faith is that Christ arose in body, and that we will, too. Therefore, our bodily labor is "not in vain" (1 Cor 15:58). Rather, the work we do now in helping build for the Kingdom is going somewhere. What happens now extends into the future: we need to invite people to the banquet now or we might not see them at the end.[131]

This realization heightens our concern for the fate of the poor now and it should motivate us to work against the harmful effects of imposing a simplistic Golden Straitjacket gospel upon developing countries right now. However, this will require careful work and attention to events and cautious participation in trying to steer them. While we should be skeptical of the free trade gospel, we should also be skeptical of claims that state socialism guarantees help to the poor. Christians might study the Asian economic development story more closely to scrutinize the ways in which interventionist states there helped to foster economic growth and industrialization, but there too we should be cautious about supporting the coercive role of governments or ignoring the potential negative effects of mass industrialization. At the same time, there is no reason why the churches should not put their weight behind promoting reforms within the World Trade Organization that would support trade practices to truly help poor farmers, even when that might require trimming subsidies for American or European agribusinesses over time. Instead of looking to the Golden Straitjacket gospel as a substitute form of glad tidings for the poor, those of us who live in abundance need to embody the fullness of the good news in our own economic thinking and practice so that we may share the abundance.

131. Wright, *Surprised by Hope.*

CHAPTER 9

From Easter to Ascension: Global Political Communion

The time of the forty days [from Easter to the Ascension] is . . . no longer a time of servitude but of sovereignty—sovereignty, precisely, over time as something that the Son receives from the Father. This time, now his, reveals all the fullness of eternity that is in it. . . . The mode of time revealed during the forty days remains the foundation for every other mode of his presence in time, in the Church, and in the world. His manner of being, revealed during those days, is the ultimate form of his reality.

—Hans Urs von Balthasar[1]

Parade Magazine recently ran a cover story on "The Race to Own the Arctic" that reframed the specter of global climate change as an opportunity rather than a threat. According to the story, until recently "the Arctic's wealth—which may include up to 25 percent of the earth's oil and gas reserves—was too difficult to reach. But now the North Pole is warming twice as fast as the rest of the planet, according to the Intergovernmental Panel on Climate Change."[2] If the ice continues to recede, reported *Parade*, we can look forward to Arctic oil imports, Arctic diamond mines, and Arctic seaborne shipping, as the old Northwest Passage finally opens to global seafarers—what National Public Radio

1. Von Balthasar, *Theology of History*, 86–87.
2. Reiss, "Race to Own the Arctic," 4–5, quote at 4.

called "business opportunities."[3] But these business opportunities also coincide with political problems, since Russia, the United States, Canada, Norway, and Denmark are competing to lay claim to territorial waters. A Russian submarine "planted a flag on the ocean floor and returned home to congratulations from President Vladimir Putin," while the Canadian prime minister said that he "understands the first principle of Arctic sovereignty: Use it or lose it."[4] Meanwhile, American Coast Guard ships are mapping the ocean floor north of Alaska in advance of securing territorial claims.[5] In light of escalating rhetoric, armed conflicts over Arctic territory are easily imaginable.

Climate concerns and the battle over the Arctic highlight three issues in the globalization of politics. First, increasing global interactions draw our attention to global problems, like climate change, that transcend the capacity of territorial states to address them. Ecological problems illustrate the "tragedy of the commons": because the world is organized into territorial states that claim sovereign authority over territory (analogous to private property), no authoritative political actors are looking out for the common areas that no one state controls because they are not claimed as sovereign territory.[6] If climate change is a serious threat, it would affect the whole globe in problematic ways, yet the nation-state system that governs our world politically often fails to address it, because no one state has a compelling interest in resolving problems that it only partially creates.[7] No authoritative global political community and no authoritative global political actors exist *above* the state that can compel states to take action, so the response to global problems such as climate change often lags, because responses require the cooperation of many states. Although the United Nations and multilateral systems exist, they are only able to function to the extent that sovereignty over issues is delegated to them. And, as we will see, states jealously protect their sovereignty, even in the face of global problems. Second, then, territoriality appears to be alive and well. Each of the states bordering the Arctic is eager to claim chunks of the region in order to capture untapped wealth below the receding

3. Inskeep, "Blasting for Diamonds in Yellowknife."

4. Inskeep, "Nations Jostle for a Share of the Arctic."

5. Reiss, "Race," 5; Inskeep, "Nations Jostle."

6. Amstutz, *International Ethics*, 197–98; Hardin, "Tragedy of the Commons," 1243–48.

7. Held, "Reframing Global Governance," 240; Kudrle, "Globalization by the Numbers," 349.

ice. Despite a great deal of commentary on the de-territorialization of politics due to globalization, it appears that territorial state sovereignty still matters when it comes to claiming resources. However, at the same time, people are increasingly nomadic: as of 2005 roughly 3 percent of the world's population, or 190 million people, lived outside their country of birth.[8] While state sovereignty remains fixed territorially, people and ideas are moving. Third, then, globalization is also reshaping and challenging the agency, power, and identity of territorial states. Migrations of people, transnational corporations, non-governmental organizations, criminal organizations, and terrorist groups all challenge the modern system of sovereignty. The Arctic situation illustrates the power shift: while states scramble to lay claim to territories, corporations are already operating mines and opening ports in previously ice-bound areas. It also illustrates an identity shift: one's reaction to the news about the Arctic will likely depend upon whether one identifies more with corporations or with non-governmental organizations. Where a businessperson sees opportunity, a Greenpeace activist sees environmental crisis. Such globalized identities—a global business identity as opposed to a global environmentalist identity—will often divide people and will even divide Christian communities. Despite a common faith identity, Christians vigorously disagree over whether climate change is even an issue. Our loyalties to Al Gore or to climate skeptics threaten to transcend our loyalty to Christ.

But a Christian's identity in the Kingdom of God—our ultimate political identity—should transcend and direct all earthly loyalties and identities. And although that identity does not dictate stances on complex policy debates, it ought to foster common concerns rooted in common identity. The story of the forty days after Easter is a story of the resurrected Jesus claiming authority, power, and identity—sovereignty—in establishing his Kingdom. At the same time, Jesus brings the church into being in his community of disciples. Yet the way in which Jesus does this is most unusual, as it centers upon the simultaneous presence and absence of his body. We find in the days leading up to Jesus' Ascension some powerful clues about how the church is to be political, and it turns out that these clues encourage us to re-imagine the globalization of politics and improvise hopeful practices of politics today.

8. "Snapshot."

GLOBALIZATION RECONFIGURING AUTHORITY, POWER, AND IDENTITY

Globalization is reshaping political authority, political agency, and political identity across the world. "There is no question," writes Friedman, that in the globalization system . . . a certain degree of decision-making is moved out of each country's political sphere into the global market sphere, where no one person, country, or institution can exert exclusive political control."[9] This decision-making in the age of globalization raises several questions: Where does final authority for political decisions reside? Who has political power in global structures and institutions? Where is the political community that claims our highest allegiance and identity? And how does the church relate to global political issues and embody global community?

Authority

A brief history shows how the present situation of political authority under globalization constitutes a halt or reversal to the modern trend that flattened political space by consolidating authority in one dominant institution. Some even suggest that we might now be seeing the rise of "neo-medieval" forms of multilayered politics.[10] As medieval European Christendom waned, political authority was indeed flattened from complex, overlapping medieval patchworks of authority to one dominant stratum of authority that was christened "the state."[11] Modern kings, princes, rulers, and republics arose to challenge the authority of the church, as state-making kings cut down not only the authority of the Pope and the Holy Roman Empire *above* them but also the authority of the nobility and towns or city-states *below* them.[12] The successors to these rulers became the core of sovereign states that we know today, both for material reasons, because the state became the most effective unit at capturing revenue in order to make war; and for constitutive reasons, because sovereign state institutions (and later their corresponding "nations") became

9. Friedman, *Lexus and the Olive Tree*, 191.

10. Sassen, "Places and Spaces of the Global," 79–105; Bull, *Anarchical Society*, 254–76.

11. Cavanaugh, *Theopolitical Imagination*, 101; Milbank, "On Complex Space."

12. Van Creveld, *Rise and Decline of the State*, 59–125.

sites of loyalty and identity in modern Europe.[13] The state (and later the nation-state) thus claimed the middle by monopolizing power and seizing authority from those who challenged it on behalf of the church or on behalf of more localized authorities. At the same time, these emergent states expanded outside Europe in imperial quests for spices, gold, and prestige. The rise of the Spanish, English, and French monarchies and the rise of the Dutch Republic in the early modern period fit this pattern particularly well. By the end of the nineteenth century the European states had exported this conception of the nation-state worldwide as they imposed sovereignty upon virtually every territory in the world (leaving only the North and South Polar Regions untouched by claims to sovereignty). While these moves had begun with "private" authorities such as trading companies or mercenaries acting to extend state authority, colonial and post-colonial states eventually laid claim to "public" authority over territory.[14] Thus, conceptions of "public space," "private property," and "nationhood" gradually came to dominate the way people around the world imagined politics, as the state claimed public authority over an "imagined community" called the nation or civil society and defined by state boundaries.[15] Part of the reason for acceptance of this authority, as Bill Cavanaugh has argued, was the widespread belief that the state provided order by suppressing violent disorder, creating a paradox in the application of violence to curb violence, namely, the "violent creation of order."[16] Nonetheless, the state's claim to legitimacy was widely accepted as a necessity in strife-torn times. Whether entirely accurate or not, the classic defense of the need for the state is well articulated by Bruce Porter's statement: "Without the state, internal anarchy or foreign oppression threaten; with the state, we risk internal bondage to keep at bay the anarchy of war, both civil and international."[17] As Thomas Hobbes famously said, life without a strong sovereign power would be "solitary, poor, nasty,

13. Tilly, *Coercion, Capital, and European States*; Tilly, "Reflections on the History of European State-Making," 3–83; Porter, *War and the Rise of the State*; Cavanaugh, *Theopolitical Imagination*, 9–52; Spruyt, *Sovereign State and Its Competitors*, 151–80.

14. Thomson, *Mercenaries, Pirates, and Sovereigns*, 69–154.

15. Taylor, *Secular Age*, 159–211; Anderson, *Imagined Communities*; Opello and Rosow, *Nation-State*, 77–120; Kratochwil, "Of Systems, Boundaries, and Territoriality," 27–52; Sassen, *Territory, Authority, Rights*, 31–73.

16. Cavanaugh, *Theopolitical Imagination*, 9–52; Cavanaugh, "Killing for the Telephone Company." Cohen et al., "Paradoxical Nature of State Making," 901–10.

17. Porter, *War*, 21.

brutish and short." Yet strong sovereign powers have authorized the killing of millions of their own citizens in the twentieth century alone.

But now globalization appears to challenge this conventional centralized authority from above and below. So are we entering a world where
the authority of the state is eroding at the supranational and sub-national
levels? I believe Stanford University political scientist Stephen Krasner is
correct to say that the effect of globalization (for the foreseeable future,
anyway) "will be to alter the scope of state authority rather than to generate some fundamentally new way to organize political life."[18] While political globalization reshapes state agency and reconfigures identities, it has
not yet begun to replace the state with an alternative form of authority.[19]
Friedman actually uses the best label to describe the current system as
"global *governance* . . . without global *government*."[20] The distinction here
is between modes of organization and the highest authoritative mode of
organization at the world level. There is no world government. However,
there are many forms of cooperative world governance between the governments of the members of the state system.

In fact, states themselves have authorized global political institutions
that carry out governance on their behalf. In other words, globalization
emerges not only from above and below state authorities but it also spreads
horizontally, between state authorities to extend their delegated authority
across the globe. We do not just have economic, ecological, or cultural
forces that are pressing globalization upon resistant state actors, but we
also have the authoritative political actors of the current day constituting
a global system that serves their interests, in global institutions such as
the United Nations, the International Monetary Fund, or the World Bank.
As Cavanaugh correctly notes, these institutions "represent a voluntary
loss of sovereignty for the nation-state," which does "not mean the end
of the state project, but rather its generalization across space."[21] Much of
this governance places states in the position to regulate economic affairs,
allowing them to construct and regulate global markets and allowing
stronger states to pressure weaker state actors toward "market-friendly"

18. Krasner, "Think Again," 20–29, quote at 20.

19. Cohen, *Resilience of the State*; Paul, "States, Security Function, and the New Global
Forces;" Campbell, "States, Politics, and Globalization."

20. Friedman, *Lexus and the Olive Tree*, 206. Emphasis in original. Note, however,
that these terms were used much earlier in Rosenau and Czempiel, *Governance without
Government*; Held, "Political Globalization," 94–102, describes a "multicentric" system.

21. Cavanaugh, *Theopolitical Imagination*, 104.

policies that benefit the dominant powers. For instance, the history of global expansion by Spain, Portugal, Holland, France, and Britain from the sixteenth to the eighteenth centuries illustrates the important role these governments played in authorizing and promoting global expansion aimed at economic gain for their home populations.[22] Mostly on this historical basis, world-systems analysts contend that a global system of states has always served the interests of the core countries by pitting peripheral states against each other to supply core markets, where capital was accumulated.[23] The very definition of a global capitalist system, in world-systems theory, requires states that serve the interests of the world economy, prioritize the market, and serve capitalist interests. On the opposite side, Robert Gilpin and others argue that states still dominate world markets, focusing primarily on autonomous political concerns that determine economic outcomes.[24] Yet the historical coincidence of global markets and state structures in the modern period suggests a kind of reciprocal relationship in which economic interests or political interests dominate at different times and in different ways. Sometimes market forces drive the agenda, at other times states drive the agenda, and often these two go together in the same direction, as in the case of earlier global imperialism.[25] It is telling that more recent events in Pietra Rivoli's story of the "travels of a t-shirt in the global economy" were "less about competitive markets than . . . about politics, history, and creative maneuvers to avoid markets."[26] Thus, it is more accurate to say that states and the global market exist in a dialectical bond, each dependent on the other, illustrating the thesis of Karl Polanyi.[27] As Polanyi put it, "The road to the free market was opened and kept open by an enormous increase in

22. Landes, *Wealth and Poverty of Nations*, 60–181; Abernethy, *Dynamics of Global Dominance*.

23. Wallerstein, *Politics of the World-Economy*, 27–30, 80–82; Hardt and Negi, *Empire*, 3–201.

24. Gilpin, *Global Political Economy*, 362–76; Waltz, *Theory of International Politics*, 129–60; Waltz, "Globalization and Governance," 693–700.

25. See Friedman, *Lexus and the Olive Tree*, 13, and Friedman, *Longitudes*, 4–5, on the balance "between nation-states and global markets." This is a common theme in the field of international political economy, as a glance at a few leading textbook titles shows: Strange, *States and Markets*; Schwartz, *States versus Markets*; Grieco and Ikenberry, *State Power and World Markets: International Political Economy*.

26. Rivoli, *Travels*, x, also see 211–13.

27. Ibid., 213; Gray, *False Dawn*, 1–54, 210–11.

continuous, centrally organized and controlled interventionism."[28] States not only fostered markets in order to gain in wealth, argued Polanyi, but they also tamed them with social legislation when unbridled commodity, currency, and capital markets threatened to undercut political stability.[29] States remain the authoritative political actors mediating transnational forces. They are the funnel through which other concerns must be channeled in order to actually affect people, all of whom remain citizens of one state or another. However, transnational corporations, ecological groups, or identity movements empowered by globalization often pressure states to act for their interests.

The case of nationalist movements illustrates how globalization both upholds state authority and empowers new actors. Achieving sovereign statehood is a desirable goal for many nationalist groups—Kurds, Chechens, Kosovars, Palestinians, and Darfurians, among others—which suggests that they see the state as a vehicle to achieving political agency in the current system. At the same time, these groups are increasingly able to network globally to gain support for their causes. Transnational networks of peoples actually empower people to take collective action at key moments in "contentious politics" such as protests, creating a kind of "globalization from below" that pressures state authorities to modify their policies.[30] The current "Save Darfur" campaign is an example of this global mobilization across borders, in which international activists support indigenous movements.[31] But the challenge of such global political movements is less to the authority of states than to their power and their claims upon human identity.[32]

Power

States still retain power to act within the global system, but are facing increasing challenges from other global actors. From above the state, the

---

28. Polanyi, *Great Transformation*, 140.

29. On regulation, see ibid., 76, 201–19.

30. Tarrow, *New Transnational Activism*; Porta et al., *Globalization from Below*.

31. For a skeptical view of NGO's roles in Mexico's Zapatista movement and in Nigeria, see Bob, *Marketing of Rebellion*.

32. Scholte, *Globalization*, 185–223, fails to make this distinction between official legal authority and the empowerment of non-state actors and thus overstates the challenge to sovereignty. Globalization does not challenge sovereignty itself but it does make it more difficult for states to effectively uphold claims to sovereignty in many areas.

power of supranational organizations is mostly lacking, and their authority only extends to areas in which states permit them to operate.[33] While some worry about a "democratic deficit," in which the citizens of states have only limited information about (and only indirect power over) the workings of distant international organizations in which governments have a voice without gaining input or facing scrutiny back home, such organizations have limited power.[34] That is to say, decisions made at the World Trade Organization headquarters in Geneva affect the government and people of Canada, yet who in Canada elected the bureaucrats representing Canada at the WTO, or the bureaucrats who work for the WTO? Still, the power of the WTO is less intimidating when we realize that its entire annual budget is rather small. In the year 2000, the amount of money the WTO spent in a year was equivalent to the amount of money Duke University spent in two weeks.[35] The WTO also depends upon state cooperation and has no way of enforcing any of its rulings apart from authorizing states to impose sanctions on one another for violations of trade rules. Likewise, both the authority and power of the United Nations is limited. Not only is its authority limited to that delegated by nation states, but it also has limited financial resources. The entire United Nations system spent approximately $18 billion in 2004, while the United States' federal government spent over $2.2 trillion in that same year. If the United Nations were one of the fifty states in 2004, it would have ranked 28th in total spending, between the spending levels of the state governments of Oregon and Colorado.[36] While lack of accountability of organizations such as the United Nations might be an issue, they scarcely have the power to challenge powerful states—and only when other states use them to do so.

By contrast, some transnational economic actors do have growing capacities to challenge state power. After working with Bill Clinton in his first term on economic policy, political operative James Carville said, "I used to think that if there was reincarnation, I wanted to come back as the President or the Pope or as a .400 baseball hitter. But now I would like to

33. Drezner, *All Politics Is Global*, 64–68, offers a helpful typology of universal, club, and regional governmental organizations.

34. Keohane, "Governance in a Partially Globalized World," 1–13.

35. Ibid., 6–7.

36. "Total UN System Estimated Expenditures"; U. S. Census Bureau, "States Ranked by Revenue and Expenditure."

come back as the bond market. You can intimidate everybody."[37] Carville constantly heard during discussions of economic policy in 1993 that certain policies would upset the bond market, and he lamented this constant check on the Clinton team's plans. Do bond markets or other financial markets put limits on governments? Is the growth of global commerce straining states' capacities to tax and spend? Is the welfare state in retreat? Do transnational corporations, sub-state terrorist groups, movements of peoples, or non-governmental organizations illustrate a trend toward the devolution of power downward? Although a vast amount of literature in political science has sprung up to answer such questions since the publication of *The Lexus and the Olive Tree*—a body of literature that we cannot review here—Friedman made three early claims about globalization and government.[38]

First, Friedman championed Carville's claim about the power of financial markets with a vengeance. He imagines a conversation in which the U. S. Treasury Secretary lectures the prime minister of Malaysia about the electronic herd of fast-paced global investors: "The Electronic Herd cuts no one any slack. No one. It does not recognize anyone's unique circumstances. The herd knows only its own rules. But the rules of the herd are pretty consistent—they're the rules of the Golden Straitjacket."[39] There is no question that global financial markets have increased their capacity to pressure governments in places like Malaysia, particularly in matters of exchange rate policy, but it is not clear that this fundamentally alters the *authority* of states as the ultimate regulators of commerce, money, and movements of people. Several recent books and articles in political science suggest that states retain some autonomy to uphold policies that challenge global financial institutions, even when they are increasingly pressured by financial markets or global economic institutions to institute economic policies that line up with investors' interests.[40] Even developing countries facing pressure to adopt the Washington Consensus have found small spaces for alternatives in recent years.[41]

37. Uchitelle, "Ideas and Trends."

38. Berger, "Globalization and Politics," 43–62, was an early review. Since its publication, dozens of books and hundreds of articles have appeared to answer these questions.

39. Friedman, *Lexus and the Olive Tree*, 113.

40. Mosley, *Global Capital and National Governments*; Weiss, *Myth of the Powerless State*; but also see Strange, *States and the Diffusion of Power*; and Tabb, *Economic Governance*.

41. Grugel et al., "Beyond the Washington Consensus?"

Second, Friedman argues that globalization helps empower transnational terrorists. Even before the attacks of September 11, 2001, Friedman argued that terrorism was a global threat because of the rise of "super-empowered angry men and women." "What makes them super-empowered," he says, "is their genius at using the networked world, the Internet, and the very high technology they hate, to attack us."[42] "Globalization not only makes it possible for them to attack the United States as individuals, it not only gives them the motivation to do it," wrote Friedman, "it also gives them the logic. The logic is that their own states don't represent the real power structure anymore. The relevant power structure is global."[43] Friedman's colleague David Brooks also credits terrorist groups with being "open-source decentralized conglomerations of small, quasi-independent groups" with "postnational Silicon Valley-style organizational methods" that challenge centralized states.[44] Such globalized terrorist networks directly challenge states from below: "They merely seek to weaken states, so they can prosper in the lawless space created by the collapse of law and order."[45] By making it easier to network outside of state authority, globalization thus empowers violent challengers to states, even if those violent challengers are unlikely to form alternative authorities.[46] It also appears that terrorist threats have actually "led to a strengthening of state power, extension of the state's role in the field of internal security, and increased intervention in people's daily lives. . . ."[47] After 9/11, the United States tightened border security, immigration and visa policies, and surveillance of international communications. And the fact remains that any person crossing an international border must produce proof of citizenship—except in places where normal passport controls have been waived by states, as in the European Union and except in places where state authorities lack the capacity to enforce their legal right to maintain border controls. As one economist notes, "Rules on cross-border labor flows are determined almost always unilaterally (rather than multilaterally as in other areas of economic exchange) and

42. Friedman, *Longitudes*, 33.
43. Ibid., 403.
44. Brooks, "Insurgent Advantage," A27.
45. Ibid.
46. Matthew and Shambaugh, "Limits of Terrorism," 617–27.
47. Cohen, *Resilience*, 146.

remain highly restrictive."[48] Apart from the capacity challenges posed by large-scale movements of people, the legal authority to control their movement—to lay a claim on them—remains with the state, except where it is delegated, and it can be taken back.

Third, Friedman also argues that non-governmental organizations (NGOs) help produce coalitions that can pressure corporations or governments for change.[49] The number of international NGOs—defined as "mostly nongovernment, private sector but public interest, sometimes volunteer, for the most part nonprofit" organizations—has grown rapidly from 832 in 1951 to over 40,000 today.[50] In support of his claim, Friedman cites the successful global campaign to ban landmines that was largely driven by an email advocacy campaign led by Jody Williams, who was later awarded the Nobel Peace Prize for her efforts.[51] Some have gone beyond Friedman to argue that a global civil society is forming in which activist groups connect in solidarity across borders, but there is some reason to doubt that a global society of activist groups will replace states anytime soon in governing, policing, or providing social services.[52] Rather, it is clear that these non-governmental groups remain in a dialectical relationship with the state system, existing to pressure it to take action rather than taking action directly themselves.[53] In the end, Jody Williams' supporters had to lobby governments to sign a treaty banning landmines, and after the treaty was signed they had to monitor compliance with it, since states could just sign the agreement and then do nothing. However, in weaker states, it is possible that NGOs can also undermine state power by taking over relief or health functions that normally reside under government authority.[54] The government of Myanmar

48. Rodrik, *One Economics*, 240.

49. Friedman, *Lexus and the Olive Tree*, 169, 206–11.

50. Cusimano et al., "Private-Sector Transsovereign Actors: MNCs and NGOs," 257–58.

51. Friedman, *Lexus and the Olive Tree*, 14; Friedman, *Longitudes*, 5–6; Williams, "International Campaign to Ban Landmines."

52. Mathews, "Power Shift," 50–66; Keck and Sikkink, *Activists Beyond Borders*; Colás, *International Civil Society*, 64–109; Drezner, *All Politics is Global*, 19–22.

53. Keck and Sikkink, *Activists*, 13. Their model assumes that non-governmental organizations in state A will recruit others in state B and state B itself to pressure the government of state A.

54. Kaplan, *Ends of the Earth*, 408, 430–33, noted the large role of NGOs in Cambodia in the early 1990s, to the point where a deputy provincial governor wanted them to enter in order to help the government. Thanks to Luke Thompson for recalling this passage.

demonstrated its power by denying relief groups permission to enter the country after a massive typhoon in May 2008. It seems that states still retain authority and some power to compel private authorities to bend to their wishes.

Despite the ways, then, in which transnational financial markets, transnational migrations of people, transnational corporations, and transnational activist or terrorist groups can challenge states' effective power, the state retains its legal authority to monitor and control the movements of money, people, and goods that cross its borders—as well as the legal right to use deadly force within its borders—even when that right cannot always be effectively exercised. This suggests that states are targets for other actors exercising power on a global basis. For example, global corporations work by pressuring states to shape institutions such as the World Trade Organization: as we noted in the last chapter, software and pharmaceutical companies persuaded states to push the WTO to include protection of intellectual property rights. We also saw how the United States invaded Iraq and how global oil corporations are now entering the country. To put it simply, if the oil companies had authority they might have invaded themselves, but they depend upon states to control the political spaces in which they explore, drill, export, and refine. Yet corporations can also lobby governments and bend their policies to favor their interests.

In some cases, private corporations have even taken over functions previously held by public, state authority. The most interesting recent cases involve the outsourcing of state security functions to private mercenary groups, which have played large roles in Iraq. This is a direct reversal of the trend toward consolidation of military authority and power within the centralized state, but it is unclear if this trend will continue. If the sharply increased use of private security firms in Iraq turns out to be a long-term trend that extends to other states, it would constitute the most serious challenge to state power since the early modern period. As the *New York Times* reported, Iraq has seen "the most extensive use of private contractors on the battlefield since Renaissance princes hired private armies to fight their battles."[55] The question is whether this is a harbinger of the future.[56] Either way, the globalization of political

55. Broder and Risen, "Armed Guards in Iraq Occupy a Legal Limbo."

56. For careful analysis of this question, see Singer, *Corporate Warriors*; and Avant, *Market for Force*, 253–64. Avant concludes that "The market for force . . . has not made

authority and power toward complex "neo-medieval" patterns reinforces the church's need to find itself politically.

Identity

Without question identity is in flux because of globalization. Shifting political identities are well-described in this striking quotation from a text on the state:

> membership in a political community becomes a fleeting and constantly moving horizon for many people rather than a secure, permanent, and lifelong identity. The imagining of politics as located in some central representation of unified, territorially based power (i.e., the state) is difficult to conjure in the minds of ever more nomadic people. . . . The nation-state promises prosperity and security within secure boundaries, which it can no longer deliver or is not any longer willing to deliver, to the poor as well as much of the working population. Therefore, although many still seek the security, prosperity, and popular sovereignty of nation-states, at the same time they seek out other identities.[57]

The rise of global identity networks is illustrated in the way that some North American evangelical Christians became part of a global social movement mobilizing behind the moral cause of climate change—not to mention global pro-life, pro-religious freedom, anti-AIDS, and anti-poverty efforts—to pressure state authorities. Evangelicalism has often functioned as a transnational social movement driven by moral concerns, notably in the Quaker and evangelical networks behind the global movement to abolish the slave trade.[58] Today, evangelicals can join global non-governmental organizations and campaigns driven by "shared principled ideas or values" that may take them in many different directions.[59] While they may be joining movements that encourage new and healthy forms of political solidarity below the state level, they might also encourage

---

states, per se, less important, but opened the way for changes in the roles states and other actors play in controlling force on the world stage" (264).

57. Opello and Rosow, *Nation-State and Global Order*, 259; for more detailed investigations of reconfigurations of citizenship, see Croucher, *Globalization and Belonging*, 43–81; and Sassen, *Territory, Authority, Rights*, 277–327.

58. Metaxas, *Amazing Grace*; Hochschild, *Bury the Chains*; Nadelmann, "Global Prohibition Regimes," 479–526.

59. Keck and Sikkink, *Activists*, 30.

unhealthy forms of solidarity.[60] The benefit of globalization is that it can challenge Christians to come into contact with other Christians globally, encouraging them to eschew narrow nationalism that glorifies one's own homeland and opening them toward concern for shared global problems, but the danger is that the complexities of globalization can trigger backlashes against it that reinforce such nationalism. Christians may network globally to promote freer immigration policies or they may network to build walls and fences. Christians may network globally to work for greenhouse gas reductions, or they may network to oppose them. They may network globally to promote free trade or to promote local economy. In either case, they are mobilizing on the basis of identity.

As communication and transportation technologies make it easier for non-state actors to network across the globe, social movements can rally for or against the threatening effects of globalization, join the "backlash," and assert local identities.[61] The struggle for identity concerns Friedman. As peoples come into contact with those different from themselves, or as they experience a perceived loss of power to global actors, they may well fear homogenization and thus reassert their particular identities. Friedman's symbol for these identities is the olive tree, which "represent[s] everything that roots us, anchors us, identifies us and locates us in this world—whether it be belonging to a family, a community, a tribe, a nation, a religion or, most of all, a place called home."[62] Thus, Friedman says, "one reason that the nation-state will never disappear, even if it does weaken, is because it is the ultimate olive tree—the expression of whom we belong to. . . ."[63] But here Christians can question the limited effects of globalization on earthly political identities. Globalization, we can say, has not gone far enough in challenging state identities: the assertion of a fundamental olive tree identity in the state contrasts with the Christian claim that we belong not to the Republic or the Nation of the United States of America or to global corporations or to global environmental causes but (in the words of the first question and answer in the Heidelberg Catechism) to our "faithful Savior Jesus Christ," who constitutes a global people. Christians believe that they find their deepest political, social, individual, and communal identity in the Jesus who died

---

60. Arquilla and Ronfeldt, "Advent of Netwar (Revisited)."

61. Friedman, *Lexus and the Olive Tree*, 327–47.

62. Ibid., 31–32.

63. Ibid., 31.

on a tree, rose again, ate with his disciples, and ascended to heaven. They therefore believe that the ultimate olive tree is not the nation-state but the church that came into being during this season.

But where is the church and how does it relate to these movements of non-state actors? While the church can support global NGO networks, it should not be reduced to being a sub-national group or civil society actor whose only political role is to pressure states.[64] Rather, as Bill Cavanaugh has stressed, the church must find its primary global political identity on its own terms.[65] The church is not just another civil society actor looking to network with others. Its power, authority, and identity transcend current political arrangements, yet its concern for embodied presence requires it to engage for justice earth now. Therefore, we can locate the church less as an alternative space to rival the state or the global market and more (in Cavanaugh's words) as a set of "alternative disciplines, imaginations or performances, because the church is not called to present itself yet as another conventional type of political arrangement. *Ecclesia* [church] is neither *polis* [city-state] nor *oikos* [economy], but an alternative which radically reconfigures the dichotomy between public and private used to domesticate the Gospel."[66] Instead, says Cavanaugh, the church is best viewed "in temporal rather than spatial terms, according to the mode of gift. Because it is enacted liturgically, the church is a series of dramatic performances, and not a state of being. The church is not a constant presence, an identifiable site firmly bounded and policed by law."[67] This unique presence of the church relies upon the tension between the absence and the presence of Christ—a tension that is dramatically re-enacted in the weeks between Easter and the Ascension of Jesus into heaven. It turns out that we find in this season a dynamic political practice that helps us re-imagine globalization and the church's mission through the stories of these weeks of the church calendar. In these forty days, while Jesus is present in the church, and while the church is his body, he is also absent from us, because he is at the right hand of the Father in heaven. As the disciples do, we must find our mission from this

---

64. The textbook I use to teach Introduction to World Politics defines the Roman Catholic Church as an NGO with a "broad-based membership" of 800 million members. Spiegel et al., *World Politics in a New Era*, 583.

65. Cavanaugh, *Torture and Eucharist*, 196, 268–69.

66. Ibid., 268–69.

67. Ibid., 269.

Jesus to whom we belong in the middle of that tension between presence and absence.

To return to the opening of this chapter, awareness of absence helps distance us from contemporary political controversies: instead of too quickly identifying Christ's presence with either corporations or environmentalists in the battle over the Arctic, we should find our identity flowing from the one to whom we belong, our ultimate olive tree. We thus identify first with God and Creation. The absence of Jesus reminds us that we should never identify worldly political agendas with his cause. Paradoxically, however, the presence of Jesus with the church reminds us that our embodied political lives matter to the cause of the reigning King. We care deeply about what happens on earth as well as in heaven, so we can hardly remain indifferent to news about possible climate change or future wars. We are to live for the embodiment of Kingdom by sharing the good news and building up the flock. And so we find our mission in communion with the Christ who is both absent and present.

RE-ENACTING THE FORTY DAYS LOCATES THE CHURCH POLITICALLY

Re-enacting the time between Jesus' Resurrection and his Ascension can help Christians to re-imagine global political community in profound ways. Cavanaugh has already made a compelling case for the "spatial story" of the Eucharist as the church's compelling alternative to globalization, but an understanding of the forty days between Easter and Ascension helps flesh out his global ecclesiology, or global understanding of the politics of the church, rooted in communion.[68] For Cavanaugh, the Body of Christ has a remarkable ability to be both global and local while practicing a true universalism or catholicity rooted in a connection to place. The gospel accounts after Easter likewise suggest that *communion* with the Risen and Ascended Christ is what constitutes the church to act globally: carrying out its mission and always attending to both Christ's resurrected bodily presence and Christ's exalted kingly absence. We find some powerful cues that empower the church's mission of witness in re-enacting the story of the forty days, which von Balthasar suggests is the model of Christ's sovereignty in the fullness of time (as we saw in the epigraph to this chapter).

68. Cavanaugh, *Theopolitical Imagination*, 116–17.

The last chapter argued that the season of Easter through Pentecost has been neglected in recent liturgical practice and theology. Liturgical historian Patrick Regan says that the fifty days after Easter were originally a time of "rejoicing in the resurrection, Ascension , bestowal of the Spirit, and founding of the Church, understood not as separate episodes succeeding each other in time, but as different facets of one and the same mystery of Jesus' exaltation as Lord."[69] Thus, this season was neither a time "after Easter" or "between Easter and Pentecost" but an entire feasting season in its own right.[70] Later an emphasis on the feast of the Ascension emerged, coming forty days after Easter and ten days before Pentecost, in line with the narrative in Acts that places the date of Jesus' ascent at that time. In the new post-Vatican II lectionary of 1969, however, the Catholic Church re-christened the season as the "Sundays *of* Easter" to emphasize a continued feast through Pentecost.[71] Moreover, this move back to historical practice reinforced the tendency to marginalize the separate Feast of the Ascension, which was already in decline because it came on a weekday and thus conflicted with the schedules of factory workers and office workers (the capitalist calendar thus trumping the liturgical one).[72] This decline in liturgical practice further contributed to Western theology's neglect of the Ascension doctrinally—a neglect documented by theologian Douglas Farrow as a harmful one for the church.[73]

Recovering the stories of this season may help address Farrow's concern by incorporating us into the political tensions they embody. The Swiss Catholic theologian Hans Urs von Balthasar, for instance, quoted at the head of this chapter, contends that these forty days are the foundation for understanding the divine relation to time, the place in the gospel narratives where Jesus' "relations with his disciples are continued, the gulf between the here and the beyond is lovingly, redeemingly bridged, and his intimacy with them is renewed: their meetings have all the ease and naturalness of human relationships, they hear and see one another, touch one another, eat together, and the historical character of the whole is taken for granted."[74] Thus, Christ is present in the forty days in familiar

69. Regan, "Fifty Days and the Fiftieth Day," 224.

70. Ibid., 223–24.

71. Ibid., 244.

72. Kleinhans, *Year of the Lord*, 58.

73. Farrow, *Ascension and Ecclesia*.

74. Von Balthasar, *Theology of History*, 83.

ways. But he is also absent in these days, appearing and disappearing in unpredictable ways until the ultimate disappearance when he ascends, constituting the church during this time after Easter. As von Balthasar notes, "All Christ's appearances during these days have explicit reference to the Church . . . the forty days were expressly intended as an introduction and initiation of the days of the Church."[75] Specifically, the post-resurrection stories give a commission to the disciples to share what they have seen with the rest of the world.[76] Thus, the season of Easter focuses on the gathering of the church and its receiving its mission around the suddenly present and suddenly absent body of Christ.[77] One sign of this church-centered focus is the fact that the lectionary replaces the Old Testament lessons during the season with passages from the book of Acts that are all about the founding events of the church. Similarly, the lectionary assigns only passages from First Peter, First John, or Revelation, which unlike Paul's epistles, address multiple churches at once. After exploring how the church finds itself politically in this season, we will then be able to re-imagine how the church relates on its own terms to the globalization of politics.

The Gospel Accounts

The pattern of close presence and distant absence, of both eating with Jesus and missing Jesus, runs throughout the gospel stories for this season. Each year on the second Sunday of Easter, for example, John 20:19–31 is read. The fearful disciples are meeting in a locked room, but Jesus shows up in the room, says "peace be with you," and shows them "his hands and his side" (vv. 19–20). He can pass through walls, yet he is also a distinctly embodied presence with scars that his disciples can touch. John reports that the disciple Thomas was not there and so he doubted his colleagues, but a week later Jesus shows up again in a room with locked doors, and this time Thomas recognizes Jesus as his Lord and God (vv. 27–28). Then Jesus responds with a bit of a rebuke that speaks to an audience outside the story: "Blessed are those who have not seen and yet have come to believe" (v. 29). After identifying with Thomas' desire to have tangible proof and admiring his declaration, the listener or reader is immediately

---

75. Ibid., 89, 94.

76. Wright, *Resurrection*, 603, 649, 660.

77. Webber, *Ancient-Future Time*, 148–58.

reminded that Jesus' body is absent to her, at least in its physical form. The narrative therefore invites potential disciples to reflect upon whether they will also declare their faith and receive this blessing, even though they cannot touch Jesus' hands and side as Thomas did. The story also points to the Eucharist as the practice in which disciples can find the presence of Christ's body, even though it is also absent. Blind faith alone is not needed: like Thomas, we can eat with Jesus; unlike Thomas, we cannot touch his hands and side. Yet this provides us the opportunity to surpass Thomas by trusting in faith without seeing and touching. We will find this stance enacted in the Eucharist, and we will find that it constitutes the church's unique way of being political, but first we must attend to the other stories of Jesus' post-resurrection appearances.

On the third Sunday of the Easter season, the church reads the accounts in Luke 24 or John 21, which also illustrate how both presence and absence shape the church's mission in communion. The Emmaus road story, unique to Luke's gospel (Luke 24:13–35), offers a double lesson. First, the risen Jesus is bodily present, walking with the two disciples, and the disciples eat in communion with him, but his identity only becomes clear when he breaks the bread. But after this surprising appearance, he disappears again: he is both with us and apart from us. Second, in terms of mission, we find two elements of early church practice in this story, both the Eucharistic breaking of the bread and the biblical teaching of Jesus, the latter of which caused the two followers to exclaim that their "hearts were burning" within them when he taught them, leading them to hurry back to Jerusalem to share the news.[78] By analogy, the church's mission is to receive this teaching, share its news, and celebrate the meal.

We find a similar pattern in Luke's next post-Easter passage (Luke 24:36–48). Here the disciples are gathered in Jerusalem and have just heard from the Emmaus travelers when Jesus shows up, startling and terrifying them, making them think it was a ghost (v. 37). But Jesus invites them, "touch me and see; for a ghost does not have flesh and bones as you see that I have" (v. 39). He shows them his hands and feet and then asks if they have anything to eat. "They gave him a piece of broiled fish, and he took it and ate in their presence" (vv. 42–43). After this, he teaches from the scriptures, and then tells the disciples that they are witnesses who are to share the story of "repentance and forgiveness of sins is to be proclaimed in his name to all nations, beginning from Jerusalem. You are

78. Ibid., 659–60.

witnesses of these things" (vv. 47–48). Once again we find the mysterious Jesus showing up to eat with his disciples before charging them with a mission to share his teaching. While his showing up is a mystery, he is no ghost. The disciples can touch his flesh and bones; he is hungry for something to eat; and he eats together with these disciples who are now to be witnesses, sharing the story.

So, too, in the final chapter of John's gospel we find a link between a Jesus who is mysteriously both absent and present and who charges his disciples with a mission (John 21:1–19). This time they are fishing in the Sea of Galilee when Jesus shows up on the shore. At first they do not recognize him, but this stranger encourages them to cast their nets on the right side of the boat, and they end up with a huge haul of fish. When John tells Peter it is Jesus, Peter dives in to swim ashore, while the rest of the disciples steer the boat in to land. The previously hidden Jesus is cooking fish and bread over a fire, and he shares this breakfast with his disciples (once they have hauled all 153 fish onto the beach). After the breakfast, Jesus restores and re-commissions Peter by making it clear that just as Jesus has fed the disciples, Peter must not only feed his flock, but he must follow Jesus on the path of discipleship and martyrdom (v. 19).

The fourth Sunday of the season is all about the good shepherd who cares for, and lays down his life for, his flock. Every year on this day, the church reads Psalm 23 and portions of John 10, hearing of the shepherd who leads us. Extended reflection on the shepherd and sheep metaphors in John 10 alone would be worthwhile, but the collect for this day in the *Book of Common Prayer* nicely reiterates the link between the shepherd and the mission in those passages: "O God, whose Son Jesus is the good shepherd of your people: Grant that when we hear his voice we may know him who calls us each by name, and follow where he leads."[79] Our mission is to listen to our shepherd's voice and follow him where he leads, even if that leads us into the valley of the shadow of death and the gate of our own cross.

But how are we to hear the voice of one who is not on earth with us in body? If Jesus is absent, who guides us? The last three Sundays in the season turn to the role of the Spirit in helping the church to hear and follow the shepherd, pointing the church toward Pentecost. The readings narrate how the disciples learned that he "would continue to remain

---

79. Episcopal Church, *Book of Common Prayer*, 225.

present with them and guide them in his physical absence."[80] Jesus promises to be present with his disciples, assuring them that the Father "will give you another Advocate, to be with you forever . . . the Spirit of truth" (John 14:16—17a). Through the Spirit, he and the Father are not just with us, but in us (vv. 18–20). Finally, he promises, "the Advocate, the Holy Spirit, whom the Father will send in my name, will teach you everything, and remind you of all that I have said to you" (v. 26). He will soon be absent, but he will remain present through the Spirit. With the encouragement that the Advocate will come, the church can carry out its mission of living out Christ's self-sacrificing love. Indeed, through the church's "oneness the glory of God may be made known in all the earth."[81]

The Ascension

Within the re-enactment of the Ascension story, we also find the connected themes of absence, presence and mission. All these can be linked to a proper understanding of the Eucharist that in turn can help us to re-imagine the church's global political role. Forty days after the resurrection, Jesus ascends into heaven (Luke 24:50–53; Acts 1:1–11), an act of great significance for a Christian view of politics. The Ascension becomes a political act, as N. T. Wright argues, when we notice two details of Luke's longer account in Acts. The bodily absence of Jesus is a founding political act for the church. First, a Jewish audience would likely connect the story to the vision in Dan 7:13 of "one like a human being coming with the clouds of heaven," finding distinct political hope. This "son of man" takes over kingship, a distinctly political claim that Jesus makes at his Ascension on the clouds.[82] Second, it was common in ancient Rome for witnesses to claim that they saw the soul of the Roman Emperor ascending after his death. However, Luke describes Jesus' entire body ascending. According to Wright, "there is then a sense that Jesus is upstaging anything the Roman emperors might imagine for themselves. He is the reality, and they are the parody."[83] By the end of the book of Acts, the gospel is being preached in Rome, which makes good the claim

---

80. Webber, *Ancient-Future Time*, 154.

81. Ibid., 157. This reference is to the message of Jesus' prayer in John 17, the text each year for the seventh and final Sunday of Easter.

82. Wright, *Surprised by Hope*, 125, 127; Wright, *Acts For Everyone*, 14.

83. Wright, *Acts For Everyone*, 14. Also see Wright, *Surprised by Hope*, 130, 133.

that Jesus "is the world's true and rightful king, sharing the very throne, and somehow even, so it seems, the identity, of the one true God."[84] The Ascension is therefore a distinctly political story, claiming that Jesus and not Caesar is Lord. It is all about authority, power, and identity claims, as Paul makes clear:

> God put this power to work in Christ when he raised him from the dead and seated him at his right hand in the heavenly places, far above all rule and authority and power and dominion, and above every name that is named, not only in this age but also in the age to come. And he has put all things under his feet and has made him the head over all things for the church, which is his body, the fullness of him who fills all in all. (Eph 1:20–23)

Although the sovereign state might claim authority today, that claim is only partial and temporary. The state does not have the final word, but King Jesus does.

For Oliver O'Donovan, therefore, "the Ascension is of great importance for political theology." [85] In his words, the Ascension was "the fulfillment of the political promise which Jesus had come to bring" and it "confirms what the whole story has been about": the divine authority of the Son of Man, the Messiah, was on this man, and now he has returned to the Father from which this authority originates.[86] Hence Jesus is at the right hand of the father, assuming the rule of the King. Because Jesus is on the throne in heaven, he has *all* authority, delegating the church to go out to the world and make disciples by baptizing and teaching people to love God and their neighbors with all their lives. And so the state's job is now to allow this mission to flourish: "the goals and conduct of secular government are to be reconceived to serve the needs of international mobility and contact which the advancement of the Gospel requires."[87] The mission of the church now takes on greater significance than the mission of the state, because the king of the church has all power.

The Ascension helps the church face the absence of its King. The church must admit that it cannot see the face of this King in heaven while it can see Caesar's face on coins used all over the world. "The disciples could embrace the flesh and bones of their risen Lord," writes O'Donovan,

84. Ibid.
85. O'Donovan, *Desire of the Nations*, 144.
86. Ibid., 145.
87. Ibid., 147.

"but they could not observe his entry into the glory of the Father. . . . To grasp the Ascension whole would mean that we should behold the glory of the Son in the Father's presence," and this is still impossible apart from momentary glimpses such as St. Stephen's.[88] Meanwhile, our kings, presidents, and prime ministers appear to govern our lives more closely than King Jesus, whom we cannot see. Christ's bodily leave-taking is essential for humbling the church in its political role and in its claims of authority or success or possession of the truth. Douglas Farrow reminds us that the Ascension helpfully corrects the church, since the danger is that we might begin to believe that Christ is completely contained within, or completely coexistent with, the church.[89] And if Christ is contained completely within the imperfect church, then his cause is in big trouble, since the church of the crusades, hypocrisy, and sex scandals has failed too many people in too many ways. Thus, says Wright, we need to "grasp firmly that the church is *not* Jesus and Jesus is *not* the church . . . that the one who is indeed present with us by the Spirit is *also* the Lord who is strangely absent, strangely other, strangely different from us and over against us."[90] The stories of Christ's disappearance therefore remind us that we must be careful about a triumphalist view of mission flowing from the church's participation in the fullness of Christ's kingship. Any triumph is not the triumph of the church but of the King, while the many failures of the church are failures of humanity. Thus, while "the Ascension is the *foundation* which determines all future time,"[91] that time, in Karl Barth's words, is "also the time of the abandonment and, in a certain respect, of the loneliness of the Church on earth."[92] We cannot blame the King for the church's failures to live out the mission; there will be loneliness because of the church's many human collapses.

---

88. Ibid., 143–44. Acts 7:56. O'Donovan points out helpfully that the biblical authors have a "general reticence" to describe the event in detail. In his gospel, Luke says only that "While he was blessing them, he withdrew from them and was carried up into heaven" (24:51). In Acts he reports a few more details, saying that Jesus "was lifted up, and a cloud took him out of their sight. While he was going and they were gazing up toward heaven, suddenly two men in white robes stood by them. They said, 'Men of Galilee, why do you stand looking up toward heaven? This Jesus, who has been taken up from you into heaven, will come in the same way as you saw him go into heaven'" (1:9–11).

89. Farrow, *Ascension and Ecclesia*, 3, 7, 11, 29, 272–73.

90. Wright, *Surprised by Hope*, 113. Emphasis in original.

91. Ibid. Emphasis in original.

92. Barth, *Dogmatics in Outline*, 128.

However, the presence of Jesus also remains after the Ascension ; his partial absence from earthly time and space correlates with his full presence in divine time and space: "He is with God."[93] Jesus did not escape into some ethereal heaven where he lives as a spirit; he is united with God in his resurrected human body. Through the Spirit, however, he also remains actively involved in our world of time and space. He is merely in another, deeper dimension of reality, united with God—a parallel dimension only separated from ours by a thin tissue. Although we cannot see his exalted body until he returns, he is still closely in touch with our world through the Spirit. The Ascension reminds us to be ready to receive the breath of this Spirit into our lives and to receive the fullness of the body in the common meal. The communion meal forms the church's heart and always recalls the Ascension; it is the vehicle of connection with the ascended Christ. Summarizing the teaching of St. Augustine, the French theologian J-. M-. R. Tillard says that "The Eucharist (1) celebrates this life *of the body* (the company of the saints) awaiting life eternal, *makes it present*, sacramentally by *making present* the personal body and blood of Christ—the head gathering its body in the power of the Spirit; (2) strengthens it and nourishes it by placing it in a true contact with its source; and (3) announces its finality and its consummation."[94] Although we find the absent body made present, we also find the present body made absent. That is, in the meal, the communicant realizes that she is still living between the present tense in which Christ is risen and the future tense in which the ascended Christ will come again. By experiencing this tension in time, she is re-centered, along with the whole community.

We must be careful not to spiritualize the ascended Jesus, not to lose the fully embodied presence that he shared, and not to spiritualize our mission.[95] We cannot forget the Eucharistic meal, which feeds our faith and nourishes us as the Spirit makes the body and blood of Christ present in the bread and the wine. In the meal, we recall that Jesus made himself known while eating with his disciples; when they encounter the resurrected Jesus, they recognize him in the cooking of fish or the breaking of bread. Thus, the practice of a common meal stems directly from

93. Barth, *Dogmatics in Outline*, 125; Wright, *Acts for Everyone*, 11; also Wright, *Surprised by Hope*, 114–16.

94. Tillard, *Flesh*, 49. Emphasis in original.

95. For example, Barth says that the church is "united with Christ only in faith and by the Holy Spirit" (Barth, *Dogmatics in Outline*, 128). But there is an embodied quality to this unity in the meal.

the situation of the disciples in the forty days. However, the disciples also find Jesus disappearing in each story, and then he ascends. Thus, says Farrow, we need "to reckon honestly with the absence of Jesus in every assertion of his presence. The church lives in the world as the community in which this absence is, or should be, acutely felt and acknowledged."[96] Farrow points out that the Ascension is the event that brings the problem of presence and absence to the fore and "necessitates the peculiar sacramental form of the people of God."[97] In other words, the Eucharistic meal is where the church can feed on Christ's body and experience his presence—yet without seeing him face-to-face. It responds to the very problem created by the Ascension. Not only, says Farrow, does the meal hold Christ's presence and absence together in tension, but it also creates an "intimate association between ecclesiology and eschatology."[98] Farrow clarifies the ecclesiological element—the church element—as the product of sacramental union with Christ: "The church, then, is marked off from the world, insofar as it is marked off, not by race or culture or even by religion . . . but by its mysterious union with one whose life, though lived *for* the world, involves a genuine break with it."[99] The eschatological element flowing from this union is clear in Paul's description of the meal for the Corinthian church: we eat the bread and drink the wine and thus "proclaim the Lord's death until he comes" (1 Cor 11:26). In that space between the Christ who has risen and the Christ who will come again, the church finds itself in a human history somewhere between the Ascension and the Second Coming. We are united temporarily with the risen Christ in the meal, but we are not yet united permanently with him in his Ascension to the presence of God.

All this suggests that the church's unique way of being political in the world is that it *embodies* global political communion. As Henri de Lubac famously wrote, "the Church produces the Eucharist, but the Eucharist also produces the Church."[100] Deeper union with God, rather than an administrative hierarchy or political arrangements, is what makes

---

96. Ibid., 265.

97. Farrow, *Ascension and Ecclesia*, 39.

98. Ibid., 3–4.

99. Ibid., 11, emphasis in original.

100. De Lubac, *Splendour of the Church*, 78. As with Tillard, de Lubac stressed how the sacrament made the church, noting that the emphasis on the organization and authority of the church was only "a partial cure because it works only from without by way of authority, instead of effective union."

the church—a union that extends upward to God-in-Christ and outward to encompass the community of the faithful.[101] The heart of the church is the Lord's Supper meal, the Eucharist—not because the meal can achieve anything but because it is the center where communion with God and with each other happens. Tillard summarizes early Christian thinking concisely: "The nature of the church is to be communion."[102] At the heart of the church is this union with the body of Jesus Christ that is constituted both vertically—through divine gift—and horizontally—through social connection between the members of the global body. The whole meal only happens because "the *nature* of God is communion."[103] And the social element is there because the meal is shared in the community. To draw on Paul's language, to "discern the body" (1 Cor 11:29) is to overcome alienation both upwardly and outwardly: it is to feed on Christ's broken body that is now ascended and to comprehend the body of Christ in the unity of the communing congregation.[104] Both types of discernment require that one is reconciled before partaking of the sacrament: if one is cut off from God or from a member of the body because of sinful division, you "eat and drink judgment against" yourself (1 Cor 11:29). You are dividing the unified body—the union between the head of the body and the members of the community all together—constituted, consecrated, and celebrated by the meal. The forty days of Easter thus frame the double mystery enacted in communion: the vertical mystery of unity with Christ and the horizontal unity of human believers united in Christ. As de Lubac said, "If the Church is thus the fullness of Christ, Christ in His Eucharist is truly the heart of the Church."[105]

But alongside this close presence and strong ecclesiology there is a sense of incompleteness and a push toward eschatology that heightens the importance of the call to spread the gospel. This is clearest in

101. De Lubac, *Catholicism*, 76. As with Tillard, de Lubac stressed how the sacrament made the church, noting that the emphasis on the organization and authority of the church was only "a partial cure because it works only from without by way of authority, instead of effective union" (76).

102. Tillard, *Flesh of the Church*, 79.

103. Zizioulas, *Being as Communion*, 134.

104. The communal context of Paul's advice to the Corinthian church is central here: it comes in the middle of a discourse on the need to overcome the shameful division between rich and poor Christians (vv. 17–22), and to focus on the body of believers (1 Cor 12–13). See Cavanuagh, *Theopolitical Imagination*, 120–21.

105. De Lubac, *Splendour of the Church*, 92.

Matthew, who implies the Ascension when he makes the final scene of his gospel the hilltop meeting in Galilee where Jesus gives his great commission (Matt 28:18—19a). The basis of the commission is Jesus' political claim to *all* heavenly and earthly authority. Because Christ is king of all, and the church participates in his fullness, the church is not to rule but to make disciples by baptizing and teaching, while the state has a limited role of providing order so the church can carry out this mission in the time before the end of the ages. While Barth suggests that now is a lonely time of abandonment, he goes on to say that the time of the Ascension and after "is the time of the great opportunity, of the task of the Church towards the world; it is the time of mission."[106] There is a heightened sense of the importance of the church's work that flows from this eschatological expectation. He is not with us but he will come again, and meanwhile the church works to invite the world to join it. One of the prayers for Ascension Day from the *Book of Common Prayer* picks up on the comforting promise of Jesus about the church's experience in time: "Almighty God, whose blessed Son our Savior Jesus Christ *ascended* far above all heavens that he might *fill* all things: Mercifully give us faith to perceive that, according to his promise, *he abides with his Church on earth, even to the end of the ages.*"[107] Jesus promises that he will be with us always, right up to the end. But the church is not constituted to sit around basking in that comfort; its job is to join the disciples who are to spread the news to "all Judea, Samaria, and to the ends of the earth" (Luke 1:8), to invite others in.

In a world of shifting political powers and loyalties, the church forms a missional community of presence-amidst-absence, united in communion with its head, that can be a compelling site of loyalty that not only discerns the body of Christ and his church but also shares his mission with the world—a mission fed by, centered upon, the communion meal. As Bill Cavanaugh describes the meal, "Christ is gift, giver, and recipient; we are simultaneously fed and become food for others."[108] When the church properly "discerns the body" by sharing itself with the world, it becomes a compelling site of primary loyalty for real people the world over. It gathers people in order to send them out with invitations to gather more people. Tillard writes that "the church of God is, as it were, the

106. Barth, *Dogmatics in Outline*, 128.

107. Episcopal Church, *Book of Common Prayer*, 226. Emphasis added.

108. Cavanaugh, *Being Consumed*, 56.

healing of the body of wounded humanity," and he warns against "reducing the church's place in the world to that of a preacher of ethics, an agent of philanthropic endeavors, a creator of magnanimous ideologies."[109] Rather, he says, "the church is essentially the presence of a space in which the fabric of the 'humanity-God-wants' is restored . . . ." This space is "an authentic, entirely gratuitous fellowship," a "communion."[110]

In its global *communion*, the church is the closest thing to a model universal political community, completely global and completely local. "The Eucharist refracts space in such a way that one becomes more united to the whole the more tied one becomes to the local," writes Cavanaugh.[111] Thus, he argues, the communion at the heart of the meal is the church's compelling alternative to globalization, a politics of authentic integration (as opposed to the false universalism of globalization, which seeks to flatten local forms by incorporating them into a global playing field). He points out that in the meal "the particular is of the utmost importance, for this particular piece of bread at this particular place and time *is* the body of Christ, and is not merely a pointer to some abstract transcendent standing behind the sign."[112] A true kind of universality is enacted in this meal: "Each consumer of the Eucharist receives the whole body of Christ, though the body remains one throughout the whole world. This is only possible because the consumer is absorbed into the body. The consumer of the Eucharist begins to walk in the strange landscape of the body of Christ, while still inhabiting a particular earthly place."[113] De Lubac writes in a similar vein, "Though only one cell of the whole body is actually present, the whole body is there virtually. The Church is in many places, yet there are not several Churches; the Church is entire in each one of its parts."[114] Locating the church as a truly global body whose members are in communion together and in communion with Christ might sound more Catholic than Protestant. However, this is ancient teaching that goes back to the early church fathers.[115] Here it helps

109. Tillard, *Flesh of the Church*, 137.

110. Ibid.

111. Cavanuagh, *Theopolitical Imagination*, 115.

112. Ibid., 119.

113. Cavanaugh, *Theopolitical Imagination*, 119–20.

114. De Lubac, *Splendour of the Church*, 86.

115. This teaching was recovered in the theology of the Protestant reformer John Calvin and more recently in the theologies of de Lubac, Tillard, and other Vatican II Catholic theologians who stressed mystical communion with Christ as the root of the

to recall that "the holy Catholic church" of the Apostles' Creed refers to an embodied universal church, not necessarily to the Roman Catholic hierarchy. True catholicity means unity and universality, an achievement of the ascended Christ in the sacrament of the meal, in which true communion happens.

RE-IMAGINING THE GLOBALIZATION OF POLITICAL AUTHORITY, POWER, AND IDENTITY

The story of the forty days from Easter to Ascension helps the church to recast three questions raised by our case study of the Arctic at the beginning of this chapter. First, how might the church respond to global issues such as climate change that transcend the authority of the territorial state system? Parts of the evangelical church recently mobilized as a social movement to pressure state authorities to reduce greenhouse gas emissions.[116] The reduction of greenhouse gas emissions may or may not be a morally defensible way to address climate change (assuming it is a reality). Our task here is not to weigh in on these complex debates. Rather, our task is to define the church's role. If the story of the forty days makes any sense, the church was not founded just to be a non-governmental organization actor lobbying governments to take action. If the voice of the church is reduced to pleading with the state to act, then we have missed the point of the story. The point of the story is that the church offers not just an ethical starting point but the practices of an embodied community rooted in global-local communion with the ascended King. The voice of the church is the voice of a group of witnesses who have been united with the risen Christ by eating with him but who also miss him and look for him to return. The church can speak to the state out of this story from the perspective of a global communion, but it also offers this story as the source of true authority, power, and identity—rooted in both presence and absence.

The embodied presence of Jesus in the meal has implications for how one thinks about ecology. Instead of worrying about the abstract cause of global environmentalism, the church cares about people in

---

church Calvin, *Institutes*, III.XX to IV.XX, 1359–1428; Smit, "Depth Behind Things"; Kerr, "Corpus Verum," 229–42; de Lubac, *Catholicism*, 25–111; de Lubac, *Splendour of the Church*, 74–92; Tillard, *Flesh*.

116. "Climate Change."

embodied communities and cares about the Creation. It is rooted concretely to earth. Unlike NGOs that benefit from environmental or other global problems—these groups grow as the problems get larger—the church's mission is to practice its unique blend of presence and absence in order to extend the love of Christ to neighbors. Because the mission of the church flows from the presence of the body of Christ, Christians care about the impact of global problems on any local groups. Unlike NGOs that leave when a problem subsides, however, the church will seek to remain and sink roots in a place. It practices a form of closer presence that will knit the inhabitants in any one place into global participation in a vertical, divine and horizontal, social body. Modeling their King, the people of the church will make themselves present to those who might be threatened and sharing meals with those who would follow. A radically local, embodied presence is part of the mission of baptizing, making disciples, and teaching.

However, radical absence also energizes the mission. As a result, the true universal church of communion does not seek to possess a place or to conquer a space for power. Unlike conventional political structures that seek to control territory, this body is knit together as a communion. So where is the church? It is everywhere that intimate communion with the absent and ascended king happens. And what is the church? It is not just an NGO that exists to pressure states, nor an institutional power structure. It is a supernatural communion between the members of the church—a truer global institution than those structures based solely on power, authority, or common identity. If the church were only a sub-state actor within civil society existing to pressure the state, then that would give state authority, power, and identity the priority. Instead, the healthy side of globalization is that it challenges the exclusive power and identity of the state and makes room for global forms of power and solidarity, creating a space for transnational connections across the world. Into that space can step the church. But this does not go far enough. The church also claims an authority that trumps the authority of the state. The ascended Christ is the highest authority, not the world's sovereign states, and the church communes with this authority.

How does the mission of the church, rooted in anticipation of the return of the ascended Christ, reframe global issues like climate change? An eschatology that defines the Second Coming of Christ as the escape of souls to a disembodied heaven will tend to denigrate the importance of caring for the creation, but a properly biblical eschatology that understands the second coming as the restoration of a new heaven and a new earth will tend to accentuate how our present treatment of the earthly Creation will extend into our resurrected future.[117] Evangelicals who are moving to understand this issue in terms of "creation care" are moving in this same direction of recognizing that our actions now will redound to our future. The specter of climate change may well be overblown by a secular, scientific ideology, but that is no reason to say, as one Christian letter-writer to *Books and Culture* said, that "it is people that are the object of God's concern, not the earth."[118] "The earth is the Lord's and the fullness thereof" (Ps 24:1 KJV). Because the restoration of God's loving rule of Creation, completed at the return of Christ, is our ultimate destiny, we will care greatly for our earthly neighbors and our shared, creational home.

Second, the church can only question the state's territorial claims and entrenchment of its exclusive sovereignty over areas of the globe, while cautiously supporting alternative types of political power that hold states accountable. In the case of the Arctic, the lure of territorial possession was evident when even the pacific Canadians were talking about claiming sovereignty over territory. Here is where Christ's body in the church forms a stark contrast with the territorial possessiveness of sovereign states. We can locate the church less as an alternative space to challenge the state and more as an embodiment of membership in one body that helps show the state its proper role.[119] The church is the truest global institution, since it is not based on power, coercion, or domination but is based on self-giving love that sustains the communion. Instead of having to claim sovereignty or "use it or lose it," the church invites people to join its re-enacted drama of becoming one in Christ's body through the church year. The church is not a space for "the violent creation of order" but an invitation to a rich banquet where the host is both present and absent—a banquet that renews the guests' in their mission to invite others in. This global church's challenge to the power of territorial state has tremendous implications for improvisational practices.

---

117. Wright, *Surprised by Hope*, 79–122.

118. Sam Naffziger, letter to the editor, 6.

119. Yoder, *Christian Witness to the State*.

Third we return to Friedman's claim that the state is the ultimate olive tree of identity—a claim that raises another question in relation to climate change: how can Christians claim to be members of a global communion and members of one body when they allow their national identity to supersede their identity in the body? How can they claim to be unified in one body when they disagree with one another on the issues raised in the Arctic? If we are not unified, how can we be a site that attracts greater loyalty than the state? A Christian businessperson might celebrate the opportunities to tap the wealth under the receding ice while a Christian ecologist might lament the damage to Creation. Should not the identity inherent in being a member of this global political communion trump one's commitment to other political identities? We could ask the same questions of other global political issues. Can one disagree so fundamentally and still remain part of the same body? Here is the encouraging part of the story of a church founded in the simultaneous absence and presence of Christ, a church founded literally in the practice of communion. We find a comforting parable in Paul's experience with the first century church in Corinth. That church was bitterly divided, factionalized between followers of different teachers (Paul or Apollos), scandalized by a man sleeping with his stepmother (1 Cor 5:1), estranged by fellow parishioners suing each other, confused that some ate foods sacrificed to idols while others did not, and (worst of all) separated by a gap between the sated rich and the hungry poor. In this context, Paul lays down his classic teaching about communion in 1 Corinthians 11 followed by his teaching on the gifts that each person brings to the body in the next two chapters. It is to this scandalously divided church that Paul says, "Now you are the body of Christ, and individually members of it" (1 Cor 12:27).[120] This does not mean that he sanctifies the divisions; quite the opposite. Instead, he teaches that the unworthy practice of the meal, failing to discern the unified body by maintaining these divisions, is what weakens, sickens, and kills the members (1 Cor 11:30). This teaching gives rise to Bill Cavanaugh's wry comment: "This might explain the condition of some of our churches."[121] Quite literally, if we commune without discerning both the social body and the divine body that is constituted in the meal, if we commune in division, we are killing ourselves. We are failing to be the body that we are intended to be. This

120. I owe this point to Harry Winters.

121. Cavanaugh, *Theopolitical Imagination*, 121.

is both a great challenge and a great comfort. The challenge is that the church too often comes to the altar with its divisions intact, failing to be united in Christ. The comfort is that, through grace, we are not called to heal those divisions on our own and that even the messed-up, divided Corinthian church was still the body of Christ. However, there remains a challenge: we must offer up our divided lives so that they can be shed and we can be united more and more in our common identity in Christ.

This does not mean that practicing the Eucharist is guaranteed to produce a united view of the climate change issue or any other contentious political concern. But it does mean that our identities—literally, what and whom we identify with—should increasingly be Christ and his church and the members of that body. We ought to be struggling, then, to frame our responses to such global political problems in ways that flow from our common identity and common story. If we are to sustain the claim that the ultimate olive tree is not the state but the church, then we will have to continue to wrestle with the globalization of political identities symbolized by the climate change issue. If we cannot produce one witness on complex policy issues, the church should at least promote its own loving, internal dialogue on such issues. The church claims that its identity flows through self-giving love, following the great shepherd, through the reception of the Holy Spirit. This identity forms a mission identity for the church, as all other political agendas are subordinated to the agenda of witnessing to this love. As the church is sent out to the world at the Ascension, it is called to bring the world back into this body. Thus, we can re-imagine how the climate change issue flows from this mission. At the very least, Christian mission encourages Christians to ask whether two conditions are true. If in fact global temperatures are climbing due to human-induced greenhouse gas emissions, that is one condition. If in fact global temperatures are rising significantly enough, we or our neighbors might be threatened by rising sea levels, desertification, shifts in agricultural viability, or a possible increase in infectious diseases, that is a second condition. If both conditions are true, then the church's mission to witness to the story to the ends of the earth will be significantly affected. Precisely because the church trusts in a transcendent, ascended king, it realizes that responses to global issues such as climate change are not up to the church's power. Rather, we can trust that the end of the story is not up to us, even as we take responsibility for acting in our part of the drama.

IMPROVISING PRACTICES OF "DISCERNING THE BODY"

Like the disciples, living the post-Easter story forces us to "discern the body" of Christ within the gathered community and in relation to our ascended Lord, while also discerning our mission. Indeed, the highest forms of authority, power, and identity for the globe reside in the ascended King of the Church who claims them alongside the Father and from whom all earthly claims to authority, power, or identity flow. But that does not mean that earthly political situations are easily handled. In fact, the dual power inherent in the simultaneous spiritual presence and bodily absence of Jesus makes the Christian approach to politics much more complicated than the approaches of those who live in a flat world of uni-dimensional political authority. As I have already implied, "discerning the body" implies that Christian churches will work to unite their understandings of global political issues in order to forge a united witness. This does not imply that exact agreement on the details of policies will flow from the study of scripture and tradition. But it does require that the diverse branches of the Christian churches see how their witness to the political realms must flow from their Eucharistic unity in Christ. Instead of Christians sniping at one another about whether climate change is a myth or an urgent reality, we might then find Christians taking a break from public lobbying on the issue while engaging in quiet internal discussions.

Indeed, we might learn from John Roth's story. In the fall of 2004, Roth, a Mennonite historian, noticed that Mennonites were divided by clashing bumper stickers and political signs: Bush-Cheney 2004 vs. Kerry-Edwards 2004. Seeing this experience as a sign of real division within the Mennonite Church USA, in which the church took its cues more from partisan politics than from its common witness, Roth proposed that his denomination take a five-year sabbatical from partisan political involvement while entering into "a disciplined period of spiritual retreat"[122] that would allow the church to carry on a conversation that might develop a common language that would offer "a public witness for ourselves and to the world that the church—not the Democratic or Republican party—is our most fundamental point of reference."[123] To use our terms here, such

---

122. Roth, "Reflections on 'Speaking to Government.'"
123. Ibid.

a temporary withdrawal from partisan advocacy on issues might be helpful to discerning the body of Christ relative to the issues.

In discerning the body, we also see that the body of Christ is a global and universal body. Discerning a global body suggests that Christians support authentic globalization and affirm what O'Donovan called "international mobility" that can advance the church's mission of proclaiming the good news of God's love in word and deed. Two of Roth's concrete ideas about the five-year sabbatical suggest how one might learn to help discern a global body. First, he suggests that churches could "develop partnership with a sister congregation in Colombia or India or Indonesia," thereby practicing the kind of embodied presence that Christ demonstrates in the forty days. [124] Long- and short-term exchanges between such churches would practice a healthy kind of globalization that deepens our understanding of what it means to be part of global political communion. One hopes that these contacts might promote true global political solidarity that is mediated by Christ more than by the nation-state and that might inform our understanding of issues such as climate change. Second, Roth suggested that his Mennonite brothers and sisters should "cultivate a global awareness through the lens" of denominational agencies "rather than NPR or Fox."[125] Here, he touches on the role of contrasting media outlets—the stereotypically liberal National Public Radio as opposed to the stereotypically conservative Fox News—in constructing one's view of the world in narrative contexts other than the global story of Christ and his church. Part of constructing a common identity in the body of Christ is to find ways of narrating the world's events through the lens of this truer story. At this point, the church has an advantage, because it is already practicing some of these forms of healthy globalization, and it has a global outlook. At one level, then, we might find it surprising to hear that the official position of the current Pope, Benedict XVI, is that climate change is a "matter of grave importance for the entire human family."[126] "Conservative" ideology, allegedly Benedict's stance, typically excludes concern for the issue. But the concern makes sense for the head of a church that is has an identity that is truly global and that can narrate the world's events through the lens of a global communion.

124. Ibid.

125. Ibid.

126. Benedict XVI, "Letter to the Ecumenical Patriarch of Constantinople." Benedict XVI, "General Audience."

Christians also discern a body with a remarkable mission and social vision. That mission is to invite others into the body so that it can grow until its head returns to govern it fully. But the church's growth must be qualitative and deeply spiritual, not merely a growth in numbers of shallow, affiliated members. The social vision is part of communion and mission. In line with ancient tradition, John Calvin noted how social solidarity and unity is embodied in the communion meal, and how that meal forges such solidarity:

> We shall benefit very much from the Sacrament if this thought is impressed upon our minds: that none of the brethren can be injured, despised, rejected, abused, or in any way offended by us, without at the same time, injuring, despising, and abusing Christ by the wrongs we do; that we cannot disagree with our brethren without at the same time disagreeing with Christ; that we cannot love Christ without loving him in the brethren; that we ought to take the same care of our brethren's bodies as we take of our own; for they are members of our body; and that, as no part of our body is touched by any feeling of pain which is not spread among all the rest, so we ought not allow a brother to be affected by any evil, without being touched by compassion for him. . . . For what sharper goad could there be to arouse mutual love among us than when Christ, giving himself to us, not only invites us by his own example to pledge and give ourselves to one another, but inasmuch as he makes himself common to all, also makes all of us one in himself.[127]

This meal constitutes the strongest solidarity imaginable, while globalization reminds us that our brothers and sisters live close to home and on every continent. As John Zizioulas writes, "It is the nature of the Eucharist to transcend not only divisions occurring within a local situation but also the very division which is inherent in the concept of geography: the division of the world into local places."[128] So we find the church's common identity, common power, and common authority in a meal, a feasting on the body and blood of the one who is in heaven, who comes near, and who yet will come again. In this shared meal, the church receives its global mission to go out into all the world with the story of what happened to this Jesus who humbly preached love but was slain, this Jesus who rose again and ascended into heaven. The mission is to invite the

127. Calvin, *Institutes* XVII.38, 1415–16.
128. Zizioulas, *Being as Communion*, 257.

world to enter this story so that its scattered members can become united with God in the fullness of time.

As the church goes out to witness, it enters a world in which not only governments operate but also networks of transnational corporations, terrorist groups, non-governmental organizations, and migrating peoples. As these globalizing forces continue to challenge state power, the global political communion of the church can offer a different kind of stability (rooted in absence) and a different kind of challenge (rooted in presence). How that political communion will look in practice will vary on the situation, but the community forged in the forty days after Easter is the global political community for which the world is searching.

CHAPTER 10

Pentecost, Catholicity, and Global Cultures

Globality . . . means merely that everyone everywhere may feed on McDonald's hamburgers and watch the latest made for TV docudrama.
—Zygmunt Bauman[1]

We cannot understand catholicity as an ecclesiological notation unless we understand it as a Christological reality. . . . It is Christ's *unity and it is* His *catholicity that the church reveals in her being Catholic.*
—John Zizioulas[2]

It is hard to imagine a place less globalized in its culture than Saudi Arabia. Under the influence of conservative Islamic religious leaders, the government bans all women in the Kingdom from driving. Even foreign women must keep their hair covered in public at all times. Strict execution of Islamic law is the hallmark of the Saudi state. Religious police—known as "committees for the promotion of virtue and suppression of vice"—patrol the streets. Yet, in private, anyone in the Kingdom with a regular television antenna or satellite dish can pick up the Saudi-owned

1. Bauman, *Life in Fragments*, 24; cited in Cray, "Postmodernism: Mutual Society in Crisis," 72.

2. Zizioulas, *Being as Communion*, 158–59, emphasis in original.

MBC channel, as my family did, while we were living just offshore from Saudi Arabia in Bahrain.[3] Every day during the Muslim holy month of Ramadan in 2004, MBC played *Oprah, Friends, Seinfeld, Malcolm in the Middle*, and other reruns of American television shows. Every night at ten and midnight, the channel showed American movies. All of these were broadcast in English, with Arabic subtitles. In just a few months watching MBC in Bahrain, we saw a number of scenes that challenge strict Muslim teachings. One night we watched *Pleasantville*, whose theme is sexual liberation (as illustrated by characters that become colorized in an otherwise repressed, black-and-white world). On another night, we watched *Grosse Point Blank*, whose hero is a professional hit man. In December 2004, we viewed *Shadowlands*, the dramatization of the relationship between C. S. Lewis and his American wife, Joy, a story beloved by many Christians (and now, it seems, many Saudi Muslims). You know that the consumption of cultural products has become globalized when you can watch such Hollywood products so freely even in Saudi Arabia.

The globalization of culture often seems synonymous with Americanization or homogenization. The homogenizing, soul-flattening, corrupting effects of McDonalds, Hollywood, and strip malls are by now a staple of popular commentary (Professor Bauman's comment above being a typical example of an academic comment). Illustrating this same conceit, Thomas Friedman tells the story of walking along the waterfront in Doha, Qatar, enjoying the authentic Arabian Gulf architecture. Rounding a corner, he sees a Taco Bell, which ruins the whole experience for him. Worst of all, he says, "it was crowded."[4] Friedman takes this to be unhealthy, a sign that Qatar went too far in absorbing this part of American culture. While Friedman raises legitimate concerns about the globalization of American popular culture overtaking local cultures, there may be a positive side to the spread of a culture of movies, television, fast food, and shopping malls. We academics tend toward an elitist mode that disdains mass culture, but I know from experience that the spread of a mass culture allows people of different cultures to find a common vernacular for connection. When our family wanted to meet Bahraini families in Bahrain for the first time, a common meeting place was at the food court of one of the landmarks there: the giant Seef Mall. When I wanted to get

3. Since this was first written, the Saudi-owned MBC network added other channels to its satellite lineup.

4. Friedman, *Lexus and the Olive Tree*, 278.

to know the students in my classes at the University of Bahrain, I asked them about some of their favorite movies, television shows, or music, and they were eager to share these. Meeting new people in Bahrain, we found that the conversation often turned to movies or television. We spent a good portion of one evening celebrating the exploits of Michael Jordan and other NBA stars with a local family. So, even though we grew up thousands of miles away from each other, we had enough culture in common to start a conversation. Culture can be partly defined as a social glue that gives people a sense of common meaning—a framework for connection. In that sense, American popular culture helps function as a global culture—at least in a superficial way. The examples I just mentioned are, of course, superficial ones, rooted in the consumption of electronic media. In this same vein, Friedman says, unapologetically, that "the wretched of the earth want to go to Disney World, not to the barricades. They want the Magic Kingdom, not *Les Misérables*."[5]

Culture as identity-forming goes deeper than Disney. In fact, we could define culture as a "cult" or symbolic "revelation system," a "cultivation" that "tills" human identities, and as a "corporate symbolic dwelling place" or an "incarnation of corporate spirit."[6] Cultures mediate beliefs about the ultimate meaning of life; they form humans; and they define identity in relation to the social groups in which we belong. Religions, languages, art, and historical narratives embody deeper meanings that polite conversation about movies can hardly reveal. You become aware of this when you hear the call to prayer five times a day in a Muslim country. "Allahu Akbar," goes the call, broadcasting a reminder that "God is greater" than what you see around you. The spread of shopping malls, English language, pop music videos, and McDonalds would seem to undermine this religious culture and threaten to replace it with a superficial culture. In fact, many conservative Muslims fear that the decadent, shallow West is seducing their children into the shallow world of self-absorbed consumption. But then our family heard the call to prayer piped over the public address system in Seef Mall, and we saw a noticeable decrease in traffic as shoppers took time out from shopping to pray in the mall's prayer room. We also saw men and women sitting at Starbucks, chatting over their tea and lattés, but they wore traditional Arabic dress—long white robes and head coverings for men, all black robes and head coverings for women.

5. Ibid., 364.

6. Kavanaugh, *Following Christ in a Consumer Society*, 70.

We heard Arabic spoken all around us—much of it by people chatting on their mobile phones. We were reminded that cultural changes are subtle, that they may be experienced in different ways, and that our "foreign cultural grammar" might not be displacing deeper Arabic and Islamic patterns.[7] We were reminded that some things had not changed: many people still prayed, even at the mall. They retained their native tongue. Perhaps they were incorporating American cultural elements into their own hybrid.

Were we witnessing the flourishing of a cultural hybrid or was it simply a stage along the way of American cultural imperialism or a step toward cultural homogeneity? Were we experiencing a momentary respite from an inevitable clash of civilizations? Although we will investigate these questions in a moment, I believe that the re-enacting of Pentecost helps the church re-imagine another way of thinking and acting vis-à-vis cultural globalization. The Pentecost feast gives us a glimpse of a healthy balance of global and local, universal and unique, general and particular. It is the birth date of a church that embodies Christ's catholicity in the Spirit and which demonstrates a true cultural unity that preserves diversity. The church has practiced a healthy, authentic blend of "glocalization" (globalization plus localization) since its formal inauguration at Pentecost.[8] It turns out that the universal church offers a model of cultural globalization that the current practices of media-driven globalization fail to match. The translation movement initiated at Pentecost promotes neither uniformity nor absolute plurality but instead a unity-in-diversity that is the model for authentic cultural globalization.

HOMOGENIZATION, CULTURAL IMPERIALISM, CLASHING CIVILIZATIONS, OR BLENDING HYBRIDS?

The debate over the globalization of culture illustrates how there is a compelling need for the church's Spirit-induced unity these days. The debate itself, much like the world, reminds one of the world after Babel. People are talking past one another without understanding. In the cacophony of voices, however, we hear at least four views of the globalization of culture: 1) homogenization—the allure to mass populations of a

7. Larsson, *Race to the Top*, 89.

8. Friedman, *Lexus and the Olive Tree*, 295–97, implies that he coined the term glocalization, but credit belongs to sociologist Robertson, "Glocalization."

mass culture of McWorld, strip malls, Disney, and movie theaters, 2) the imposition of American cultural ideas through forceful cultural imperialism, 3) a backlash in the "clash of civilizations" and a retreat to local communities, or 4) some kind of hybridity, a mix of local and global, of particular and universal, of familiar and exotic, that allegedly liberates people to construct their own identities and to construct peaceful blends of cultures.[9]

First, many critics blame globalization for homogenizing the world's cultures into a standardized, uniform global cultural straitjacket. This goes beyond the symbolic spread of fast food chains and extends to a deeper infrastructure of standardized practices that organize daily life.[10] Those who worry about homogenization find a surprising ally in Friedman, who states their case quite clearly. He writes, "When unrestrained globalization uproots cultures and environments, it destroys the necessary underlying fabric of communal life. . . ." And he worries that traditional cultures could "get steamrolled by globalization."[11] He even argues that "the profit motive. . . can too easily lead to the commercialization and exploitation of every cultural icon" (what Marx called commodification).[12] This concern for lost identity goes deeper than the shallowness of shopping malls and extends to the decline of traditional languages and the increasing uniformity of food—all of which raise questions of community and identity that are central to the globalization of culture. Because personal names express personal identity, the fact that Indian call center employees must Americanize their names disturbs the Indian novelist Arundhati Roy. She makes the call centers into metaphors for India's loss of soul in its opening to globalization: "The Call Center Colleges train their students to speak in American and British accents. They have to read foreign papers so they can chitchat about the news or the weather. On duty they have to change their given names. Sushma becomes Suzie,

---

9. Barber, *Jihad vs. McWorld*; Rothkopf, "In Praise of Cultural Imperialism?"; Huntington, *Clash of Civilizations*; Kraidy, *Hybridity*; Pieterse, *Globalization and Culture*; Kirby, *Vulnerability and Violence*, 101–5.

10. Marling, *How "American" is Globalization?* 144–204. A number of scholars have argued that the nineteenth and twentieth centuries saw the emergence of global cultural or normative standards, often linked to international institutions. For a readable historical treatment of this argument see Iriye, *Global Community*. Also see Boli and Thomas, eds., *Constructing World Culture*; Lechner and Boli, *World Cultur*; and Bartky, *One Time Fits All*.

11. Friedman, *Lexus and the Olive Tree*, 302.

12. Ibid., 299.

Govind becomes Jerry, Advani becomes Andy. (Hi! I'm Andy. Gee, hot day, innit? Shoot how can I help ya?).”[13] By effacing their names, these workers lose some of their particular identity. The loss of local native languages is also a common concern that Friedman shares.[14] Similarly, the spread of American cuisine also threatens local food cultures. Here, too, the critics of globalization have waxed eloquent. A Uruguayan writer minces no words here: “Garbage disguised as food is colonizing palates everywhere and annihilating local cooking traditions in the process. Fine dining, the joy of eating, cultivated and diversified over thousands of years in some countries, constitutes a collective patrimony that finds its way to everyone's hearth, not only to the tables of the rich. Such traditions, such signs of cultural identity, such celebrations of life are being steamrollered by the globalization of hamburgers, the dictatorship of fast food.”[15] Although Friedman is more sanguine about McDonald's, he shares this concern about homogenization. While he might not approve of the actions of the French farmer Jose Bové, who famously tore down a McDonald's restaurant in southern France in 1999, he can understand the worry about the loss of traditional cuisines.[16]

Second, the middle class economic culture of “McWorld” has few passionate allies among intellectuals, but there are those who would favor the spread of American culture.[17] Although few American professors would argue for the values of American popular culture, quite a few are willing to praise the emphasis of American political culture on freedom. David Rothkopf, for example, argues “in praise of cultural imperialism,” contending that “it is in the economic and political interests of the United States to ensure that if the world is moving toward a common language it be English; that if the world is moving toward common telecommunications, safety, and quality standards, they be American; that if the world is becoming linked by television, radio, and music, the programming be American; and that if common values are being developed, they be values with which Americans are comfortable.”[18] This vision could be

13. Roy, *Power Politics*, 83–84.

14. Friedman, *Lexus and the Olive Tree*, 303–4.

15. Galeano, *Upside-Down*, 253–54.

16. Friedman, *Lexus and the Olive Tree*, 302–3, on the loss of true corner bakeries.

17. As Eric Schlosser's book *Fast Food Nation* and the documentary film *Super Size Me* illustrate.

18. Rothkopf, “In Praise,” 45.

the mission statement of the recent Bush Administration's foreign policy, where the promotion of economic and political freedom—especially in the Middle East—became the stated goals. A kind of cultural imperialism, a confidence in the rightness of expanding this culture, drives the foreign policy elites who operate as if Francis Fukuyama were right: there is no alternative to liberal democracy, and it is our job to help it take root in the Middle East and around the world.[19] President George W. Bush expressed this view most forcefully and most recently on Memorial Day 2008, saying that America was "the greatest nation on earth and the last best hope for mankind."[20] Responding to this type of American exceptionalist rhetoric, a British observer of American political culture noted "the paradox of a nation that preaches universalist values which, however, are wielded in the service of national rather than international causes."[21] In this view, the story of the globalization of culture is partly the story of forceful Americanization that is allegedly good for the world, political-cultural imperialism straight up.

Third, however, the United States threatens at times to fulfill Samuel Huntington's prediction of a "clash of civilizations" between the Judeo-Christian West and the Islamic world. Many American Christians even seem to relish this possibility, hoping that the "Judeo-Christian" values of the West triumph over "Islamo-fascism." Support for the wars against Afghanistan and Iraq was solid in evangelical Christian communities, in part because the U.S. was seen as bringing "freedom" to these countries. Many American Christians feel that their religious values and their cultural values run together. Defending the modern West against Islamic extremism is seen as central to upholding Christian identity. Thus, many Americans have embraced Huntington's diagnosis of the 9/11 terrorist attacks as the lashing out of a civilization resentful of Western modernity. Furthermore, Philip Jenkins even speculates that the growth of Christianity in the global South might cause conflicts with rapidly growing Muslim communities in developing countries.[22] The backlash against globalization, on this view, is in part an attempt to defend traditional cultural identities against the threat of cultural and religious invasion.

19. Fukuyama, *End of History*.

20. From "President Bush Attends Arlington National Cemetery Memorial Day Commemoration."

21. Crockatt, *After 9/11*, 221.

22. Jenkins, *Next Christendom*, 5–6, 163–90.

Instead of a culture of shared consumption or forceful imposition of American values, this view sees cultures in conflict. Similarly, much of the anti-globalization movement thus turns to the local, where cultural identity can be preserved against global corporations and U. S. foreign policy.[23] Even Friedman is forced to admit that increased global communication might actually lead to increased conflict: "We are now seeing and hearing one another faster and better, but with no corresponding improvement in our ability to learn from, or understand, one another. So integration, at this stage, is producing more anger than anything else."[24] Globalization often breeds cultural clashes rather than cultural homogeneity.

Fourth, however, some observers also see the potential for creative understandings between cultures to emerge, for cultural hybrids to be constructed by increasingly cosmopolitan individuals who will be increasingly liberated to select the best from the world's cultures in their quest for happiness.[25] Friedman also takes this view at times, arguing that "the global juggernauts of McDonald's or Taco Bell . . . proliferate because they offer people something they want."[26] Instead of global homogenization, some predict global hybridization, a diversity of blends, more cultural choices.[27] People around the world can choose from wider varieties of global cultures—more Hollywood and Bollywood flicks, more foreign and independent films, and more television programs—and so can everyone else in the world. Simply stated, this view argues that globalization means more choices, with fewer restrictions, therefore, it must be good. "Each can be the architect of his own future—if he's allowed to be," writes one advocate of this view.[28] Tyler Cowen makes the argument explicitly in terms of culture: over time, he says, "cross-cultural exchange . . . will support innovation and creative human energies."[29] Examples of

23. Mander and Goldsmith, eds., *Case Against the Global Economy*; Korten, *When Corporations Rule the World*.

24. Friedman, *Longitudes*, 169.

25. Legrain, "Cultural Globalization is not Americanization;" Cowen, *Creative Destruction*; Crothers, *Globalization and American Popular Culture*, 142–49; Marling, *How "American"?* 81–143, 205.

26. Friedman, *Lexus*, 294.

27. Bhagwati, *In Defense of Globalization*, 109–16; Pieterse, *Globalization and Culture*, 74–83; Nye, "Globalization is about Blending not Homogenizing," 23.

28. Larsson, *Race to the Top*, 136.

29. Cowen, *Creative*, 17.

such cultural exchanges and hybrids are numerous, but one of the more bizarre recent examples was the appearance of scantily clad cheerleaders from the Washington Redskins football team at a cricket match in modest India.[30] Yet hybridization can also promote particular values of female modesty: in 2005, the *New York Times* reported that a Syrian company was successfully marketing a doll in the Middle East who looked very much like Barbie but came dressed in a long black cloak with a headscarf and her own prayer mat.[31] Global sports loyalties may even rival political loyalties in hybridization. In Iraq, a *Washington Post* reporter noticed graffiti on walls in a village in southern Iraq: "'Long live Moqtada,' one slogan reads. 'All of us will sacrifice to defend Sadr,' another declares. In green is written, 'Yes, yes to Islam.' Next to it in blue, a little out of place, is scrawled, 'Long live Real,' a show of support for the Spanish soccer team Real Madrid."[32] If hybridity theorists are correct, graffiti for popular sports teams or rap groups may eventually match localized political and religious slogans (such as for a local Shi'a leader in Iraq). And while such mixed-up hybrids are interesting examples of cultural diffusion and creative synthesis, do they enrich both cultures? When everyone who wants Big Macs, satellite television, global soccer, Barbies, or cheerleaders gets them, the world may be more peaceful.[33]

Are global McDonaldization, the global imperialism of freedom, a global clash of civilizations, or a global hodge-podge of liberating mélange the only choices? I want to argue that the church's global mission after Pentecost offers another, more compelling alternative in the face of the confusion over global culture. However, we must address a deeper problem than our discussion so far has indicated: much of the globalization of culture is driven by electronic media that promote shallow engagements between cultures and make it more difficult to properly imagine and practice the reality of a global-local church. Globalized culture may lack depth. American writer Peter Hessler noticed the shallowness of global electronic interaction while in China during and after the attacks of September 11, 2001. After the attacks, many shops were selling or renting pirated videos of news footage of the attacks, for

---

30. Varadarajan, "India's Game, U.S. Spice"; Wax, "Redskins Cheerleaders Shake Up Cricket in Modest India."

31. Zoepf, "Bestseller in Mideast."

32. Shadid, "In a Land Without Order."

33. Friedman, *Lexus and the Olive Tree*, 248–75.

entertainment. "And there was something particularly warped about the images being sold as movies in a city like Wenzhou," he writes, "which had so many trade links with the outside world. . . . It wasn't surprising that the attacks became just another American-style product. Over the next month, I collected other 9/11 goods: a 'Bush vs. bin Laden' video game, Osama bin Laden key chains."[34] Hessler noticed how the lack of personal interaction and the shallowness of electronic communication turned the foreign spectacle into a commodity. This same problem drives Friedman to a sober realization: "We are technologically closer—and culturally and politically as far apart as ever. . . . Maybe the Internet, fiber optics, and satellites are, together, like a high-tech Tower of Babel. It's as though God gave us all the tools to communicate and none of the tools to understand."[35] Yet Friedman continues to celebrate these tools, even as global media continue to market global brands and deep communication is lacking.

Branding is a shallow form of communication but it threatens the church. To introduce the problem of global branding for the church, consider the following little multiple choice quiz. Who said the following? "[Global communication] is a form of communication that transcends national boundaries and languages and reaches to the hearts and minds of people. Global communication must speak personally to every individual; at the same time its message must be universal."[36] Was it: (A) Billy Graham, (B) Pope John Paul II, (C) the Archbishop of Canterbury, (D) the Ecumenical Patriarch of Constantinople or (E) an advertising executive? The correct answer, it turns out, is (E): it was the president of Japan's largest ad agency, speaking in a language that mimics the language of Pentecost's catholicity. Instead of a message of good news that speaks both personally and globally—instead of the Christian gospel of repentance and renewal—this executive is preaching a shallower gospel that tries to sell corporate products. The global pervasiveness of advertising raises a serious question: Is it possible that global media and advertising do a better job at embodying compelling messages than the church? The Catholic political scientist Michael Budde has pointed out that global media companies now rival or even surpass the power of the church. When you compare the identity-forming power of Disney/ABC/ESPN,

34. Hessler, *Oracle Bones*, 322.

35. Friedman, *Longitudes*, 390–91.

36. Budde, *(Magic) Kingdom of God*, 42–43.

Viacom, Universal Vivendi, Time Warner, Bertelsmann, General Electric, Sony, and News Corp with the identity-forming power of the global-local church, it looks like the church may be in trouble.[37] "What is at risk," writes Budde, "is not any particular interpretation of the gospel but the capacity to think, feel, and experience in ways formed by the Christian story."[38] Whereas each of these corporations is worth tens of billions of dollars and each controls film or television studios, news channels, sports programming, magazines, newspapers, and book publishers, how many resources for identity-formation does the church command? How effective is it in broadcasting its message and forming young and old into its story? The Christian message itself is being advertised globally in ways that fail to do justice to the depth of its message. If the marketers and advertisers shape us more than the Christian story does, then we may be losing the very grammar of faith, the narrative of discipleship. The Nike Swoosh or the Golden Arches threaten to overtake the cross as a meaningful symbol.

What kind of story, if any, are the global media giants forming us into? More specifically, what do they seek to form our children into? As we saw in chapter 6, consumption has become an urgent necessity in the global economy and consumerism is becoming a global culture.[39] It is thus necessary to "brand" youth into loyalty to corporate images early on, turning even young children into consumers.[40] As one child marketing expert put it, "The plain fact of the matter is that businesses have only two major sources of new customers. . . . Either they are switched from competitors, or they are developed from childhood."[41] Therefore, selling to kids is big business in the present and it can generate sales for the long-term future. I will never forget flying into Kuwait in 1994 and chatting about the Chicago Bulls basketball team with a little Kuwaiti boy who was playing on his Nintendo and wearing Michael Jordan gear. Although he was becoming global consumer, we also had something to talk about.

It makes one wonder if the church can form us and our children in a compelling story of the Kingdom that might rival global branding.

37. For a list of the top ten global media corporations, see Kirby, *Vulnerability*, 112–13.

38. Budde, *(Magic) Kingdom of God*, 15.

39. Ibid., 26.

40. On branding, see Beaudoin, *Consuming Faith*; Klein, *No Logo*, 1–85; Quart, *Branded*; Schor, *Born to Buy*, 25–27.

41. McNeal, *Children as Consumers*, quoted in Quart, *Branded*, 51.

Re-enacting the Pentecost story might help us to re-imagine ourselves in ways that transcend global corporate branding, to re-connect us to a world-historical story, and even to captivate us and our kids. Re-enacting the Pentecost story also demonstrates how the global-local church's hopeful alternatives transcend the current views that cultural globalization equals homogenization, that it equals cultural imperialism, that it creates a cultural backlash and localism, or that it promotes freedom. In the end, we must trust that the Holy Spirit blows through the church and forms it. But if the wind blows, will we hear it?

Re-Enacting Pentecost

Pentecost, taking a prefix from the Greek word for fifty, marked the fiftieth day after the feast of unleavened bread in Passover. It is the Jewish holiday of Shavuot (Festival of Weeks) which celebrates the first fruits of the harvest being brought into the Temple, the culmination of forty nine days of feasting. It was on this feast day that the Holy Spirit, sounding like a "violent wind" (Acts 2:2), descended on the disciples in their room and on that same day Peter preached his sermon in Jerusalem to the many Jewish pilgrims celebrating the feast. Right from the beginning, then, the church calendar was linked to the Jewish liturgical cycle, and this holiday was part of the calendar along with Easter.[42] As with the Jewish festival, the Pentecost feast is better understood as secondary to, and a culmination of, the paschal feast, which is the center of the calendar.[43] We noted in the last chapter that early Christian tradition also did not distinguish between the various elements of Christ's triumph but chose instead to celebrate them for the entire fifty days. Although it is essential to remember the outpouring of the Spirit, there is a danger in detaching the Pentecost story from the earlier chapters of Christ's triumph and making the Holy Spirit into some kind of independent agent who works outside of the Father and the Son.[44] A free-floating Spirit would threaten to turn the church into a disembodied group separated from the body of Jesus. Hence, the Catholic lectionary assigns the same selection from

---

42. Dix, *Shape of the Liturgy*, 337; Schmemann, *For the Life of the World*, 56.

43. Cobb, "History," 463–64, 471, registers this concern, which is the post-Vatican II view of the season. See Catholic Church, *Catechism of the Catholic Church*, sections 1163, 1168, and 1169 (329, 331).

44. O'Donovan, *Desire of the Nations*, 161; Zizioulas, *Being as Communion*, 126–32.

1 Corinthians 12 each year, a selection which begins with Paul's point that "no one can say 'Jesus is Lord' except by the Holy Spirit" (v. 3b).

The lectionary gospel texts for Pentecost Sunday also emphasize the close bonds between Father, Son, and Spirit. In John 20, for instance, Jesus breathes on the disciples and tells them to "receive the Holy Spirit" (v. 22). The Spirit is literally the Father's and the Son's breath upon the disciples.[45] In John 14, he tells the disciples that if they have seen him, they have seen the Father (v. 9), and he tells them that the Father will send the Spirit in his (Jesus') name (v. 26). With John, we must see the bonds of unity here, being careful not to posit some ethereal Spirit that works outside of the Trinity. Instead, we must understand Pentecost as closely connected to the rest of the year and the rest of Christ's work. Oliver O'Donovan, for example, links the church's birth at Pentecost to the Ascension, the link "through which the Exaltation was opened to the participation of his community."[46] As he puts it, "the whole authorization of the church is conveyed by the Spirit, so that Pentecost can be seen as the moment at which the church comes to participate in the authority of the ascended Christ."[47] Because this authority flows from union with the Father and Son, the Spirit-empowered church recapitulates in its sacraments all of the events of the coming of the Kingdom in the person of Jesus.[48] But Pentecost marks the point at which the church begins this ministry of re-enacting Christ's work, because the church is "the gift of the Holy Spirit, giving social form to the triumph of Christ."[49] This social form is evident in the "astonishing variety" of gifts that all come from "the same Spirit", "the same Lord", and the "same God" for the "common good" of the church body, which is also Christ's body (1 Cor 12:4–7).[50] The diversity of gifts and the unity of the body are integrally linked: "For just as the body is one and has many members, and all the members of the body, though many, are one body, so it is with Christ. For in the one Spirit

45. I take this as textual evidence for the Western view in the *filioque* controversy that split the Eastern Orthodox off from the West by 1054 A.D. The Western church held that the Spirit proceeds from both the Father and the Son, while the East held that the Spirit proceeded only from the Father.

46. O'Donovan, *Desire of the Nations*, 161.

47. Ibid., 162.

48. Ibid., 172–90.

49. Ibid., 169.

50. "Astonishing variety" comes from Christian Reformed Church, *Our World*, Section 29.

we were all baptized into one body—Jews or Greeks, slaves or free—and we were all made to drink of one Spirit" (1 Cor 12–13). Unity-in-diversity and diversity-in-unity is an essential mark of the Spirit's presence.

The Pentecost story itself not only dramatically illustrates this union of diverse gifts, but it also adds elements of eschatology and mission. The dramatic re-enactment of unity-amidst-plurality is the first thing we encounter in the story. When the Holy Spirit came, there were "God-fearing Jews from every nation under heaven" in Jerusalem, and each of them heard the disciples speaking to them in their own language (Acts 2:5-6). Quite literally, the curse of Babel was overcome, but not through the return of all peoples into one language; instead, the plurality of tongues remained, but the message from the newly empowered disciples made sense in the native vernacular of "Parthians, Medes, Elamites, and residents of Mesopotamia, Judea and Cappadocia, Pontus and Asia, Phrygia and Pamphylia, Egypt and the parts of Libya belonging to Cyrene, and visitors from Rome, both Jews and proselytes, Cretans and Arabs" (Acts 2:9–11a). Unlike Islam, which insists that the Qur'an is untranslatable, Christianity from its beginning has insisted that its message is translatable into the vernacular of any group. Diversity of languages is preserved at the origin of the church and throughout the Christian story. The preservation of diversity-in-unity has profound implications for how we will re-imagine the globalization of the church as a mode of translation that "gathers people from every tongue, tribe, and nation into the unity of the body of Christ."[51]

The eschatological dimensions of Pentecost become clear when Peter stands up to deliver his sermon to the pilgrims in Jerusalem. He asserts that the words of the prophet Joel were now being fulfilled: "In the last days it will be, God declares, that I will pour out my Spirit upon all flesh, and your sons and your daughters shall prophesy, and your young men shall see visions, and your old men shall dream dreams" (Acts 2:17, Joel 2:28). The Spirit's movements, or Peter's description of them, suggest that we, like those in Jerusalem in Peter's day, await an imminent end to history. The Spirit enables the apostles' message to be heard through the gift of tongues and translation. And that message is urgent: we are living in the last days.

Pentecost moves the church from an internal mission of communion to an external mission of proclamation of the good news of Jesus'

---

51. Christian Reformed Church, *Our World*, Section 30.

death, resurrection, and ascension. At Pentecost, the church discovers anew that Jesus' words before his ascension have been fulfilled: "But you will receive power when the Holy Spirit has come upon you; and you will be my witnesses in Jerusalem, in all Judea and Samaria, and to the ends of the earth" (Acts 1:8). The outpouring of the Spirit is the sign that confirms or seals these promises. So in these last days, with the resurrected Jesus abiding close at hand, the church is to bear witness to the rest of the globe. What is this extension of a witnessing church to look like? The church that formed in response to Peter's sermon was marked by several distinct practices that embodied its mission: They "devoted themselves to the apostles' teaching and fellowship, to the breaking of bread and the prayers" (Acts 2:42). Biblical teaching and preaching (reiterating the core of Peter's sermon), economic sharing, communion, and prayer mark the church's unique witness to the world—a care and concern for the unity and membership that also extends outward in invitations to the rest of the world.

My own denomination expresses the outward dimension of Spirit-empowered mission particularly well in a contemporary testimony recited by our congregation in a Pentecost liturgy: "Anointed and sent by the Spirit, the church is thrust into the world, ambassadors of God's peace, announcing forgiveness and reconciliation, proclaiming the good news of grace. Going before them and with them, the Spirit convinces the world of sin and pleads the cause of Christ."[52] This presence of the Spirit in the mission of the church reminds us that the work is not up to the church but only flows from the empowering of the Spirit. Thus, the Spirit takes primacy over institutional modes of the church, nudging it toward a universal order that extends toward the ends of the earth. "The ordering of the church's life," writes O'Donovan, "follows its authorization as a 'catholic' social reality by the Holy Spirit. The catholic identity of the church derives from the progress of the Spirit's own mission. It is therefore always larger than its ordered structures, taking its shape from the new ground that the Spirit is possessing. It remains for the church's structures to catch up with this mission, to discern what the Spirit has done, and construct such ordered links of community as will safeguard brotherly love."[53] In tandem with the outward thrust of the Spirit's work,

---

52. Ibid. The language about convincing of sin and pleading Christ's cause evokes Jesus' teachings about the Spirit in John 14–16.

53. O'Donovan, *Desire of the Nations*, 169–70.

then, is an inward thrust for the church body, which is knit together in the "communion [*koinonia*] of the Holy Spirit" (2 Cor 13:13)—the same type of communion that the early church practiced by "holding all things in common [*koinos*]" (Acts 2:42). In addition to breaking bread in communion and embodying communion in economic sharing, the church practices proclamation and prayer.[54] While proclamation and prophecy speak to the world, as Peter did, prayer speaks with and listens to God, finding the source of all power in God. This entails listening for God and waiting upon the Spirit in community, as the apostles did before the Spirit was poured out (Acts 2:1). In both proclaiming and listening, "the church's authority mirrors Christ's own, establishing God's Kingdom by God's word."[55] There is no question that clear global communication of the good news of Christ's death and resurrection must do better than the shallow gospels of global media firms.

The ultimate mission statement for the church comes from Jesus in Matthew 28, and we can reiterate three points from this text for the mission of the church relative to globalization.[56] First, Jesus commands the disciples to "make disciples of all nations" (v. 19a), highlighting the dimension of universality and catholicity at the birth of the church: people from *all* nations are to be made into disciples, going beyond the confines of Judaism in Palestine and extending to all the Gentiles, a move that requires the disciples to translate their teaching into diverse cultural contexts. Second, Jesus commands his disciples to baptize them "in the name of the Father and of the Son and of the Holy Spirit"— reiterating the role of the Spirit within the communion of persons in this work. It is not solely up to the church to do its work on its own. As Jesus reminds them, he will be with them until the end through the Spirit's work. Third, the church is to "teach everything" that he commanded—the teachings of the gospels—summarized by the command to love God and love their neighbors.

All three elements of the season come together in a unity of the church's work: the Spirit's work through diversity, eschatology, and mission. The work of Christ breathes the Spirit into the church; there is no

54. Yoder, *Body Politics*, 14–27, argues that the Lord's Supper was primarily, even solely, an economic act. See O'Donovan, *Desire of the Nations*, 186–90, on prophecy and prayer.

55. O'Donovan, *Desire of the Nations*, 187.

56. In the lectionary, this passage is read once every three years on Trinity Sunday, the Sunday following Pentecost.

separation between the Spirit's work and the Son's work. The church thus participates in the life of God through the Spirit.[57] The church first does this by embodying unity-in-diversity, reversing Babel through the gift of translation, speaking to the nations and in prayer with God (aided by the Spirit that prays for us and with us—Rom 8:22–27). The prophecy of our sons and daughters reminds us that we are in the "last days," prompting the church to continue in its mission of proclamation to all peoples, to the ends of the earth, while embodying the hope of unity in its own body, which in turn is the body of Christ (both absent and present).

It is all there: the internal mission of embodying loving unity, the external mission of proclamation to "all the nations," the testimony to Christ's work, the sense of eschatological urgency, and the overcoming of Babel in the very embodiment of the global Church. Here is the beginning of a model for re-imagining the globalization of culture by viewing it through the church of Pentecost.

RE-IMAGINING THE GLOBALIZATION OF CULTURE

"Almighty God," begins the prayer for Pentecost Sunday in the *Book of Common Prayer*, "on this day you opened the way of eternal life to every race and nation by the promised gift of your Holy Spirit: Shed abroad this gift throughout the world by the preaching of the Gospel, that it may reach to the ends of the earth."[58] This prayer reminds us that the church was born global in a dual sense: it will encompass all peoples, bringing unity in diversity, and it will extend to uttermost parts of the earth. We might say, then that the church is already engaged in cultural globalization, but in its own peculiar way that calls it out from the world. John Howard Yoder writes that "the original meaning of the word *ecclesia* [the New Testament Greek word for "church"] is political; it is literally a 'called meeting,' an assembly, such as a town meeting, convened to do business, to deliberate on behalf of the entire society."[59] But this calling out can only occur in the Spirit. As theologian John Zizioulas writes, "the Spirit is not something that 'animates' a Church that already exists. The Spirit

57. O'Donovan, *Desire of the Nations*, 187: "So finally we characterize the Pentecostal church simply by its participation in the divine speech, which is at the same time God's speech to us and ours to him, reflecting the two natures of Christ in hypostatic union."

58. Episcopal Church, *Book of Common Prayer*, 227.

59. Yoder, *Body Politics*, 2; Clapp, *Peculiar People*, 80–81.

makes the Church *be*."[60] Under the Spirit's power only, the global church is called out to re-imagine the world's globalization of cultures and practice its own form of being global. We can see this in four movements.

First, the church is called to move beyond homogeneity and toward practicing true catholicity and true glocalization: toward a global-local blend. The presence of Jews from "all nations" at Pentecost was a reminder that the church needed to embody an extensive unity that crossed the world. But in the early church this required intensive work in adapting a unique culture that knitted Jews and Gentiles together, a major preoccupation of the epistles of the New Testament. This concern continues today. John Paul II recognized that "cultures also run the risk of being homogenized if they are not accepted and respected in their originality and richness, but forcefully adapted to the needs of the market and fashion."[61] By contrast, however, the church has been globalizing in a healthy way that preserves local identity and language while also maintaining catholicity. It practices a catholicity that reflects the character of Christ through the Spirit—a communion with his body through a universal (catholic) community that is both local and global.[62] This practice does not originate from the human effort to respect diversity. Rather, it flows from the Eucharistic unity described in the last chapter. Flowing from this unity, Zizioulas notes that in early church practice it was "possible to apply the term 'catholic' both to the local and universal realms at the same time."[63] Each local community of the church embodied the "full eschatological unity of all in Christ," knitting together rich and poor, Greek and Jew, slave and free in a united body that was Christ's body in that place—a sign of the liberation that was already breaking in to the world through the church.[64] The gathering of the church was also universal in uniting diverse groups across the known world.

The church's catholicity is therefore both extensive and intensive. It is both concerned to cross geographical boundaries and to attend closely to the unity of all those in the local parish. To the extent that the true church has always struggled to keep doing this, we can say without exaggeration that it has been practicing a healthy form of "glocalization" for

---

60. Zizioulas, *Being*, 132.

61. John Paul II, "Address to the Sixth Public Session."

62. Zizioulas, *Being as Communion*, 131.

63. Ibid., 154.

64. Ibid., 154–55, 247–48.

almost two thousand years. In each place the church enters, it creates an embodied, local presence in its worship and work. If the church is to be truly local, "it must absorb and use all the characteristics of a given local situation and not impose an alien culture on it."[65] Christian communities have always adapted to the local conditions in which they find themselves, and even the intellectual culture of Western Christianity has changed over time, as its center of gravity shifted from Rome, to Ireland, to Europe, to North America and now again to Africa and Asia.[66] Rather than requiring people to convert to a culture in order to join the community, the church has always adapted its culture to suit local needs and concerns. These local needs and concerns will differ widely, but translation into their diversity is the very starting place of true unity in the Spirit-led Church. However, these indigenous concerns were also challenged at those places where they still contributed to division and fragmentation. To truly be the church, the body needed to embody the unity of Christ in that place.[67] Neither absolute uniformity nor absolute plurality was celebrated in the church. Rather, the unity-in-diversity begun at Pentecost—the knitting together of factions into the one body of Christ—was to be maintained as a sign of Christ's work of reconciliation, the beginning, not so much of a reversal of Babel, but of a new Jerusalem that people from every tribe, language, and nation will join. By re-enacting Pentecost and maintaining this sign of unity, the church participates in a healthy globalization that avoids homogenization and absolute pluralism. At its best, the church offers a coherent community that is simultaneously global and local. Unlike the "parody of true catholicity" we see in globalization, the church provides the real thing.[68]

Second, the Spirit calls the church to re-imagine the problem of cultural imperialism by understanding its interactions with culture as part of a translation movement instead. When the Christian church comes into contact with a local culture for the first time, it inevitably has an impact. The Spirit's blowing, we recall, sounded like a violent wind. Christians hope that the impact will be for the better, but we must confess that missionary efforts often led to cultural breakdowns. Chinua Achebe's masterful novel *Things Fall Apart* reminds us of political and

---

65. Ibid., 254.

66. Walls, *Missionary Movement*, 7–29.

67. Zizioulas, *Being as Communion*, 225.

68. Cavanaugh, *Being Consumed*, 71.

cultural consequences that resulted from Christian missionaries entering Nigeria. Tribes and families were divided, social structures changed.
The main character of Achebe's novel, a proud warrior named Okonkwo,
ends up clashing with missionaries after seeing his son stolen away to the
new faith. His suicide symbolizes the collapse of traditional African culture in the face of this new imperial onslaught. The arrival of the church
and the gospel can be like the arrival of a fire, and resulting changes can
sometimes be catastrophic to old ways of life, as Achebe reminds us. But
that change can also be liberating for people. Achebe himself was edu-
cated at Anglican mission schools, and he depicts the ritual sacrifice of
children as an important part of traditional culture that was rejected after
missionaries arrived. Only the most doctrinaire cultural relativist could
justify child sacrifice as "diverse" culturally appropriate behavior worthy
of preserving. This is not to argue in favor of Western cultural imperialism, but it is to argue that the arrival of the church (if not the state!) can
be good news for a culture, or at least better news than the arrival of
foreign militaries or merchants.

After years of secular education, often including assignments of
Achebe's book, many mainline Christians feel guilty over missions today,
and believe that they were part of a program of "cultural imperialism."[69]
But Yale Divinity School professor Lamin Sanneh, himself an African
convert to Christianity, argues that Westerners need to get over their
liberal guilt complex. He points out that missionaries in Africa were
engaged in a translation movement that actually preserved indigenous
languages. And, he argues, "Colonial rule was irreparably damaged by
the consequences of vernacular translation. . . ."[70] That is, the translation
of the Bible by missionaries was liberating, not oppressive. Translation of
the Bible into indigenous languages also has a dynamic cultural impact,
according to Sanneh, both "destigmatizing" a local culture or affirming
it and "relativizing" it, opening up that "culture up to the demand and
need for change."[71] Sanneh points out that many missionaries faced challenges from followers who learned the new scriptures and criticized their
Western counterparts when they failed to observe the teachings of Jesus.
Using their own languages they were able to assert their power and to

69. For a revision of this view, see a forthcoming book by Jay Riley Case, *Evangelicals
in the World*.

70. Sanneh, "Christian Missions," 331.

71. Ibid., 332.

bring social change. So we should resist a simplistic understanding of the church's role in global culture, and we should be open to the possibility that it has played a constructive role at times. This is not to justify imperialism, but simply to recognize that things are more complicated than they seem, and traditional cultures don't always "fall apart" but actually pull together when their languages are translated into writing. We must hold open the possibility that the gospel can work within a culture to bring changes for the better. The African church is now starting to teach the Western churches, and Christianity is no longer a predominantly Western religion but an African, Asian, and Latin American one, and a Pentecostal one at that.[72] The Spirit blows where it will, even to the ends of the earth. Here we recall the centrality of the mystery of tongues—the simultaneous translation of the Apostles' teaching into the local vernacular of the various Jewish pilgrims in Jerusalem. A central truth of the Spirit's working is that the unity of Christ is preserved through a multiplicity of languages. Missions scholar Andrew Walls notes "a delightful paradox that the more Christ is translated into the various thought forms and life systems form our national identities, the richer all of us become in our common Christian identity."[73] Our catholicity is actually enriched by increasing the plurality within Christ's unity. Instead of seeking to impose American culture on the world, then, Christians' time would be better spent learning a foreign language in order to translate the gospel or to receive it from another language. The church is, in part, a translation movement.

Third, the Spirit calls the church to re-imagine the clash of civilizations through a vision of the always-Global, Spirit-filled church that existed from the beginning of Christian history. If we define globalization as integration across continents, we can see that the new church was global from its beginning at Pentecost, starting with Jews from all over and extending to Arab converts (Acts 2:11).[74] A central theme of the book of Acts is that the apostles are to spread the message not just in Judea and Samaria (the Holy Land) but "to the ends of the earth" (Acts 1:8)—extending the blessing upon Israel so that all nations may join in union with God, an outward movement that demonstrates the universality of God's concern. The promise that started with Abraham—that "all

72. Jenkins, *Next Christendom*; Sanneh, *Disciples of All Nations*.

73. Walls, *Missionary Movement*, 54.

74. Goudzwaard, *Globalization*, 19–20; Lott, "Is Globalization Christian?"

the families of the earth shall be blessed" through him (Gen 12:3)—is fulfilled when "every tribe and race and people and nation" (Rev 5:9, 7:9) worship at the throne of the Lamb. This final end reflects the movement God's uniting from Abraham onward, part of a globalizing movement that connected cultures across the earth. Theologian John Zizioulas sees this movement of unity as a central work of the Spirit in the church. As he puts it, "to reveal Christ's whole Body in history means to meet the demonic powers of division which operate in history. A Christological catholicity which is seen in the context of this encounter with the anti-catholic powers of the world cannot be a *static* but a *dynamic catholicity*" that "depends constantly upon the Holy Spirit" and not upon human powers.[75] The church's "call to catholicity is a call not to a progressive conquest but to a 'kenotic' [emptying] experience of the fight with the anticatholic demonic powers and a continuous dependence upon the Lord and His Spirit. . . . A catholic Church in the world . . . lives in humility and service and above all in constant worship and prayer."[76] We are reminded again of the *koinonia* [communion] of the Spirit that was to be incarnated in the Body of the Son. The unity of the church is a sign that the promise to Abraham is coming true, depending on the Spirit's breath, in contrast to the powers of division and fragmentation that seem to dominate history. "All cultures in one way or other share in this fallen and disintegrated world, and therefore all of them include elements which need to be transcended. If the church in its localization fails to present an image of the Kingdom in this respect, it is not a Church."[77]

Yet, apart from the Spirit, it is difficult to realize or see this unity in practice, since it does not appear to exist in typical political terms. Thus, conventional media tend to miss the global unity of Christianity and tend reinforce the assumption that Christianity is only a Western religion. However, historians of the global church have helped us to see the extensive catholicity of the church in practice in history.[78] Not only was the church globalizing from its beginning but it now reaches closer to "ends of the earth," still embodying the unity of the Spirit (as much as it is humanly possible to sustain), and this should calm our fears of a global

75. Zizioulas, *Being as Communion*, 160 (emphasis in original) and 161.

76. Ibid., 161–62.

77. Ibid., 255.

78. Bediako, "New Christian World"; Jenkins, *Next Christendom*; Berger, "Four Faces"; Sanneh, *Disciples of All Nations*.

clash of civilizations. Because Samuel Huntington identifies Christianity with the West, he fails to consider how Christianity is growing and becoming (again) a non-Western religion.[79] The rise of a truly global church challenges Huntington's predictions to the extent that Christians live in every major civilization and cut across those allegedly impermeable cultural-religious barriers. These Christians and others have the potential to form a bridge across civilizational boundaries in the transnational church.[80] As part of this global church, the American evangelical church might even listen to its brothers and sisters in ways that will lead it to sometimes praise and sometimes criticize the U. S. government in solidarity with its brothers and sisters in the church abroad. Although this sounds a long way off, a church that lives out of the Pentecost story can more easily imagine itself as a global communion.

Fourth, the Spirit helps the church to re-imagine global cultural hybrids from the perspective of true communion. John Paul II once described the end product of mainstream globalized culture this way: "The result is a cultural product, bearing a superficial syncretism, imposing a new scale of values, derived from criteria that are regularly arbitrary, consumerist and opposed to any kind of openness to the Transcendent."[81] While this might sound harsh, his concern was that "the market as an exchange mechanism has become the medium of a new culture."[82] As we noted at the beginning of this chapter, we often flatten the definition of culture to the consuming of commodities marketed through global media conglomerates. But culture encompasses more than the consumption of Big Macs, Starbucks coffee, or Disney films. If these market commodities become the primary vehicle for cultural exchange, then we are in danger of reducing culture to items that can be bought or sold, excluding the deeper communion with God and each other that material cultural can nourish, through the Spirit. The communion of the Spirit, ushering us into the love of the Father and the grace of Jesus (1 Cor 13:13) is not something that you can download—at least, not yet. Instead, it requires constant participation in the body of Christ, entering into the communion through eating the Eucharist meal, through participating in the life of the body. "It is not insignificant," says Zizioulas, "that the

---

79. Jenkins, *Next Christendom*, 5–6, 15–38.

80. On this idea, see Waalkes, "Prescience and Paradigms."

81. John Paul II, "Address to the Sixth Public Session."

82. John Paul II, "Address of the Holy Father."

Spirit has always, since the time of Paul been associated with the notion of communion."[83]

To the extent that hybridized identities participate in this type of communion, they could be embraced, but discernment is necessary here. Another Greek Orthodox theologian has made the case in just the terms we are using here, "avoiding the simplistic interpretations which see globalization and post-modernity only as a melting-pot, or, to the contrary, only as an inevitable clash of civilizations. . . ."[84] Instead, he argues, the church should consider whether theories of cultural hybridization "converge in a fruitful way with those elements of the Christian experience that are able to build a culture of coexistence and social justice. The challenge here is to learn how to become faithful listeners to the Spirit who blows wherever it pleases."[85] How does the reconciliation evident in the Spirit's work compare to this hybridity? On the one hand, it gives us an encouraging glimpse of harmony between cultures globally. On the other hand, the global market of electronic media creates a world in which everyone's identity is a mixed-up jumble of global and local elements that differs for each person. It empowers people to create their own hybrids. By contrast, the church is a community of coherent communion in the Spirit, diverse yet truly unified. Graced by the Holy Spirit, the worshipping church already participates in the worship of the Ascended Christ, as a community that participates in his body. Because the church has always been a globalized community that provides such a deeply rooted identity, it should be able to respond well to the Babel of contemporary globalized culture. To the homeless or lost, the church offers community and direction. To people sick of fast food, the church offers a meal that gives a foretaste of what communion with God is like and that goes deeper than the branding of global media corporations, in flesh-and-blood, embodied local communities that are also part of the universal body of Christ.

IMPROVISING PRACTICES: BINDING, LOOSING, TRANSLATING

John Howard Yoder notes that Jesus only uses the world *ecclesia* twice in the gospels. In Matthew 16, Jesus promises that he will build his church

83. Zizioulas, *Being as Communion*, 130–31.

84. Papathanasiou, "Reconciliation: The Major Conflict in Post-Modernity."

85. Ibid.

on the rock of Peter. And in Matthew 18, he explains a process of reconciliation between his followers. In both places, he says that he is giving the power to "bind and loose" to Peter and/or the disciples. Yoder interprets this to mean that the church is called to engage in moral discernment (similar to the rabbinical meaning of binding) and reconciliation (loosing, or releasing from obligations).[86] Binding or discernment confronts what is wrong while loosing offers the chance of reconciliation between those who wronged each other. Both of these practices offer powerful ways of fostering a distinctive global-local culture that the church can offer the world.

On the one hand, churches that practice "loosing" bear witness to the Kingdom in a world of deep cultural division.[87] They practice reconciliation rather then seek to impose homogeneity or create conflict. Yoder interprets the concept of "loosing" to mean that whoever the church forgives will also be forgiven in heaven. Reconciliation here and now participates in the reconciliation of all things that is the destiny of Creation.[88] If we take John 20:23 into account—"If you forgive the sins of any, they are forgiven them; if you retain the sins of any, they are retained"—we find an inextricable link between our forgiving others and God's forgiving us. We must be reconciling with each other if we hope to face God someday. The communion within the church is the sign that extends outward to the communion and reconciliation of the world itself. People hoping to find "peace with God" will be more likely to find it in a community of people at peace with each other, and at peace with God. To obtain that peace, reconciliation must happen. People must confess their sins to each other and be restored to fellowship. To fully practice this process with an eye toward reconciliation would be a radical departure from the polite culture of most North American churches, and it would certainly provide a striking contrast to the globalized culture of McWorld. Although liturgical churches symbolically "pass the peace" before the Eucharist as a way of enacting a gesture of forgiveness before going to the table, and Catholic and Orthodox believers also practice the sacrament of confession or reconciliation, it is not clear how seriously these practices are taken. While Yoder argues that this process should be vested in the church as a whole and not just in priests, at least those

86. Yoder, *Body Politics*, 2.

87. Sanneh, *Disciples*, 286–87.

88. Ibid., 2–3. In support of this interpretation, see the entirety of Matthew 18.

churches engage in a practice where one human can forgive another in God's name.[89] Most Protestants are far too willing to believe that this action must only occur in their "heart," rather than being embodied with real words and actions. If forgiveness is just between us and God, then how will the world see it? If churches started putting reconciliation into practice, it would proclaim a Kingdom identity that not only goes much deeper than anything offered by McWorld but also demonstrates how to reconcile differences and breaches of the peace. By regularly confessing to each other, resolving conflicts directly, and reconciling, the church would create a powerful cultural witness.

In a world full of conflict, a church that practices reconciliation can be an ark of salvation. It is hard to imagine cultures more at odds than those of the black majority in South Africa and those of the white minority regime. Yet the apartheid regime in South Africa came to a peaceful end, in part because of the work of the Truth and Reconciliation Commission, one of whose founders was Anglican Archbishop Desmond Tutu. The goal of reconciliation is at heart of the gospel message. Of course, applying it to public life outside the church may lead to failure, where it is detached from the sustaining narrative provided by the preaching of the whole gospel and the context of communion.[90] Yet there is no question that Tutu's effort illustrates the power of the "loosing" church to help end serious clashes between victims and perpetrators. In a small way, the world saw the power of reconciliation to heal relationships. Of course, the church failed in Rwanda, which was one of the most "Christian" countries in Africa (at least defined by the number of churches relative to population). Yet it was unable to bring reconciliation between the Hutu and Tutsi groups, and some church leaders even allowed the 1994 genocide of Tutsis to go forward.[91] The church alone is not going to save the world through its ministry of reconciliation, but it can sometimes, with the Spirit's help, begin to heal the divides between its members, bring in new members, and thereby bring greater peace. There is no guarantee of success, but the

---

89. Ibid., 3.

90. Thanks to Steve Martin for sharpening this point. See the critique of Donald Shriver's book *Forgiveness in Politics* by Amstutz, "After the Death Squads." Amstutz focuses on the practical efficacy of forgiveness in public-political life. However, if we were there to judge the crucifixion by the standard of efficacy, we would have found it wanting as a strategy for politics. Martyrdom seems like failure, yet it was ultimately success for Jesus and the early church.

91. Katongole, "Christianity, Tribalism, and the Rwandan Genocide."

church bears witness in its culture of "loosing," and it hopes that this culture can bring identity both to victims and to perpetrators of evil.

Reconciliation starts small, but its effects can ripple outward. Father Elias Chacour, an Israeli Arab Melkite Christian, tells a story from his first few weeks in ministry in Ibillin, an Arab village within northern Israel. A feud between two families had nearly destroyed the church to which he had been assigned. The people were so distracted by their anger at each other that it was distracting them from their worship. On Palm Sunday, Father Chacour became so fed up with the parishioners from the two families that he rushed to the back of the sanctuary at the end of the service and locked the door. He returned to the front of the church, now full of shocked worshippers, and told his parishioners that he would not let them go until they reconciled with each other. After a tense silence lasting several minutes, the families finally patched up their differences and the joy of Easter broke out a week early. Father Chacour continued to preach reconciliation, extending it to relations between Palestinians and Israelis.[92] Reconciliation started within the church but can spread outward to the world. Although a message of reconciliation will never be a popular message in bitter conflicts like the Palestinian-Israeli war, it may be the only way out, and it is certainly what the church ought to be preaching and practicing. The world's cultures need it. We all need it.

At a global level, ecumenical efforts to repair relations between Christian churches, if motivated by the spirit of true reconciliation, can reinforce this witness. Two noteworthy ventures are the Evangelicals and Catholics Together movement and the Catholic Church's efforts to repair the rift with Orthodoxy. As he announced his continuation of the latter effort to reach out to the Orthodox, the new Pope Benedict XVI pointedly asked, "how can we communicate with the Lord if we don't communicate among ourselves?"[93] This question cuts straight to the role of the Spirit in breeding unity through communion, a reality in which the practice of reconciliation participates. If the church does practice reconciliation, it shows to the world how neither homogenization nor conflict has the final say. Rather, peaceful, harmonious difference can be reconciled with unity. But, while we must make the effort, this can only be a gift of the Spirit.

92. Chacour and Hazard, *Blood Brothers*, 176–79; Chacour and Jensen, *We Belong to the Land*, 28–33; Cartwright, "Being Sent."

93. Fisher, "Pope Vows."

The church also practices binding. This practice of discernment can help us act more carefully in a world of global branding and hybridity. Careful discernment is necessary to hear the blowing of the Spirit and to test the global marketing of cultural commodities. John Paul II asks, "The discernment, which we are called to exercise as disciples of Christ, has for its primary object the inevitable human, cultural, and spiritual impact . . . of globalization. What is the image of man (that globalization) proposes and even imposes? What culture does it favor? Is there room for the experience of faith and the interior life?"[94] The church ought to be concerned with the shallowness of marketing and electronic modes of cultural interaction. One small way in which churches might exercise cultural discernment is to provide deep cultural experiences in worship or programs. A generation of people raised on a steady diet of instant messaging, blogging, online shopping, and Facebook will be hungry for "faith and the interior life." Therefore, churches that cultivate a diet of rich faith food can expect to reach people disenchanted with the emptiness of the electronic media culture of global branding.

My own congregation experienced qualitative growth as it increasingly included visual arts in its weekly worship and observation of the liturgical year. To cite just one instance, an icon of the Holy Trinity, based on Rublev's icon in traditional Orthodox style, created a powerful means of pondering the mystery of the three-in-one Godhead. I am convinced that in our world awash with images, we are growing accustomed to shallow reflection on the visual. If a picture does not speak to us immediately, we ditch it. Yet God invites us into contemplation of his mysteries through the visual. Our churches ought to be bringing people deeper into the mysteries of God. Father Henri Nouwen spent several hours sitting in the Hermitage Museum in St. Petersburg observing and pondering Rembrandt's painting of the father embracing the younger son from the story of the Prodigal Son, managing to write an entire book from his reflections on details in the painting.[95] Churches offering this kind of depth will surely speak to the needs of people used to shallowness. There is discernment here: In a shallow global culture, churches of depth bear witness to the coming Kingdom. They embody a deeper culture that will give global surfers a solid rock of refuge. They point those people living on the surface to that day when there will be no more death or mourning

94. John Paul II, "Address to the Sixth Public Session."
95. Nouwen, *Return of the Prodigal Son.*

or crying or pain (Rev 21:4). By helping connect our neighbors' lives to the larger story told in Pentecost and Advent, where we glimpse the end of the story, we can help them experience their lives as coherent stories.[96] The biggest problem with hybridity is that it often fails to offer such coherence that allows people to construct stable identities rooted in such a global story. An understanding of Pentecost can remind us that we all have an internal and external mission in the church: we are to practice reconciliation and foster communion while inviting others to join that communion to the ends of the earth before the end of time.

Another practice stemming from Pentecost is the practice of translation. Pentecost was a translation movement right at the beginning, allowing everyone to hear the apostles in their own tongues. So, too, the church's external mission might be understood best as struggling to communicate in terms not unlike those described by the Japanese advertising executive earlier in this chapter, in ways that move listeners, not unlike those who heard Peter and were "cut to the heart" (Acts 2:37). This ability to speak meaningfully while also speaking personally to individuals and speaking broadly to the universal world is a gift of the Spirit. But this gift is at the root of the church's ability from the beginning to move from Judea and Samaria to the ends of the earth. The church has always struggled to translate the gospel into terms that communicate the good news effectively. In an age of globalization, that struggle grows in urgency. And in an age that even Friedman fears is returning us to the conditions of Babel, the church must struggle to translate in ways that transcend the shallow movements of cultural trends that occur only through electronic media. Instead, the church's members will want to share the message in person, and many will need to learn to translate as they travel for long- and short-term missions to others in the world, whether that means Nigerians and Koreans traveling to North America or North Americans traveling to Nigeria or South Korea. Not only will the global church need to continue to do "missions," but it will continue to need to struggle to translate. God does not speak only Hausa, or Korean, or English. Every language will be heard around the throne. Meanwhile, we need to keep translating.

---

96. MacIntyre, *After Virtue*, 204–25, argues that people need to be part of a larger narrative that frames their lives within a meaningful journey through the end of life. At their best, churches do that for their members.

314 The Fullness of Time in a Flat World

Peter's Pentecost sermon tells us that we are in the "last days," and this energizes the church's mission. The church is composed of people who have been called out to form a community centered on the preaching of the Word and the practice of the sacraments. As such, this makes for a peculiar culture. For example, Rodney Clapp points out in his book, *A Peculiar People* that "the church is the only institution that regularly celebrates the hope of its demise, the hope that it will not endure forever."[97] Unlike other global institutions that seek to perpetuate themselves, the church catholic is united with Christ in his absence and looks forward to being joined with him in his full resurrected and ascended presence some day, when the church will be fulfilled. The church tells a story that transcends the story of God's people on earth. It hopes for the day when, in Clapp's words, "there will no longer be any distinction between the church and the world."[98] As the global church regularly gathers, it prays that the Father's Kingdom will come "on earth as in heaven," which means that the church would no longer be called out from the nations but would be united with God in the new heaven and the new earth when the nations are united in worship.

Here we are reminded of Jesus' words that he will be with the disciples "to the end of the age" (Matt 28:20). Reflecting on the importance of eschatology for the mission of the church, Sam Wells writes that the church "simply operates with a different timescale from the rest of society. For the Church, that is the eschatological perspective."[99] This perspective is part of what the Spirit brings as it blows. Because the church already knows the end of the story—the world worshipping the Lamb in a new heaven and a new earth—it is freed to improvise, because it knows that it cannot make a mistake that would stop the work of the Spirit. Rather, it can work energetically knowing the end of the story that it has already been given. Thus the church can immerse itself "in the 'triviality' of the world" in the same way that "God has immersed himself in his world through Israel, Christ and the Church. . . ."[100] By engaging the messiness of daily life with the end in view, the church can help participate in this story, practicing reconciliation and discernment in ways that show our love for God and our neighbors. Wells puts it this way: "Because

97. Clapp, *Peculiar People*, 116.
98. Ibid.
99. Wells, *Transforming Fate into Destiny*, 172.
100. Ibid., 179.

[Christians] are not anxious about creating a propitious end to the story, they can spend their time doing things that witness their faith that the story has already been assigned an end. Christians stand out from the world because of the practices they have developed which express their faith in the world's purpose."[101] We already know the end of the story in the future, but we bear witness to it in the present by recalling and recapitulating how that end was brought about in the past, in the life, death, resurrection, and exaltation of Christ—the Fullness of Time.

The "called out ones" are indeed a peculiar people who are called to participate in this fullness through prophecy and prayer, the forms of communication with the world and with God.[102] In these last days, the church's young men and young women prophesy, telling the world the truth about its condition in God's eyes and speaking "a word from God to the church as it is placed here and now."[103] The church is called to preach Peter's Pentecost sermon over and over, hoping that some listeners will be "cut to the heart" (Acts 2:37). "Through the spiritual exegesis of Scripture, the church looks to Jesus of Nazareth as portrayed in the biblical drama in order to discover itself and find its way in the world as a distinctive people under the authority of Christ the King. It is in the quest to interpret reality through the Christological lens of Scripture that God discloses himself and becomes effectual in and through the church's manifold witness."[104] One of the most powerfully prophetic things the church can do is witness to the true end of history: not a fearful apocalypse but the triumph of the Kingdom of peace, a new heavens and a new earth, the restoration of Creation. "The prayers of the church seek one thing only, the final manifestation of God's rule on earth. . . . Prayer is invocation of the Spirit, calling upon God's power now to witness to God's power then."[105] When the church prays, "your Kingdom come, your will be done, on earth as it is in heaven" it is asking that this power and authority of the Kingdom be present on earth. While demonstrations of such power do happen in the Spirit, they also might not, and thus the church is taught in its prayer to be patient, to be faithful, and to endure,

---

101. Ibid.
102. O'Donovan, *Desire of the Nations*, 186–89.
103. Ibid., 188.
104. Hollon, *Everything is Sacred*, 196.
105. Ibid., 189. Emphasis in original.

like the churches in the book of Revelation. Attentive prayer is another proper posture for the church constituted at Pentecost.

As the church goes out into Ordinary Time, it maintains this vigilance right on through to Advent. And so the spiral renews itself again, until one day the spiral will cease, for all will be at rest in the Kingdom.

Conclusion

The contrast between *kairos* time and *chronos* time runs through this book. *Chronos* time speaks of the flat world: the world without eschatological hope, the world of hot money and cash values, the world of ravenous global eating, the world of alienating work, the world of restless global consuming, the world of U. S. military hegemony, the world of coercive free trade, the world of political communities in flux, and the world of globalized media. But the church can re-describe this world within the narrative of *kairos* time, the liturgical year and its modes of participation in Christ's fullness, which helps us to re-imagine our predicament on the world stage and to improvise ethical responses accordingly. *Kairos* time remains more closely attuned to the rhythms of embodied people in local places. It attends to human relationships and natural cycles. For instance, the Islamic world retains some of this understanding of time in its liturgical practices. The five daily calls for prayer remain tied to the position of the sun in the local place one is situated, with the first prayer coming just before sunrise and the final prayer coming just before sunset. Similarly, the times for fasting during the month of Ramadan depend upon the rising and the setting of the sun. A Muslim can break her fast only when the sun sets in the locality where she lives and prays. And the timing of the month itself is tied to the movements of the moon, since it is based on the Islamic calendar, a lunar reckoning of time which is approximately eleven days shorter than the Western Gregorian calendar, making Ramadan fall ten to eleven days earlier each year in the Western calendar. When our family lived in Bahrain, the fasting month started around October 15. In 2009 it will start around August 22. A few years later it will begin in July. My point here is simply to illustrate how some of these Muslim liturgical practices are tied to changing natural cycles and rhythms—in contrast to Western Christian liturgical practices that are more abstracted from such cycles and rhythms, and in stark contrast to standardized time, which seeks to eliminate such variation in favor of homogeneous, standardized time.

However, in this book I did not argue that we should emulate Islam and link the practices of the church year to natural rhythms and seasons in local places. For example, many Christians associate Christmas with winter, Epiphany with winter light, and Easter with springtime. One problem with those associations is that many Christians living in the southern hemisphere experience these holidays in the opposite seasons. The seasonal links are not universal, whereas the gospel narratives re-enacted in each season can be universal. I have also tried to avoid a nostalgia for the enchanted times of the medieval era that can sometimes tinge those who criticize the modern.[1] Neither the connections with natural cycles nor a simple return to the past are the keys to recovering practices of *kairos* time. Instead, the way toward recovering the fullness of time is to enter imaginatively into the liturgical year's gospel narratives in the present, to repeat the story each year in unique ways, to step into the spiral of the church year, and to enter into the dramatic re-enactments of Jesus' imminent coming, his birth, his self-revelation to the world, his work, his temptation and suffering, his passion and death, his glorious resurrection, his fleeting appearances and disappearances, and his breathing of the Spirit upon the church—something that we can do at any time and in any place. If the church attends carefully to these events in the drama it will naturally attune itself to local places and local times. After all, the drama calls us to embodiment in emulation of Jesus. Precisely because the fullness of God entered into the womb of Mary in Nazareth, there is a dramatic affirmation of both timely place and embodied time. By analogy, disciples emulate Jesus and "stand in readiness, trying to understand the signs of the times, and the message they convey . . ." receiving time as a gift that requires careful attention to the local places where they reside.[2] "It is the essence of grace that it places the individual in particular Christological situations," writes von Balthasar, not "vague and hazy" situations, but specific stories with concrete settings and real choices.[3] Members of the church can literally find themselves in any of the stories

1. Chesterton, "Outline of Sanity"; Milbank, "On Complex Space"; Pickstock, "Liturgy, Art, and Politics."

2. Von Balthasar, *Theology of History*, 120, also 72.

3. Ibid., 72–73.

of Jesus so that they can find their ethical compass for issues such as globalization. By listening to the gospel narratives being re-enacted in worship, one can place oneself in the story and figure out how to improvise ethical responses to the dilemmas one faces. This liberates the church to respond to globalization creatively, improvising responses as situations emerge.

These "Christological situations" can inform the Christian response to any ethical challenge, not just globalization. When Christians encounter these stories being re-enacted in worship, they come into contact with the fullness of truth that allows them to put everything else in perspective.[4] By re-enacting these Christological stories, the church year puts one in contact with the universal truth that is also a singular: God entering into time, redeeming it, and transforming our relationship to it. As in the Eucharist, paradoxically, the more one is connected to this universal truth the more one is connected to one's particular situation. The spiral of the Christian year brings both repetition and variety, both universality and particularity.

The liturgical year is thus far more than a political statement.[5] Observance of the calendar is part of the worship of God, and, although the worship of God might well fire our political imaginations, no human agenda should become its rationale. The rationale for worship, to quote one writer on liturgy and politics, "lies solely in the praised lordship of Christ, who happens to rule not an original horde of individual believers but a body of fellow-citizens."[6] The liturgical year is not an instrument that we "use" to derive social lessons to impart to worshippers.[7] Rather than changing or employing the calendar for our purposes, the calendar changes *us* to pursue God's purposes. Therefore, worshippers must learn to read the world from within the Christological situations they enter within the year.[8] This book provides only one example of such a reading.

4. Rodney Clapp, *Peculiar People,* 94–113; Hollon, *Everything Is Sacred,* 164–97.

5. Wannenwetsch, *Political Worship,* 21–31.

6. Wannenwetsch, "Liturgy," 89.

7. For a problematic example of an approach "*employing* certain Sundays in Ordinary Time for the *promotion* of social justice," see Baldovin, "Liturgical Year: Calendar for a Just Community," 441. Emphasis added. Also see Avila, *Worship and Politics,* 81, where he insists upon "the necessity of restructuring the Eucharist according to our situation of dependence."

8. Hollon, *Everything Is Sacred,* 193: "Throughout the Christian year, as pastors all over the world follow the lectionary and struggle to lead their congregations through the preached Word, the light of the omnipresent Christ shines in a multitude of human situations."

I invite other readings of how the events of the Christian calendar help us re-imagine other pressing ethical issues, or how they can help us re-imagine globalization in other ways. There are many other ways for us to re-imagine the world as we enter deeply into the specific Christological stories of the gospels. Because we find the fullness of God in those narratives, we have all we need.

ORDINARY TIME: TIME FOR ASSIMILATION AND MISSION

After celebrating Pentecost, the body of Christian citizens enters into the liturgical period called Ordinary Time, which lasts over half of the regular calendar year, from June until late November or early December. Liturgists have pointed out for years that the word "ordinary" technically refers to the numbering of the Sundays after Pentecost, but in common usage the term also conveys a sense of commonplace time after the extraordinary events enacted throughout the liturgical year.[9] As Joyce Ann Zimmerman puts it, this season offers "the opportunity to 'catch up' with ourselves in order to digest, appropriate, and live out what we have experienced through celebration."[10] Ordinary time is partly a time for assimilation, to allow the dynamic events of the year thus far—Christ's birth, the manifestation of his glory, his suffering, passion, death, and resurrection—to sink in. All these themes are recapitulated through the rest of the year, making this a time of teaching and grasping intellectually what has been experienced liturgically. By assimilating the themes, the church begins to live them out in the world, in its mission.

Like the disciples, the church also experiences the time after Pentecost as a time of mission. It is clear in this season that the church is being sent out into the world to invite the world to participate in the fullness that the church has experienced, in advance of the final appearance of Christ. In the most literal sense, the current church is living between the time of Pentecost and the time of the Advent all the time. We live after the disciples experienced the miraculous outpouring of the breath of Jesus into their lives in Jerusalem but before Jesus comes again. So what does the church do in the meantime? It depends upon the Spirit to carry out its work in the world, resting in the assurance that its work is not in vain. As Advent reminds us, Jesus promised to return. This heightened sense

9. Webber, *Ancient-Future Time*, 167–76, uses the common meaning.

10. Zimmerman, *Liturgy as Living Faith*, 124.

of meaningful time forms a compelling contrast to global standardized time. It is precisely because the church confesses to finding the fullness of God in the heart of time that it marks time differently. By living in liturgical time, by marking time according to the appearance of Jesus, and by counting the Sundays between Pentecost and Advent, the church demonstrates that it lives by an alternative narrative that guides its mission.

In chapter 1, I identified four general ways in which the alternative narrative of the church year responds to globalization. Each of these is a way of fleshing out the mission of the church in relation to globalization, as we have seen in the chapters of this book.

First, the alternative narrative of the church year drama—the story of the redeeming reign of God that has already begun—helps the church to find itself and figure out what to do in relation to ethical challenges such as globalization. By finding itself in the christological drama, the church is empowered to think outside the confines of the given system, reframing globalization and nurturing improvisational practices. To those who claim that history gives us only one political option, we found that Advent liberates us to appreciate God breaking into time and liberating us to imagine other alternatives. To those who argue that U.S. hegemony liberates others, the church contends out of Holy Week that humiliation brings exaltation, that it must live non-violently, disengage from hegemonic domination, and be prepared for martyrdom. To those who argue that free trade is the only alternative that liberates the poor, the church responds that practices such as fair trade do better in emulating the good news of Easter. To those who worry that globalization will overwhelm local cultures or cause a backlash, the church demonstrates how Pentecost empowers a healthy blend of universal and local cultures.

Second, practicing the liturgical year can also help the church live in liturgical time rather than limiting itself to the standardized, uniform measures of contemporary secular time. Practices such as Lenten fasting remind us that we can break out of the ceaseless cycle of "24 hours a day, 7 days a week, 365 days a year time" and begin to enter spaces of rest and retreat by ceasing from the busy, everyday practices of work and consumption. It might even be necessary at times to flee to the desert to embody alternatives of liturgical time and to re-direct our participation in God's economy, so that we live in a proper sacramental relation to things rather than as restless consumers. We must make space for God to enter our time. Seasons of preparation help Christians begin to live peaceably with time, to receive God's time as an abundant gift rather than a scarce commodity. Instead of seeing time as bleak and standardized, one begins to see time as rich and full. Advent, for instance, helps us to experience time, not as a blank space, but as a winding road full of surprises and gifts. This same posture toward time, Mary's expectant waiting, should extend into ordinary time, as we wait for the final Advent of Christ.

Third, the slowness of time is something that the season of ordinary time helps the church to embody in a world that claims to move always at warp speed. After moving through the life of Christ rather quickly, from December through May or June, the pace slows for over half of the year. The seasons of preparation—Advent and Lent—also help nurture Christians in disciplines of patience and waiting, slowing the church down by breaking from the restless cycles of working, shopping, and eating. Likewise, a healthy respect for Creation as an epiphany of God will help us to change our eating habits, to slow down our machine-like consumption of food and help us re-enter into a proper sacramental relationship with God, in which we allow God to be revealed in the very food we eat. Planting, growing, and harvesting our own local food would slow us down and re-connect our eating to the land. So, too, an approach that frames work in liturgical time, an approach that listens for God's voice in work, will start to look different than attitudes toward work that value it solely in terms of money. Unfortunately, however, we found that monetary values threaten to overtake the world by putting a price tag on everything. Thankfully, though, the Christmas story shocks us into attending to concrete circumstances, to relationships, and to the humility demonstrated by Jesus. By taking time to re-enact this story each year, the church slows down enough to ponder these mysteries and to learn that the Kingdom comes through the self-emptying love modeled by the baby Jesus.

Finally, all of this happens in a moral community formed by the shared experience of the liturgical year. Christianity is not an individualistic enterprise. Instead, the practices of the Christian year themselves help to form a people with a political theology—a shared constitution and a shared mission in the world that far transcends the mission of the United States of America or any other political entity. When the church gathers, it becomes the people of God, united in communion with its head through the gift of the Spirit, a community of wholeness.[11] Significantly,

11. Lohfink, *Does God Need the Church?* 223, 273–90.

then, the season of ordinary time is broken by one major feast day, All Saints' Day on November 1, which commemorates the communion of the saints, the church on earth and in heaven.[12] The prayer for the day in the *Book of Common Prayer* reminds us of the significance of the embodied community of the church: "Almighty God, you have knit together your elect in one communion and fellowship in the mystical body of your Son Christ our Lord: Give us grace so to follow your blessed saints in all virtuous and godly living, that we may come to those ineffable joys that you have prepared for those who truly love you."[13] This global communion unites its living and dead members in communion with Christ, forming a community of social solidarity that runs deeper than all other earthly communities. Its members' joyful resistance to the Powers helps to show the world what it means to find true community, to find the fullness of time right in the midst of daily life, to find the fullness of God right in the midst of a worshiping Christian congregation. The mission of the church in ordinary time is to invite the world to join this fullness.

12. Webber, *Ancient-Future Time*, 175.

13. Episcopal Church, *Book of Common Prayer*, 245.

Appendix: A Brief Overview of the Liturgical Year

The Christmas Cycle: The Mystery of Christ's Incarnation

Season	Themes	Dates in the Gregorian Calendar
Advent	Christ's Coming	The four Sundays prior to December 25
Christmas	Christ's Incarnation	December 25–January 5
Epiphany	Christ's Appearance in Glory	January 6
Sundays after Epiphany or Ordinary Time	Beginnings of Christ's Ministry	January 7–February or March

The Easter Cycle: The Mystery of Christ's Suffering, Death,
Resurrection, Ascension, and Descent in the Spirit

Season	Themes	Dates in the Gregorian Calendar
Lent	Christ's Temptation and Suffering	February or March–April* (The forty week-days prior to Easter)
Holy Week	Christ's Passion and Death	March or April*
Easter Sunday	Christ's Resurrection	March or April*
Sundays of Easter	Christ's Appearances and Ascension	The forty days after Easter

Season	Themes	Dates in the Gregorian Calendar
Pentecost	The Descent of the Spirit	The fiftieth day after Easter
Trinity Sunday	The Father, Son, and Holy Spirit	The Sunday after Pentecost

The Sundays of the Year: Counting the Time after Pentecost

Season	Themes	Dates in the Gregorian Calendar
Ordinary Time	Recapituating all previous themes The Mission to Spread the Gospel	Late May– late November (until the First Sunday of Advent)

* Easter's date always varies. Based on the Jewish lunar calendar, it always falls on the Sunday after the first full moon of the Jewish pascha (Passover) season, which reminds us of how Christian liturgical time flows out of Jewish liturgical time.

Bibliography

Abernethy, David B. *The Dynamics of Global Dominance: European Overseas Empires, 1415–1980.* New Haven, CT: Yale University Press, 2000.

"Address to a Joint Session of Congress and the American People." September 20, 2001. Online: http://georgewbush-whitehouse.archives.gov/news/releases/2001/09/2001-0920-8.html.

Agence France. "Oil Ministry and Untouched Building in Ravaged Baghdad." *Sydney Morning Herald*, April 16, 2003. Online: http://www.smh.com.au/articles/ 2003/ 04/16/1050172643895.html.

Aliber, Robert Z. *The New International Money Game.* 6th ed. Chicago: University of Chicago Press, 2002.

Allen, Horace T. *On Common Ground: The Story of the Revised Common Lectionary.* Norwich, UK: Canterbury, 1998.

Amsden, Alice H. *Escape from Empire: The Developing World's Journey through Heaven and Hell.* Cambridge, MA: MIT Press, 2007.

———. *The Rise of the "The Rest": Challenges to the West from Late Industrializing Countries.* New York: Oxford University Press, 2001.

Amstutz, Mark R. "After the Death Squads." *Books and Culture* 3 (1997) 25–27.

———. *International Ethics.* 2nd ed. Lanham, MD: Rowman & Littlefield, 2005.

Anderson, Benedict R. *Imagined Communities: Reflections on the Origin and Spread of Nationalism.* 2nd ed. London: Verso, 1991.

Anderson, Jenny, and Vikas Bajaj. "Wary of Risk, Bankers Sold Shaky Mortgage Debt." *New York Times*, December 6, 2007, national edition, A1.

Andrews, Edmund L. "Fed and Regulators Shrugged as the Subprime Crisis Spread." *New York Times*, December 18, 2007, national edition, A1.

Aquinas, Thomas. *Summa Theologiae.* In *St. Thomas Aquinas on Politics and Ethics: A New Translation, Backgrounds, Interpretations,* edited by Paul E. Sigmund. New York: Norton, 1988.

———. *The Summa Theologica of St. Thomas Aquinas,* 2nd ed. 1920. Translated by Fathers of the English Dominican Province. Kevin Knight, 2008. Online: http:// www.newadvent.org/summa/3124.htm.

Arendt, Hannah. *The Human Condition.* New York: Anchor, 1959.

Aristotle. *The Politics.* Translated by T. A. Sinclair. New York: Penguin, 1981.

Armijo, Leslie Elliot. "Mixed Blessing: Expectations about Foreign Capital Flows and Democracy in Emerging Markets." In *Financial Globalization and Democracy in Emerging Markets*, edited by Leslie Elliot Armijo, 17–50. New York: Bedford, 1999.

Arquilla, John, and David Ronfeldt. "The Advent of Netwar (Revisited)." In *Networks and Netwars: The Future of Crime, Terror, and Insurgency*, edited by John Arquilla, 1–28. Santa Monica, CA: Rand, 2001.

Ashcraft, Adam B., and Til Schuermann. "Understanding the Securitization of Subprime Mortgage Credit." Federal Reserve Bank of New York, Staff Report no. 318, March 2008. Online: http://www.newyorkfed.org/research/staff_reports/sr318.pdf.

"Ask the White House." February 9, 2004. Online: http://georgewbush-whitehouse .archives.gov/ask/20040209.html.

Associated Press. "Amish Way Might be the Better Way When it Comes to Farming, Says Study." *The [Canton] Repository*, June 6, 2003.

——. "Countrywide Failed to Survive Slump." *CNN Money.com*. Online: http:// money.cnn.com/news/newsfeeds/articles/newstex/AFX-0013–22203675.htm.

Atlas, Riva D., and Mary Williams Walsh. "Pension Officers Putting Billions into Hedge Funds." *New York Times*, November 27, 2005. Online: http://ww.nytimes .com/2005/11/27/business/yourmoney/27hedge.html.

"At O'Hare, President Says 'Get On Board: Remarks by the President to Airline Employees O'Hare International Airport, Chicago, Illinois." September 27, 2001. Online: http:// georgewbush-whitehouse.archives.gov/news/releases/2001/09/20010927-1.html.

Augsburger, David. *Dissident Discipleship: A Spirituality of Self-Surrender, Love of God, and Love of Neighbor*. Grand Rapids: Brazos, 2006.

Avant, Deborah D. *The Market for Force: Consequences of Privatizing Security*. New York: Cambridge University Press, 2005.

Avila, Rafael. *Worship and Politics*. Translated by Alan Neely. Maryknoll, NY: Orbis, 1981.

Babcock, Michael A. "If This Be Imperialism . . ." *Seattle Post-Intelligencer*, August 19, 2005. Online: http://seattlepi.nwsource.com/opinion/237165_ imperialop.html.

Bacevich, Andrew J. *American Empire: The Realities and Consequences of U.S. Diplomacy*. Cambridge, MA: Harvard University Press, 2002.

Bader-Saye, Scott. "Figuring Time: Providence and Politics." In *Liturgy, Time, and the Politics of Redemption*, edited by C. C. Pecknold and Randi Rashkover, 91–111. Grand Rapids: Eerdmans, 2006.

Bailey, Kenneth E. *Jesus Through Middle Eastern Eyes: Cultural Studies in the Gospels*. Downers Grove, IL: InterVarsity, 2008.

Bajaj, Vikas, and Floyd Norris. "Central Bankers to Lend Billions in Credit Crisis." *New York Times*, December 13, 2007, national edition, A1.

Bakke, Dennis W. *Joy at Work: A Revolutionary Approach to Fun on the Job*. Seattle: PVG, 2005.

Barber, Benjamin. *Jihad vs. McWorld: How Globalism and Tribalism Are Reshaping the World*. New York: Random House, 1992.

Baldovin, John F. "The Liturgical Year: Calendar for a Just Community." In *Between Memory and Hope: Readings on the Liturgical Year*, edited by Maxwell E. Johnson, 429–44. Collegeville, MN: Liturgical, 2000.

Barber, Mike. "Mistrial Ends Watada Court-Martial." *Seattle Post-Intelligencer*, February 7, 2007. Online: http://seattlepi.nwsource.com/local/302733_ courtmartial07ww.html.

Barboza, David. "China Inflation Exacting a Toll Across the U. S." *New York Times*, February 1, 2008, national edition, A1.

Barrett, Christopher B. "Markets, Social Norms, and Governments in the Service of Environmentally Sustainable Economic Development: The Pluralistic Stewardship Approach." *Christian Scholar's Review* 33 (2000) 435–54.

Barry, Christian, and Sanjay G. Reddy. *International Trade and Labor Standards: A Proposal for Linkage*. New York: Columbia University Press, 2008.

"Bartering Gains Steam." *National Public Radio*, July 16, 2008. Online: http://www.npr .org/templates/story/story.php?storyId=92602005.

Bartky, Ian. *One Time Fits All: The Campaigns for Global Uniformity*. Stanford: Stanford University Press, 2007.

Barth, Karl. *Dogmatics in Outline*. Translated by G. T. Thomson. New York: Harper & Row, 1959.

Bass, Dorothy C. *Receiving the Day: Christian Practices for Opening the Gift of Time*. San Francisco: Jossey-Bass, 2000.

Bateman, Bradley W. "There are Many Alternatives: Margaret Thatcher in the History of Economic Thought." *Journal of the History of Economic Thought* 24 (2002) 307–11.

Bauman, Zygmunt. *Life in Fragments*. Oxford: Blackwell, 1995.

BBC News. "The U.S. Sub-Prime Crisis in Graphics." British Broadcasting Corporation, November 21, 2007. Online: http://news.bbc.co.uk/2/hi/business/7073131.stm.

Beaudoin, Tom. *Consuming Faith: Integrating Who We Are with What We Buy*. Lanham, MD: Sheed & Ward, 2003.

Bediako, Kwame. "A New Christian World: Reading the Signs of the Kingdom Amid Global Politics." Lecture at Symposium on Religion and Politics, Calvin College, April 30, 2004.

Begbie, Jeremy S. *Theology, Music and Time*. New York: Cambridge University Press, 2000.

Bello, Walden. "Building an Iron Cage: The Bretton Woods Institutions, the WTO, and the South." In *Views from the South: The Effects of Globalization and the WTO on Third World Countries*, edited by Sarah Anderson, 54–90. Chicago: Food First, 2000.

Benedict XVI. "General Audience." September 5, 2007. Online: http://www.vatican.va/ holy_father/benedict_xvi/audiences/2007/documents/hf_ben-xvi_aud_20070905 _en.html.

———. "Letter of His Holiness Benedict XVI to the Ecumenical Patriarch of Constantinople on the Occasion of the Seventh Symposium of the Religion, Science, and the Environment Movement." September 1, 2007. Online: http://www.vatican .va/holy_father/benedict_xvi/letters/2007/documents/hf_ben-xvi_let_20070901 _symposium-environment_en.html.

Berger, Peter. "Four Faces of Global Culture." *National Interest* 49 (1997) 23–29.

Berger, Suzanne. "Globalization and Politics." *Annual Review of Political Science* 3 (2000) 43–62.

Berkhof, Hendrik. *Christ and the Powers*. Translated by John Howard Yoder. Scottdale, PA: Herald, 1977.

Bernard of Clairvaux. *St. Bernard's Sermons for the Seasons and Principal Festivals of the Year*. Vol. 1, translated by a priest of Mount Mellary. Dublin: Browne & Nolan, 1923.

Bernstein, Peter L. *Against the Gods: The Remarkable Story of Risk*. New York: Wiley, 1998.

Berry, Wendell. "A Bad Big Idea." In *Sex, Economy, Freedom and Community*, 45–52. New York: Pantheon, 1993.

———. "The Burden of the Gospels." In *The Way of Ignorance and Other Essays*, 127–40. Washington, DC: Shoemaker & Hoard, 2005.

———. "Christianity and the Survival of Creation." In *Sex, Economy, Freedom and Community*, 93–116. New York: Pantheon, 1993.

———. *The Gift of Good Land: Further Essays Cultural and Agricultural.* San Francisco: North Point, 1981.

———. "God and Country." In *What Are People For?* 95–102. San Francisco: North Point, 1990.

———. "Healing." In *What Are People For?* 9–16. San Francisco: North Point, 1990.

———. "Is Life a Miracle?" In *Citizenship Papers*, 181–90. Washington, DC: Shoemaker & Hoard, 2004.

———. "The Pleasures of Eating." In *What Are People For?* 145–52. San Francisco: North Point, 1990.

———. "The Purpose of a Coherent Community." In *The Way of Ignorance and Other Essays*, 69–80. Washington, DC: Shoemaker & Hoard, 2005.

———. "Renewing Husbandry." In *The Way of Ignorance and Other Essays,* 91–104. Washington, DC: Shoemaker & Hoard, 2005.

———. "Two Economies." In *On Moral Business*, edited by Max L. Stackhouse et al., 827–35. Grand Rapids: Eerdmans, 1999.

———. "The Whole Horse." In *Citizenship Papers*, 113–26. Washington, DC: Shoemaker and Hoard, 2004.

Bhagwati, Jagdish. *In Defense of Globalization.* New York: Oxford University Press, 2004.

Black Gold. DVD. Directed by Marc Francis and Nick Francis. San Francisco: California Newsreel, 2006.

Blaise, Clark. *Time Lord: Sir Sandford Fleming and the Creation of Standard Time.* New York: Pantheon, 2000.

Bob, Clifford. *The Marketing of Rebellion: Insurgents, Media, and International Activism.* New York: Cambridge University Press, 2005.

Boli, John, and George M. Thomas, editors. *Constructing World Culture: International Nongovernmental Organizations Since 1875.* Stanford, CA: Stanford University Press, 1999.

Bonanno, Mike, and Andy Bichlbaum. *The Yes Men.* DVD. Directed by Chris Smith, Dan Ollman, and Sarah Price. Santa Monica, CA: MGM Home Entertainment, 2005.

Bongiorni, Sara. *A Year Without "Made in China": One Family's True Life Adventure in the Global Economy.* Hoboken, NJ: Wiley, 2007.

Borgmann, Albert. "The Moral Complexion of Consumption." *Journal of Consumer Research* 26 (2000) 418–22.

Bouma-Prediger, Steve. *For the Beauty of the Earth: A Christian Vision for Creation Care.* Grand Rapids: Baker Academic, 2001.

Bradsher, Keith. "Ending Tariffs Is Only the Start." *New York Times*, February 28, 2006, national edition, C1.

Brakke, David. *Athanasius and Asceticism.* Baltimore: Johns Hopkins University Press, 1998.

Bray, Marianne. "The New Faces of Outsourcing." *CNN.com*, October 25, 2005. Online: http://www.cnn.com/2005/WORLD/asiapcf/09/14/india.eye.outsourcing/index.html.

Broder, John M., and James Risen. "Armed Guards in Iraq Occupy a Legal Limbo." *New York Times*, September 20, 2007, national edition, A1.

Brooks, David. "Good News About Poverty." *New York Times*, November 27, 2004. Online: http://www.nytimes.com/2004/11/27/opinion/27brooks.html.

———. "The Insurgent Advantage." *New York Times*, May 18, 2007, national edition, A27.

Brown, Michael Barratt. *Fair Trade: Reform and Realities in the International Trading System*. London: Zed, 1983.

Brown, Tricia Gates. "Christian Peacemaker Teams: An Introduction." In *Getting in the Way: Stories from Christian Peacemaker Teams*, edited by Tricia Gates Brown, 11–16. Scottdale, PA: Herald, 2005.

Brubaker, Pamela K., et al. "Introduction." In *Justice in a Global Economy: Strategies for Home, Community, and World*, edited by Pamela K. Brubaker et al., 1–16. Louisville: Westminster John Knox, 2006.

Brueggemann, Walter. "Always in the Shadow of Empire." In *The Church as Counterculture*, edited by Michael L. Budde and Robert W. Brimlow, 39–58. Albany: SUNY, 2000.

Bryan, Christopher. *Render to Caesar: Jesus, the Early Church, and the Roman Superpower*. New York: Oxford University Press, 2005.

Buchholz, Todd G. *From Here to Economy: A Shortcut to Economic Literacy*. New York: Plume, 1995.

Budde, Michael L. *The (Magic) Kingdom of God: Christianity and Global Culture Industries*. Boulder, CO: Westview, 1997.

Buechner, Frederick. *The Magnificent Defeat*. New York: Seabury, 1966.

———. *Wishful Thinking: A Seeker's ABC*. 2nd ed. New York: HarperCollins, 1993.

Bull, Hedley. *The Anarchical Society: A Study of Order in World Politics*. New York: Columbia University Press, 1977.

Burtless, Gary, et al. *Globaphobia: Confronting Fears about Open Trade*. Washington, DC: Brookings Institution, 1998.

Calvin Institute of Christian Worship. "Psalter Hymnal #309." *Christian Classics Ethereal Library*. Online: http://www.hymnary.org/hymn/PsH/309.

Calvin, John. *Institutes of the Christian Religion, Books III.XX to IV.XX*. Translated by Ford Lewis Battles. Edited by John T. McNeill. Philadelphia: Westminster, 1960.

Campbell, John L. "States, Politics, and Globalization: Why Institutions Still Matter." In *The Nation State in Question*, edited by T. V. Paul et al., 234–59. Princeton: Princeton University Press, 2003

Camus, Albert. *The Plague*. Translated by Stuart Gilbert. New York: Vintage International, 1991.

Carter, Jimmy. "Subsidies' Harvest of Misery." *Washington Post*, December 10, 2007. Online: http://www.washingtonpost.com/wp-dyn/content/article/2007/12/09/AR-2007120900911.html.

Cartwright, Michael G. "Being Sent: Witness." In *The Blackwell Companion to Christian Ethics*, edited by Stanley Hauerwas and Samuel Wells, 481–94. Malden, MA: Blackwell, 2004.

Case, Jay Riley. *Evangelicals in the World: The American Evangelical Missionary Movement and World Christianity, 1815–1920*. New York: Oxford University Press, forthcoming.

Catholic Church. *Lectionary for Mass (U.S.)*. Collegeville, MN: Liturgical, 1970.

———. *The Catechism of the Catholic Church*. New York: Image, 1995.

Cathy, S. Truett. "Chick-fil-A's Closed-on-Sunday Policy." Online: http://www.truettcathy
.com/pdfs/Closed%20on%20Sunday.pdf.

Cavanaugh, William T. *Being Consumed: Economics and Christian Desire.* Grand Rapids:
Eerdmans, 2008.

———. "Killing for the Telephone Company: Why the Nation-State Is Not the Keeper
of the Common Good." In *In Search of the Common Good,* edited by Dennis P.
McCann and Patrick D. Miller, 301–32. New York: T. & T. Clark, 2005.

———. *Theopolitical Imagination: Discovering the Liturgy as a Political Act in an Age of
Global Consumerism.* New York: T. & T. Clark, 2002.

———. *Torture and Eucharist: Theology, Politics, and the Body of Christ.* Oxford: Blackwell, 1998.

———. "The Unfreedom of the Free Market." In *Wealth, Poverty, and Human Destiny,*
edited by Doug Bandow and David L. Schindler, 103–28. Wilmington, DE: ISI,
2003.

Celizic, Mike. "More and More Couples Finding Surrogates in India." *Today Show,* February 20, 2008. Online: http://today.msnbc.msn.com/id/ 23252624/?GT1=43001.

Chacour, Elias, and David Hazard. *Blood Brothers.* 2nd ed. Grand Rapids: Chosen, 2003.

Chacour, Elias, and Mary Jensen. *We Belong to the Land: The Story of a Palestinian Israeli
Who Lives for Peace and Reconciliation.* San Francisco: Harper, 1992.

Chan, Simon. *Liturgical Theology: The Church as Worshipping Community.* Downer's
Grove, IL: InterVarsity, 2006.

Chanda, Nayan. *Bound Together: How Traders, Preachers, Adventurers, and Warriors
Shaped Globalization.* New Haven: Yale University Press, 2007.

Chandler, Alfred D. Jr. *The Visible Hand: The Managerial Revolution in American Business.* Cambridge, MA: Belknap, 1977.

Chandrasekaran, Rajiv. *Imperial Life in the Emerald City: Life Inside Iraq's Green Zone.*
New York: Knopf, 2007.

"Characteristics of New Privately Owned One-Family Houses Completed: 1990 to 2005."
2007 Statistical Abstract of the United States, page 11. Online: http://www. census
.gov/prod/2006pubs/07statab/construct.pdf.

Chea, Terence. "China's Air Pollution Reaches U.S. Skies." *Associated Press,* July 28, 2006.
Online: http://apnews.myway.com/article/20060728/D8J53RV01.html.

Chesterton, G. K. "The Outline of Sanity." In *The Collected Works of G. K. Chesterton,* vol.
V. San Francisco: Ignatius, 1987.

China Blue. DVD. San Francisco: Teddy Bear Films, 2005.

Chomsky, Noam. *Hegemony or Survival: America's Quest for Global Dominance.* New
York: Holt, 2004.

Christian Peacemaker Teams. "CPT Release: We Mourn the Loss of Tom Fox." *Christian
Peacemaker Teams,* March 10, 2006. Online: http://www.cpt.org/iraq/response /06
-10-03statement.htm.

Christian Peacemaker Teams Founding Conference. "Mission Statement." *Christian
Peacemaker Teams.* Online: http://cpt.org/about/mission.

Christian Reformed Church. *Our World Belongs to God: A Contemporary Testimony.*
Online: http://www.crcna.org/pages/our_world_spirit.cfm.

Claiborne, Shane. *The Irresistible Revolution: Living as an Ordinary Radical.* Grand
Rapids: Zondervan, 2006.

Claiborne, Shane, and Chris Haw. *Jesus for President: Politics for Ordinary Radicals.*
Grand Rapids: Zondervan, 2008.

Clapp, Rodney. *A Peculiar People: The Church as Culture in a Post-Christian Society.* Downers Grove, IL: InterVarsity, 1996.

Clark, Andrew. "Bear Stearns Chief Steps Down Over Sub-Prime Loss." *The Guardian*, January 10, 2008. Online: http://www.guardian.co.uk/business/2008/jan/09/subprimeloss.

"Climate Change: An Evangelical Call to Action." *Evangelical Climate Initiative*. Online: http://christiansandclimate.org/learn/call-to-action/.

Cobb, Peter G. "The History of the Christian Year." In *The Study of Liturgy*, edited by Cheslyn Jones et al., 455–71. New York: Oxford University Press, 1992.

Cohen, Samy. *The Resilience of the State: Democracy and the Challenge of Globalization.* Boulder, CO: Lynne Rienner, 2006.

Cohen, Yousef R., et al. "The Paradoxical Nature of State Making: The Violent Creation of Order." *American Political Science Review* 75 (1981) 901–10.

Colás, Alejandro. *International Civil Society: Social Movements in World Politics.* Malden, MA: Blackwell, 2002.

Committee to Study War and Peace. "Report from the Committee to Study War and Peace to Synod 2006." *Christian Reformed Church of North America.* Online: http://www.crcna.org/site_ uploads/uploads/osjha/2006_warandpeace.pdf.

Conyers, A.J. *The Eclipse of Heaven: Rediscovering the Hope of a World Beyond.* Downer's Grove, IL: InterVarsity, 1992.

Cowen, Tyler. *Creative Destruction: How Globalization Is Changing the World's Cultures.* Princeton: Princeton University Press, 2002.

Coyne, Brendan. "Investment Company Challenged on Social Responsibility." *The New Standard*, July 6, 2005. Online: http://newstandardnews.net/content/index.cfm/items/2051.

Craddock, Fred B., et al. *Preaching through the Christian Year, Year A: A Comprehensive Commentary on the Lectionary.* Philadelphia: Trinity, 1992.

Cray, Graham. "Postmodernism: Mutual Society in Crisis." In *Building a Relational Society: New Priorities for Public Policy*, edited by Nicola Baker, 65–82. Burlington, VT: Arena, 1996.

Crockatt, Richard. *After 9/11: Cultural Dimensions of American Global Power.* New York: Routledge, 2007.

Cross, Gary. *Time and Money: The Making of a Consumer Culture.* London: Routledge, 1993.

Crothers, Lane. *Globalization and American Popular Culture.* Lanham, MD: Rowman & Littlefield, 2007.

Croucher, Sheila L. *Globalization and Belonging: The Politics of Identity in a Changing World.* Lanham, MD: Rowman & Littlefield, 2004.

Cusimano, Maryann K., et al. "Private-Sector Transsovereign Actors: MNCs and NGOs." In *Beyond Sovereignty: Issues for a Global Agenda*, edited by Maryann Cusimano Love, 255–82. New York: Bedford/St. Martin's, 2000.

Cumings, Bruce. "The Origins and Development of the Northeast Asian Political Economy: Industrial Sectors, Product Cycles, and Political Consequences." *International Organization* 38 (1984) 1–40.

Dawn, Marva J. *A Royal "Waste" of Time: The Splendor of Worshiping God and Being Church for the World.* Grand Rapids: Eerdmans, 1999.

———. *Keeping the Sabbath Wholly: Ceasing, Resting, Feasting, Embracing.* Grand Rapids: Eerdmans, 1989.

Day, Dorothy. "Blood on Our Coal." In *By Little and By Little: The Selected Writings of Dorothy Day*, edited by Robert Ellsberg, 249–51. New York: Knopf, 1983.

Dean, Cornelia. "Study Sees 'Global Collapse' of Fish Species." *New York Times*, November 3, 2006. Online: http://www.nytimes.com/2006/11/03/science/03fish.html?scp=1 &sq=study+sees+global+collapse+of+fish+species&st=nyt.

DeCarlo, Jacqueline. *Fair Trade: A Beginner's Guide*. Oxford: Oneworld, 2007.

De Graaf, John, et al. *Affluenza: The All-Consuming Epidemic*. 2nd ed. San Francisco: Berrett-Koehler, 2005.

De la Dehesa, Guillermo. *What Do We Know about Globalization? Issues of Poverty and Income Distribution*. Malden, MA: Blackwell, 2007.

Della Porta, Donatella, et al. *Globalization from Below: Transnational Activists and Protest Networks*. Minneapolis: University of Minnesota Press, 2006.

De Lubac, Henri. *Catholicism: Christ and the Common Destiny of Man*. Translated by Lancelot C. Shephard and Elizabeth Englund. San Francisco: Ignatius, 1988.

———. *The Splendour of the Church*. Translated by Michael Mason. Glen Rock, NJ: Paulist, 1956.

DePree, Max. *Leadership Is an Art*. New York: Doubleday, 1989.

———. *Leadership Jazz*. New York: Dell, 1992.

D'Innocenzio, Anne. "Wal-Mart Session Addresses Critics." *The [Canton] Repository*, November 5, 2005, B–6.

Dix, Gregory. *The Shape of the Liturgy*. London: Dacre, 1945.

Dobnik, Verena. "Churches Offer Help in Mortgage Crisis." *Boston Globe*, May 18, 2008. Online: http://www.boston.com/realestate/news/articles/2008/05/18/churches_offer _help_in_mortgage_crisis/.

Dollar, David, and Aart Kraay. "Growth Is Good for the Poor." *World Bank Policy Research Working Paper* No. 2587 (April 2001). Online: http://ssrn.com/abstract=632656.

Dolnick, Sam. "Giving Birth Is Latest Job Outsourced to India." *The [Canton] Repository*, December 31, 2007, A-8.

Dowlah, C. A. F. *Backwaters of Global Prosperity: How Forces of Globalization and GATT/ WTO Trade Regimes Contribute to the Marginalization of the World's Poorest Nations*. New York: Praeger, 2004.

Doyle, Michael. "Kant, Liberal Legacies, and Foreign Affairs, Part I." *Philosophy and Public Affairs* 12 (1983) 205–35.

———. "Kant, Liberal Legacies, and Foreign Affairs, Part II." *Philosophy and Public Affairs* 12 (1983) 323–53.

Dreher, Rod. *Crunchy Cons*. New York: Crown Forum, 2006.

Drezner, Daniel W. *All Politics Is Global: Explaining International Regulatory Regimes*. Princeton: Princeton University Press, 2007.

———. "Bottom Feeders." *Foreign Policy* 121 (2000) 64–70.

———. "Globalization and Policy Convergence." *International Studies Review* 3 (2001) 53–78.

Dylan, Bob. "Union Sundown." On *Infidels*. 1983. Sony Entertainment. 4607272. Compact Disc.

Easterly, William. *The Elusive Quest for Growth: Economists' Adventures and Misadventures in the Tropics*. Cambridge, MA: MIT Press, 2002.

Eichengreen, Barry. *Capital Flows and Crises*. Cambridge: MIT Press, 2003.

———. "Financial Instability." In *Global Crises, Global Solutions*, edited by Bjorn Lomberg, 251–80. New York: Cambridge University Press, 2004.

———. *Globalizing Capital: A History of the International Monetary System*. Princeton: Princeton University Press, 1998.

Eilperin, Juliet. "World's Fish Supply Running Out, Researchers Warn." *Washington Post*, November 3, 2006. Online: http://www.washingtonpost.com.

Elliott, Kimberly Ann, and Richard B. Freeman. *Can Labor Standards Improve under Globalization?* Washington, DC: Institute for International Economics, 2003.

Episcopal Church. *Book of Common Prayer*. New York: Church Hymnal Corp., 1979.

Fackler, Martin. "Sharp Sell-Off Sweeps Asian Markets." *New York Times,* November 12, 2007. Online: http://www.nytimes.com/2007/11/12/business/12cnd-marts.html ?scp=1&sq=Sharp%20Sell-off%20sweeps%20asian%20markets&st=cse.

Faiola, Anthony. "Where Every Meal is a Sacrifice." *Washington Post*, April 28, 2008, A1. Online: http://www.washingtonpost.com/wp-dyn/content/story/2008/04/27/ST2008042702198.html.

Farrow, Douglas. *Ascension and Ecclesia: On the Significance of the Doctrine of the Ascension for Ecclesiology and Christian Cosmology*. Grand Rapids: Eerdmans, 1999.

Ferguson, Niall. *Colossus: The Rise and Fall of the American Empire*. New York: Penguin, 2004.

———. "The Empire Slinks Bank." *New York Times Magazine*, April 27, 2003. Online: http://www.nytimes.com/2003/04/27/magazine /27EMPIRE.html.

Finger, Thomas. "An Anabaptist/Mennonite Theology of Creation." In *Creation and the Environment: An Anabaptist Perspective on a Sustainable World*, edited by Calvin Redekop, 154–69. Baltimore: Johns Hopkins University Press, 2000.

Fisher, Ian. "Pope Vows to Try to End Split With the Orthodox." *New York Times,* May 30, 2005. Online: http://www.nytimes.com/2005/05/30/international/europe/30pope .html?_r=1&scp=1&sq=Pope%20Vows%20to%20Try%20to%20End%20Split%20With%20the%20Orthodox&st=cse&oref=slogin.

Fishman, Ted C. *China, Inc.: How the Rise of the Next Superpower Challenges America and the World*. New York: Scribner, 2005.

Floyd, Shawn. "Morally Serious Pedagogy." *Christian Scholar's Review* 36 (2007) 245–61.

Fodor, James, and Stanley Hauerwas. "Performing Faith: The Peaceable Rhetoric of God's Church." In *Performing the Faith: Bonhoeffer and the Practice of Non-Violence* by Stanley Hauerwas. Grand Rapids: Brazos, 2004.

Forbes, Bruce David. *Christmas: A Candid History*. Berkeley: University of California Press, 2007.

Forest, Jim. *The Ladder of the Beatitudes*. Maryknoll, NY: Orbis, 1999.

Fowl, Stephen E. *Philippians*. Grand Rapids: Eerdmans, 2005.

Fridell, Gavin. *Fair Trade Coffee: The Prospects and Pitfalls of Market-Driven Social Justice*. Toronto: University of Toronto Press, 2007.

Friedman, Thomas L. *The Lexus and the Olive Tree*. New York: Anchor, 2000.

———. *Longitudes and Attitudes: The World in the Age of Terrorism*. New York: Anchor, 2003.

———. "Protesting for Whom?" *New York Times,* April 24, 2001. Online: http://www .nytimes.com/2001/04/24/opinion/24FRIE.html.

———. "The Power of Green." *New York Times Magazine*, April 15, 2007. Online: http:// www.nytimes.com/2007/04/15/magazine/15green.t.htm.

———. *The World Is Flat: A Brief History of the Twenty-first Century*. New York: Farrar, Straus & Giroux, 2005.

———. *The World Is Flat: A Brief History of the Twenty-first Century.* 3rd ed. New York: Picador, 2007.

———. *Hot, Flat, and Crowded: Why We Need a Green Revolution—And How It Can Renew America.* New York: Farrar, Straus & Giroux, 2008.

Fukuyama, Francis. *The End of History and the Last Man.* New York: Free, 1992.

———. "The End of History." *National Interest* 16 (1989) 3–18.

———. "Reflections on The End of History, Five Years Later." In *After History? Francis Fukuyama and His Critics,* edited by Timothy Burns, 239–58. Lanham, MD: Rowman & Littlefield, 1994.

Fuller, Reginald H. *Preaching the Lectionary: The Word of God for the Church Today.* Collegeville, MN: Liturgical, 1984.

Galeano, Eduardo. *Upside Down: A Primer for the Looking-Glass World.* Translated by Mark Fried. New York: Picador, 2000.

Garson, Barbara. *Money Makes the World Go Around: One Investor Tracks Her Cash Through the Global Economy.* New York: Penguin, 2001.

Gay, Craig. *Cash Values: Money and the Erosion of Meaning in Today's Society.* Grand Rapids: Eerdmans, 2003.

———. *The Way of the (Modern) World, or, Why It's Tempting to Live as If God Doesn't Exist.* Grand Rapids: Eerdmans, 1998.

Gentleman, Amelia. "India Nurtures Business of Surrogate Motherhood." *New York Times,* March 10, 2008. Online: http://query.nytimes.com/gst/fullpage. html?res= 9B05EED91138F933A25750C0A96E9C8B63&scp=1&sq=India%20Surrogate%20 Business&st=nyt.

Giddens, Anthony. *Runaway World: How Globalization Is Reshaping Our Lives.* 2nd ed. New York: Routledge, 2003.

Gill, Eric. *A Holy Tradition of Working.* West Stockbridge, MA: Lindisfarne, 1983.

Gilpin, Robert M. *Global Political Economy.* Princeton: Princeton University Press, 2001.

———. *War and Change in World Politics.* New York: Cambridge University Press, 1981.

Giridharadas, Anand. "Outsourcing Works, So India is Exporting Jobs." *New York Times,* September 25, 2007. Online: http://www.nytimes.com/2007/09/25/business/ worldbusiness/25outsource.html.

Gish, Peggy. *Iraq: A Journey of Hope and Peace.* Scottdale, PA: Herald, 2004.

Glyn, Andrew. *Capitalism Unleashed: Finance, Globalization, and Welfare.* New York: Oxford University Press, 2006.

Goodchild, Philip. "Capital and Kingdom: An Eschatalogical Economy." In *Theology and the Political: The New Debate,* edited by Creston Davis, John Milbank, and Slavoj Žižek, 127–52. Durham: Duke University Press, 2005.

———. *Theology of Money.* London: SCM, 2007.

Goodman, Peter S., and Phillip P. Pan. "Chinese Workers Pay for Wal-Mart's Low Prices." *Washington Post,* February 8, 2004. Online: http://www.washingtonpost.com/ac2/ wp-dyn/A22507-2004Feb7?language=printer.

Goudzwaard, Bob, *Globalization and the Kingdom of God.* Grand Rapids: Baker, 2001.

Goudzwaard, Bob, et al. *Hope in Troubled Times: A New Vision for Confronting Global Crises.* Grand Rapids: Baker, 2007.

Gray, John. *False Dawn: The Delusions of Global Capitalism.* New York: New, 1998.

Gray, Madison J. "P. Diddy's Clothing Line Allegedly Tied to Sweatshop." *The [Canton] Repository,* October 29, 2003, A-6.

Greenhouse, Steven. "Nike Shoe Plant in Vietnam Is Called Unsafe for Workers." *New York Times*, November 8, 1997. Online: http://query.nytimes.com/gst/ fullpage .html?res=9A06EEDC1539F93BA35752C1A961958260.

Greenhouse, Steven, and David Leonhardt. "Real Wages Fail to Match a Rise in Productivity." *New York Times,* August 28, 2006. Online: http://www.nytimes .com/2006/08/28/business/28wages.html?scp=2&sq=%22real+wages+fail+to+ma tch%22&st=nyt.

Grieco, Joseph M., and G. John Ikenberry. *State Power and World Markets: International Political Economy.* New York: Norton, 2003.

Griffiths, Brian J. "Trade, Aid, and Domestic Reform in the Fight Against Global Poverty." In *Globalization and the Good*, edited by Peter Heslam, 16–28. Grand Rapids: Eerdmans, 2004.

Gross, Daniel. "Behind that Sense of Job Insecurity." *New York Times*, September 10, 2006, national edition, C4.

Grugel, Jean, et al. "Beyond the Washington Consensus? Asia and Latin America in Search of More Autonomous Development." *International Affairs* 84 (2008) 499–517.

Grynbaum, Michael. "Stocks Drop Sharply Amid Subprime Woes." *New York Times*, January 11, 2008. Online: http://www.nytimes.com/2008/01/11/business/11cnd-stox .html?_r=1&hp&oref=slogin.

Guroian, Vigen. *Ethics after Christendom: Toward an Ecclesial Christian Ethic.* Grand Rapids: Eerdmans, 1994.

Haggard, Stephan. *Pathways from the Periphery: The Politics of Growth in the Newly Industrializing Countries.* Ithaca: Cornell University Press, 1990.

Haley, P. Edward. *Strategies of Dominance: The Misdirection of U.S. Foreign Policy.* Baltimore: Johns Hopkins University Press, 2006.

Halteman, Matthew C. "Compassionate Eating as Care of Creation." *Humane Society of the United States Website*, Animals and Religion Section. Online: http://www.hsus .org/web-files/PDF/religion/ar-halteman_book_lowres2.pdf.

Hansen, Richard P. "Finding God's Will, or Hearing God's Voice?" *Books and Culture* 9 (2003).

Harder, James M. "The Violence of Global Marketization." In *Teaching Peace: Nonviolence and the Liberal Arts*, edited by J. Denny Weaver and Gerald Biesecker Mast, 179–93. Lanham, MD: Rowman & Littlefield, 2003.

Hardin, Garrett. "The Tragedy of the Commons." *Science* 162 (1968) 1243–48.

Hardt, Michael, and Antonio Negri. *Empire.* Cambridge: Harvard University Press, 2000.

Hardy, Lee. *The Fabric of This World: Inquiries into Calling, Career Choice, and the Design of Human Work.* Grand Rapids: Eerdmans, 1990.

Harford, Tim. "Yes, We Have Bananas. We Just Can't Ship Them." *New York Times*, December 16, 2005. Online: http://www.nytimes.com/2005/12/16/opinion/16-Harford.html.

Harvey, David. *The Condition of Postmodernity.* Cambridge, MA: Blackwell, 1989.

———. *Spaces of Hope.* Berkeley: University of California Press, 2000.

Hauerwas, Stanley. "The Nonviolent Terrorist: In Defense of Christian Fanaticism." In *The Church as Counterculture*, edited by Michael L. Budde and Robert W. Brimlow, 89–104. Albany: SUNY, 2000.

———. "Work as Co-Creation: A Critique of a Remarkably Bad Idea." In *In Good Company: The Church as Polis*. Notre Dame: University of Notre Dame Press, 1995.

Hauerwas, Stanley, and Samuel Wells, editors. *The Blackwell Companion to Christian Ethics*. Malden, MA: Blackwell, 2004.

Hauerwas, Stanley, and Romand Coles. *Christianity, Democracy, and the Radical Ordinary: Conversations Between a Radical Democrat and a Christian*. Theopolitical Visions 1. Eugene, OR: Cascade, 2007.

Haugen, Gary. *Good News about Injustice*. Downers Grove, IL: InterVarsity, 1999.

Healy, Nicholas M. *Church, World and the Christian Life: Practical-Prophetic Ecclesiology*. New York: Cambridge University Press, 2000.

———. "Practices and the New Ecclesiology: Misplaced Concreteness?" *International Journal of Systematic Theology* 5 (2003) 287–308.

Heilbroner, Robert L. *The Making of Economic Society, Revised for the 1990's*. 8th ed. Englewood Cliffs, NJ: Prentice Hall, 1989.

Held, David. "Political Globalization." In *Globalization and State Power: A Reader*, edited by Joel Krieger, 94–102. New York: Pearson-Longman, 2006.

———. "Reframing Global Governance: Apocalypse Soon or Reform!" In *Globalization Theory: Appraoches and Controversies*, edited by David Held and Anthony McGrew, 240–60. Malden, MA: Polity, 2007.

Held, David, et al. *Global Transformations: Politics, Economics, and Culture*. Stanford, CA: Stanford University Press, 1999.

Henry, Clement M., and Robert Springborg. *Globalization and the Politics of Development in the Middle East*. New York: Cambridge University Press, 2001.

Hessler, Peter. *Oracle Bones: A Journey Between China's Past and Present*. New York: HarperCollins, 2006.

Hobson, J. A. *Richard Cobden, the International Man*. New York: Holt, 1919.

Hochschild, Adam. *Bury the Chains: Prophets and Rebels in the Fight to Free an Empire's Slaves*. Boston: Houghton Mifflin, 2005.

Hoekman, Bernard. "Development and Trade Agreements: Beyond Market Access." In *Global Trade and Poor Nations: The Poverty Impacts and Policy Implications of Liberalization*, edited by Bernard Hoekman and Marcello Olarreaga, 225–46. Washington, DC: Brookings Institution, 2007.

Hoekman, Bernard, and Marcello Olarreaga. "The Challenges to Reducing Poverty through Trade Reform: Overview." In *Global Trade and Poor Nations: The Poverty Impacts and Policy Implications of Liberalization*, edited by Bernard Hoekman and Marcello Olarreaga, 11–30. Washington, DC: Brookings Institution, 2007.

Hollon, Brian C. *Everything Is Sacred: Spiritual Exegesis in the Political Theology of Henri de Lubac*. Theopolitical Visions 3. Eugene, OR: Cascade, 2008.

Holt, Jim. "It's the Oil." *London Review of Books,* October 18, 2007. Online: http://www.lrb.co.uk/v29/n20/holt01_.html.

Hopkins, Gerard Manley. "God's Grandeur." *Bartleby.Com*. Online: http://www.bartleby.com/122/7.html.

Horne, James E., and Maura McDermott. *The Next Green Revolution: Essential Steps to a Healthy, Sustainable Agriculture*. New York: Food Products, 2001.

Horsley, Richard. *Jesus and Empire: The Kingdom of God and the New World Order*. Minneapolis: Fortress, 2003.

Huntington, Samuel P. *The Clash of Civilizations and the Remaking of World Order*. New York: Touchstone, 1996.

Ignatieff, Michael. "The Burden." *New York Times Magazine*, January 5, 2003. Online: http://query.nytimes.com/gst/fullpage.html?res=9B03E6DA143FF936A35752C0 A9659C8B63&scp=1&sq=The%20Burden&st=cse.

Ikenberry, G. John. *After Victory: Institutions, Strategic Restraint, and the Rebuilding of Order after Major Wars*. Princeton: Princeton University Press, 2001.

———. "Globalization as American Hegemony." In *Globalization Theory: Approaches and Controversies*, edited by David Held and Anthony McGrew, 41–61. Malden, MA: Polity, 2007.

Inskeep, Steve. "Blasting for Diamonds in Yellowknife." *National Public Radio*, September 4, 2007. Online: http://www.npr.org/templates/story/story.php? toryId=14161630.

———. "Nations Jostle for a Share of the Arctic." *National Public Radio*, September 4, 2007. Online: http://www.npr.org/templates/story/story.php?story Id=14092469.

Iriye, Akira. *Global Community: The Role of International Organizations in the Making of the Contemporary World*. Berkeley: University of California Press, 2002.

Jackson, Rob. *The Earth Remains Forever: Generations at a Crossroads*. Austin: University of Texas Press, 2002.

Jaffee, Daniel. *Brewing Justice: Fair Trade Coffee, Sustainability, and Survival*. Berkeley: University of California Press, 2007.

James, Harold. *The Roman Predicament: How the Rules of International Order Create the Politics of Empire*. Princeton: Princeton University Press, 2006.

Jenkins, Philip. *The Next Christendom: The Coming of Global Christianity*. New York: Oxford University Press, 2002.

Joachim, David S. "Sparing Paper Checks That Last Trip to the Bank." *New York Times*, November 9, 2006, national edition, C10.

John Paul II. "Address of the Holy Father to the Pontifical Academy of Social Sciences." April 27, 2001. Online: http://www.vatican.va/holy_father /john_paul_ii/speeches/ 2001/documents/hf_jp-ii_spe_20010427_pc-social-sciences_en.html.

———. "Address to the Sixth Public Session of the Pontifical Academies of Theology and of St. Thomas Aquinas." November 8, 2001. Online: http://www.vatican.va/ holy_father/john_paul_ii/speeches/2001/november/documents/hf_jp-ii_spe _20011108_pontificie-accademie_en.html.

———. *Centesimus Annus*. Online: http://www.vatican.va/edocs/ENG0214/_INDEX .htm.

———. *Laborem Exercens*. Online: http://www.vatican.va/edocs/ENG0217/__P1.htm.

Johnson, Chalmers. *Blowback: The Costs and Consequences of American Empire*. New York: Holt, 2000.

———. "The Developmental State: Odyssey of a Concept." In *The Developmental State*, edited by Meredith Woo-Cumings, 32–60. Ithaca, NY: Cornell University Press, 1999.

———. "The Sorrows of Empire: Militarism, Secrecy, and the End of the Republic." In *The Politics of Globalization: A Reader*, edited by Mark Kesselman, 330–34. Boston: Houghton Mifflin, 2007.

Johnson, D. Gale. "Food Security and World Trade Prospects." *American Journal of Agricultural Economics* 80 (1998) 941–47.

Johnson, Kirk. "Bringing in the Harvest, without a Farm in Sight." *New York Times*, October 27, 2003. Online: http://www.nytimes.com/2003/10/27/ nyregion/27FARM.html.

Johnson, Maxwell E. "Preparation for Pascha? Lent in Christian Antiquity." In *Between Memory and Hope: Readings on the Liturgical Year*, edited by Maxwell E. Johnson, 207–22. Collegeville, MN: Liturgical, 2000.

Jomo, K.S. "Rethinking the Role of Government Policy in Southeast Asia." In *Rethinking the East Asian Miracle,* edited by Joseph Stiglitz and Shahid Yusuf, 461–508. New York: Oxford University Press, 2001.

Jordan, Mary. "The Cappuccino Effect: Quality Beans Revive Guatemala's Coffee Industry." *Washington Post,* October 17, 2004, A1. Online: http:// www.washingtonpost.com/ ac2/wp-dyn/A38740–2004Oct16?language=printer.

Jordan, Mary, and Kevin Sullivan. "Very Little Trickles Down: Free Trade Has Failed to Lift Mexicans Out of Poverty." *Washington Post Weekly Edition,* March 31–April 6, 2003.

Kanigel, Robert. *The One Best Way: Frederick Winslow Taylor and the Enigma of Efficiency.* New York: Penguin, 1997.

Kant, Immanuel. "Idea for a Universal History with a Cosmopolitan Purpose." In *Kant's Political Writings,* edited by Hans Reiss, 41–53. Translated by H. B. Nisbet. New York: Cambridge University Press, 1970.

Kapstein, Ethan B. "Winners and Losers in the Global Economy." *International Organization* 54 (2000) 359–84.

Katongole, Emmanuel M. "Christianity, Tribalism, and the Rwandan Genocide." *Logos* 8 (2005) 67–93.

Kavanaugh, John F. *Following Christ in a Consumer Society: The Spirituality of Cultural Resistance.* Rev. ed. Maryknoll, NY: Orbis, 1991.

Keck, Margaret E., and Kathryn Sikkink. *Activists Beyond Borders: Transnational Advocacy Networks in International Politics.* Ithaca: Cornell University Press, 1998.

Kennedy, Paul. *Preparing for the Twenty-First Century.* New York: Random House, 1993.

Keohane, Robert O. "Governance in a Partially Globalized World." *American Political Science Review* 95 (2001) 1–13.

Keohane, Robert O., and Joseph S. Nye. "Globalization: What's New? What's Not? And So What?" *Foreign Policy* 118 (2000) 104–19.

Kerr, Nathan R. "Corpus Verum: On the Ecclesial Recovery of Real Presence in John Calvin's Doctrine of the Eucharist." In *Radical Orthodoxy and the Reformed Tradition: Creation: Covenant, and Participation,* edited by James K. A. Smith and James Olthuis, 229–42. Grand Rapids: Baker, 2005.

Kierkegaard, Soren. *Repetition: An Essay in Experimental Psychology.* Translated by Walter Lowrie. New York: Harper and Row, 1964.

Kiker, Douglas. "Bush Econ Adviser: Outsourcing OK." *CBS News.* Online: http://www .cbsnews.com/stories/2004/02/13/opinion/main600351.shtml.

Kindleberger, Charles P. *Manias, Panics, and Crashes: A History of Financial Crises.* 4th ed. New York: Wiley, 2000.

Kinzer, Stephen W. *Overthrow: America's Century of Regime Change from Hawaii to Iraq.* New York: Times, 2006.

Kirby, Peadar. *Vulnerability and Violence: The Impact of Globalization.* London: Pluto, 2006.

Klein, Naomi. *No Logo: Taking Aim at the Brand Bullies.* New York: Picador, 1999.

Kleinhans, Theodore J. *The Year of the Lord: The Church Year: Its Customs, Growth and Ceremonies.* St. Louis: Concordia, 1967.

Kluver, Randolph, and Wayne Fu. "The Cultural Globalization Index." *Foreign Policy,* February 2004. Online: http://www.foreignpolicy.com/story/cms.php?story_id =2494.

Knight, Douglas H. *The Eschatalogical Economy: Time and the Hospitality of God.* Grand Rapids: Eerdmans 2006.

Kohli, Atul. *State-Directed Development: Political Power and Industrialization in the Periphery.* New York: Cambridge University Press, 2004.

Korten, David. *When Corporations Rule the World.* 2nd ed. Bloomfield, CT: Kumarian, 2001.

Kraidy, Marwan. *Hybridity, or the Cultural Logic of Globalization.* Philadelphia: Temple University Press, 2005.

Kramer, Andrew E. "Deals with Iraq are Set to Bring Oil Giants Back." *New York Times,* June 19, 2008. Online: http://www.nytimes.com/2008/06/19/world/middleeast/19Iraq .html.

Krasner, Stephen D. "State Power and the Structure of International Trade." *World Politics* 20 (1976) 317–47.

———. "Think Again: Sovereignty." *Foreign Policy* 121 (2001) 20–29.

Kratochwil, Friedrich. "Of Systems, Boundaries, and Territoriality: An Inquiry into the Formation of the States System." *World Politics* 39 (1986) 27–52.

Kraybill, Donald. *The Upside-Down Kingdom.* Scottdale, PA: Herald, 1978.

Kristof, Nicholas D. "Following God Abroad." *New York Times,* May 21, 2002. Online: http://www.nytimes.com/2002/05/21/opinion/21KRIS.html.

———. "God on their Side." *New York Times,* September 27, 2003. Online: http://www .nytimes.com/2003/09/27/opinion/27KRIS.html.

Krugman, Paul. "Don't Cry for Me, America." *New York Times,* January 18, 2008, national edition, A23.

———. "French Family Values." *New York Times,* July 29, 2005. Online: http://www .nytimes.com/2005/07/29/opinion/29krugman.html?incamp=article_popular&oref =slogin.

Kudrle, Robert. "Globalization by the Numbers: Quantitative Indicators and the Role of Policy." *International Studies Perspectives* 5 (2004) 341–55.

Kuttner, Robert. *Everything for Sale: The Virtues and Limits of Markets.* New York: Knopf, 1997.

Lal, Deepak. *In Praise of Empires: Globalization and Order.* New York: Palgrave, 2004.

Landes, David S. *The Wealth and Poverty of Nations: Why Some Are So Rich and Some So Poor.* New York: Norton, 1998.

Landler, Mark. "Deutsche Bank's Hit from Subprime Crisis Not as Dire as Expected." *International Herald Tribune,* October 3, 2007. Online: http://www.iht.com/articles/ 2007/10/03/business/dbank.php.

———. "Losses at Deutsche Bank Reflect Depth of Credit Crisis." *International Herald Tribune,* April 29, 2008. Online: http://www.iht.com/articles/2008/04/29/business/ bank.php.

Larsson, Tomas. *The Race to the Top: The Real Story of Globalization.* Washington, DC: Cato Institute, 2001.

Leax, John. "Lent," In *Epiphanies: Stories for the Christian Year,* 2nd ed., edited by Eugene H. Peterson and Emilie Griffin, 79–108. Grand Rapids: Baker, 2003.

Lechner, Frank J., and John Boli. *World Culture: Origins and Consequences.* Malden, MA: Blackwell, 2005.

Legrain, Philippe. "Cultural Globalization is not Americanization." *Chronicle of Higher Education,* May 9, 2003, B7–B10.

Life and Debt. DVD. Directed by Stephanie Black. New York: New Yorker Films, 2001.

Lindsey, Brink. "Grounds for Complaint? Understanding the Coffee Crisis." Cato Institute Trade Briefing Paper no. 16, May 6, 2003. Online: http://www.freetrade .org/pubs/briefs/tbp-016.pdf.

Littrell, Mary Ann, and Marsha Ann Dickson. *Social Responsibility in the Global Market: Fair Trade of Cultural Products.* Thousand Oaks, CA: Sage, 1999.

Locke, John. *Second Treatise of Government.* Indianapolis: Hackett, 1980.

Lohfink, Gerhard. *Does God Need the Church? Toward a Theology of the People of God.* Translated by Linda M. Maloney. Collegeville, MN: Liturgical, 1999.

Long, D. Stephen. *Divine Economy: Theology and the Market.* London: Routledge, 2000.

Lorge, Elizabeth M. "New Archbishop Pledges to Find More Chaplains." *U.S. Army,* January 29, 2008. Online: http://www.army.mil/-news/2008/01/29/7187-new-archbishop-pledges-to-find-more-chaplains.

Lott, Jeremy. "Is Globalization Christian?" *Books and Culture* 8 (2002).

Löwith, Karl. *Meaning in History.* Chicago: University of Chicago Press, 1949.

MacIntyre, Alasdair. *After Virtue: A Study in Moral Theory.* 2nd ed. Notre Dame: University of Notre Dame Press, 1984.

Mallaby, Sebastian. "The Pain, and Gain, of the Subprime Meltdown." *Washington Post,* August 13, 2007. Online: http://www.washingtonpost.com/wp-dyn/content/ article/2007/08/12/AR2007081200815.html.

Mander, Jerry, and Edward Goldsmith, editors. *The Case Against the Global Economy: And For a Turn to the Local.* San Francisco: Sierra Club, 1996.

Mandelbaum, Michael. *The Case for Goliath: How America Acts as the World's Government in the Twenty-First Century.* New York: Public Affairs, 2005.

Mandle, Jay R. *Globalization and the Poor.* New York: Cambridge University Press, 2003.

Marling, William H. *How "American" Is Globalization?* Baltimore: Johns Hopkins University Press, 2006.

Marx, Karl. "Economic and Philosophic Manuscripts of 1844." In *The Marx-Engels Reader,* 2nd ed., edited by Robert C. Tucker. New York: Norton, 1978.

Mather, Clive. "Combining Principle with Profit: A Business Response to the Challenges of Globalization." In *Globalization and the Good,* edited by Peter Heslam, 29–40. Grand Rapids: Eerdmans, 2004.

Mathews, Jesssica T. "Power Shift." *Foreign Affairs* 76 (1997) 50–66.

Matthew, Richard, and George Shambaugh, "The Limits of Terrorism: A Network Perspective." *International Studies Review* 7 (2005) 617–27.

McCarraher, Eugene. "Me, Myself, and Inc.: 'Social Selfhood,' Corporate Humanism, and Religious Longing in Management Theory, 1908–1956." In *Figures in the Carpet: Finding the Human Person in the American Past,* edited by Wilfred E. McClay, 185–231. Grand Rapids: Eerdmans, 2007.

McClendon, James William, Jr. *Doctrine: Systematic Theology, Vol. 2.* Nashville: Abingdon, 1994.

McGrew, Anthony. "Organized Violence in the Making (and Remaking) of Globalization." In *Globalization Theory: Approaches and Controversies,* edited by David Held and Anthony McGrew, 15–40. Malden, MA: Polity, 2007.

McGurn, William. "Creative Virtues of the Economy." In *Is the Market Moral? A Dialogue on Religion, Economics, and Justice,* edited by E.J. Dionne Jr., Jean Bethke Elshtain, and Kayla Drogosz, 129–44. Washington, DC: Brookings Institution, 2003.

————. "Pulpit Economics." *First Things* 122 (2002) 21–25.

McKibben, Bill. *Deep Economy: The Wealth of Economies and the Durable Future.* New York: Times Books, 2007.

McLaren, Brian D. *Everything Must Change: Jesus, Global Crises, and a Revolution of Hope.* Nashville: Thomas Nelson, 2007.

"Measuring Globalization." *Foreign Policy* (May/June 2005) 52–60.

Merton, Thomas. *Love and Living.* New York: Harvest, 1979.

———. *Seasons of Celebration.* New York: Farrar, Straus & Giroux, 1965.

Metaxas, Eric. *Amazing Grace: William Wilberforce and the Heroic Campaign to End Slavery.* New York: HarperOne, 2007.

Metz, Johann-Baptist. *Faith in History and Society: Toward a Practical Fundamental Theology.* Translated by David Smith. New York: Seabury, 1980.

———. "Messianic or 'Bourgeois Religion?'" In *Faith and the Future: Essays on Theology, Solidarity, and Modernity,* by Johann-Baptist Metz and Jürgen Moltmann, 17–29. Maryknoll, NY: Orbis, 1995.

Milbank, John. "Can a Gift Be Given? Prolegomena to a Future Trinitarian Metaphysic." *Modern Theology* 11 (1995) 119–61.

———. "On Complex Space." In *The Word Made Strange: Theology, Language, Culture,* 268–92. Malden, MA: Blackwell, 1997.

———. *Theology and Social Theory: Beyond Secular Reason.* Cambridge, MA: Blackwell, 1990.

Mill, John Stuart. *Principles of Political Economy.* Edited by W. J. Ashley. New York: Augustus M. Kelley, 1965.

Millman, Gregory J. *The Vandals' Crown: How Rebel Currency Traders Overthrew the World's Central Banks.* New York: Free, 1995.

Miller, Vincent J. *Consuming Religion: Christian Faith and Practice in a Consumer Culture.* New York: Continuum, 2003.

Mills, Paul S. "The Ban on Interest: Dead Letter or Radical Solution?" *Cambridge Papers* 1:4 (March 1993). Online: http://www.jubilee-centre.org/document.php?id=3.

Milner, Helen V. "Globalization, Development, and International Institutions: Normative and Positive Perspectives." *Perspectives on Politics* 3 (2005) 833–54.

Moroney, Stephen K., et al. "Cultivating Humility in Students: Teaching Practices Rooted in Christian Anthropology." In *The Schooled Heart: Moral Formation in American Higher Education,* edited by Michael Beaty and Douglas V. Henry, 171–90. Waco, TX: Baylor University Press, 2007.

Mosley, Layna. *Global Capital and National Governments.* New York: Cambridge University Press, 2003.

Murphy, Cullen. *Are We Rome? The Fall of an Empire and the Fate of America.* Boston: Houghton-Mifflin, 2007.

Myers, Bryant L. *Walking with the Poor: Principles and Practices of Transformational Development.* Maryknoll, NY: Orbis, 1999.

Nadelmann, Ethan A. "Global Prohibition Regimes: The Evolution of Norms in International Society." *International Organization* 44 (1990) 479–526.

Naffziger, Sam. Letter to the editor. *Books and Culture* 13 (2007) 6.

Nardone, Richard M. *The Story of the Christian Year.* New York: Paulist, 1991.

Naroff, Joel. "Foreword." In *A Year Without "Made in China,"* by Sara Bongiorni. Hoboken, NJ: Wiley, 2007.

Nation, Mark Thiessen. "Washing Feet: Preparation for Service." In *The Blackwell Companion to Christian Ethics*, edited by Stanley Hauerwas and Samuel Wells, 441–52. Malden, MA: Blackwell, 2004

The National Security Strategy of the United States of America. September 2002. Online: http://www.whitehouse.gov/nsc/nss/2002/nss.pdf.

Nelson, Robert H. *Economics as Religion: From Samuelson to Chicago and Beyond.* University Park, PA: Penn State University Press, 2001.

———. "What is 'Economic Theology'?" *Princeton Seminary Bulletin* 25 (2004) 58–79.

Nexon, Daniel H., and Thomas Wright. "What's at Stake in the American Empire Debate." *American Political Science Review* 101 (2007) 253–71.

Nicholls, Alex, and Charlotte Opal. *Fair Trade: Market-Driven Ethical Consumption.* Thousand Oaks, CA: Sage, 2004.

Norris, Floyd. "Credit Crisis Puts Global Finance to the Test." *International Herald Tribune*, August 9, 2007. Online: http://www.iht.com/articles/2007/08/09/business/liquidity.php.

"Not by Their Bootstraps Alone." *The Economist*, May 12, 2001, 52.

Nouwen, Henri. *The Return of the Prodigal Son: A Story of Homecoming.* New York: Image, 1994.

Nye, Joseph S. "Globalization is about Blending not Homogenizing." *Washington Post Weekly Edition*, October 14–20, 2002.

Ocampo, José Antonio, et al. "Capital Market Liberalization and Development." In *Capital Market Liberalization and Development*, edited by Joseph E. Stiglitz and José Antonio Ocampo, 1–47. New York: Oxford University Press, 2008.

O'Donovan, Oliver. *The Desire of the Nations.* New York: Cambridge University Press, 1996.

Office of Management and Budget. *Budget of the U.S. Government, Fiscal Year 2009.* Washington, DC: Government Printing Office, 2008. Online: http://www.whitehouse.gov/omb/budget/fy2009/pdf/budget.pdf.

Olson, Elizabeth. "Myanmar Tests Resolve of I.L.O. on Enforcing Standards." *New York Times*, June 5, 2001. Online: http://query.nytimes.com/gst/fullpage.html?res=9A0CE7DD123FF936A35755C0A9679C8B63&scp=1&sq=Myanmar+Tests+REsolve&st=nyt.

Opello, Jr. Walter C., and Stephen J. Rosow. *The Nation-State and Global Order.* 2nd ed. Boulder, CO: Lynne Rienner, 2004.

Oromia Coffee Farmers Cooperative Union. "About Us." Online: http://www.oromiacoffeeunion.org/aboutus.html.

Papathanasiou, Athanasios N. "Reconciliation: The Major Conflict in Post-Modernity: An Orthodox Contribution to Missiological Dialogue." Conference on World Mission and Evangelism, World Council of Churches, Athens, Greece, May 9–16, 2005. Online: http://www.oikoumene.org/uploads/media/PLEN_11_doc2_Papathanasiou.doc.

Pettis, Michael. "Will Globalization Go Bankrupt?" *Foreign Policy* 126 (2001) 52–59.

Phillips, Kevin. *Bad Money: Reckless Finance, Failed Politics, and The Global Crisis of American Capitalism.* New York: Viking, 2008.

Pickstock, Catherine. "Liturgy, Art and Politics." *Modern Theology* 16 (2000) 159–80.

Pieper, Josef. *In Tune With the World: A Theory of Festivity.* Translated by Richard and Clara Winston. 1963. Reprint, South Bend, IN: St. Augustine's, 1999.

————. *Leisure, The Basis of Culture.* Translated by Gerald Malsbary. 1948. Reprint, South Bend, IN: St. Augustine's, 1998.

Pieterse, Jan Nederveen. *Globalization and Culture: Global Mélange.* Lanham, MD: Rowman & Littlefield, 2005.

Polak, Paul. *Out of Poverty: What Works When Traditional Approaches Fail.* San Francisco: Berrett-Koehler, 2008.

Polanski, Sandra. *Winners and Losers: Impact of the Doha Round on Developing Countries.* Washington, DC: Carnegie Endowment for International Peace, 2006. Online: http://www.carnegieendowment.org/files/BWfinal.pdf.

Polanyi, Karl. *The Great Transformation: The Political and Economic Origins of Our Time.* Boston: Beacon, 1957.

Pollan, Michael. *The Omnivore's Dilemma: A Natural History of Four Meals.* New York: Penguin, 2006.

Pomeranz, Kenneth, and Steven Topik. *The World that Trade Created: Society, Culture, and the World Economy, 1400s-Present.* Armonk, NY: M. E. Sharpe, 1999.

Porter, Bruce. *War and the Rise of the State: The Military Origins of Modern Politics.* New York: Free, 1994.

"President Bush Attends Arlington National Cemetery Memorial Day Commemoration." *White House*, May 26, 2008. Online: http://georgewbush-whitehouse.archives.gov/news/releases/2008/05/20080526.html.

"President Discusses War on Terrorism." November 8, 2001. Online: http://georgewbush-whitehouse.archives.gov/news/releases/2001/11/20011108-13.html.

Przeworski, Adam, and James Vreeland. "The Effect of IMF Programs on Economic Growth." *Journal of Development Economics* 62 (2000) 385–421.

Quart, Alisa. *Branded: The Buying and Selling of Teenagers.* New York: Basic, 2003.

Ramirez-Vallejo, Jorge. "A Break for Coffee." *Foreign Policy* 132 (2002) 26–27.

Rasmussen, Ib. *Monty Python's Flying Circus: Just the Words, Episode 30.* Online: http://www.ibras.dk/montypython/episode30.htm#4.

Raynolds, Laura T., and Douglas L. Murray. "Fair Trade: Contemporary Challenges and Future Prospects." In *Fair Trade: The Challenges of Transforming Globalization*, edited by Laura T. Raynolds, Douglas L. Murray, and John Wilkinson, 223–34. New York: Routledge, 2007.

Raynolds, Laura T., and John Wilkinson. "Fair Trade in the Agriculture and Food Sector: Analytical Dimensions." In *Fair Trade: The Challenges of Transforming Globalization*, edited by Laura T. Raynolds, Douglas L. Murray, and John Wilkinson, 33–47. New York: Routledge, 2007.

Raynolds, Laura, et al., editors. *Fair Trade: The Challenges of Transforming Globalization.* New York: Routledge, 2007.

Reed, Larry. "A Ten-Trillion-Dollar Stewardship." In *Globalization and the Kingdom of God*, edited by James W. Skillen, 61–81. Grand Rapids: Baker, 2001.

Regan, Patrick. "The Fifty Days and the Fiftieth Day." In *Between Memory and Hope: Readings on the Liturgical Year*, edited by Maxwell E. Johnson, 223–46. Collegeville, MN: Liturgical, 2000.

————. "The Three Days and the Forty Days." In *Between Memory and Hope: Readings on the Liturgical Year*, edited by Maxwell E. Johnson, 125–42. Collegeville, MN: Liturgical, 2000.

Reiss, Bob. "The Race to Own the Arctic." *Parade Magazine*, June 1, 2008, 4–5.

Ricks, Thomas. "Empire or Not? A Quiet Debate Over U.S. Role." *Washington Post*, August 21, 2001, A1.

Riedlmayer, Andras. "Yes, the Oil Ministry Was Guarded!" *Iraq War and Archaeology Blog*, May 7, 2003. Online: http://iwa.univie.ac.at/oilministry.html.

Rivoli, Pietra. *The Travels of a T-Shirt in the Global Economy*. New York: Wiley, 2005.

Robbins, Lionel. *A History of Economic Thought: The LSE Lectures*. Edited by S. G. Medema and W. Samuels. Princeton: Princeton University Press, 1998.

Robertson, Roland. "Glocalization: Time-Space and Homogeneity-Heterogeneity." In *Global Modernities*, edited by Mike Featherstone, Scott Lash, and Roland Robertson, 25–44. Thousand Oaks, CA: Sage, 1995.

Robinson, Tim. *Work, Leisure and the Environment: The Vicious Circle of Overwork and over Consumption*. Northampton, MA: Edward Elgar, 2006.

Rodrik, Dani. *One Economics, Many Recipes: Globalization, Institutions, and Economic Growth*. Princeton: Princeton University Press, 2007.

———. "Trading in Illusions." *Foreign Policy* 123 (2001) 54–62.

Rosenau, James N., and Ernst-Otto Czempiel, editors. *Governance without Government: Order and Change in World Politics*. New York: Cambridge University Press, 1992.

Roth, John D. "Reflections on 'Speaking to Government.'" *Mennonite Church USA*, July 6, 2005. Online: http://www.mennoniteusa.org/Home/About/ Statementsandresolutions/Government/tabid/116/Default.aspx#3.

Rothkopf, David. "In Praise of Cultural Imperialism?" *Foreign Policy* 107 (1997) 38–53.

Roy, Arundhati. *Power Politics*. Expanded ed. Boston: South End, 2001.

Roy, Olivier. *Globalized Islam: The Search for a New Ummah*. New York: Columbia University Press, 2004.

Rubin, Beth A. *Shifts in the Social Contract: Understanding Change in American Society*. Thousand Oaks, CA: Pine Forge, 1996.

Rutledge, Fleming. *The Bible and the New York Times*. Grand Rapids: Eerdmans, 1998.

Sageman, Marc. *Understanding Terror Networks*. Philadelphia: University of Pennsylvania Press, 2004.

Sahadi, Jeanne. "CEO Pay: 364 Times More Than Workers." *CNN*, August 29, 2007. Online: http://money.cnn.com/2007/08/28/news/economy/ceo_pay_workers/index.htm.

Samuelson, Robert J. "A Baffling Global Economy." *Washington Post*, July 16, 2008. Online: http://www.washingtonpost.com/wp-dyn/content/article/2008/07/15/AR 2008071502428.html.

Sanneh, Lamin. "Christian Missions and the Liberal Guilt Complex." *Christian Century* (April 8, 1987) 330–34.

———. *Disciples of All Nations: Pillars of World Christianity*. New York: Oxford University Press, 2008.

Sassen, Saskia. "The Places and Spaces of the Global: An Expanded Analytic Terrain." In *Globalization Theory: Approaches and Controversies*, edited by David Held and Anthony McGrew, 79–105. Malden, MA: Polity, 2004.

———. *Territory, Authority, Rights: From Medieval to Global Assemblages*. Princeton: Princeton University Press, 2006.

Sayers, Dorothy L. *The Mind of the Maker*. London: Methuen, 1941.

Schlosser, Eric. *Fast Food Nation*. Boston: Houghton-Mifflin, 2001.

———. "A Side Order of Human Rights." *New York Times*, April 6, 2005. Online: http://www.nytimes.com/2005/04/06/opinion/06schlosser.html.

Schluter, Michael. "Risk, Reward, and Responsibility: A Biblical Critique of Global Capital Markets." In *Globalization and the Good,* edited by Peter Heslam, 66–78. Grand Rapids: Eerdmans, 2004.

Schmemann, Alexander. *For the Life of the World: Sacraments and Orthodoxy.* Crestwood, NY: St. Vladimir's Seminary, 1973.

Schmidt, Leigh Eric. *Consumer Rites: The Buying and Selling of American Holidays.* Princeton: Princeton University Press, 1995.

Schneider, John R. *The Good of Affluence: Seeking God in a Culture of Wealth.* Grand Rapids: Eerdmans, 2002.

Scholte, Jan Aarte. *Globalization: A Critical Introduction.* New York: Palgrave, 2005.

Schor, Juliet B. *Born to Buy: The Commercialized Child and the New Consumer Culture.* New York: Scribner, 2005.

———. "Civic Engagement and Working Hours: Do Americans Really Have More Free Time than Ever Before?" Paper prepared for presentation at Conference on Civic Engagement in American Democracy, September 26–28, 1997, Portland, Maine. Online: http://www.swt.org/putok.htm.

———. *The Overworked American: The Unexpected Decline of Leisure.* New York: Basic, 1991.

Schut, Michael, editor. *Simpler Living, Compassionate Life: A Christian Perspective.* Denver: Living the Good News, 1999.

Schwartz, Herman M. *States Versus Markets: History, Geography, and the Development of the International Political Economy.* New York: St. Martin's 1994.

Second Vatican Council. "Constitution on the Sacred Liturgy." In *The Documents of Vatican II,* edited by Walter M. Abbott, S.J. New York: America, 1966.

Sedgwick, Peter H. *The Market Economy and Christian Ethics.* New York: Cambridge University Press, 1999.

Seeton, Melissa Griffy. "Students: Prepare for Global Economy." *The Repository,* Canton, Ohio, March 23, 2007, B-3.

———. "Students: Prepare for Global Economy." *The Repository,* Canton, Ohio, March 23, 2007. Online: http://www.cantonrep.com/index.php?ID=343815.

SERRV International. "Our History." *A Greater Gift.* Online: http://www.agreatergift .org/AboutUs/OurHistory.aspx.

Shadid, Anthony. "In a Land Without Order, Punishment Is Power." *Washington Post,* October 22, 2006. Online: http://www.washingtonpost.com/wp-dyn/content/article/ 2006/10/21/AR2006102101048.html.

Sharlet, Jeff. "Soldiers of Christ I: Inside America's Most Powerful Megachurch." *Harper's Magazine,* May 2005. Online: http://www.harpers.org/SoldiersOfChrist.html.

Sherrard, Philip. *The Eclipse of Man and Nature.* West Stockbridge, MA: Lindisfarne, 1987.

Shiva, Vandana. "War Against Nature and the People of the South." In *Views from the South: The Effects of Globalization and the WTO on Third World Countries,* edited by Sarah Anderson, 91–125. Chicago: Food First, 2000.

Sider, Ronald J. *Christ and Violence.* Eugene, OR: Wipf and Stock, 2001.

———. "God's People Reconciling." *Christian Peacemaker Teams.* Online: http://www .cpt.org/resources/writings/sider.

Sine, Tom. *Mustard Seed versus McWorld: Reinventing Life and Faith for the Future.* Grand Rapids: Baker, 1999.

Singer, Peter W. *Corporate Warriors: The Rise of the Privatized Military Industry*. Ithaca: Cornell University Press, 2004.

Sittser, Gerald L. *The Will of God as a Way of Life*. Grand Rapids: Zondervan, 2000.

Skocpol, Theda. "Will 9/11 and the War on Terror Revitalize American Civic Democracy?" *PS: Political Science and Politics* 35 (2002) 537–40.

Smit, Laura. "'The Depth Behind Things': Toward a Calvinist Sacramental Theology." In *Radical Orthodoxy and the Reformed Tradition: Creation: Covenant, and Participation,* edited by James K. A. Smith and James Olthuis, 205–27. Grand Rapids: Baker, 2005.

Smith, Alisa, and J. B. McKinnon. *The 100-Mile Diet: A Year of Local Eating*. Toronto: Vintage Canada, 2007.

Smith, James K. A. *Introducing Radical Orthodoxy: Mapping a Post-Secular Theology*. Grand Rapids: Baker, 2004.

Smith, Robert, and Adam Davidson. "Analysis: Lenders, Investors, Buyers Fed Loan Crisis." *National Public Radio*, May 27, 2008. Online: http://www.npr.org/templates/story/story.php?storyId=90840961&sc=emaf.

"Snapshot: Global Migration." *New York Times,* June 22, 2007. Online: http://www.nytimes.com/ref/world/20070622_CAPEVERDE_GRAPHIC.html.

Solomon, Robert. *Money on the Move: The Revolution in International Finance Since 1980*. Princeton: Princeton University Press, 1999.

Southgate, Douglas. *World Food Economy*. Malden, MA: Blackwell, 2005.

Spiegel, Steven L., et al. *World Politics in a New Era*. 3rd ed. Belmont, CA: Wadsworth, 2004.

Spruyt, Hendrik. *The Sovereign State and Its Competitors*. Princeton: Princeton University Press, 1994.

Stafford, Tim. "Good Morning, Evangelicals! Meet Ted Haggard, the NAE's Optimistic Champion of Ecumenical Evangelism and Free-Market Faith." *Christianity Today*, November 2005. Online: http://www.christianitytoday.com/ct/2005/november/20.41.html.

Stiglitz, Joseph. *Globalization and Its Discontents*. New York: Norton, 2002.

———. *Making Globalization Work*. New York: Norton, 2006.

Stoll, Steven. "Postmodern Farming, Quietly Flourishing." *Chronicle of Higher Education*, June 21, 2002, B7–B9.

Strange, Susan. *States and Markets*. 2nd ed. New York: Continuum, 1998.

———. *States and the Diffusion of Power in the World Economy*. New York: Cambridge University Press, 1996.

Streitfield, David. "A Global Need for Grain That Farms Can't Fill." *New York Times*. March 9, 2008. Online: http://www.nytimes.com/2008/03/09/business/worldbusiness/09crop.html.

Tabb, William K. *Economic Governance in the Age of Globalization*. New York: Columbia University Press, 2004.

Talley, Thomas J. "Constantine and Christmas." In *Between Memory and Hope: Readings on the Liturgical Year*, edited by Maxwell E. Johnson, 265–72. Collegeville, MN: Liturgical, 2000.

———. *The Origins of the Liturgical Year*. 2nd ed. Collegeville, MN: Liturgical, 1991.

Tarrow, Sidney. *The New Transnational Activism*. New York: Cambridge University Press, 2005.

Taylor, Charles. *A Secular Age*. Cambridge, MA: Belknap, 2007.

————. *Modern Social Imaginaries.* Durham: Duke University Press, 2004.

Terry, Benjamin. Review of *Richard Cobden: The International Man*, by J. A. Hobson. *The Journal of Political Economy* 28 (1920) 256–61.

Thayer, Bradley, and Christopher Layne. *American Empire: A Debate.* New York: Routledge, 2006.

Thomas, Cal. "The Tom Fox Tragedy." *Townhall.com*, March 14, 2006. Online: http://www.townhall.com/columnists/CalThomas/2006/03/14/the_tom_fox_tragedy.

Thomas, Scott. *The Global Resurgence of Religion and the Transformation of International Relations.* New York: Palgrave Macmillan, 2005.

Thomson, Janice E. *Mercenaries, Pirates, and Sovereigns: State-Building and Extraterritorial Violence in Early Modern Europe.* Princeton: Princeton University Press, 1996.

TIAA-CREF. "CREF Social Choice Account." Online: http://www.tiaa-cref.org/pdf/fact_sheets/cref_social_choice.pdf.

Tillard, John-Marie-Roger. *Flesh of the Church, Flesh of Christ: At the Source of the Ecclesiology of Communion.* Translated by Madeleine Beaumont. Collegeville, MN: Liturgical, 2001.

Tilly, Charles. *Coercion, Capital, and European States, A.D. 990–1990.* Boston: Blackwell, 1990.

————. "Reflections on the History of European State-Making." In *The Formation of National States in Western Europe*, edited by Charles Tilly, 3–83. Princeton: Princeton University Press, 1975.

Tolson, Jay. "The New American Empire?" *U.S. News and World Report*, January 13, 2003, 35–40.

Toppen, Joel. "Fixing Globalization: A Review Essay." *Christian Scholar's Review* 33 (2004) 379–90.

"Top Ten Products to Battle Consumerism." *The Onion.* Online: http://www.theonion.com/content/magazine/top_10_products_to_battle.

"Total UN System Estimated Expenditures." *Global Policy Forum.* Online: http://www.globalpolicy.org/finance/tables/system/tabsyst.htm.

Trudeau, G. B. *Doonesbury.* November 26, 1996. Online: http://www.amureprints.com/img1/doonesbury/1996/db961126.gif.

Uchitelle, Louis. "Goodbye, Production (And Maybe Innovation)." *New York Times*, December 24, 2006, national edition, B4.

————. "Ideas and Trends: The Bondholders Are Winning; Why America Won't Boom." *New York Times*, June 12, 1994. Online: http://query.nytimes.com /gst/fullpage.html?res=9C0CE1DF113AF931A25755C0A962958260.

UNESCO. "Survey on National Cinematography: Summary." No pages. Online: http://www.unesco.org/culture/industries/cinema/html_eng/survey.shtml.

United International. "Exxon, Shell: Iraq Oil Law Needed for Deal." *United International*, February 13, 2008. Online: http://www.upi.com/International_ Security/Energy/Briefing/2008/02/13/exxon_shell_iraq_oil_law_needed_for_deal/9680.

U. S. Census Bureau. "States Ranked by Revenue and Expenditure Total Amount and Per Capita Total Amount: 2004." *Census Bureau.* Online: http://www.census.gov/govs/state/04rank.html.

Van Creveld, Martin. *The Rise and Decline of the State.* New York: Cambridge University Press, 1999.

Van Dyk, Leanne, editor. *A More Profound Alleluia: Theology and Worship in Harmony.* Grand Rapids: Eerdmans, 2005.

Vanhoozer, Kevin J. *The Drama of Doctrine: A Canonical-Linguistic Approach to Christian Theology*. Louisville: Westminster John Knox, 2005.

Varadarajan, Tunku. "India's Game, U.S. Spice." *New York Times,* April 15, 2008. Online: http://www.nytimes.com/2008/04/15/opinion/15varadarajan.html.

Vatican II Council. "Decree *Ad Gentes:* On the Mission Activity of the Church." December 7, 1965. Online: http://www.vatican.va/archive/hist_councils/ii_vatican_council/documents/vat-ii_decree_19651207_ad-gentes_en.html.

Von Balthasar, Hans Urs. *A Theology of History.* San Francisco: Ignatius, 1994.

————. *Theo–Drama: Theological Dramatic Theory, Vol. 1: Prolegomena.* Translated by Graham Harrison. San Francisco: Ignatius, 1988.

Waalkes, Scott. "Money or Business? A Case Study of Christian Virtue Ethics in Corporate Work." *Christian Scholar's Review* 38 (2008) 15–40.

————. "Prescience and Paradigms." *Fides et Historia* 36 (2004) 104–9.

Wadell, Paul J. *Friendship and the Moral Life.* Notre Dame: Notre Dame University Press, 1989.

Wade, Robert. *Governing the Market: Economic Theory and the Role of Government in East Asian Industrialization.* Princeton: Princeton University Press, 1990

Wade, Robert Hunter. "America's Empire Rules an Unbalanced World." In *Globalization and State Power: A Reader,* edited by Joel Kriger, 129–32. New York: Pearson, 2006.

————. "What Can Economics Learn from East Asian Success?" *Annals of the American Academy of Political and Social Science* 505 (1989) 68–79.

Wallerstein, Immanuel. *The Politics of the World-Economy: The States, the Movements, and the Civilizations.* New York: Cambridge University Press, 1984.

Walls, Andrew. *The Missionary Movement in Christian History.* Maryknoll, NY: Orbis, 1996.

Walsh, Brian J., and Sylvia C. Keesmaat. *Colossians Remixed: Subverting the Empire.* Downers Grove, IL: InterVarsity, 2004.

Waltz, Kenneth N. "Globalization and Governance." *Political Science and Politics* 32 (1999) 693–700.

————. *Theory of International Politics.* New York: McGraw-Hill, 1979.

Wang, Robert. "Panelists: Time for Action, Not Fear: Don't Ignore Foreclosure." *The Repository,* Canton, Ohio, April 29, 2008, B1.

Wannenwetsch, Bernd. *Political Worship: Ethics for Christian Citizens.* Translated by Margaret Kohl. New York: Oxford University Press, 2004.

————. "Liturgy." In *The Blackwell Companion to Political Theology,* edited by Peter Scott and William T. Cavanaugh, 76–90. Malden, MA: Blackwell, 2004.

Watson, Adam. *The Evolution of International Society.* New York: Routledge, 1992.

Wax, Emily. "Redskins Cheerleaders Shake Up Cricket in Modest India." *Washington Post,* April 19, 2008. Online: http://www.washingtonpostcom/wp-dyn/content/article/2008/04/18/AR2008041803577.html.

Webber, Robert E. *Ancient-Future Time: Forming Spirituality through the Christian Year.* Grand Rapids: Baker, 2004.

Weil, Martin, and Michael Alison Chandler. "Virginian Taken Hostage in Iraq Is Found Dead." *Washington Post,* March 11, 2006. Online: http://www. washingtonpost.com/wp-dyn/content/article/2006/03/10/AR2006031001935.html.

Weiner, Eric J. "Foreclosure-Proof Homes?" *Los Angeles Times*, December 3, 2007. Online: http://www.latimes.com/news/opinion/sunday/commentary/la-oe-weiner 3dec03,0,5261681.story?coll=la-sunday-commentary.

Weiner, Tim. "In Corn's Cradle, U.S. Imports Bury Family Farms." *New York Times*, February 26, 2002. Online: http://www.nytimes.com/2002/02/26/international/Americas/26CORN.html.

Weiss, Linda. *The Myth of the Powerless State*. Ithaca, NY: Cornell University Press, 1998.

Weiss, Rick. "Report Targets Costs of Factory Farming." *Washington Post*, April 30, 2008. Online: http://www.washingtonpost.com/wp-dyn/content/article/2008/04/29/AR 2008042902602.html.

Weller, Christian E., and Adam Hersh. "Free Markets and Poverty." *American Prospect* 13 (2002). Online: http://www.prospect.org/cs/articles?article=free_markets_and _poverty.

Wells, Samuel. *God's Companions: Reimagining Christian Ethics*. Malden, MA: Blackwell, 2006.

———. *Improvisation: The Drama of Christian Ethics*. Grand Rapids: Brazos, 2004.

———. *Transforming Fate into Destiny: The Theological Ethics of Stanley Hauerwas*. Eugene, OR: Cascade, 2004.

Wesche, Kenneth Paul. "ΘΕΩΣΙΣ [Theosis] in Freedom and Love: The Patristic Vision." In *The Consuming Passion: Christianity and the Culture of Consumption*, edited by Rodney Clapp, 118–28. Downers Grove, IL: InterVarsity, 1998.

Westmoreland-White, Michael. "The Watada Case and Just War Theory." *Levellers Blog*, February 8, 2007. Online: http://levellers.word .com/2007/ 02/08/the-watada-case-just-war-theory.

Whalen, Michael D. *Seasons and Fasts of the Church Year: An Introduction*. New York: Paulist, 1993.

White, Lynn B. Jr. "The Historical Roots of Our Ecologic Crisis." *Science* 155 (967) 1203–7.

Wicker, Brian. "Introduction." In *Witnesses to Faith? Martyrdom in Christianity and Islam*, edited by Brian Wicker, 1–14. Burlington, VT: Ashgate, 2006.

Wilkins, Jennifer. "Think Globally, Eat Locally." *New York Times*, December 18, 2004. Online: http://www.nytimes.com/2004/12/18/opinion/18wilkins.html.

Wilkinson, John, and Gilberto Mascharenas. "Southern Social Movements and Fair Trade." In *Fair Trade: The Challenges of Transforming Globalization*, edited by Laura T. Raynolds, Douglas L. Murray, and John Wilkinson, 125–37. New York: Routledge, 2007.

Will, George F. "Seattle Mounts Its Own Version of Storming the Winter Palace." *Seattle Post-Intelligencer*, December 9, 1999. Online: http://seattlepi.nwsource.com/opinion/will071.shtml

Williams, Jody. "The International Campaign to Ban Landmines: A Model for Disarmament Initiatives?" *Nobel Prize Web site*, September 3, 1999. Online: http://nobelprize .org/nobel_prizes/peace/articles/williams/index.html.

Wink, Walter. *The Powers That Be: Theology for a New Millennium*. New York: Doubleday, 1999.

Winkler, Gabriele. "The Appearance of Light at the Baptism of Jesus and the Origins of the Feat of Epiphany: An Investigation of Greek, Syriac, Armenian, and Latin Sources." In *Between Memory and Hope: Readings on the Liturgical Year*. Edited by Maxwell E. Johnson, 291. Collegeville, MN: Liturgical, 2000.

Woods, Ngaire. *The Globalizers: The IMF, The World Bank, and Their Borrowers*. Ithaca, NY: Cornell University Press, 2006.

Wolf, Martin. *Why Globalization Works*. New Haven: Yale University Press, 2003.

Wolin, Sheldon S. *Politics and Vision: Continuity and Innovation in Western Political Thought*. Expanded ed. Princeton: Princeton University Press, 2004.

Wolterstorff, Nicholas. *Until Justice and Peace Embrace*. Grand Rapids: Eerdmans, 1983.

World Bank. *The East Asian Miracle: Economic Growth and Public Policy*. New York: Oxford University Press, 1993.

———. "The State of Sustainable Coffee." *World Bank Website*, October 14, 2003. Online: http://go.worldbank.org/VF8O554Loo.

"World Wide Military Expenditures," *GlobalSecurity.org*. Online: http://www.global-security.org/military/world/spending.htm.

Wright, N. T. *Acts for Everyone*. Louisville: Westminster John Knox, 2008.

———. *Christians at the Cross: Finding Hope in the Passion, Death, and Resurrection of Jesus*. Ijamsville, MD: The Word Among Us, 2007.

———. *The Resurrection of the Son of God*. Minneapolis: Fortress, 2003.

———. *Surprised by Hope: Rethinking Heaven, the Resurrection, and the Mission of the Church*. New York: HarperOne, 2007.

Yergin, Daniel, and Joseph Stanislaw. *The Commanding Heights: The Battle for the World Economy*. 3rd ed. New York: Touchstone, 2002.

Yoder, John Howard. *Body Politics: Five Practices of the Christian Community Before the Watching World*. Scottsdale, PA: Herald, 2001.

———. *The Christian Witness to the State*. Newton, KS: Faith and Life, 1964.

———. *The Original Revolution: Essays on Christian Pacifism*. Scottsdale, PA: Herald, 1972.

———. *The Politics of Jesus: Vicit Agnus Noster*. 2nd ed. Grand Rapids: Eerdmans, 1994.

———. *The Priestly Kingdom: Social Ethics as Gospel*. Notre Dame: Notre Dame University Press, 1984.

York, Tripp. "Dirty Basins, Dirty Disciples, and Beautiful Crosses: The Politics of Foot-washing." *Liturgy* 20 (2005) 11–18.

———. *The Purple Crown: The Politics of Martyrdom*. Scottsdale, PA: Herald, 2007.

Zimmerman, Joyce Ann. *Liturgy As Living Faith: A Liturgical Spirituality*. Scranton, PA: University of Scranton Press, 1993.

Žižek, Slavoj. "Denying the Facts, Finding the Truth." *New York Times*, January 5, 2007, national edition, A-17.

Zizioulas, John D. *Being as Communion: Studies in Personhood and the Church*. Crestwood, NY: St. Vladimir's Seminary Press, 1985.

Zoepf, Katherine. "Bestseller in Mideast: Barbie with a Prayer Mat." *New York Times*, September 22, 2005. Online: http://www.nytimes.com/2005/09/22/international/middleeast/22doll.html.

Index